AN APOLOGY
FOR THE LIFE
OF
COLLEY CIBBER

Bust of COLLEY CIBBER

An Apology
FOR THE
Life of
Colley Cibber

WITH AN HISTORICAL VIEW
OF THE STAGE
DURING HIS OWN TIME

Written by Himself

Edited, with an Introduction, by
B. R. S. FONE

ANN ARBOR
The University of Michigan Press

To My Parents
Abbie and Reginald Fone
The best of all my teachers

PREFACE

An edition of Cibber's *Apology* is long overdue. The work, valuable to the scholar of seventeenth- and eighteenth-century theater, and useful and interesting to the student and the general reader, has not been edited for seventy-five years; the text of the first edition, which I present here, has never been edited, nor has it been available since it first appeared in 1740.

My introduction does not pretend to be "new," for there is little new to say that Richard Hindry Barker has not said in his excellent *Mr. Cibber of Drury Lane* (New York, 1939), a book to which those interested not only in Cibber but in the theater of the period can turn with profit and reward. But since the *Apology* has not, for so long, been easily accessible, I have tried to bring together in one place those facts which Barker, Lowe, and other scholars have found, adding, where appropriate, notes and my own comments on the book. I have contented myself with a discussion of the worth of the book, its value as a theatrical document, and something of its history. In short, for those unfamiliar with the text and its background, I hope to give perspective, for the student, clarification, and for the scholar, a gathering of material which, though perhaps familiar, will not be unwelcome.

I am indebted to many for the aid given me in preparing a textually accurate book. I should first like to thank Professor Edward L. McAdam, Jr., of New York University, who was responsible for starting me on my work with Cibber, and who has very kindly read the manuscript, offering many helpful suggestions. A debt for kind words also must be paid to Mr. George Milne. Dean George Winchester Stone, and Professor Dan H. Laurence, of New York University, and Professor Robert Halsband, of Columbia University, have been of great aid, and my thanks go to them.

I would like to thank Mr. William B. Long, of the City College, who also read my text and made many valuable suggestions, Mr. Ralph Manogue, of Queens College, for invaluable aid in the collation, and Mr. George Marcelle for his very helpful work on the manuscript and his comments on the text. To Miss Anne Finkler, of the Classics Department at the City College, go my thanks for her kindness in helping at short notice with Cibber's classical allusions. To Miss Constantina Michalos, who has excellently typed the manuscript with care and attention, go my special thanks. To Mrs. Frances Monson McCoullough, I owe a debt of gratitude of long standing.

My researches have been materially aided by the staffs of many libraries, among them the New York Public Library, Yale University Library, the Harvard University Libraries, the libraries of the British Museum and Oxford University, and the Library of the City University of New York. A generous grant from City University has substantially helped my work on the book, and I thank Professor Edmond L. Volpe, chairman of the Department of English, for his kindness in recommending me for that aid.

There is one further debt that neither thanks nor books can pay: to Seymour Pitcher, professor of English and General literature at Harpur College of the State University of New York, a fine man, a great teacher, a dear friend.

The City College
New York City

B.R.S.F.

INTRODUCTION

Cibber's *Apology* is not widely read now; nevertheless, it does not deserve to be ignored, even though it chronicles a period in the theater which has never been much regarded. We seldom read Rowe's *Ambitious Stepmother* (1701) now, or Hill's *Fatal Vision* (1716), or hear Gay's opera *Achilles* (1733), but the era is, in stage history, of first importance. Here the English stage grew; the great playhouses were established, the great traditions born, and Cibber was there to participate in the ferment, in part to shape it, and, what is for us important, he was there to write about it. The *Apology* is a record of the complicated beginnings of the modern theater, and it remains, despite criticism, in many ways the best.

Critics have always objected to the *Apology;* earlier critics because it was written by Cibber, later because it seemed vain, pert, and neither lucid nor elegantly written. Though we might wish for a more Addisonian style, we can hardly condemn a book which gives so clear a picture of so interesting a man, and in the bargain provides an original chronicle of the times. While the *Apology* may be everything an autobiography should not be, its very faults in that genre may be its greatest virtues as theater history. For the *Apology*, while telling of forgotten plays, tells when these plays were acted, and who spoke their turgid lines. And more happily, the book recalls performances by actors so good that even base metal seemed golden in their speech—actors of whom, save for Cibber, we would know nothing. And of course we must not forget that the *Apology* gives us a portrait of a man who, despite ridicule, was one of the most influential members of the theatrical world—as actor, manager, and playwright—who for some forty years was a central figure on the London stage. There can be no doubt that Cibber's book is one of the most important and indispensable accounts of a vital period in English theatrical history. His title tells us all: *An Apology for the Life of Mr. Colley Cibber, Comedian, and Late Patentee of the Theatre Royal. With an Historical View of the Stage During His Own Time. Written by Himself.*

Every reader knows that it is this same Colley Cibber who was placed on the "throne of Dullness" by Pope. This Cibber, too, was castigated by Fielding, despised by Dennis, and made the butt of attacks throughout his life.[1] When Cibber was made poet laureate in 1730, for example, his appointment was greeted with laughter in some quarters, anger in others, and satires by Johnson and Pope. Johnson observes:

> *Augustus still survives in Maro's strain*
> *And Spenser's verse prolongs Eliza's reign;*
> *Great George's acts let tuneful Cibber sing;*
> *For Nature form'd the Poet for the King.*[2]

As usual, Johnson's barbs are not only double-edged but carry subtle poison. Pope, more poisonously still, insists:

> *In Merry old England, it once was a Rule*
> *The King had his Poet, and also his Fool.*
> *But now we're so frugal, I'd have you know it,*
> *That Cibber can serve both for Fool and Poet.*[3]

Cibber's name, therefore, has come down as that of a poseur and clown. And indeed the reader who takes up his verses—and knows them to be the utterance of the laureate—can only be appalled. His plays are never seen and, with perhaps the exception of *The Careless Husband* (1704), can add nothing good to the portrait. But the reader of the *Apology* will find that there is more to Cibber than a bad poet and a hack playwright. Because he is so likable, one cannot but conclude that perhaps injustice

has, somehow, been done. That Cibber decided to defend himself in his book is not surprising. That it became more than mere
rebuttal redounds to his credit and to our good fortune.

Cibber's life is excellently and definitively recorded in R.H.
Barker's *Mr. Cibber of Drury Lane* (New York, 1939), but as
reported by himself in this edition of the *Apology*, some comment may be welcome to the reader unfamiliar with the out-
lines of his career—especially, since Cibber's tale is not always
entirely clear, and after 1733 is untold.

Cibber was born in 1671, and in time he went on, as he enter-
tainingly tells us, to meager schooling—six years only—for he
did not go up to the university. Instead, he went to London and
saw his first play, and there, at nineteen, he "imbib'd an inclination for the stage..." (p. 37). Casting aside all further pretensions to any other career, he joined the Theatre Royal in
1689/90.

His success was slight. Moreover, there was no salary, for he
was only an apprentice. His first role of any consequence was
as the chaplain in Otway's *Orphan* (1680). Other small parts
followed, and eventually he was gratified to hear himself praised
by Congreve when he substituted for Kynaston as Lord Touchwood in *The Double Dealer* (1694). In 1693, before this success
and with no prospects, Cibber married Katherine Shore. Since
he was poor, earning twenty shillings a week, his wife went
on the stage and began a career for herself.

Despite Congreve's praise, advancement did not come and
poverty still threatened. Cibber decided to create a part for
himself. Written in 1696, *Love's Last Shift*, with the author as
Sir Novelty Fashion the fop, immensely pleased the town, established Cibber as a new playwright, and gave him a character
which was to remain his for the rest of his career. Cibber the
foppish fool—Sir Novelty, Lord Foppington, and a score of
others—was to become a fixture of the stage.

We know that Cibber was, to his sorrow, no dashing rake.
He had no money, no family, and little education. Without these
advantages he had only one resource: his wits. He was, as the
episode of *Love's Last Shift* tells, a man always willing to grasp

the nearest way. He was a speculator and a gambler, and sur-
prisingly often he won his throw. So it was that he came to the
stage at nineteen. So it was that through an accident, tradition
says, he won his first salary.[4] And so it was that at twenty-five he
had a play acclaimed by the Lord Chamberlain and applauded
by all London, a play now generally regarded to be the first of
the sentimental comedies and which held the stage for a century.[5] Some years later Dennis said that the play was too good
and that Cibber must have stolen it.[6]

After *Love's Last Shift*, Cibber's life was a succession of roles
played and plays written: *Woman's Wit* (1697), Lord Foppington in *The Relapse, Xerxes* (1699), and a dozen other roles, and
four more plays, until by 1704 he had become an actor-manager
at Drury Lane. His rise to responsibility came about through
his growing influence with Christopher Rich, the patentee.

The *Apology* tells in detail about this period and the years
following. It is a complicated story of plots and counterplots,
machinations and intrigues, among Cibber, Rich, Swiney, Wilks,
and others, which runs through various unions and divisions
of the theater to the overthrow of Rich and the triumph of the
actor-managers. It is best to let the book speak for itself rather
than to try here to penetrate the thicket of tangled events.

In the years between 1717 and 1730 Cibber became increas-
ingly unpopular and quarreled with Pope, Fielding, Dennis, and
the Jacobite journalist Nathaniel Mist; perhaps this explains the
spotty coverage given the period in the *Apology*. He also saw
several plays fail during this time, though *The Non-Juror* (1717)
was received with favor, and Cibber attributed his later appointment as laureate to the popular reception of its Whig sentiments.
Nevertheless, there is some evidence to show that he was losing
interest and, more likely, patience with his role as manager.

In 1730, three years before his retirement, the indignities he
suffered at the hands of Mist and other enemies were impres-
sively assuaged, for he was made poet laureate. Cibber, usually
vain about his achievements and ready to gloss over his short-
comings, does not elaborate on his good fortune in the *Apology*.
Perhaps the ridicule which followed his appointment led him to

discretion, or perhaps he felt some of the dignity which clings to the title, despite the general inferiority of its holders, and was moved to silence. What is sure is that he recognized what all the world was saying, that is, that his poems were bad, and he candidly admitted it.

In 1733 Cibber was sixty-five. He was the laureate. He was the most famous comedian of his time, the effective head of Drury Lane, and a successful playwright as well. At the height of everything, he chose to retire, feeling his age, perhaps, or as I have suggested, losing patience with the frantic world of the theater. Wilks, Cibber's partner with Booth, had died in 1732, and Booth had sold half his share in the patent to John Highmore. Cibber was left with Highmore and John Ellis, Wilks' executor, neither of whom was experienced in theater management in the way that Wilks and Booth had been. With his two cronies gone, and new partners to contend with, it was not unreasonable of Cibber to decide to retire. In 1733 he sold his interest to Highmore for three thousand guineas.[7]

Once out of the theater, Cibber pursued his duties as laureate. There is no reason to think that he took the post lightly. Though his verses were inept, he took seriously the job of turning out birthday odes for the king, of celebrating royal triumphs, and of grieving over royal sorrows. Dr. Johnson tells us that "his friends gave out that he *intended* his birthday *Odes* to be bad: but that was not the case, Sir; for he kept them many months by him, and a few years before he died he shewed me one of them, with great solicitude to render it as perfect as might be, and I made some corrections, to which he was not very willing to submit."[8]

Because he was laureate, Cibber was admitted to the best circles. Though Dr. Johnson did not respect Cibber because he was a player—" 'Now, Sir, to talk of *respect* for a *player!*' (smiling disdainfully)"[9]—his post did allow him to frequent the salons of the noble. He dined with Chesterfield, was seen with the Duke of Newcastle, and appeared at Court. The world was open to him, and if one looks through these years one sees Cibber gambling, preening, flattering the ladies, and being an intimate of the great and famous. And there was little wonder, for though Walpole did not consider him a gentleman of "the first fashion,"[10] Cibber was great and famous. He was what he had always wanted to be: he was known. It probably did not matter to him, at least he did not show it, whether or not he was liked.

Because he was well known, we may presume, he began his book. He started writing in 1737, and the first copies reached the town in 1740. Almost immediately controversy began, and he was soon deep in quarrels with his old enemies Pope and Fielding. These encounters were to fiill Cibber's life until Pope's death. The roster of pamphlets shows something of the extent of the exchange: *A Letter from Mr. Cibber to Mr. Pope* (1742); *The Egoist; or Colley Upon Colley* (1743); *A Second Letter from Mr. Cibber to Mr. Pope* (1743); *Another Occasional Letter from Mr. Cibber to Mr. Pope* (1744). And, of course, there was *The Dunciad* and Fielding's *Joseph Andrews*.

During this time he returned, despite his "retirement," to the stage. His occasional appearances were welcomed not so much because of his skill, which was decayed, but because he was a venerable name from the past and, for the young, a curiosity. And despite his retirement Cibber remained interested in the theater, attending it, prompting young actors and actresses with advice, passing judgment on new plays, weighing the merits of new performers (he did not like Garrick), and acting, in short, the theatrical patriarch. In 1745 Cibber finally made his last appearance on the stage, in his own play, *Papal Tyranny in the Reign of King John*. It was deservedly unsuccessful, and Cibber's portrayal of the evil Cardinal Pandulph was not well received. Cibber was seventy-four, and after the closing of his play he left the stage for good.

But the old man was not to be deterred by mere theatrical failure. He sought out company everywhere, and since he was familiar in society, he felt the need of new elations and closer associations. He solved the first problem at Bath, where he had written much of the *Apology*, by becoming, with Beau Nash, one of the company of elderly rakes. He ogled the ladies, sang their praises, and even went so far as to fall hopelessly in love with Mrs. Chudleigh, the toast of the season. To some, this behavior may seem childish, almost senile, but it is characteristic of Cibber, and we know at least that the insolent fire had not yet died.

The story of Cibber's last years becomes a record of his friendships and his life in the town. Cibber the actor, playwright, and apologist is now gone, and only the laureate, writing, enjoying his post, and entertaining himself with the theater and with his noble friends is left. Cibber appears in these last years to be somehow more charming, less waspish, than before. He is kinder, and more benign, and yet lively to the end.

Of his friends a few names remain to be recorded. In 1740 he met and admired Peg Woffington, whose fame as an actress was to grow from that year. He thought highly of her, and when Garrick stole her away there may have been some rancor. But apparently Cibber was not too distraught, and soon he embarked on another flirtatious friendship, this time with Mrs. Pilkington, an adventuress and poet of sorts, who had been a friend to Swift until scandal excluded her from his company, and who found in Cibber a friend and patron. Mrs. Pilkington is not remembered as a poet, but she was apparently charming, and Cibber was not adverse to the flattery she so lavishly heaped upon him in return for his introductions to the rich and the great.

Cibber continued to write even in his last years. In 1747 he completed *The Character and Conduct of Cicero*, which is long and undistinguished. It was much admired by Samuel Richardson, with whom Cibber became close, close enough to object to the novelist about Clarissa's death. In 1748 he wrote *The Lady's Lecture, A Theatrical Dialogue*, and in 1751 *A Rhapsody on the Marvellous*—all now forgotten.

It is clear from the sparse evidence that little of Cibber's life after the *Apology* need concern us. The life had been lived and chronicled, and what remained was a happy retirement filled with those inconsequentia which made life pleasant and which were indeed, the very stuff and fabric of his plays. He finally came, in age, to live the life he had written of in youth. And clearly, despite the flaws and careless indiscretions, despite Pope and Fielding, despite himself, he lived it very well. He died, quite as happily, on December 11, 1757.

He was a speculator, a social climber—vain and inclined to envy—yet he was, as his book shows, a man who could be frank and probably likable as well. Wits, will, and determination drove him, and in consequence he became the most distinguished co-median of his day, the effective and efficient master of Drury Lane, and a shaping force in the English theater. As Johnson had observed, Colley Cibber was no blockhead. He knew what he wanted, and he tried the wind until he found the way.

The *Apology*, published by John Watts in quarto, for a guinea, appeared on April 7, 1740. It was taken up, read, discussed, praised, attacked, and ridiculed. It infuriated Pope, further alienated Fielding, and provided a brisk, candid, and gossipy portrait of theater life. Probably, the public did not await the book with the same trepidation with which Boswell's *Johnson* was anticipated, but the *Apology* gave many cause to gossip and refueled old quarrels and lighted new ones.

The book was successful enough to call for a second edition, again published by Watts—on May 14, 1740—this time in oc-tavo at five shillings. Cibber made some corrections in this edi-tion, revised a little, and let some new printer's errors appear. For accuracy, there is little reason to prefer one edition over the other. Two editions appeared in the same year in Dublin, "re-printed" by George Faulkner, probably pirated, and later in 1740 Cibber began proceedings against Robert Walker who also tried to pirate the book.[11]

Two years later, in 1742, an abbreviated version, much re-written, called "The Life of Mr. Colley Cibber" appeared in a collection of essays, *A History of the Stage*. There was no new complete edition until 1750, when Cibber sold his copy-right to Robert Dodsley.[12] *The Laureat* observes that "from such a Pile of undigested incoherent Ideas huddled together by the *Misnomer* of a History" Cibber raised "a contribution on the Town (if Fame says true) of Fifteen hundred Pounds."[13] This amount came to Cibber in the first year alone, so that when he sold the copyright he was apparently satisfied with his proceeds.

The third edition, octavo, of 1750 was followed in 1756 by a fourth in two volumes, duodecimo, this too published by Dodsley. This was the last edition in Cibber's lifetime.

The book remained popular and was reprinted in 1822, 1826, 1829, 1830, and 1889. The most important of these editions are Edmund Bellchambers' (1822), "with many Critical and Explanatory Notices," and Robert W. Lowe's, in two volumes (1889).

Bellchambers' edition was the first to be annotated. Bellchambers liked the *Apology* but despised Cibber, and his notes reflect this; in addition, they are perfunctory and sometimes incorrect. Lowe, on the contrary, annotated carefully and objectively. He corrected Bellchambers' errors, added a great deal of information, and cleared up many problems, but some of his information is now outdated, inappropriate, or in rare instances in error. For modern taste, perhaps, he overannotates, but the book is a useful source for theatrical information relevant to the *Apology*—such as his reprints of Aston's *Brief Supplement* and the *Historial Histrionica*.[14] He also included Bellchambers' useful memoirs of actors and actresses and a good supplemental chapter on Cibber's later life. He reprinted the second edition, which he compared with the first. Only a handful of variants are recorded, however, and some inaccuracies have crept into the text and into the variants. Nevertheless, Lowe's book is the first edition which can in any way satisfy modern requirements for a definitive text. The Grolier Society reprinted Lowe's volumes in a limited edition of 150 copies. The twentieth century has seen three other reprints: the Everyman edition (1914, 1938), textually flawed and out of print, and the Golden Cockeral Press two-volume edition (1925), a modernized version of the text of 1756.

Cibber's book was bound to be received with less than objectivity. His quarrels with Pope and Fielding insured that, and their vehement reaction to the book perhaps obscures the fact that it was popular, as Cibber's profits show. Benjamin Victor, a friend of Cibber's and closely involved with the theater, commented in 1761 that the *Apology* had been "universally read and justly admired. . . ."[15] Walpole, though he thought Cibber's writings to be generally "pert and dull," declared the book inimitable and asserted that it "deserved immortality."[16] Johnson described the *Apology* as "very entertaining." Further, when Boswell insisted, "You will allow his *Apology* to be very well done," Johnson replied: "Very well done to be sure, Sir. That book is a striking proof of the justice of Pope's remark: 'Each might his several province well command,/ Would all but stoop to what they understand.'"[17] Johnson did not like Cibber, and Pope would have been infuriated to be used in his defense, but the point is well taken. Cibber knew what he was doing. It will probably never be known why Swift sat up all night to finish the book, for he liked Cibber no better than Johnson did, but it may have been because he recognized that Cibber was an authority and because the story was candidly told. The exiled dean was no doubt grateful for the memories that Cibber revived, and sometimes, perhaps, even gleeful. Thus, Cibber's enemies were not able to damn the book entirely, and *The Laureat* grudgingly admitted that "There are some good things in thy Book, old Colley. . . ."[18]

But as often happened, Cibber's enemies were more vociferous and famous than his friends, and it is the remarks of his enemies which posterity recalls. Pope, in an often-quoted letter to the Earl of Orrery set the tone: "And Cibber himself is the honestest Man I know, who has writ a book of his *Confessions*, not so much to his Credit as St. Augustine's, but full as True & as open. Never had Impudence and Vanity so faithful a Professor. I honour him next to my Lord."[19]

Some of the most vicious and keenest criticism appeared in *The Laureat*, where an anonymous writer asserted that "this long and labour'd Performance of our most celebrated Laureat, is something over-rated; and that if this work of his were to be dissected by a good Pen, . . . it would appear a most wretched and imperfect Skeleton, void of almost every Thing necessary either to delight or instruct."[20] On Cibber's comment that the world, having seen him in the acting guise of others for so long, should now be pleased to see him in his own shape, *The Laureat* critic gibed: "I think, the world would not have been inflamed with any violent curiosity. . . ." His motives, the writer continued, "which have prompted him thus to strip himself and dance naked before the People, were the same that incited him to act upon the stage, *Interest* and *Vanity*. . . . Colley Cibber is not the Character he pretends to be in this Book, but a mere *Charleton*, a *Persona Dramatis*, a Mountebank, a Counterfeit Colley. . . ."[21] Earlier in his tirade the writer had slyly noted that Cibber said in the *Apology* that *"he should write his own Life, and be laugh'd at;* the prophecy is fulfill'd. . . ."[22]

A pamphlet in which Fielding may have had a hand was entitled *The Tryal of Colley Cibber* (1740), written by "T. Johnson." "Lo! He hath Written a Book," is the epigraph, and some pages later the writer declared: "and tho' some imagined it would be confined only to the Theatre, yet certain it is that this valuable Work hath much greater Matters in View, and may as properly be stiled an Apology for the Life of One Who hath played a very comical Part, which, tho' Theatrical hath been acted on a much larger Stage than *Drury-Lane*."[23] The information in the book, he continued, is such that "there are several Particulars which no one can know without reading it, and which very probably may not reach Posterity in any other History."[24] (It is nice to note parenthetically that this is precisely one of the reasons why we now value the *Apology*.)

The writer of the *Tryal* chided Cibber on his style, a legitimate complaint: "He who commits his Thoughts to Paper without being able methodically to range them . . . gives us an Instance of the most intemperate Abuse of his own Time. . . ." Finally, again turning Cibber's words, the writer pointed out that in the *Apology* Cibber had urged that his book would show whether he was or was not a blockhead, "a point in which the Reader is by this Time well settled."[25] Dr. Johnson absolved Colley of this charge.

If Fielding did have something to do with the *Tryal*,[26] he did not reveal it. He was far more open in other publications, among them *The Champion*, a periodical, wherein he attacked Cibber for his style; in the issue for May 17, 1740, he put Cibber on trial for the murder of the English tongue. Later, in 1741, *An Apology for the Life of Mrs. Shamela Andrews* by Coney Keyber effectively choked two singing birds, and the crown of it all came in 1742, when in *Joseph Andrews* Fielding noted that Cibber must have lived the life he did in order to apologize for it. The battery was done, and to an extent, Cibber had deserved it.

To offset the attacks, a few later opinions may be mentioned. Once factionalism and controversy had died, a more objective view began to emerge. The earliest careful annotator of the book, Edmund Bellchambers, observed (while he meanly attacks Cibber: "He became in the zenith of his notoriety a drunkard, a fornicator, and an atheist")[27] that "to the justice of his general views very little can be added. He has delineated the stage, during his long intimacy with it, in a copious and impartial manner, and whatever earnestness he betrays in support of its primitive institution, is always coupled with a warm exposure of its contemptible management. Nothing is more liable to corrupt and debase the public mind than licentious amusements. . . . Cibber saw this evil with a clear and honest eye and some of the best pages of his *Apology* are those that were penned to correct it."[28]

Lowe in 1889 briefly commented that "Colley Cibber's famous autobiography has always been recognized as one of the most delightful books of its class . . . ,"[29] and the writer who called himself "John o'London" in *T-P's Weekly* for August 8, 1914, reviewing the Everyman edition, rejoiced that the *Apology*, "of neglected books . . . one of the most remarkable," will be read again. It is, he continued, "a first-rate, salty, and orginating [sic] piece of work, suffused with good sense, gusto, and convincing judgement. It is the only vindication that Cibber now needs against the malignity of Pope and the coldness of Johnson."

William Carew Hazlitt also spoke in its defense. In an "Appreciation" printed in the Everyman text he insisted that "Cibber is a most amusing biographer: happy in his own good opinion, the best of all others; teeming with animal spirits, and uniting the self-sufficiency of youth with the garrulity of age."[30]

Modern opinion is well expressed by Edgar Johnson: The *Apology* is "a collection of theatrical memoirs, of brilliant dramatic portraits and skilful analyses of the actor's art; an informal and gossipy history of the stage . . . all as light and trivial and gay, and as sensible and keen in an everyday, wordly way as its author."[31]

The *Apology*, then, is clearly one of the most important documents of the eighteenth-century stage. Since Cibber was one of the best actors, most prolific playwrights, and shrewdest managers, his voice is certainly authoritative. Often our knowledge of some areas of theatrical history—characters of actors, performances, backstage machinations—is based solely on his information.

Cibber offers mainly three things in the *Apology:* an autobiographical account of his life, a history of the theater as he saw it from 1690 to 1733, and a collection of portraits, anecdotes, and observations about actors and acting. That these things are in an almost haphazard arrangement and in a remarkably un-Augustan style has been remarked since the book appeared, and there is no reason to defend him against these criticisms. The essence of Cibber's book is digression, and one chapter, for example, will find him dealing with events which occurred in 1698, 1704, and 1728. Yet there is always a connection, and, if the various chapters are surveyed, it is clear that Cibber covers, in one way or another, the major events of four decades with remarkable thoroughness. Though his method may not be chronological, or even logical, yet he does effectively present the information he intends to offer, and he gives a picture of his character as well. We see him in a variety of situations and roles, acting, on and off stage, flattering, cajoling, insulting, writing, managing. Time is telescoped, chronology ignored, yet the final effect is neither unpleasant nor even really confusing. I will not attribute the multi-faceted sense of event to any subtlety in Cibber's technique. I am sure he digressed because his mind was not one which proceeded logically from event to event. Nevertheless, the theme of the book is still clear, for as Cibber moves backward and forward in time, comparing events of 1695 with those of 1728, comparing the united company of 1694 with the united theater under the actor managers, comparing the divided theater with the united company, his point emerges. The playhouse is most successful when unified. A playhouse under divided management cannot stand. Two playhouses lead only to the corruption of the stage.[32] This thesis is put forward so often that it becomes abundantly clear that Cibber is writing not only his life, but also a warning and manual for other managers and for the theater itself.

Further, out of the digressions Cibber himself emerges. And this is an achievement of the shifting chronology. Again and again, we see Cibber the wise, Cibber the generous, Cibber the patient. Whether he is quite literally giving the shirt off his back, or making up a deficit out of his pocket, whether he influences Rich beneficently or guides the actor-managers to success, always it is Cibber who is the effective influence behind the scenes.

That there is vanity here, not even Cibber would deny. But there is also much truth, and an attempt to explain as clearly, and in as good light as possible, of course, the events of a complex time. If Cibber—arguing a case wisely before the Court in Chancery, or graciously making amends to Doggett, or patiently bearing the abuse of the senior actors at Drury Lane—appears as a sympathetic figure, then all to the good. Cibber is absolutely candid when he tells us that vanity has always been a part of his disposition, but this does not mean that his account could not be truthful.

If Cibber errs, as the notes will show that he sometimes does, it is not, I think, from malice, but simply from faulty memory. Some events are, no doubt, colored by animosity. It is true for example that he did not like Powell, and that he objected to Wilks. But his treatment of them, though biased, is never malicious. Delightfully human as he was, Cibber could not be impartial. And in a time when partiality and attack were a literary staple, one ought not expect him to be. It is pleasing to see that Cibber is far less likely to attack, far less likely to defame or dismiss, than those who vilified him.

No doubt one could point out that his judgments on the actors of the early Restoration are more favorable than on those in his own time. But then, he is looking back fifty years, to the idols of youth. No one can blame him for a rosy perspective, and his comments as an actor on his own contemporaries are the more useful by being candid.

Except for his attack on Fielding as a broken wit—and he had some provocation—Cibber is seldom bitter, seldom unfair. He is sometimes envious, often shrewd, and even scheming, but he redeems himself by always being human and engaging. Cibber never fails to charm and to communicate enthusiasm and delight. These things the reader catches and shares. And best of all, he is always readable.

Cibber is readable, though, not because he writes well, but because he writes with character. One cannot speak of Cibber's style, for if he has one, it is badly faulted. He is discursive, ungrammatical. Metaphors take wing and fall in confusion. Language is used with an almost charming disregard for its meaning. "Thus, when he says . . . *Satire is angrily particular*, every Dunce of a Reader knows he means angry with a particular person; or when he says . . . a *Moral Humanity*, can't you strike Moral out, and let humanity stand by itself, or put Virtue in its Place?"[33] The reader will no doubt note more examples. But we need not carp over style; it too is Cibber, and its one redeeming quality is that, as we perceive Johnson in a sonorous phrase, so we know Cibber better when his weak periods limp to their pert, frank, and amusing close.

Certain elements in the *Apology* should be considered which tell something of his talents, his prose, and his verse. He says that "such learning as that school could give me is the most I pretend to (which, tho' I have not utterly forgot, I cannot say

I have much improv'd by study) ..." (p. 9). With his six years
of formal education as his only training, Cibber was drawn to
the stage. One should not be too shocked, then, to find deficiencies in his writing. He was no linguist, his classical training
was slight, even his knowledge of drama does not seem extensive. It is curious to note that of the many Shakespearean quotations in the Apology, all save a few come from *Hamlet* or
Othello; most of his Latin is drawn from Horace and Virgil.

Another moment catches him typically: "I resolv'd to leave
nothing unattempted, that might shew me in some new Rank
or Distinction. Having then no other Resources, I was at last
reduc'd to write a character for myself" (p. 118). Cibber was
unschooled, yet brave, and also eager for fame; the *Apology* tells
something of the man who, when a youth, sought to rise by
any way at all, even by writing a play as his own starring vehicle.
There is courage there, foolishness too, yet one must respect
the frankness of his admission and remember that he was com-
peting at the top level with Dryden, Congreve, and Southerne,
and at the second level with Mrs. Behn, Shadwell, and many
others. Cibber was, after all, only twenty-five when he wrote
a rare work—*Love's Last Shift*. It is not a great one, but it is
theatrically important—better than many credit it with being.
It is funny, it has stageworthy moments, and Sir Novelty Fashion
is a most excellent fop. Sentimental comedy was probably born
with this play. Cibber intuitively sensed what the audience
wanted. It is just this sort of moment that displays him so vividly.
It is this intuition which leads us through the *Apology* and
which characterizes the man. It is not tact, nor diplomacy, but
a sixth sense that impelled him to do the right thing for himself at the right time. A real character lives in these pages.
Whether it is always truly Cibber we cannot know, but he is
far too alive for such a quibble.

What are invariably—and truly—called the best things in the
book are Cibber's descriptions of "several theatrical characters." Cibber creates character well. Betterton is drawn in detail.
Kynaston appears, and Cibber describes his person, his character, the roles he played, and his talents, until little is left that we

want to know. Sandford, Leigh, the great Mrs. Barry, are all portrayed in detail and with a happy remembrance brought about by the passing years. Cibber makes it clear that these were gods for him and that the stage never saw their kind again. As Barker has observed,[34] Cibber's vision is not so clear when he looks to a mellowed past. It is sharper, more biting and critical, when he tells of his own times.

The first five chapters of the book are the best because they are the most vivid. But the last chapters become more detailed, for Cibber tells of a period—1695 to 1733—when he was on hand to observe. These chapters are more specific and more particular. Petty quarrels, minor events, rivalries, and backstage schemes are recounted. Here the struggle between the Lord Chamberlain and the theaters is described. Here Rich the villain is created, Cibber the hero is born. Here are reported the daily details of the battle between the two stages and, gradually, the triumph of the actor-managers. The characters are so numerous and their roles so various that some confusion is inevitable. Yet in back of this little world, in back of the maneuverings of Rich and Swiney, of Wilks, Steele, and Cibber, even the most casual reader can see the strong tradition of the English stage being built. He can sense that, despite the king-making and the toppling of thrones, there was a dedication of spirit and talent. And that, of course, is why Cibber's book—the chronicle, some say, of a coxcomb, of a vain and envious fool, a detailed account of feuds and lesser men—is still engaging, for it tells frankly and without deception not only the life of its author, but what it was like before the curtain rose.

A NOTE ON THE OFFICIAL STATUS
OF THE THEATER

The *Apology* is not only an autobiography, but a chronicle of the relations between the stage and the government. A brief chronology of important events will make the official status of the theater clear.

1660 Davenant and Killigrew receive a patent from Charles II. They thus become servants of the King, and legally responsible to him and his officers. The patent in effect gave them a monopoly on plays, players, and acting, though they were to some extent under the control of the Master of the Revels, Sir Henry Herbert.

1662 Killigrew and Herbert agree on payment of a fee to the Master of the Revels for each new play.

1682 The two companies are united under one patent.

1695 The two companies separate and a license is issued to the dissenting actors at Lincoln's Inn Fields. The principle of patent *and* license is now established; it will become the lever that the actor-managers later use in their rise to power.

1695 The Lord Chamberlain rules that actors cannot leave their respective companies without his permission. His action is taken under the presumption that the actors are, under the patent, King's servants.

1696 The Lord Chamberlain orders all plays to be licensed, and
/97 to be submitted to the Master of the Revels for examination and, if necessary, censoring.

In the eighteenth century interference by the Lord Chamberlain becomes common and is further strengthened by the following:

1709 Rich is silenced by the Lord Chamberlain.

1714 The order of silence is revoked and Rich's patent is restored.

1715 Sir Richard Steele is granted a patent by the Lord Chamberlain.

During this time, as well, the Lord Chamberlain continues to exercise control over the performance of plays until, in 1737, the Licensing Act achieves a settlement and clearly established the Lord Chamberlain's power as censor.

It should not be thought that there was no opposition to these
events. Indeed, much of Cibber's book is concerned with
the efforts of the patentees and the managers to circumvent
the authority of the Lord Chamberlain. But that is, in effect, the story of the development of the theater from an
independent group to a licensed and controlled entity,
allied gradually, and often by constraint, with the crown.
It is to Cibber's credit that he was among those who fought
to establish and maintain the freedoms of the theater.

A NOTE ON THE TEXT

The following text is that of the first edition of 1740, which
has not been reprinted since that year. Though Cibber made
some changes in the second edition, they are not rewritings
in the sense that his changes in *Love's Last Shift* (1696) for the
1721 edition of his plays were, but are corrections and gram-
matical changes. It is the first, not the second, edition which is,
even in this minor way, historically important, and it seems appropriate to use that as the copy text. Since there has never
been a complete collation with the London editions, in which,
presumably, Cibber might have had a hand, I feel justified in
offering the first edition with the historical collation to be found
in the notes.

   I have, save for a few emendations, reproduced the text as it
appears in the first edition, modernizing only the long "s." Punc-
tuation, spelling, and italicized words remain unchanged, save
where some obvious printer's error has led me to correct the
defect.

THE CONTENTS.

TO A CERTAIN GENTLEMAN[1]

SIR,

Because I know it would give you less Concern, to find your Name in an impertinent Satyr, then before the daintiest Dedication of a modern Author, I conceal it.

Let me never talk so idly to you, this way; you are, at least, under no necessity of taking it to yourself: Nor when I boast of your Favours, need you blush to have bestow'd them. Or may I now give you all the Attributes, that raise a wise, and good-natur'd Man, to Esteem, and Happiness, and not be censured as a Flatterer by my own, or your Enemies.---- I place my own first; because as they are the greater Number, I am afraid of not paying the greater Respect to them. Yours, if such there are, I imagine are too well-bred to declare themselves: But as there is no Hazard, or visible Terror, in an Attack, upon my defenceless Station, my Censurers have generally been persons of an intrepid Sincerity. Having therefore shut the Door against them, while I am thus privately addressing you, I have little to apprehend, from either of them.

Under this Shelter, then, I may safely tell you, That the greatest Encouragement, I have had to publish this Work, has risen from the several Hours of Patience you have lent me, at the Reading it. It is true, I took the Advantage of your Leisure, in the Country, where moderate Matters serve for Amusement; and there indeed, how far your Good-nature, for an old Acquaintance, or your Reluctance to put the Vanity of an Author out of countenance, may have carried you, I cannot be sure; and yet Appearances give me stronger Hopes: For was not the Complaisance of a whole Evening's Attention, as much as an Author of more Importance ought to have expected? Why then was I desired the next Day, to give you a second Lecture? Or why was I kept a third Day, with you, to tell you more of the same Story? If these Circumstances have made me vain, shall I say, Sir, you are accountable for them? No, Sir, I will rather so far flatter myself, as to suppose it possible, That your having been a Lover of the Stage (and one of those few good Judges, who know the Use, and Value of it, under a right Regulation) might incline you to think so copious an Account of it a less tedious Amusement, than it may naturally be, to others of different good Sense, who may have less Concern, or Taste for it. But be all this as it may; the Brat is now born, and rather, than see it starve, upon the Bare Parish Provision, I chuse thus clandestinely, to drop it at your Door, that it may exercise One of your Many Virtues, your Charity, in supporting it.

If the World were to know, into whose Hands I have thrown it, their Regard to its Patron might incline them, to treat it as One of his Family: But in the Consciousness of what I *am*, I chuse not, Sir, to say who You *are*. If your Equal, in Rank, were to do publick Justice to your Character, then indeed, the Concealment of your Name might be an unnecessary Diffidence: But am I, Sir, of Consequence enough, in any Guise, to do Honour to Mr.----? were I to set him, in the most laudable Lights, that Truth, and good Sense could give him, or his own Likeness would require; my officious Mite would be lost in that general Esteem, and Regard, which People of the first Consequence, even of different Parties, have a Pleasure, in paying him. Encomiums to Superiors, from Authors of lower Life, as they are naturally liable to Suspicion, can add very little Lustre, to what before was visible to the publick Eye: Such Offerings (to use the Stile they are generally dress'd in) like *Pagan* Incense, evaporate, on the Altar, and rather gratify the Priest, than the Deity.

But you, Sir, are to be approach'd in Terms, within the Reach of common Sense: The honest Oblation of a cheerful Heart, is as much as you desire, or I am able to bring you: A Heart, that has just Sense enough, to mix Respect, with Intimacy, and is never more delighted, than when your rural Hours of Leisure admit me, with all my laughing Spirits, to be my idle self, and in the whole Day's Possession of you! Then, indeed, I have Reason to be vain; I am, then, distinguish'd, by a Pleasure too great, to be conceal'd, and could almost pity the Man of graver Merit, that dares not receive it, with the same unguarded Transport! This Nakedness of Temper the World may place, in what Rank of Folly, or Weakness they please; but till Wisdom, can give me something, that will make me more heartily happy, I am content, to be gaz'd at, as I am, without lessening my Respect, for those, whose Passions may be more soberly cover'd.

Yet, Sir, will I not deceive you; 'tis not the Lustre of your publick Merit, the Affluence of your Fortune, your high Figure in Life, nor those honourable Distinctions, which you had rather deserve than be told of, that have so many Years made my plain Heart hang after you: These are but incidental Ornaments, that, 'tis true, may be of Service to you, in the World's Opinion; and though, as one among the Crowd, I may rejoice, that Providence has so deservedly bestow'd them; yet my particular Attachment has risen from a meer natural, and more engaging Charm, The Agreeable Companion! Nor is my Vanity half so much gratified, in the *Honour*, as my Sense is in the *Delight* of your Society! When I see you lay aside the Advantages of Superiority, and by your own Cheerfulness of Spirits, call out all that Nature has given me to meet them; then 'tis I taste you! then Life runs high! I desire! I possess you!

Yet, Sir, in this distinguish'd Happiness, I give not up my farther Share of that Pleasure, or of that Right I have to look upon you, with the publick Eye, and to join in the general Regard so unanimously pay'd to that uncommon Virtue, your *Integrity!* This, Sir, the World allows so conspicuous a Part of your Character, that, however invidious the Merit, neither the rude License of Detraction, nor the Prejudice of Party, has ever, once, thrown on it the least Impeachment, or Reproach. This is that commanding Power, that in publick Speaking, makes you heard with such Attention! This it is, that discourages, and keeps silent the Insinuations of Prejudice, and Suspicion; and almost

renders your Eloquence an unnecessary Aid, to your Assertions:
Even your Opponents, conscious of your *Integrity*, hear you
rather as a Witness, than an Orator---- But this, Sir, is drawing
you too near the Light, *Integrity* is too particular a Virtue to be
cover'd with a general Application. Let me therfore only talk
to you, as at *Tusculum*² (for so I will call that sweet Retreat,
which your own Hands have rais'd) where like the fam'd Orator
of old, when publick Cares permit, you pass so many rational,
unbending Hours: There! and at such Times, to have been
admitted, still plays in my Memory, more like a fictitious, than
a real Enjoyment! How many golden Evenings, in that Theatrical Paradise of water'd Lawns, and hanging Groves, have I
walk'd, and prated down the Sun, in social Happiness! Whether
the Retreat of *Cicero*, in Cost, Magnificence, or curious Luxury
of Antiquities, might not out-blaze the *Simplex Munditiis*³, the
modest Ornaments of your *Villa*, is not within my reading to
determine: But that the united Power of Nature, Art, or Ele-
gance of Taste, could have thrown so many varied Objects, into
a more delightful Harmony, is beyond my Conception.

When I consider you, in this View, and as the Gentleman of
Eminence, surrounded with the general Benevolence of Mankind; I rejoice, Sir, for you, and for myself; to see *You*, in this
particular Light of Merit, and myself, sometimes, admitted to
my more than equal Share of you.

If this *Apology* for my past Life discourages you not, from
holding me, in your usual Favour, let me quit this greater
Stage, the World, whenever I may, I shall think This the best-
acted Part of any I have undertaken, since you first condescended to laugh with,

    SIR,
          Your most obedient,
               most oblig'd, and
                   most humble Servant,

Novemb. 6.
 ¹739
                        COLLEY CIBBER

An
Apology
for the
Life *of Mr.* Colley Cibber, & c.

CHAP. I[1]

You know, Sir, I have often told you, that one time or other I should give the Publick some Memoirs of my own Life; at which you have never fail'd to laugh, like a Friend, without saying a word to dissuade me from it; concluding, I suppose, that such a wild Thought could not possibly require a serious Answer. But you see I was in earnest. And now you will say, the World will find me, under my own Hand, a weaker Man than perhaps I may have pass'd for, even among my Enemies.---- With all my Heart! my Enemies will then read me with Pleasure, and you, perhaps, with Envy, when you find that Follies, without the Reproach of Guilt upon them, are not inconsistent with Happiness.---- But why make my Follies publick? Why not? I have pass'd my Time very pleasantly with them, and I don't recollect that they have ever been hurtful to any other Man living. Even admitting they were injudiciously chosen, would it not be Vanity in me to take Shame to myself for not being found a Wise Man? Really, Sir, my Appetites were in too much haste to be happy, to throw away my Time in pursuit of a Name I was sure I could never arrive at.

Now the Follies I frankly confess, I look upon as, in some

measure, discharged; while those I conceal are still keeping the
Account open between me and my Conscience. To me the
Fatigue of being upon a continual Guard to hide them, is more
than the Reputation of being without them can repay. If this
be Weakness, *defendit numerus*,[2] I have such comfortable Numbers on my side, that were all Men to blush, that are not Wise,
I am afraid, in Ten, Nine Parts of the World ought to be out of
Countenance: But since that sort of Modesty is what they don't
care to come into, why should I be afraid of being star'd at, for
not being particular? Or if the Particularity lies in owning my
Weakness, will my wisest Reader be so inhuman as not to pardon
it? But if there should be such a one, let me, at least, beg him to
shew me that strange Man, who is perfect! Is any one more
unhappy, more ridiculous, than he who is always laboring to be
thought so, or that is impatient, when he is not thought so?
Having brought myself to be easy, under whatever the World
may say of my Undertaking, you may still ask me, why I give
myself all this trouble? Is it for Fame, or Profit[3] to myself, or
Use or Delight to others? For all these Considerations I have
neither Fondness nor Indifference: If I obtain none of them, the
Amusement, at worst, will be a Reward that must constantly go
along with the Labour. But behind all this, there is something
inwardly inciting, which I can not express in few Words; I
must therefore a little make bold with your Patience.

A Man who has pass'd above Forty Years of his Life upon a
Theatre, where he has never appear'd to be Himself, may have
naturally excited the Curiosity of his Spectators to know what
he really was, when in no body's Shape but his own; and whether
he, who by his Profession had so long been ridiculing his Bene-
factors, might not, when the Coat of his Profession was off,
deserve to be laugh'd at himself; or from his being often seen in,
the most flagrant, and immoral Characters; whether he might not
see as great a Rogue, when he look'd into the Glass himself,
as when he held it to others.

It was, doubtless, from a Supposition that this sort of Curiosity
wou'd compensate their Labours, that so many hasty Writers
have been encourag'd to publish the Lives of the late Mrs. *Old-*

field, Mr. *Wilks*, and Mr. *Booth*,[4] in less time after their Deaths than one cou'd suppose it cost to transcribe them.

Now, Sir, when my Time comes, lest they shou'd think it worth while to handle my Memory with the same Freedom, I am willing to prevent its being so odly besmear'd (or at best but flatly white-wash'd) by taking upon me to give the Publick This, as true a Picture of myself as natural Vanity will permit me to draw: For, to promise you that I shall never be vain, were a Promise that, like a Looking-glass too large, might break itself in the making: Nor am I sure I ought wholly to avoid that Imputation, because if Vanity be one of my natural Features, the Portrait wou'd not be like me without it. In a Word, I may palliate, and soften, as much as I please; but, upon an honest Examination of my Heart, I am afraid the same Vanity which makes even homely People employ Painters to preserve a flattering Record of their Persons, has seduced me to print off this *Chiaro Oscuro* of my mind.

And when I have done it, you may reasonably ask me, of what Importance can the History of my private Life be to the Publick? To this, indeed, I can only make you a ludicrous Answer, which is, That the Publick very well knows, my Life has not been a private one; that I have been employ'd in their Service, ever since many of their Grandfathers were young Men; And tho' I have voluntarily laid down my Post, they have a sort of Right to enquire into my Conduct, (for which they have so well paid me) and to call for the Account of it, during my Share of the Administration in the State of the Theatre. This Work, therefore, which I hope, they will not expect a Man of my hasty Head shou'd confine to any regular Method: (For I shall make no scruple of leaving my History, when I think a Digression may make it lighter, for my Reader's Digestion.) This Work, I say, shall not only contain the various Impressions of my Mind, (as in *Louis the Fourteenth* his Cabinet you have seen the growing Medals of his Person from Infancy to Old Age,) but shall likewise include with them the *Theatrical History of my Own Time*, from my first Appearance on the Stage to my last *Exit*.[5]

If then what I shall advance on that Head, may any ways contribute to the Prosperity or Improvement of the Stage in being, the Publick must of consequence have a Share in its Utility.

This, Sir, is the best Apology I can make for being my own Biographer. Give me leave therefore to open the first Scene of my Life, from the very Day I came into it; and tho' (considering my Profession) I have no reason to be asham'd of my Original; yet I am afraid a plain dry Account of it, will scarce admit of a better Excuse than what my brother *Bays* makes for Prince *Prettyman* in the *Rehearsal*, viz, *I only do it, for fear I should be thought to be no body's Son at all;*[6] for if I have led a worthless Life, the Weight of my Pedigree will not add an Ounce to my intrinsic Value. But be the Inference what it will, the simple Truth is this.

I was born in *London*, on the 6th of *November* 1671, in *Southampton-Street*, facing *Southampton-House*.[7] My Father, *Caius Gabriel Cibber*, was a native of *Holstein*, who came into *England* some time before the Restoration of King *Charles* II. to follow his Profession, which was that of a Statuary, & c. The *Basso Relievo* on the Pedestal of the Great Column in the City, and the two Figures of the *Lunaticks*, the *Raving* and the *Melancholy*, over the Gates of *Bethlehem-Hospital*, are no ill Monuments of his Fame as an Artist.[8] My Mother[9] was the Daughter of *William Colley*, Esq; of a very ancient Family of *Glaiston* in *Rutlandshire*, where she was born. My Mother's Brother, *Edward Colley*, Esq; (who gave me my Christian Name) being the last Heir Male of it, the Family is now extinct. I shall only add, that in *Wright's* History of *Rutlandshire*, publish'd in 1684, the *Colley's* are recorded as Sheriffs and Members of Parliament from the Reign of *Henry* VII. to the latter end of *Charles* I. in whose Cause chiefly Sir *Antony Colley*, my Mother's Grandfather, sunk his Estate from Three Thousand to about Three Hundred *per Annum*.

In a Year 1682, at little more than ten Years of Age, I was sent to the Free-School of *Grantham* in *Lincolnshire*, where I staid till I got through it, from the lowest Form to the uppermost. And such Learning as that School could give me, is the most I pretend to (which, tho' I have not utterly forgot, I can not say I have much improv'd by Study) but even there I remember I was the same inconsistent Creature I have been ever since! always in full Spirits, in some small Capacity to do right, but in a more frequent Alacrity to do wrong; and consequently often under a worse Character than I wholly deserv'd: A giddy Negligence always possess'd me, and so much, that I remember I was once whip'd for my *Theme*, tho' my Master told me, at the same time, what was good of it was better than any Boy's in the Form. And (whatever Shame it may be to own it) I have observ'd the same odd Fate has frequently attended the course of my later Conduct in Life. The unskilful openness, or in plain Terms, the Indiscretion I have always acted with from my Youth, has drawn more ill-will towards me, than Men of worse Morals and more Wit might have met with. My Ignorance, and want of Jealousy of Mankind has been so strong, that it is with Reluctance I even yet believe any Person, I am acquainted with, can be capable of Envy, Malice, or Ingratitude: And to shew you what a Mortification it was to me, in my very boyish Days, to find my self mistaken, give me leave to tell you a School Story.

A great Boy, near the Head taller than my self, in some wrangle at play had insulted me; upon which I was fool-hardy enough to give him a Box on the Ear; the Blow was soon return'd with another, that brought me under him, and at his Mercy. Another Lad, whom I really lov'd, and thought a good-natur'd one, cry'd out with some warmth, to my Antagonist (while I was down) Beat him, beat him soundly! This so amaz'd me, that I lost all my Spirits to resist, and burst into Tears! When the Fray was over I took my Friend aside, and ask'd him, How he came to be so earnestly against me? To which, with some glouting[10] Confusion, he reply'd, Because you are always jeering, and making a Jest of me to every Boy in the School. Many a Mischief have I brought upon my self by the same Folly in riper Life. Whatever Reason I had to reproach my Companion's declaring against me, I had none to wonder at it, while I was so often hurting him: Thus I deserv'd his Enmity, by my not having Sense enough to know I *had* hurt him; and he hated me, because he had not Sense enough to know, that I never *intended* to hurt him.

As this is the first remarkable Error of my Life I can recollect, I cannot pass it by without throwing out some farther Reflections upon it; whether flat or spirited, new or common, false or true, right or wrong, they will be still my own, and consequently like me; I will therfore boldly go on; for I am only oblig'd to give you my *own*, and not a *good* Picture, to shew as well the Weakness, as the Strength of my Understanding. It is not on what I write, but on my Reader's Curiosity I relie to be read through: At worst, tho' the Impartial may be tir'd, the Ill-natur'd (no small number) I know will see the bottom of me.

What I observ'd then, upon my having undesignedly provok'd my School-Friend into an Enemy, is a common Case in Society; Errors of this kind often sour the Blood of Acquaintance into an inconceivable Aversion, where it is little suspected. It is not enough to say of your Raillery, that you intended no Offense; if the Person you offer it to has either a wrong Head, or wants a Capacity to make that distinction, it may have the same effect as the Intention of the grossest Injury: And in reality if you know his Parts are too slow to return it in kind, it is a vain and idle Inhumanity, and sometimes draws the Aggressor into difficulties not easily got out of: Or to give the Case more scope, suppose your Friend may have a passive Indulgence for your Mirth, if you find him silent at it; tho' you were as intrepid as *Caesar*, there can be no Excuse for your not leaving it off. When you are conscious that your Antagonist can give as well as take, then indeed the smarter the Hit the more agreeable the Party: A Man of cheerful Sense, among Friends will never be grave upon an Attack of this kind, but rather thank you that you have given him a Right to be even with you: There are few Men (tho' they may be Masters of both) that on such occasions had not rather shew their Parts than their Courage, and the Preference is just; a Bull-Dog may have one, and only a Man can have the other. Thus it happens, that in the coarse Merriment of common People, when the Jest begins to swell into earnest; for want of this Election you may observe, he that has least Wit generally gives the first Blow. Now, as among the better sort, a readiness of Wit is not always a Sign of intrinsic Merit; so the want of that readiness is no Reproach to a Man of plain Sense and Civility, who therefore (methinks) should never have these lengths of Liberty taken with him. Wit there becomes absurd, if not insolent; ill-natur'd I am sure it is, which Imputation a generous Spirit will always avoid, for the same Reason that a Man of real Honour will never send a Challenge to a Cripple. The inward Wounds that are given by the inconsiderate Insults of Wit, to those that want it, are as dangerous as those given by Oppression to Inferiors; as long in healing, and perhaps never forgiven. There is beside (and little worse than this) a mutual Grossness in Raillery, that sometimes is more painful to the Hearers that are not concerned in it, than to the Persons engag'd. I have seen a couple of these clumsy Combatants drub one another with as little Manners or Mercy as if they had two Flails in their Hands; Children at play with Case-knives could not give you more Apprehension of their doing one another Mischief. And yet when the Contest has been over, the Boobys have look'd around them for Approbation, and upon being told they were admirably well match'd, have sat down (Bedawb'd as they were) contented, at making it a drawn Battle. After all that I have said, there is no clearer way of giving Rules for Raillery than by Example.

There are two Persons now living,[11] who tho' very different in their manner, are, as far as my Judgment reaches, complete Masters of it; the one of a more polite and extensive Imagination, the other of a Knowledge more closely useful to the Business of Life: The one gives you perpetual Pleasure, and seems always to be taking it; the other seems to take none, till his Business is over, and then gives you as much as if Pleasure were his only Business. The one enjoys his Fortune, the other thinks it first necessary to make it; though that he will enjoy it then, I cannot be positive, because when a Man has once pick'd up more than he wants, he is apt to think it a Weakness to suppose he has enough. But as I don't remember ever to have seen these Gentlemen in the same Company, you must give me leave to take them separately.

The first of them, then, has a Title, and--- no matter what; I am not to speak of the great, but the happy part of his Character, and in this one single light; not of his being an illustrious, but a delightful Companion.

In Conversation he is seldom silent but when he is attentive, nor ever speaks without exciting the Attention of others; and tho' Man might with less displeasure to his Hearers, engross the Talk of the Company, he has a Patience in his Vivacity that chuses to divide it, and rather gives more Freedom than he takes; his sharpest Replies having a mixture of Politeness that few have the command of; his Expression is easy, short, and clear; a stiff or study'd Word never comes from him; it is in a simplicity of Style that he gives the highest Surprize, and his Ideas are always adapted to the Capacity and Taste of the Person he speaks to: Perhaps you will understand me better if I give you a particular Instance of it. A Person at the University, who from being a Man of Wit, easily became one of his Acquaintance there, from that Acquaintance found no difficulty in being made one of his Chaplains: This Person afterwards leading a Life that did no great Honour to his Cloth, oblig'd his Patron to take some gentle notice of it; but as his Patron knew the Patient was squeamish, he was induc'd to sweeten the Medicine to his Taste, and therefore with a smile of good-humour told him, that if to the many Vices he had already, he would give himself the trouble to add one more, he did not doubt but his Reputation might still be set up again. Sir *Crape*, who could have no Aversion to so pleasant a Dose, desiring to know what it might be, was answered, *Hypocrisy, Doctor, only a little Hypocrisy!* This plain Reply can need no Comment; but *ex pede Herculem*,[12] he is every where proportionable. I think I have heard him since say, the Doctor thought Hypocrisy so detestable a Sin that he dy'd without committing it. In a word, this Gentleman gives Spirit to Society the Moment he comes into it, and whenever he leaves it, they who have Business have then leisure to go about it.

Having often had the Honour to be my self the Butt of his Raillery, I must own I have receiv'd more Pleasure from his lively manner of raising the Laugh against me, than I could have felt from the smoothest flattery of a serious Civility. Tho' Wit flows from him with as much ease as common Sense from another, he is so little elated with the Advantage he may have over you, that whenever your good Fortune gives it against him, he seems more pleas'd with it on your side than his own. The only advantage he makes of his Superiority of Rank is, that by always waving it himself, his inferior finds he is under the greater Obligation not to forget it.

When the Conduct of social Wit is under such Regulations, how delightful must those *Convivia*, those Meals of Conversation be, where such a Member presides; who can with so much ease (as Shakespeare phrases it) *set the Table in a roar*.[13] I am in no pain that these imperfect Out-lines will be apply'd to the Person I mean, because every one that has the Happiness to know him, must know how much more in this particular Attitude is wanting to be like him.

The other Gentleman, whose bare interjections of Laughter have Humour in them, is so far from having a Title, that he has lost his real name, which some Years ago he suffer'd his Friends to railly him out of; in lieu of which they have equipp'd him with one they thought had a better sound in good Company. He is the first man of so sociable a Spirit, that I ever knew capable of quitting the Allurements of Wit and Pleasure, for a strong Application to Business; in his Youth (for there was a Time when he was young) he set out in all the hey-day Expences of a modish Man of Fortune; but finding himself over-weighted with Appetites, he grew restiff, kick'd up in the middle of the Course, and turn'd his Back upon his Frolicks abroad, to think of improving his Estate at home: In order to which he clapt Collars upon his Coach-horses, and that their Mettle might not run over other People, he ty'd a Plough to their Tails, which tho' it might give them a more slovenly Air, would enable him to keep them fatter in a foot pace, with a whistling Peasant beside them, than in full trot, with a hot-headed Coachman behind them. In these unpolite Amusements he has laughed like a Rake, and look'd about him like a Farmer for many Years. As his Rank and Station often find him in the best Company, his easy Humour, whenever he is call'd to it, can still make himself the Fiddle of it.

And tho' some say, he looks upon the Follies of the World like too severe a Philosopher, yet he rather chuses to laugh, than to grieve at them; to pass his time therefore more easily in it, he often endeavours to conceal himself, by assuming the Air and Taste of a Man in fashion; so that his only Uneasiness seems to be, that he can't quite prevail with his Friends to think him a worse Manager, than he really is; for they carry their Raillery to such a height, that it sometimes rises to a Charge of downright Avarice against him. Upon which head it is no easy matter to be more merry upon him, than he will be upon himself. Thus while he sets that Infirmity in a pleasant Light, he so disarms your Prejudice that, if he has it not, you can't find in your Heart to wish he were without it. Whenever he is attack'd where he seems to lie so open, if his Wit happens not to be ready for you, he receives you with an assenting Laugh, till he has gain'd time to whet it sharp enough for a Reply, which seldom turns out to his disadvantage. If you are too strong for him (which may possibly happen from his being oblig'd to defend the weak side of the Question) his last Resource is to join in the Laugh, till he has got himself off by an ironical Applause of your Superiority.

If I were capable of Envy, what I have observ'd of this Gentleman would certainly incline me to it; for sure to get through the necessary Cares of Life, with a Train of Pleasures at our Heels, in vain calling after us, to give a constant Preference to the Business of the Day, and yet be able to laugh while we are about it, to make even Society the subservient Reward of it, is a State of Happiness which the gravest Precepts of moral Wisdom will not easily teach us to exceed. When I speak of Happiness, I go no higher than that which is contain'd in the World we now tread upon; and when I speak of Laughter, I don't

simply mean that which every Oaf is capable of, but that which
has its sensible Motive and proper Season, which is not more
limited than recommended by that indulgent Philosophy,

Cum ratione insanire.[14]

When I look into my present Self, and afterwards cast my Eye
round all my Hopes, I don't see any one Pursuit of them that
shou'd so reasonably rouze me out of a Nod in my Great Chair,
as a call to those agreeable Parties I have sometimes the Happiness to mix with, where I always assert the equal Liberty of
leaving them, when my Spirits have done their best with them.

Now, Sir, as I have been making my way for above Forty
Years through a Crowd of Cares, (all which, by the Favour of
Providence, I have honestly got rid of) is it a time of Day for
me to leave off these Fooleries, and to set up a new Character?
Can it be worth my while to waste my Spirits, to bake my
Blood, with serious Contemplations, and perhaps impair my
Health, in the fruitless Study of advancing myself into the
better Opinion of those very---very few Wise Men that are
as old as I am? No, the Part I have acted in real Life, shall
be all of a piece.

------*Servetur ad imum,*
Qualis ab incepto processerit.[15] *Hor.*

I will not go out of my Character, by straining to be wiser than
I *can* be, or by being more affectedly pensive than I *need* be;
whatever I am, Men of Sense will know me to be, put on what
Disguise I will; I can no more put off my Follies, than my Skin;
I have often try'd, but they stick too close to me; nor am I sure
my Friends are displeas'd with them; for, besides that in this
Light I afford them frequent matter of Mirth, they may possibly be less uneasy at their *own* Foibles, when they have so old
a Precedent to keep them in countenance: Nay, there are some
frank enough to confess, they envy what they laugh at; and
when I have seen others, whose Rank and fortune have laid a sort
of Restraint upon their Liberty of pleasing their Company, by

pleasing themselves, I have said softly to myself,---- Well, there
is some Advantage in having neither Rank nor Fortune! Not but
there are among them a third Sort, who have the particular
Happiness of unbending into the very Wantonness of Good-
humour, without depreciating their Dignity: He that is not
Master of that Freedom, let his Condition be never so exalted,
must still want something to come up to the Happiness of his
Inferiors who enjoy it. If *Socrates* cou'd take pleasure in playing
at *Even or Odd* with his Children, or *Agesilaus*[16] divert himself
in riding the Hobby-horse with them, am I oblig'd to be as
eminent as either of them before I am as frolicksome? If the
Emperor *Adrian*,[17] near his death, cou'd play with his very Soul,
his *Animula*, &c. and regret that it could no longer be compan-
ionable; if Greatness, at the same time, was not the Delight he
was so loth to part with, sure then these cheerful Amusements
I am contending for, must have no inconsiderable share in our
Happiness; he that does not chuse to live his own way, suffers
others to chuse for him. Give me the Joy I always took in the
End of an old Song,

My Mind, my Mind is a Kingdom to me![18]

If I can please myself with my own Follies, have I not a plentiful
Provision for Life? If the World thinks me a Trifler, I don't
desire to break in upon their Wisdom; let them call me any Fool,
but an Unchearful one! I live as I write; while my Way amuses
me, it's as well as I with it; when another writes better, I can
like him too, tho' he shou'd not like me. Not our great Imitator
of *Horace* himself can have more Pleasure in writing his Verses,
than I have in reading them, tho' I sometimes find myself there
(As Shakespeare terms it) *dispraisingly* spoken of:[19] If he is a
little free with me, I am generally in good company, he is as
blunt with my Betters; so that even here I might laugh in my
turn. My Superiors, perhaps, may be mended by him; but, for
my part, I own myself incorrigible: I look upon my Follies as
the best part of my Fortune, and am more concern'd to be a
good Husband of Them, than of That; nor do I believe I shall
ever be rhim'd out of them. And, if I don't mistake, I am sup-

ported in my way of thinking by *Horace* himself, who, in excuse
of a loose Writer, says,

> *Praetulerim scriptor delirus, inersque videri,*
> *Dum mea delectent, mala me, aut denique fallant,*
> *Quam sapere, et ringi----*[20]

which, to speak of myself as a loose Philospher, I have thus ventur'd to imitate:

> *Me, while my laughing Follies can deceive,*
> *Blest in the dear Delirium let me live,*
> *Rather than wisely know my Wants, and grieve.*

We had once a merry Monarch of our own, who thought chearfulness so valuable a Blessing, that he would have quitted one of
his Kingdoms where he cou'd not enjoy it; where, among many
other hard Conditions they had ty'd him to, his sober Subjects
wou'd not suffer him to laugh on a *Sunday;* and tho' this might
not be the avow'd Cause of his Elopement, I am not sure, had he
no other, that this alone might not have serv'd his turn; at least,
he has my hearty Approbation either way; for had I been under
the same Restriction, tho' my staying were to have made me his
Successor, I shou'd rather have chosen to follow him.

How far his Subjects might be in the right, is not my Affair
to determine; perhaps they were wiser than the Frogs in the
Fable, and rather chose to have a Log, than a Stork for their
King; yet I hope it will be no offense to say, that King *Log* himself must have made but a very simple Figure in History.

The Man who chuses never to laugh, or whose becalm'd Passions know no Motion, seems to me only in the quiet State of
a green Tree; he vegetates, 'tis true, but shall we say he lives?
Now, Sir, for Amusement.----Reader, take heed! for I find a
strong impulse to talk impertinently; if therefore you are not as
fond of seeing, as I am of shewing myself in all my Lights, you
may turn over two Leaves together, and leave what follows to
those who have more Curiosity, and less to do with their Time,
than you have.----- As I was saying then, let us, for Amusement,

advance this, or any other Prince, to the most glorious Throne,
mark out his Empire in what Clime you please, fix him on the
highest Pinnacle of unbounded Power; and in that State let us
enquire into his degree of Happiness; make him at once the
Terror and the Envy of his Neighbors, send his Ambition out
to War, and gratify it with extended Fame and Victories; bring
him in triumph home, with great unhappy Captives behind him,
through the Acclamations of his People, to repossess his Realms
in Peace. Well, when the Dust has been brusht from his Purple,
what will he do next? Why, this envy'd Monarch (who, we will
allow to have a more exalted Mind than to be delighted with the
trifling Flatteries of a congratulating Circle) will chuse to retire, I presume, to enjoy in private the Contemplation of his
Glory; an Amusement, you will say, that well becomes his
Station! But there, in that pleasing Rumination, when he has
made up his new Account of Happiness, how much, pray, will be
added to the Balance more than as it stood before his last Expedition? From what one Article will the Improvement of it appear?
Will it arise from the conscious Pride of having done his weaker
Enemy an Injury? Are his Eyes so dazzled with false Glory,
that he thinks it a less Crime in him to break into the Palace of
his Princely Neighbor, because he gave him time to defend it,
than for a Subject feloniously to plunder the House of a private
Man? Or is the Outrage of Hunger and Necessity more enormous than the Ravage of Ambition? Let us even suppose the
wicked Usage of the World, as to that Point, may keep his Conscience quiet; still what is he to do with the infinite Spoil that his
imperial Rapine has brought home? Is he to sit down, and vainly
deck himself with the Jewels which he has plunder'd from the
Crown of another, whom Self-defence had compell'd to oppose
him? No, let us not debase his Glory into so low a Weakness.
What Appetite, then, are these shining Treasures food for? Is
their vast Value in feeling his vulgar Subjects stare at them, wise
Men smile at them, or his Children play with them? Or can the
new Extent of his Dominion add a Cubit to his Happiness? Was
not his Empire wide enough before to do good in? And can it
add to his Delight that now no Monarch has such room to do

mischief in? But farther; even if the great *Augustus*, to whose Reign such Praises are given, cou'd not enjoy his Days of Peace, free from the Terrors of repeated Conspiracies, which lost him more Quiet to suppress, than his Ambition cost him to provoke them. What human Eminence is secure? In what private Cabinet then must this wondrous Monarch lock up his Happiness, that common Eyes are never to behold it? Is it, like his Person, a Prisoner to its own Superiority? Or does he at last poorly place it in the Triumph of his injurious Devastations? One Moment's Search into himself will plainly shew him, that real and reasonable Happiness can have no Existence without Innocence and Liberty. What a Mockery is Greatness without them? How lonesome must be the Life of that Monarch, who, while he governs only by being fear'd, is restrain'd from letting down his Grandeur sometimes to forget himself, and to humanize him into the Benevolence and Joy of Society? To throw off his cumbersome Robe of Majesty to be a Man without Disguise, to have a sensible Taste of Life in its Simplicity, till he confess, from the sweet Experience, that *dulce est desipere in loco*,[21] was no Fool's Philosophy. Or if the gawdy Charms of Pre-eminence are so strong that they leave him no Sense of a less pompous, tho' a more rational Enjoyment, none sure can envy him, but those who are the Dupes of an equally fantastick Ambition.

My Imagination is quite heated and fatigued, in dressing up this Phantome of Felicity; but I hope it has not made me so far misunderstood, as not to have allow'd, that in all the Dispensations of Providence, the Exercise of a great and virtuous Mind is the most elevated State of Happiness: No, Sir, I am not for setting up Gaity against Wisdom; nor for preferring the Man of Pleasure to the Philosopher; but for the shewing, that the Wisest, or Greatest Man, is very near an unhappy Man, if the unbending Amusements I am contending for, are not sometimes admitted to relieve him.

How far I may have over-rated these Amusements, let graver Casuists decide; whether they affirm, or reject, what I have asserted, hurts not my Purpose; which is not to give Laws to

others; but to shew by what Laws I govern myself: If I am mis-
guided, 'tis Nature's Fault, and I follow her, from this Persuasion; That as Nature has distinguish'd our Species from the mute
Creation, by our Risibility, her Design must have been, by that
Faculty, as evidently to raise our Happiness, as by our *Os Sublime*[22] (our erected Faces) to lift the Dignity of our Form above
them.

Notwithstanding all I have said, I am afraid there is an absolute Power, in what is simply call'd our Constitution, that will
never admit of other Rules for Happiness, than her own; from
which (be we never so wise or weak) without Divine Assistance,
we only can receive it: So that all this my Parade, and Grimace
of Philosophy, has been only making a mighty Merit of following my own Inclination. A very natural Vanity! Though it is
some sort of Satisfaction to know it does not impose upon me.
Vanity again! However, think It what you will that has drawn
me into this copious Digression, 'tis now high time to drop it:
I shall therefore in my next Chapter return to my School, from
whence, I fear, I have too long been Truant.

It often makes me smile, to think how contentedly I have sate myself down, to write my own Life; nay, and with less Concern for what may be said of it, than I should feel, were I to do the same for a deceas'd Acquaintance. This you will easily account for, when you consider, that nothing gives a Coxcomb more Delight, than when you suffer him to talk of himself; which sweet Liberty I here enjoy for a whole Volume together! A Privilege, which neither cou'd be allow'd me, nor wou'd become me to take, in the Company I am generally admitted to;[2] but here, where I have all the Talk to myself, and have no body to interrupt or contradict me, sure, to say whatever I have a mind other People shou'd know of me, is a Pleasure which none but Authors, as vain as myself, can conceive.--- But to my History.

However little worth notice the Life of a School-boy may be suppos'd to contain; yet, as the Passions of Men and Children have much the same Motives, and differ very little in their Effects, unless where the elder Experience may be able to conceal them: As therefore what arises from the Boy, may possibly be a Lesson to the Man, I shall venture to relate a Fact, or two, that happen'd while I was still at School.

In *February*, 1684-5, died King *Charles* II. who being the only King I had ever seen, I remember (young as I was) his Death made a strong Impression upon me, as it drew Tears from the Eyes of Multitudes, who look'd no further into him than I did: But it was, then, a sort of School-Doctrine to regard our Monarch as a Deity; as in the former Reign it was to insist he was accountable to this World, as well as to that above him. But what, perhaps, gave King *Charles* II. this peculiar Possession of so many Hearts, was his affable and easy manner in conversing; a Quality that goes farther with the greater Part of Mankind than

many higher Virtues, which, in a Prince, might more immediately regard the publick Prosperity. Even his indolent Amusement of playing with his Dogs, and feeding his Ducks, in St.
James's Park, (which I have seen him do) made the common
People adore him, and consequently overlook in him, what, in
a Prince of a different Temper, they might have been out of
humour at.

I cannot help remembering one more Particular in those times,
tho' it be quite foreign to what will follow. I was carry'd by my
Father to the Chapel in *Whitehall;* where I saw the King, and his
royal Brother the then Duke of *York*, with him in the Closet,
and present during the whole Divine Service. Such Dispensation, it seems, for his Interest, had that unhappy Prince, from his
real Religion, to assist at another, to which his Heart was so utterly averse.---- I now proceed to the Facts I promis'd to speak of.

King *Charles* his Death was judg'd, by our School-master, a
proper Subject to lead the Form I was in, into a higher kind of
Exercise; he therefore enjoin'd us, severally, to make his Funeral
Oration: This sort of Task, so entirely new to us all, the Boys receiv'd with Astonishment, as a Work above their Capacity; and
tho' the Master persisted in his Command, they one and all, except
myself, resolv'd to decline it. But I, Sir, who was ever giddily
forward, and thoughtless of Consequences, set myself roundly
to work, and got through it as well as I could. I remember to this
Hour, that single Topick of his Affability (which made me
mention it before) was the chief Motive that warm'd me into
the Undertaking; and to shew how very childish a Notion I
had of his Character at that time, I rais'd his Humanity, and Love
of those who serv'd him, to such height, that I imputed his Death
to the Shock he receiv'd from the Lord *Arlington's* being at the
point of Death, about a Week before him.[3] This Oration, such as
it was, I produc'd the next Morning: All the other Boys pleaded
their Inability, which the Master taking rather as a mark of their
Modesty than their Idleness, only seem'd to punish, by setting
me at the Head of the Form: A Preferment dearly bought!
Much happier had I been to have sunk my Performance in the
general Modesty of declining it. A most uncomfortable Life I

led among 'em, for many a Day after! I was so jeer'd, laugh'd
at, and hated as a pragmatical Bastard (School-boys Language)
who had betray'd the whole Form, that scarce any of 'em wou'd
keep me company; and tho' it so far advanc'd me into the Master's Favour, that he wou'd often take me from the School, to
give me an Airing with him on Horseback, while they were
left to their Lessons; you may be sure, such envy'd Happiness
did not encrease their Good-will to me: Notwithstanding which,
my Stupidity cou'd take no warning from their Treatment. An
Accident of the same nature happen'd soon after, that might have
frighten'd a Boy of a meek Spirit, from attempting any thing
above the lowest Capacity. On the 23d of *April* following,
being the Coronation-Day of the new King, the School petition'd the Master for leave to play; to which he agreed, provided any of the Boys wou'd produce an *English* Ode upon
that Occasion.---- The very Word, *Ode,* I know, makes you
smile already; and so it does me; not only because it still makes
so many poor Devils turn Wits upon it, but from a more
agreeable Motive; from a Reflexion of how little I then thought
that, half a Century afterwards, I shou'd be call'd upon twice
a Year, by my Post,[4] to make the same kind of Oblations to an
unexceptionable Prince, the serene Happiness of whose Reign
my halting Rhimes are still unequal to--- This, I own, is Vanity
without Disguise; but, *Haec olim meminisse juvat:*[5] The rememberance of the miserable Prospect we had then before us, and
have since escap'd by a Revolution, is now a Pleasure, which,
without that Rememberance, I cou'd not so heartily have enjoy'd. The Ode I was speaking of fell to my Lot, which, in
about half an Hour I produc'd. I cannot say it was much above
the merry Style of *Sing! Sing the Day, and sing the Song,* in
the Farce:[6] Yet, bad as it was, it serv'd to get the School a Play-
day, and to make me not a little vain upon it; which last Effect so
disgusted my Play-fellows, that they left me out of the Party
I had most mind to be of, in that Day's Recreation. But their
Ingratitude serv'd only to increase my Vanity; for I consider'd
them as so many beaten Tits, that had just had the Mortification of seeing my Hack of a *Pegasus* come in before them. This

low Passion is so rooted in our Nature, that sometimes riper
Heads cannot govern it. I have met with much the same silly
sort of Coldness, even from my Contemporaries of the Theatre,
from having the superfluous Capacity of writing myself the
Characters I have acted.

Here perhaps, I may again seem to be vain; but if all these
Facts are true (as true they are) how can I help it? Why am I
oblig'd to conceal them? The Merit of the best of them is not
so extraordinary as to have warn'd me to be nice upon it; and
the Praise due to them is so small a Fish, it was scarce worth
while to throw my Line into the Water for it. If I confess my
Vanity while a Boy, can it be Vanity, when a Man, to remember
it? And if I have a tolerable Feature, will not that as much belong
to my Picture, as an Imperfection? In a word, from what I have
mentioned, I wou'd observe only this; That when we are conscious of the least comparative Merit in ourselves, we shou'd take
as much care to conceal the Value we set upon it, as if it
were a real Defect: To be elated, or vain upon it, is shewing
your Money before People in want; ten to one, but some who
may think you have too much, may borrow, or pick your
Pocket before you get home. He who assumes Praise to himself,
the World will think overpays himself. Even the Suspicion of
being vain, ought as much to be dreaded as the Guilt itself.
Caesar was of the same Opinion, in regard to his Wife's Chastity.
Praise, tho' it may be our due, is not like a *Bank-Bill*, to be paid
upon Demand; to be valuable, it must be voluntary. When we
are dun'd for it, we have a Right and Privilege to refuse it. If
Compulsion insists upon it, it can only be paid as Persecution in
Points of Faith is, in a counterfeit Coin: And who, ever, believ'd
Occasional Conformity to be sincere? *Nero*, the most vain Coxcomb of a Tyrant that ever breath'd, cou'd not raise an unfeigned
Applause to his Harp by military Execution: Even where Praise
is deserv'd, Ill-nature and Self-conceit (Passions, that poll a
majority of Mankind) will with less reluctance part with their
Mony, than their Approbation. Men of the greatest Merit are
forc'd to stay 'till they die, before the World will fairly make
up their Account: Then, indeed, you have a Chance for your

full Due, because it is less grudg'd when you are incapable of enjoying it: Then, perhaps, even Malice shall heap Praises upon your Memory; tho' not for your sake, but that your surviving Competitors may suffer by a Comparison. 'Tis from the same Principle that *Satyr* shall have a thousand Readers, where *Panegyric* has one. When I therefore find my Name at length, in the Satyrical Works of our most celebrated living Author, I never look upon those Lines as Malice meant to me, (for he knows I never provok'd it) but Profit to himself: One of his Points must be, to have many Readers: He considers that my Face and Name are more known than those of many thousands of more consequence in the Kingdom: That therefore, right or wrong, a Lick at the *Laureat*⁷ will always be a sure Bait, *ad captandum vulgus*,⁸ to catch him little Readers: And that to gratify the Unlearned, by now and then interspersing those merry Sacrifices of an old Acquaintance to their Taste, is a piece of quite right Poetical Craft.

But as a little bad Poetry, is the greatest Crime he lays to my charge, I am willing to subscribe to his opinion of *it*. That this sort of Wit is one of the easiest ways too, of pleasing the generality of Readers, is evident from the comfortable Subsistance which our weekly Retailers of Politicks have been known to pick up, merely by making bold with a Government that had unfortunately neglected to find their Genius a better Employment.

Hence too arises all that flat Poverty of Censure and Invective, that so often has a Run in our publick Papers, upon the Success of a new Author; when, God knows, there is seldom above one Writer among hundreds in being at the same time, whose Satyr a Man of common Sense ought to be mov'd at. When a Master in the Arts is angry, then, indeed, we ought to be alarm'd! How terrible a Weapon is Satyr in the Hand of a great Genius? Yet even there, how liable is Prejudice to misuse it? How far, when general, it may reform our Morals, or what Cruelties it may inflict by being angrily particular, is perhaps above my reach to determine. I shall therefore only beg leave to interpose what I feel for others, whom it may personally have fallen upon. When I read those mortifying Lines of our most eminent Author, in his Character of *Atticus*[9] (*Atticus*, whose Genius in Verse, and whose Morality in Prose, has been so justly admir'd) though I am charm'd with the Poetry, my Imagination is hurt at the Severity of it; and tho' I allow the Satyrist to have had personal Provocation, yet, methinks, for that very Reason, he ought not to have troubled the Publick with it: For, as it is observ'd in the 242d *Tattler*,[10] "In all Terms of Reproof, where the Sentence appears to arise from Personal Hatred, or Passion, it is not then made the Cause of Mankind, but a Misunderstanding between two Persons." But if such kind of Satyr has its incontestable Greatness; if its exemplary Brightness may not mislead inferior Wits into a barbarous Imitation of its Severity, then I have only admir'd the Verses, and expos'd myself, by bringing them under so scrupulous a Reflexion: But the Pain which the Acrimony of those Verses gave me, is, in some measure, allay'd, in finding that this inimitable Writer, as he advances in Years, has since had Candour enough to celebrate the same Person for his visible Merit. Happy Genius! whose Verse, like the Eye of Beauty, can heal the deepest Wounds with the least Glance of Favour.

Since I am got so far into this Subject, you must give me leave to go thro' all I have a mind to say upon it; because I am not sure, that in a more proper Place, my Memory may be so full of it. I cannot find, therefore, from what Reason, Satyr is allow'd more License than Comedy, or why either of them (to be admir'd) ought not to be limited by Decency and Justice. Let *Juvenal* and *Aristophanes* have taken what Liberties they please, if the Learned have nothing more than their Antiquity to justify their laying about them, at that enormous rate, I shall wish they had a better Excuse for them! The Personal Ridicule and Scurrility thrown upon *Socrates*, which *Plutarch* too condemns; and the Boldness of *Juvenal*, in writing real Names over guilty Characters, I cannot think are to be pleaded in right of our modern Liberties of the same kind. *Facit indignatio versum*,[11] may be a very spirited Expression, and seems to give a Reader hopes of a lively Entertainment: but I am afraid Reproof is in

unequal Hands, when Anger is its Executioner; and tho' an out-
rageous Invective may carry some Truth in it, yet it will never
have that natural, easy Credit with us, which we give to the
laughing Ironies of a cool Head. The Satyr that can smile *circum
praecordia ludit*,[12] and seldom fails to bring the Reader quite
over to his Side, whenever Ridicule and Folly are at variance.
But when a Person satyriz'd is us'd with the extremest Rigour,
he may sometimes meet with Compassion, instead of Contempt,
and throw back the Odium that was design'd for him, upon the
Author. When I would therefore disarm the Satyrist of this
Indignation, I mean little more, than that I wou'd take from him
all private or personal Prejudice, and wou'd still leave him as
much general Vice to scourge as he pleases, and that with as
much Fire and Spirit as Art and Nature demand to enliven his
Work, and keep his Reader awake.

Against all this it may be objected, That these are Laws which
none but phlegmatick Writers will observe, and only Men of
Eminence should give. I grant it, and therefore only submit them
to Writers of better Judgment. I pretend not to restrain others
from chusing what I don't like; they are welcome (if they please
too) to think I offer these Rules, more from an Incapacity to
break them, than from a moral Humanity. Let it be so! still, That
will not weaken the strength of what I have asserted, if my Assertion be true. And though I allow, that Provocation is not
apt to weigh out its Resentments by Drachms and Scruples, I
shall still think, that no publick Revenge can be honourable,
where it is not limited by Justice; and, if Honour is insatiable
in its Revenge, it loses what it contends for, and sinks itself, if
not into Cruelty, at least into Vain-glory.

This so singular Concern which I have shewn for others, may
naturally lead you to ask me, what I feel for myself, when I
am unfavourably treated by the elaborate Authors of our daily
Papers. Shall I be sincere? and own my Frailty? Its usual Effect
is to make me vain! For I consider, if I were quite good for
nothing, these Pidlers in Wit would not be concern'd to take
me to pieces, or (not to be quite so vain) when they moderately
charge me with only Ignorance, or Dulness, I see nothing in

That which an honest Man need be asham'd of: There is many a good Soul, who, from those sweet Slumbers of the Brain, are never awaken'd by the least harmful Thought; and I am sometimes tempted to think those Retailers of Wit may be of the same Class; that what they write proceeds not from Malice, but Industry; and that I ought no more to reproach them, than I would a Lawyer that pleads against me for his Fee; that their Detraction, like Dung, thrown upon a Meadow, tho' it may seem at first to deform the Prospect, in a little time it will disappear of itself, and leave an involuntary Crop of Praise behind it.

When they confine themselves to a sober Criticism upon what I write; if their Censure is just, what Answer can I make to it? If it is unjust, why should I suppose that a sensible Reader will not see it, as well as myself? Or, admit I were able to expose them, by a laughing Reply, will not that Reply beget a Rejoinder? And though they might be Gainers, by having the worst on't, in a Paper War, that is no Temptation for me to come into it. Or (to make both sides less considerable) would not my bearing Ill-language, from a Chimney-sweeper, do me less harm, than it would be to box with him, tho' I were sure to beat him? Nor indeed is the little Reputation I have, as an Author, worth the trouble of a Defence. Then, as no Criticism can possibly make me worse than I really am; so nothing I say of myself can possibly make me better: When therefore a determin'd Critick comes arm'd with Wit and Outrage, to take from me that small Pittance I have, I would no more dispute with him, than I would resist a Gentleman of the Road, to save a little Pocket-Money. Men that are in want themselves, seldom make a Conscience of taking it from others. Whoever thinks I have too much, is welcome to what share of it he pleases: Nay, to make him more merciful (as I partly guess the worst he can say of what I now write) I will prevent even the Imputation of his doing me Injustice, and honestly say it myself, *viz.* That of all the Assurances I was ever guilty of, this, of writing my own Life, is the most hardy. I beg his Pardon!--- Impudent is what I shou'd have said! That thro' every Page there runs a Vein of Vanity and Impertinence, which no *French Ensigns memoires* ever came up to; but, as this is a common Error, I presume the Terms of *Doating Trifler, Old Fool*, or *Conceited Coxcomb*, will carry Contempt enough for an impartial Censor to bestow on me; that my Style is unequal, pert, and frothy, patch'd and party-colour'd, like the Coat of an *Harlequin;* low and pompous, cramm'd with Epithets, shrew'd with Scraps of second-hand *Latin* from common Quotations; frequently aiming at Wit, without ever hitting the Mark; a mere Ragoust, toss'd up from the Offals of other Authors: My Subject below all Pens but my own, which, whenever I keep to, is flatly dawb'd by one external Egotism: That I want nothing but Wit, to be as an accomplish'd a Coxcomb here, as ever I attempted to expose on the Theatre: Nay, that this very Confession is no more a sign of my Modesty, than it is a Proof of my Judgment; that, in short, you may roundly tell me, that--- *Cinna* (or *Cibber*) *vult videri Pauper, et est Pauper*.

> When humble *Cinna* cries, *I'm Poor and Low*,
> You may believe him--- he is really so.[13]

Well, Sir Critick! and what of all this? Now I have laid myself at your Feet, what will you do with me? Expose me? Why, dear Sir, does not every Man that writes, expose himself? Can you make me more ridiculous than Nature has made me? You cou'd not sure suppose, that I would lose the Pleasure of Writing, because you might possibly judge me a Blockhead, or perhaps might pleasantly tell other People they ought to think me so too. Will not they judge as well from what *I* say, as from what *You* say? If then you attack me merely to divert yourself, your Excuse for writing will be no better than mine. But perhaps you may want Bread: If that be the Case, even go to Dinner, i' God's name!

If our best Authors, when teiz'd by these Triflers, have not been Masters of this Indifference, I shou'd not wonder if it were disbeliev'd in me; but when it is consider'd that I have allow'd, my never having been disturb'd into a Reply, has proceeded as much from Vanity as from Philosophy, the Matter then may not seem so incredible: And, though I confess, the complete Revenge of making them Immortal Dunces in Immortal Verse, might be glorious; yet, if you will call it Insensibility in me, never to have winc'd at them, even that Insensibility has its Happiness, and what could Glory give me more? For my part, I have always had the Comfort to think, whenever they design'd me a Disfavour, it generally flew back into their own Faces, as it happens to Children when they squirt at their Play-fellows against the Wind. If a Scribbler cannot be easy, because he fancies I have too good an Opinion of my own Productions, let him write on, and mortify; I owe him not the Charity to be out of temper myself, merely to keep him quiet, or give him Joy: Nor, in reality, can I see, why anything misrepresented, tho' believ'd of me by Persons to whom I am unknown, ought to give me any more Concern, than what may be thought of me in *Lapland:* 'Tis with those with whom I am to *live* only, where my Character can affect me; and I will venture to say, he must find out a new way of Writing that will make me pass my Time *there* less agreeably.

You see, Sir, how hard it is for a Man that is talking of himself, to know when to give over; but if you are tired, lay me aside till you have a fresh Appetite; if not, I'll tell you a Story.

In the Year 1730, there were many Authors, whose Merit wanted nothing but Interest to recommend them to the vacant *Laurel*,[14] and who took it ill, to see it at last conferr'd upon a Comedian; insomuch, that they were resolv'd, at least, to shew Specimens of their superior Pretensions, and accordingly enliven'd the publick Papers with ingenious Epigrams, and satyrical Flirts, at the unworthy Successor: These Papers, my Friends, with a wicked Smile, would often put into my Hands, and desire me to read them fairly in Company: This was a Challenge which I never declin'd, and, to do my doughty Antagonists justice, I always read them with as much impartial Spirit, as if I had writ them myself. While I was thus beset on all sides, there happen'd to step forth a poetical Knight-Errant to my Assistance, who was hardy enough to publish some compassionate Stanzas in my Favour.[15] These, you may be sure, the

Raillery of my Friends could do no less than say, I had written to myself. To deny it, I knew would but have confirm'd their pretended Suspicion: I therefore told them, since it gave them such Joy to believe them my own, I would do my best to make the whole Town think so too. As the Oddness of this Reply was, I knew, what would not be easily comprehended, I desired them to have a Day's Patience, and I would print an Explanation to it: To conclude, in two Days after I sent this Letter, with some doggerel Rhimes at the bottom,

To the Author of the Whitehall Evening-Post.

SIR,

The Verses to the Laureat, in yours of *Saturday* last, have occasion'd the following Reply, which I hope you'll give a place in your next, to shew that we can be quick, as well as smart, upon a proper Occasion: And, as I think it the lowest Mark of a Scoundrel to make bold with any Man's Character in Print, without subscribing the true Name of the Author; I therefore desire, if the Laureat is concern'd enough, to ask the Question, that you will tell him my Name, and where I live; till then, I beg leave to be known by no other than that of,

Your Servant,

Monday, Jan. 11, 1730.

FRANCIS FAIRPLAY.

These were the Verses.

I.

Ah, hah! Sir *Coll*, is that thy Way,
    Thy own dull Praise to write?
And wou'd'st thou stand so sure a Lay?
    No, that's too stale a Bite.

II.

Nature, and Art, in thee combine,
   Thy Talents here excel:
All shining Brass thou dost outshine
   To play the Cheat so well.

III.

Who sees thee in *Iago's* Part,
   But thinks thee such a Rogue?
And is not glad, with all his Heart,
   To hang so sad a Dog?

IV.

When *Bays* thou play'st, Thyself thou art;
   For that by Nature fit,
No Blockhead better suits the Part,
   Than such a Coxcomb Wit.

V.

In *Wronghead* too, thy Brains we see,
   Who might do well at Plough;
As fit for Parliament was he,
   As for the Laurel, Thou.

VI.

Bring thy protected Verse from Court,
   And try it on the Stage;
There it will make much better Sport,
   And set the Town in Rage.

VII.

There Beaux, and Wits, and Cits, and Smarts,
   Where Hissing's not uncivil,
Will shew their Parts, to thy Deserts,
   And send it to the Devil.

VIII.

But, ah! in vain, 'gainst Thee we write,
  In vain thy Verse we maul!
Our sharpest Satyr's thy Delight,
  For--- Blood! thou'lt stand it all.

IX.

Thunder, 'tis said, the Laurel spares;
  Nought but thy Brows could blast it:
And yet--- O curst, provoking Stars!
  Thy Comfort is, thou *hast* it.

This, Sir, I offer as a Proof, that I was seven Years ago the same cold Candidate for Fame, which I would still be thought; you will not easily suppose I could have much Concern about it, while, to gratify the merry Pique of my Friends, I was capable of seeming to head the Poetical Cry then against me, and at the same time of never letting the Publick know, till this Hour, that these Verses were written by myself: Nor do I give them you as an Entertainment, but merely to shew you this particular Cast of my Temper.

When I have said this, I would not have it thought Affectation in me, when I grant, that no Man worthy of the Name of an Author, is a more faulty Writer than myself; that I am not Master of my own Language, I too often feel, when I am at a Loss for Expression: I know too that I have too bold a Disregard for that Correctness, which others set so just a Value upon: This I ought to be asham'd of, when I find that Persons, of perhaps colder Imaginations, are allow'd to write better than myself. Whenever I speak of any thing that highly delights me, I find it very difficult to keep my Words within the Bounds of Common Sense: Even when I write too, the same Failing will sometimes get the better of me; of which I cannot give you a stronger Instance, than in that wild Expression I made use of in the first Edition of my Preface to the *Provok'd Husband;* where,

*A Line in the Epilogue to the *Nonjuror*.[16]

speaking of Mrs. *Oldfield's* excellent Performance in the Part of
Lady *Townly*, my Words ran thus, *viz. It is not enough to
say, that here she outdid* her usual *Outdoing.*---- A most vile
Jingle, I grant it! You may well ask me, How could I possibly
commit such a Wantonness to Paper? And I owe myself the
Shame of confessing, I have no Excuse for it, but that, like a
Lover in the Fulness of his Content, by endeavouring to be
floridly grateful, I talk'd Nonsense. Not but it makes me smile
to remember how many flat Writers have made themselves brisk
upon this single Expression; wherever the Verb, *Outdo*, could
come in, the pleasant Accusative, *Outdoing*, was sure to follow
it. The provident Wags knew, that *Decies repetita placeret:*[17] so
delicious a Morsel could not be serv'd up too often! After it
had held them nine times told for a Jest, the Publick has been
pester'd with a tenth Skull, thick enough to repeat it. Nay, the
very learned in the Law, have at last facetiously laid hold of it!
Ten Years after it first came from me, it serv'd to enliven the
Eloquence of an eminent Pleader before the House of Parliament! What Author would not envy me so frolicksome a Fault,
that had such publick Honours paid to it?

After this Consciousness of my real Defects, you will easily
judge, Sir, how little I presume that my Poetical Labours may
outlive those of my mortal *Contemporaries.*

At the same time that I am so humble in my Pretensions to
Fame, I would not be thought to undervalue it; Nature will
not suffer us to despise it, but she may sometimes make us too
fond of it. I have known more than one good Writer, very near
ridiculous, from being in too much Heat about it. Whoever intrinsically deserves it, will always have a proportionable Right
to it. It can neither be resign'd nor taken from you by Violence.
Truth, which is unalterable, must (however his Fame may be
contested) give every Man his Due: What a Poem weighs, it
will be worth; nor is it in the Power of Human Eloquence,
with Favour or Prejudice, to increase or diminish its Value.
Prejudice, 'tis true, may a while discolour it; but it will always
have its Appeal to the Equity of good Sense, which will never
fail, in the end, to reserve all false Judgment against it. Therefore

when I see an eminent Author hurt, and impatient at an impotent Attack upon his Labours, he disturbs my Inclination to admire him; I grow doubtful of the favourable Judgment I have made of him, and am quite uneasy to see him so tender, in a Point he cannot but know he ought not himself to be judge of; his Concern indeed, at another's Prejudice, or Disapprobation, may be natural; but, to own it, seems to me a natural Weakness. When a Work is apparently great, it will go without Crutches; all your Art and Anxiety to heighten the Fame of it, then becomes low and little. He that will bear no Censure, must be often robb'd of his due Praise. Fools have as good a Right to be Readers, as Men of Sense have, and why not to give their Judgments too? Methinks it would be a sort of Tyranny in Wit, for an Author to be publickly putting every Argument to death that appear'd against him; so absolute a Demand for Approbation, puts us upon our Right to dispute it; Praise is as much the Reader's Property, as Wit is the Author's; Applause is not a Tax paid to him as a Prince, but rather a Benevolence given to him as a Beggar; and we have naturally more Charity for the dumb Beggar, than the sturdy one. The Merit of a Writer, and a fine Woman's Face, are never mended by their talking of them: How amiable is she that seems not to know she is handsome.

   To conclude: all I have said upon this Subject is much better contained in six Lines of a Reverend Author, which will be an Answer to all critical Censure for ever.

> Time is the Judge; Time has nor Friend, nor Foe;
> False Fame will wither, and the True will grow:
> Arm'd with this Truth, all Criticks I defy,
> For, if I fall, by my own Pen I die.
> While Snarlers strive with proud, but fruitless Pain,
> To wound Immortals, or to slay the Slain.[18]

I am now come to that Crisis of my Life, when Fortune seem'd to be at a Loss what she should do with me. Had she favour'd my Father's first Designation of me, he might then, perhaps, have had as sanguine hopes of my being a Bishop, as I afterwards conceiv'd of my being a General, when I first took Arms, at the Revolution. Nay, after that, I had a third Chance too, equally as good, of becoming an Under-proper of the State. How, at last, I came to be none of all these, the Sequel will inform you.

About the Year 1687, I was taken from School to stand at the Election of Children into *Winchester* College; my being, by my Mother's side, a Descendent of *William* of *Wickam*, the Founder, my Father (who knew little how the World was to be dealt with) imagined my having that Advantage, would be Security enough for my Success, and so sent me simply down thither, without the least favourable Recommendation or Interest, but that of my naked Merit, and a pompous Pedigree in my Pocket. Had he tack'd a Direction to my Back, and sent me by the Carrier to the Mayor of the Town, to be chosen Member of Parliament there, I might have had as much chance to have succeeded in the one, as the other. But I must not omit in this place, to let you know, that the Experience which my Father then bought, at my Cost, taught him, some Years after, to take a more judicious care of my younger Brother, *Lewis Cibber*, whom, with the Present of a Statue of the Founder, of his own making, he recommended to the same College. This Statue now stands (I think) over the School Door there, and was so well executed, that it seem'd to speak----for its Kinsmen. It was no sooner set up, than the Door of Preferment was open to him.

Here, one wou'd think, my Brother had the Advantage of me,

in the Favour of Fortune, by this his first laudable Step into the World. I own, I was so proud of his Success, that I even valued myself upon it; and yet it is but a melancholy Reflexion to observe, how unequally his Profession and mine were provided for; when I, who had been the Outcast of Fortune, could find means, from my Income of the Theatre, before I was my own Master there, to supply, in his highest Preferment, his common Necessities. I cannot part with his Memory without telling you, I had as sincere a Concern for this Brother's Well-being, as my own. He had lively Parts, and more than ordinary Learning, with a good deal of natural Wit and Humour; but, from too great a Disregard to his Health, he died a Fellow of *New College* in *Oxford*, soon after he had been ordain'd by Dr. *Compton*, then Bishop of *London*.[2] I now return to the State of my own Affair at Winchester.

After the Election, the moment I was inform'd that I was one of the unsuccessful Candidates, I blest myself to think what a happy Reprieve I had got, from the confin'd Life of a Schoolboy! and the same Day took Post back to *London*, that I might arrive time enough to see a Play (then my darling Delight) before my Mother might demand an Account of my traveling Charges. When I look back to that time, it almost makes me tremble to think what Miseries, in fifty Years farther in Life, such an unthinking Head was liable to! To ask, why Providence afterwards took more care of me, than I did of myself, might be making too Bold an enquiry into its secret Will and Pleasure: All I can say to that Point, is, that I am thankful, and amaz'd at it!

'Twas about this time I first imbib'd an Inclination, which I durst not reveal, for the Stage; for, besides that I knew it would disoblige my Father, I had no Conception of any means, practicable, to make my way to it. I therefore suppress'd the bewitching Ideas of so sublime a Station, and compounded with my Ambition by laying a lower Scheme, of only getting the nearest way into the immediate Life of a Gentleman-Collegiate. My Father being at this time employ'd at *Chattsworth* in *Derbyshire*, by the (then) Earl of *Devonshire*,[3] who was raising that Seat

from a *Gothick*, to a *Grecian*, Magnificence, I made use of the
Leisure I then had, in *London*, to open to him, by Letter, my
Disinclination to wait another Year for an uncertain Preferment
at *Winchester*, and to entreat him that he would send me, *per
saltum*, by a shorter Cut, to the University, My Father, who
was naturally indulgent to me, seem'd to comply with my Request, and wrote word, that as soon as his Affairs would permit,
he would carry me with him, and settle me in some College,
but rather at *Cambridge*, where, (during his late Residence at
that Place, in making some Statues that now stand upon *Trin-
ity* College New Library, he had contracted some Acquaintance
with the Heads of Houses, who might assist his Intentions for
me. This I lik'd better than to go discountenanc'd to *Oxford*, to
which it would have been a sort of Reproach to me, not to have
come elected. After some Months were elaps'd, my Father, not
being willing to let me lie too long idling in *London*, sent for
me down to *Chattsworth*, to be under his Eye, till he cou'd
be at leisure to carry me to *Cambridge*. Before I could set out,
on my Journey thither, the Nation fell in labour of the Revolution, the News being then just brought to *London*, That the
Prince of *Orange*, at the Head of an Army was landed in the
West.[4] When I came to *Nottingham*, I found my Father in Arms
there, among those Forces which the Earl of *Devonshire* had
rais'd for the Redress of our violated Laws and Liberties. My
Father judg'd this a proper Season, for a young Stripling to
turn himself loose into the Bustle of the World; and being himself too advanc'd in Years, to endure the Winter Fatigue, which
might possibly follow, entreated that noble Lord, that he would
be pleas'd to accept of his Son in his room, and that he would
give him (my Father) leave to return, and finish his Works at
Chattsworth. This was so well receiv'd by his Lordship, that he
not only admitted of my Service, but promis'd my Father, in
return, that when Affairs were settled, he would provide for
me. Upon this, my Father return'd to *Derbyshire*, while I, not a
little transported, jump'd into his Saddle. Thus, in one Day, all
my Thoughts of the University were smother'd in Ambition!
A slight Commission for a Horse-Officer, was the least View I

had before me. At this Crisis you cannot but observe, that the
Fate of King *James,* and the Prince of *Orange,* and that of so
minute a Being as my self, were all at once upon the Anvil:
In what shape they wou'd severally come out, tho' a good *Guess*
might be made, was not then *demonstrable* to the deepest Fore-
sight; but as my Fortune seem'd to be of small Importance to the
Publick, Providence thought fit to postpone it, 'till that of those
great Rulers of Nations, was justly perfected. Yet, had my
Father's Business permitted him to have carried me, one Month
sooner (as he intended) to the University, who knows but,
by this time, that purer Fountain might have wash'd my Imperfections into a Capacity of writing (instead of Plays and Annual
Odes) Sermons, and Pastoral Letters. But whatever Care of
the Church might, so, have fallen to my share, as I dare say it
may be now, in better Hands, I ought not to repine at my being
otherwise dispos'd of.

You must, now, consider me as one among those desperate
Thousands, who, after a Patience sorely try'd, took Arms under
the Banner of Necessity, the natural Parent of all Human Laws,
and Government. I question, if in all the Histories of Empire,
there is one Instance of so bloodless a Revolution, as that in
England in 1688, wherein Whigs, Tories, Princes, Prelates,
Nobles, Clergy, common People, and a standing Army, were
unanimous. To have seen all *England* of one Mind is to have
liv'd at a very particular Juncture. Happy Nation! who are
never divided among themselves, but when they have least to
complain of! Our greatest Grievance since that time, seems to
have been, that we cannot all govern; and 'till the Number of
good Places are equal to those, who think themselves qualified
for them, there must ever be a Cause of Contention among us.
While Great Men want great Posts, the Nation will never
want real or seeming Patriots; and while great Posts are fill'd
with Persons, whose Capacities are but Human, such Persons
will never be allow'd to be without Errors; not even the Revolution, with all its Advantages, it seems, has been able to furnish
us with unexceptionable Statesmen! for, from that time, I don't
remember any one Set of Ministers, that have not been heartily

rail'd at; a Period long enough, one would think, (if all of them
have been as bad as they have been call'd) to make a People
despair of ever seeing a good one: But as it is possible that Envy,
Prejudice, or Party, may sometimes have a share in what is
generally thrown upon 'em, it is not easy for a private Man,
to know who is absolutely in the right, from what is said against
them, or from what their Friends or Dependants may say in
their Favour: Tho' I can hardly forbear thinking, that they who
have been *longest* rail'd at, must, from that Circumstance, shew,
in some sort, a Proof of Capacity.---But to my History.

It were almost incredible to tell you, at the latter end of King
James's Time (though the Rod of Arbitrary Power was always
shaking over us) with what Freedom and Contempt the common People, in the open Streets, talk'd of his wild Measures to
make a whole Protestant Nation Papists; and yet, in the height
of our secure and wanton Defiance of him, we, of the Vulgar,
had no farther Notion of any Remedy for this Evil, than a
satisfy'd Presumption, that our Numbers were too great to be
master'd by his mere Will and Pleasure; that though he might
be too hard for our Laws, he would never to able to get the
better of our Nature; and, that to drive all *England* into Popery
and Slavery, he would find, would be teaching an old Lion to
dance.

But, happy was it for the Nation, that it had then wiser Heads
in it, who knew how to lead a People so dispos'd into Measures
for the Publick Preservation.

Here, I cannot help reflecting on the very different Deliver-
ances *England* met with, at this Time, and in the very same Year
of the Century before: Then (in 1588) under a glorious Princess, who had, at heart, the Good and Happiness of her People,
we scatter'd and destroy'd the most formidable Navy of In-
vaders, that ever cover'd the Seas: And now (in 1688) under a
Prince, who had alienated the Hearts of his People, by his absolute Measures, to oppress them, a foreign Power is receiv'd with
open Arms, in defence of our Laws, Liberties, and Religion,
which our native Prince had invaded! How widely different

were these two Monarchs in their Sentiments of Glory! But, *Tantum religio potuit suadere malorum.*[5]

When we consider, in what height of the Nation's Prosperity, the Successor of Queen *Elizabeth* came to his Throne, it seems amazing, that such a Pile of *English* Fame, and Glory, which her skilful Administration had erected, should, in every following Reign, down to the Revolution, so unhappily moulder away, in one continual Gradation of Political Errors: All which must have been avoided, if the plain Rule, which that wise Princess left behind her, had been observed, *viz. That the Love of her People was the surest Support of her Throne.* This was the Principle by which she so happily govern'd herself, and those she had the Care of. In this she found Strength to combat, and struggle through more Difficulties, and dangerous Conspiracies, than ever *English* Monarch had to cope with. At the same time that she profess'd to *desire* the People's Love, she took care that her Actions shou'd *deserve* it, without the least Abatement of her Prerogative; the Terror of which she so artfully covered, that she sometimes seem'd to flatter those she was determin'd should obey. If the four following Princes had exercis'd their Regal Authority with so visible a Regard to the Publick Welfare, it were hard to know, whether the People of *England* might have ever complain'd of them, or even felt the want of that Liberty they now so happily enjoy. 'Tis true, that before her Time, our Ancestors had many successful Contests with their Sovereigns for their *ancient Right* and *Claim* to it; yet what did those Successes amount to? little more than a Declaration, that there was such a Right in being; but who ever saw it enjoy'd? Did not the Actions of almost every succeeding Reign shew, there were still so many Doors of Oppression left open to the Prerogative, that (whatever Value our most eloquent Legislators may have set upon those ancient Liberties) I doubt it will be difficult to fix the Period of their having a real Being, before the Revolution: Or if there ever was an elder Period of our unmolested enjoying them, I own, my poor Judgment is at a loss where to place it. I will boldly say then, it is, to the Revo-

lution only, we owe the full Possession of what, 'till then, we
never had more than a perpetually contested Right to: And,
from thence, from the Revolution it is, that the Protestant Successors of King *William* have found their Paternal Care and
Maintainance of that Right, has been the surest Basis of their
Glory.

These, Sir, are a few of my political Notions, which I have
ventur'd to expose, that you may see what sort of an *English*
Subject I am; how wise, or weak they may have shewn me, is
not my Concern; lest the weight of these Matters have drawn me
never so far out of my Depth, I still flatter my self, that I have
kept a simple, honest Head above Water. And it is a solid Comfort to me, to consider that how insignificant soever my Life was
at the Revolution, it had still the good Fortune to make one,
among the many, who brought it about; and that I, now, with
my Coaevals, as well as with the Millions, since born, enjoy the
happy Effects of it.

But I must now let you see how my particular Fortune went
forward, with this Change in the Government; of which I shall
not pretend to give you any farther Account than what my
simple Eyes saw of it.

We had not been many Days at *Nottingham* before we
heard, that the Prince of *Denmark*,[6] with some other great Persons, were gone off, from the King, to the Prince of *Orange*,
and that the Princess *Anne*, fearing the King her Father's Resentment might fall upon her, for her Consort's Revolt, had withdrawn her self, in the Night, from *London*, and was then within
half a Days Journey of *Nottingham;* on which very Morning we
were suddenly alarm'd with the News, that two thousand of the
King's Dragoons were in close pursuit to bring her back Prisoner
to *London:* But this Alarm it seems was all Stratagem, and was
but a part of that general Terror which was thrown into many
other Places about the Kingdom, at the same time, with design
to animate and unite the People in their common Defense; it
then being given out, that the Irish were every where at our
Heels, to cut off all the Protestants within the Reach of their
Fury. In this Alarm our Troops scrambled to Arms in as much

Order as their Consternation would admit of, when having advanc'd some few Miles on the *London* Road, they met the
Princess in a Coach, attended only by the Lady *Churchill* (now
Dutchess Dowager of *Marlborough*)[7] and the Lady *Fitzharding*,
whom they conducted into *Nottingham*, through the Acclamations of the People: The same Night all the Noblemen, and the
other Persons of Distinction, then in Arms, had the Honour
to sup at her Royal Highness's Table; which was then furnish'd
(as all her necessary Accomodations were) by the Care, and at
the Charge of the Lord *Devonshire*. At this Entertainment,
of which I was a Spectator, something very particular surpriz'd
me: The noble Guests at the Table happening to be more in
number, than Attendants out of Liveries, could be found for,
I being well known in the Lord *Devonshire's* Family, was desir'd by his Lordship's *Maitre d'Hotel* to assist at it: The Post
assign'd me was to observe what the Lady *Churchill* might call
for. Being so near the Table, you may naturally ask me, what I
might have heard to have pass'd in Conversation at it? which
I should certainly tell you, had I attended to above two Words
that were utter'd there, and those were, *Some Wine and Water*.
These, I remember, came distinguish'd, and observ'd to my
Ear, because they came from the fair Guest, whom I took
such pleasure to wait on: Except at that single Sound, all my
Senses were collected into my Eyes, which during the whole
Entertainment wanted no better Amusement, then of steal-
ing now and then the delight of gazing on the fair Object so
near me: If so clear an Emanation of Beauty, such a commanding Grace of Aspect struck me into a Regard that had something
softer than the most profound Respect in it, I cannot see why
I may not, without offence, remember it; since Beauty, like
the Sun, must sometimes lose its Power to chuse, and shine
into equal Warmth, the Peasant and the Courtier. Now to give
you, Sir, a farther Proof of how good a Taste my first hopeful
entrance into Manhood set out with, I remember above twenty
Years after, when the same Lady had given the World four of
the loveliest Daughters, that ever were gaz'd on, even after they
were all nobly married, and were become the reigning Toasts of

every Party of Pleasure, their still lovely Mother had at the
same time her Votaries, and her Health very often took the
Lead, in those involuntary Triumphs of Beauty. However presumptuous, or impertinent these Thoughts might have appear'd at my first entertaining them, why may I not hope that
my having kept them decently secret, for full fifty Years, may
be now a good round Plea for their Pardon? Were I now qualify'd to say more of this celebrated Lady, I should conclude it
thus: That she liv'd (to all Appearance) a peculiar Favourite of
Providence; that few Examples can parallel the Profusion of
Blessings which have attended so long a Life of Felicity. A
Person so attractive! a Husband so memorably great! an Offspring so beautiful! a Fortune so immense! and a Title, which
(when royal Favour had no higher to bestow) she only cou'd
receive from the Author of Nature; a great Grandmother
without grey Hairs! [8] These are such consumate Indulgencies,
that we might think Heaven has center'd them all in one Person,
to let us see how far, with a lively Understanding, the full
Possession of them could contribute to human Happiness---- I
now return to our military Affairs.

From *Nottingham* our Troops march'd to *Oxford;* through
every Town we pass'd the People came out, in some sort of
Order, with such rural, and rusty Weapons as they had, to meet
us, in Acclamations of welcome, and good Wishes. This, I
thought, promis'd a favourable End of our Civil War, when the
Nation seem'd so willing to be all of a Side! At *Oxford* the
Prince and Princess of *Denmark* met, for the first time, after
their late Separation, and had all possible Honours paid them by
the University. Here we rested in quiet Quarters for several
Weeks, till the Flight of King *James* into *France;* when the
Nation being left to take care of it self, the only Security that
could be found for it, was to advance the Prince and Princess
of *Orange* to the vacant Throne. The publick Tranquillity being
now settled, our Forces were remanded back to *Nottingham.*
Here all our Officers, who had commanded them from their
first rising, receiv'd Commissions to confirm them in their several Posts; and at the same time, such private Men as chose to

return to their proper Business or Habitations, were offer'd their Discharges. Among the small number of those, who receiv'd them, I was one; for not hearing that my Name was in any of these new Commissions, I thought it time for me to take my leave of Ambition, as Ambition had before seduc'd me from the imaginary Honours of the Gown, and therefore resolv'd to hunt my Fortune in some other Field.

From *Nottingham* I again return'd to my Father at *Chattsworth*, where I staid till my Lord came down, with the new Honours of Duke of *Devonshire*, Lord Steward of his Majesty's Houshold, and Knight of the Garter![9] a noble turn of Fortune! and a deep Stake he had play'd for! which calls to my Memory a Story we had then in the Family, which though too light for our graver Historians notice, may be of weight enough for my humble Memoirs. This noble Lord being in the Presence-Chamber, in King *Jame's* time, and known to be no Friend to the Measures of his Administration; a certain Person in favour there, and desirous to be more so, took occasion to tread rudely upon his Lordship's Foot, which was return'd with a sudden Blow upon the Spot: For this Misdemeanour his Lordship was fin'd thirty thousand Pounds; but I think had some time allow'd him for the Payment. In the Summer preceding the Revolution, when his Lordship was retir'd to *Chattsworth*, and had been there deeply engag'd with other Noblemen, in the Measures, which soon after brought it to bear, King *James* sent a Person down to him, with Offers to mitigate his Fine, upon Conditions of ready Payment, to which his Lordship reply'd, that if his Majesty pleas'd to allow him a little longer time, he would rather chuse to play *double* or *quit* with him: The time of the intended Rising being then so near at hand, the Demand, it seems, came too late for a more serious Answer.

However low my Pretensions to Preferment were at this time, my Father thought that a little Court Favour added to them, might give him a Chance for saving the Expence of maintaining me, as he had intended at the University: He therefore order'd me to draw up a Petition to the Duke, and to give it some Air of Merit, to put it into *Latin*, the Prayer of which was,

that his Grace would be pleas'd to do something (I really forget
what) for me---- However the Duke upon receiving it, was
so good as to desire my Father would send me to *London* in the
Winter, where he would consider of some Provision for me.
It might, indeed, well require time to consider it; for I believe
it was then harder to know what I was really fit for, than to
have got me any thing I was not fit for: However, to *London*
I came, where I enter'd into my first State of Attendance and
Dependance for about five Months, till the *February* following.
But alas! in my Intervals of Leisure, by frequently seeing Plays,
my wise Head was turn'd to higher Views, I saw no Joy in
any other Life than that of an Actor, so that (as before, when a
Candidate at *Winchester*) I was even afraid of succeeding to
the Preferment I sought for: 'Twas on the Stage alone I had
form'd a Happiness preferable to all that Camps or Courts could
offer me! and there was I determin'd, let Father and Mother
take it as they pleas'd, to fix my *non ultra*.[10] Here I think my self
oblig'd, in respect to the Honour of that noble Lord, to acknowl-
edge, that I believe his real Intentions to do well for me, were
prevented by my own inconsiderate Folly; so that if my Life
did not then take a more laudable Turn, I have no one but
my self to reproach for it; for I was credibly inform'd by the
Gentlemen of his Houshold, that his Grace had, in their hearing, talk'd of recommending me to the Lord *Shrewsbury*,
then Secretary of State, for the first proper Vacancy in that
Office. But the distant Hope of a Reversion was too cold a Temptation for a Spirit impatient as mine, that wanted immediate
Possession of what my Heart was so differently set upon. The
Allurements of a Theater are still so strong in my Memory, that
perhaps few, except those who have felt them, can conceive:
And I am yet so far willing to excuse my Folly, that I am convinc'd, were it possible to take off that Disgrace and Prejudice,
which Custom has thrown upon the Profession of an Actor,
many a well-born younger Brother, and Beauty of low Fortune
wou'd gladly have adorn'd the Theatre, who by their not being
able to brook such Dishonour to their Birth, have pass'd away
their Lives decently unheeded and forgotten.

Many Years ago, when I was first in the Management of the Theatre, I remember a strong Instance, which will shew you what degree of Ignominy the Profession of an Actor was then held at---- A Lady, with a real Title, whose female Indiscretions had occasion'd her Family to abandon her, being willing, in her distress to make an honest Penny of what Beauty she had left, desir'd to be admitted as an Actress; when before she could receive our Answer, a Gentleman (probably by her Relation's Permission) advis'd us not to entertain her, for Reasons easy to be guess'd. You may imagine we cou'd not be so blind to our Interest as to make an honourable Family our unnecessary Enemies, by not taking his Advice; which the Lady too being sensible of, saw the Affair had its Difficulties; and therefore pursu'd it no farther. Now it is not hard that it shou'd be a doubt, whether this Lady's Condition or ours were the more melancholy? For here, you find her honest Endeavour, to get Bread from the Stage, was look'd upon as on Addition of new Scandal to her former Dishonour! so that I am afraid, according to this way of thinking, had the same Lady stoop'd to have sold Patches and Pomatum, in a Band-box, from Door to Door, she might, in that Occupation have starv'd, with less Infamy, than had she reliev'd her Necessities by being famous on the Theatre. Whether this Prejudice may have arisen from the Abuses that so often have crept in upon the Stage, I am not clear in; tho' when that is grossly the Case, I will allow there ought to be no Limits set to the Contempt of it; yet in its lowest Condition, in my time, methinks there could have been no great Pretence of preferring the Bandbox to the Buskin. But this severe Opinion, whether merited, or not, is not the greatest Distress that this Profession is liable to.

I shall now give you another Anecdote, quite the Reverse of what I have instanc'd, wherein you will see an Actress, as hardly us'd for an Act of Modesty (which without being a Prude, a Woman, even upon the Stage, may sometimes think it necessary not to throw off.) This too I am forc'd to premise, that the Truth of what I am going to tell you, may not be sneer'd at before it be known. About the Year 1717, a young Actress, of a desirable Person, sitting in an upper Box at the Opera, a military Gentleman thought this a proper Opportunity to secure a little Conversation with her; the Particulars of which were, probably, no more worth repeating, than it seems the *Damoiselle* then thought them worth listening to; for, notwithstanding the fine Things he said to her, she rather chose to give the Musick the Preference of her Attention: This Indifference was so offensive to his high Heart, that he began to change the Tender, into the Terrible, and, in short, proceeded at last to treat her in a Style too grossly insulting, for the meanest Female Ear to endure unresented: Upon which, being beaten too far out of her Discretion, she turn'd hastily upon him, with an angry Look, and a Reply, which seem'd to set his Merit in so low a Regard, that he thought himself oblig'd, in Honour, to take his time to resent it: This was the full Extent of her Crime, which his Glory delay'd no longer to punish, than 'till the next time she was to appear upon the Stage: There, in one of her best Parts, wherein she drew a favourable Regard and Approbation from the Audience, he, dispensing with the Respect which some People think due to a polite Assembly, began to interrupt her Performance, with such loud and various Notes of Mockery, as other young Men of Honour, in the same Place, have sometimes made themselves undauntedly merry with: Thus, deaf to all Murmurs or Entreaties of those about him, he pursued his Point, even to throwing near her such Trash, as no Person can be suppos'd to carry about him, unless to use on so particular an Occasion.

A Gentleman, then behind the Scenes, being shock'd at his unmanly Behaviour, was warm enough to say, That no Man, but a Fool, or a Bully, cou'd be capable of insulting an Audience, or a Woman, in so monstrous a manner. The former valiant Gentleman, to whose Ear the Words were soon brought, by his Spies, whom he had plac'd behind the Scenes, to observe how the Action was taken there, came immediately from the Pit, in a Heat, and demanded to know of the Author of those Words, if he was the Person that spoke them? to which he calmly reply'd, That though he had never seen him before, yet, since he

seem'd so earnest to be satisfy'd, he would do him the favour
to own, That, indeed, the Words were his, and that they would
be the last Words he should chuse to deny, whoever they might
fall upon. To conclude, their Dispute was ended the next Morning in *Hyde-Park*, where the determin'd Combatant, who first
ask'd for Satisfaction, was oblig'd afterwards to ask his Life too;
whether he mended it or not, I have not yet heard; but his
Antagonist, in a few Years after, died in one of the principal
Posts of the Government.[11]

Now though I have, sometimes, known these gallant Insulters
of Audiences, draw themselves into Scrapes, which they have
less honourably got out of; yet, alas! what has that avail'd? This
generous publick-spirited Method of silencing a few, was but
repelling the Disease, in one Part, to make it break out in another: All Endeavours at Protection are new Provocations, to
those who pride themselves in pushing their Courage to a Defiance of Humanity. Even when a Royal Resentment has shewn
itself, in the behalf of an injur'd Actor, it has been unable to defend him from farther Insults! an Instance of which happen'd in
the late King *James*'s time. Mr. *Smith* (whose Character as a
Gentleman, could have been no way impeach'd, had he not de-
graded it, by being a celebrated Actor) had the Misfortune,
in a Dispute with a Gentleman behind the Scenes, to receive a
Blow from him: The same Night an Account of this Action
was carry'd to the King, to whom the Gentleman was represented so grossly in the wrong, that, the next Day, his Majesty
sent to forbid him the Court upon it. This Indignity cast upon
a Gentleman, only for having maltreated a Player, was look'd
upon as the Concern of every Gentleman; and a Party was soon
form'd to assert, and vindicate their Honour, by humbling this
favour'd Actor, whose slight Injury had been judg'd equal to
so severe a Notice. Accordingly, the next time *Smith* acted, he
was receiv'd with a Chorus of Cat-calls, that soon convinc'd
him, he should not be suffer'd to proceed in his Part; upon which,
without the least Discomposure, he order'd the Curtain to be
dropp'd; and, having a competent Fortune of his own, thought
the Conditions of adding to it, by his remaining upon the Stage,

were too dear, and from that Day entirely quitted it.[12] I shall
make no Observation upon the King's Resentment, or on that
of his good Subjects; how far either was, or was not right, is not
the Point I dispute for: Be that as it may, the unhappy Condition
of the Actor was so far from being reliev'd by this Royal Interposition in his favour, that it was the worse for it.

While these sort of real Distresses, on the Stage, are so unavoidable, it is no wonder that young People of Sense (though
of low Fortune) should be so rarely found, to supply a Succession of good Actors. Why then may we not, in some measure,
impute the Scarcity of them, to the wanton Inhumanity of those
Spectators, who have made it so terribly mean to appear there?
Were there no ground for this Question, where could be the
Disgrace of entring into a Society, whose Institution, when not
abus'd, is a delightful School of Morality; and where to excel,
requires as ample Endowments of Nature, as any one Profession (that of holy Institution excepted) whatsoever? But, alas!
as *Shakespear* says,

> *Where's that Palace, whereinto, sometimes*
> *Foul things intrude not?*[13]

Look into St. *Peter's* at *Rome*, and see what a profitable
Farce is made of Religion there! Why then is an Actor more
blemish'd than a Cardinal? While the Excellence of the one arises
from his innocently seeming what he is not, and the Eminence
of the other, from the most impious Fallacies that can be impos'd upon human Understanding? If the best things, therefore, are most liable to Corruption, the Corruption of the
Theatre is no Disproof of its innate and primitive Utility.

In this Light, therefore, all the Abuses of the Stage, all the
low, loose, or immoral Supplements, to wit, whether, in making
Virtue ridiculous, or Vice agreeable, or in the decorated Nonsense and Absurdities of Pantomimical Trumpery, I give up
to the Contempt of every sensible Spectator, as so much
rank Theatrical Popery. But cannot still allow these Enormities
to impeach the Profession, while they are so palpably owing to
the deprav'd Taste of the Multitude. While Vice, and Farcical

Folly, are the most profitable Commodities, why should we
wonder that, time out of mind, the poor Comedian, when real
Wit would bear no Price, should deal in what would bring him
most ready Money?[14] But this, you will say, is making the Stage
a Nursery of Vice and Folly, or at least keeping an open Shop
for it.---I grant it: But who do you expect should reform
it? The Actors? Why so? If People are permitted to buy it,
without blushing, the Theatrical Merchant seems to have an
equal Right to the Liberty of selling it, without Reproach. That
this Evil wants a Remedy, is not to be contested; nor can it be
denied, that the Theatre is as capable of being preserv'd, by a
Reformation, as Matters of more Importance; which, for the
Honour of our national Taste, I could wish more attempted; and
then, if it could not subsist, under decent Regulations, by not
being permitted to present any thing there, but what were
worthy to be there, it would be time enough to consider,
whether it were necessary to let it totally fall, or effectually
support it.

Notwithstanding all my best Endeavours, to recommend the
Profession of an Actor, to a more general Favour, I doubt, while
it is liable to such Corruptions, and the Actor himself to such
unlimited Insults, as I have already mention'd, I doubt, I say,
we must still leave him a-drift, with his intrinsic Merit, to ride
out the Storm as well as he is able.

However, let us now turn to the other side of this Account,
and see what Advantages stand there, to balance the Misfortunes I have laid before you. There we shall still find some valuable Articles of Credit, that, sometimes overpay his incidental
Disgraces.

First, if he has Sense, he will consider, that as these Indignities are seldom or never offer'd him by People, that are remarkable for any one good Quality, he ought not to lay them too
close to his Heart: He will know too, that when Malice, Envy,
or a brutal Nature, can securely hide or fence themselves in a
Multitude, Virtue, Merit, Innocence, and even sovereign Superiority, have been, and must be equally liable to their Insults; that
therefore, when they fall upon him in the same manner, his

intrinsick Value cannot be diminish'd by them: On the contrary, if, with a decent and unruffled Temper, he lets them pass, the Disgrace will return upon his Aggressor, and perhaps warm the generous Spectator into a Partiality in his Favour.

That while he is conscious, that, as an Actor, he must be always in the Hands of Injustice, it does him at least this involuntary Good, that it keeps him in a settled Resolution to avoid all Occasions of provoking it, or of even offending the lowest Enemy, who, at the Expence of a Shilling, may publickly revenge it.

That, if he excels on the Stage, and is irreproachable in his Personal Morals, and Behaviour, his Profession is so far from being an Impediment, that it will be oftner a just Reason for his being receiv'd among People of condition with Favour; and sometimes with a more social Distinction, than the best, though more profitable Trade he might have follow'd, could have recommended him to.

That this is a Happiness to which several Actors, within my Memory, as *Betterton, Smith, Montfort*, Captain *Griffin*, and Mrs. *Bracegirdle* (yet living) have arriv'd at; to which I may add the late celebrated Mrs. *Oldfield*.[15] Now let us suppose these Persons, the Men, for example, to have been all eminent Mercers, and the Women as famous Milliners, we can imagine, that merely as such, though endow'd with the same natural Understanding, they could have been call'd into the same honourable Parties of Conversation? People of Sense and Condition, could not but know, it was impossible they could have had such various Excellencies on the Stage, without having something naturally valuable in them: And I will take upon me to affirm, who knew them all living, that there was not one of the number, who were not capable of supporting a variety of Spirited Conversation, tho' the Stage were never to have been the Subject of it.

That, to have trod the Stage, has not always been thought a Disqualification from more honourable Employments; several have had military Commissions; *Carlisle* and *Wiltshire* were both kill'd Captains; one, in King *William's* Reduction of *Ireland;* and the other, in his first War, in *Flanders;* and the famous *Ben. Johnson*, tho' an unsuccessful Actor, was afterwards made Poet-Laureat.[16]

To these laudable Distinctions, let me add one more; that of Publick Applause, which, when truly merited, is, perhaps, one of the most agreeable Gratifications that venial Vanity can feel. A Happiness, almost peculiar to the Actor, insomuch that the best Tragick Writer, however numerous his separate Admirers may be, yet, to unite them into one general Act of Praise, to receive at once, those thundring Peals of Approbation, which a crouded Theatre throws out, he must still call in the Assistance of the skilful Actor, to raise and partake of them.

In a Word, 'twas in this flattering Light only, though not perhaps so thoroughly consider'd, I look'd upon the Life of an Actor, when but eighteen Years of Age; nor can you wonder, if the Temptations were too strong for so warm a Vanity as mine to resist; but whether excusable, or not, to the Stage, at length I came, and it is from thence, chiefly, your Curiosity, if you have any left, is to expect a farther Account of me.

Tho' I have only promis'd you an Account of all the material Occurrences of the Theatre during my own Time; yet there was one which happen'd not above seven Years before my Admission to it,[2] which may be as well worth notice, as the first great Revolution of it, in which, among numbers, I was involv'd. And as the one will lead you into a clearer View of the other, it may therefore be previously necessary to let you know that:

King *Charles* II. at his Restoration, granted two Patents, one to Sir *William Davenant*, and the other to *Henry Killigrew*, Esq; and their several Heirs and Assigns, for ever, for the forming of two distinct Companies of Comedians: The first were call'd the *King's Servants*, and acted at the Theatre-Royal in *Drury-Lane;* and the other the *Duke's Company*, who acted at the Duke's Theatre in *Dorset-Garden*.[3] About ten of the King's Company were on the Royal Houshold-Establishment, having each ten Yards of Scarlet Cloth, with a proper quantity of Lace allow'd them for Liveries; and in their Warrants from the Lord Chamberlain, were stiled *Gentlemen of the Great Chamber:* Whether the like Appointments were extended to the Duke's Company, I am not certain; but they were both in high Estimation with the Publick, and so much the Delight and Concern of the Court, that they were not only supported by its being frequently present at their publick *Presentations*, but by its taking cognizance even of their private Government, insomuch, that their particular Differences, Pretentions, or Complaints, were generally ended by the *King*, or *Duke's* Personal Command or Decision. Besides their being thorough Masters of their Art, these Actors set forwards with two critical Advantages, which perhaps may never happen again in many Ages. The one was, their immediate opening after so long Interdiction of Plays, during the Civil War, and the Anarchy that follow'd it. What eager Appetites from so long a Fast, must the Guests of those Times have had, to that high and fresh variety of Entertainments, which *Shakespear* had left prepar'd for them? Never was a Stage so provided! A hundred Years are wasted, and another silent Century well advanced, and yet what unborn Age shall say, *Shakespear* has his Equal! How many shining Actors have the warm Scenes of his Genius given to Posterity? without being himself, in his Action, equal to his Writing! A strong Proof that Actors, like Poets, must be born such. Eloquence and Elocution are quite different Talents: *Shakespear* cou'd write *Hamlet;* but Tradition tells us, That the *Ghost,* in the same Play, was one of his best Performances as an Actor: Nor is it within the reach of Rule or Precept to complete either of them. Instruction, 'tis true, may guard them equally against Faults or Absurdities, but there it stops; Nature must do the rest: To excel in either Art, is a self-born Happiness, which something more than good Sense must be the Mother of.

The other Advantage I was speaking of, is, that before the Restoration, no Actresses had ever been seen upon the *English* Stage. The Characters of Women, on former Theatres, were perform'd by Boys, or young Men of the most effeminate Aspect. And what Grace, or Master-strokes of Action can we conceive such ungain Hoydens to have been capable of? This Defect was so well consider'd by *Shakespear,* that in few of his Plays, he has any greater Dependance upon the Ladies, than in the Innocence and Simplicity of a *Desdemona,* an *Ophelia,* or in the short Specimen of a fond and virtuous *Portia.* The additional Objects then of real, beautiful Women, could not but draw a proportion of new Admirers to the Theatre. We may imagine too, that these Actresses were not ill chosen, when it is well known, that more than one of them had Charms sufficient at their leisure Hours, to calm and mollify the Cares of Empire. Besides these peculiar Advantages, they had a private Rule or Agreement, which both Houses were happily ty'd down to, which was, that no Play acted at one House, should ever be attempted at the other. All the capital Plays therefore of *Shakes-pear*, *Fletcher*, and *Ben. Johnson*, were divided between them, by the Approbation of the Court, and their own alternate Choice:[4] So that when *Hart*[5] was famous for *Othello*, *Betterton* had no less a Reputation for *Hamlet*. By this Order the Stage was supply'd with a greater variety of Plays, than could pos-sibly have been shewn, had both Companies been employ'd at the same time, upon the same Play; which Liberty too, must have occasion'd such frequent Repetitions of 'em, by their opposite Endeavours to forestall and anticipate one another, that the best Actors in the World must have grown tedious and tasteless to the Spectator: For what Pleasure is not languid to Satiety? It was therefore one of our greatest Happinesses (during my time of being in the Management of the Stage) that we had a cer-tain number of select Plays, which no other Company had the good Fortune to make a tolerable Figure in, and consequently, could find little or no Account, by acting them against us. These Plays therefore, for many Years, by not being too often seen, never fail'd to bring us crowded Audiences; and it was to this Conduct we ow'd no little share of our Prosperity. But when four Houses are at once (as very lately they were)[6] all permitted to act the same Pieces, let three of them perform never so ill, when Plays come to be so harrass'd and hackney'd out to the common People (half of which too, perhaps would as lieve see them at one House as another) the best Actors will soon feel that the Town has enough of them.

I know it is the common Opinion, That the more Playhouses, the more Emulation; I grant it; but what has this Emulation ended in? Why, a daily Contention which shall soonest surfeit you with the best Plays; so that when what *ought* to please, can no *longer* please, your Appetite is again to be rais'd by such monstrous Presentations,[7] as dishonour the Taste of a civil-iz'd People. If, indeed, to our several Theatres, we could raise a proportionable number of good Authors, to give them all different Employment, then, perhaps, the Publick might profit from their Emulation: But while good Writers are so scarce, and undaunted Criticks so plenty, I am afraid a good Play, and

a blazing Star, will be equal Rarities. This voluptous Expedient,
therefore, of indulging the Taste with several Theatres, will
amount to much the same variety as that of a certain Oeconomist,
who, to enlarge his Hospitality, would have two Puddings, and
Two Legs of Mutton, for the same Dinner.---- But, to resume
the Thread of my History.

These two excellent Companies were both prosperous for
some few Years, 'till their Variety of Plays began to be ex-
hausted: Then of course, the better Actors (which the King's
seem to have been allow'd) could not fail of drawing the greater
Audiences. Sir *William Davenant*, therefore, Master of the
Duke's Company, to make Head against their Success, was
forc'd to add Spectacle and Musick to Action; and to introduce
a new Species of Plays, since call'd Dramatick Opera's, of which
kind were the *Tempest, Psyche, Circe*,[8] and others, all set off
with the most expensive Decorations of Scenes and Habits, with
the best Voices and Dancers.

This sensual Supply of Sight and Sound, coming in to the
Assistance of the weaker Party, it was no wonder they should
grow too hard for Sense and simple Nature, when it is consider'd how many more People there are, that can see and hear,
than think and judge. So wanton a Change of the publick Taste,
therfore, began to fall as heavy upon the King's Company,
as their greater Excellence in Action, had, before, fallen upon
their Competitors: Of which Encroachment upon Wit, several
good Prologues in those Days frequently complain'd.

But alas! what can Truth avail, when its Dependance is much
more upon the Ignorant, than the sensible Auditor? a poor Satisfaction, that the due Praise given to it, must at last, sink into
the cold Comfort of--- *Laudatur & Alget*.[9] Unprofitable Praise
can hardly give it a *Soup maigre*. Taste and Fashion, with us,
have always had Wings, and fly from one publick Spectacle to
another so wantonly, that I have been inform'd, by those, who
remember it, that a famous Puppet-shew, in *Salisbury* Change
(then standing where *Cecil-Street* now is) so far distrest these
two celebrated Companies, that they were reduc'd to petition
the King for Relief against it: Nor ought we perhaps to think

this strange, when if I mistake not, *Terence* himself reproaches
the *Roman* Auditors of his Time, with the like Fondness for
the *Funambuli*, the Rope-dancers.[10] Not to dwell too long therefore upon that Part of my History, which I have only collected,
from oral Tradition, I shall content my self with telling you,
that *Mohun*,[11] and *Hart* now growing old (for, above thirty
Years before this Time, they had severally born the King's
Commission of Major and Captain, in the Civil Wars) and the
younger Actors, as *Goodwin, Clark*,[12] and others, being impatient to get into their Parts, and growing intractable, the Audiences too of both Houses then falling off, the Patentees of each,
by the King's Advice, which perhaps amounted to a Command,
united their Interests, and both Companies into one, exclusive
of all others, in the Year 1684.[13] This Union was, however, so
much in favour of the Duke's Company, that *Hart* left the
Stage upon it, and *Mohun* surviv'd not long after.

One only Theatre being now in Possession of the whole
Town, the united Patentees impos'd their own Terms, upon the
Actors; for the Profits of acting were then divided into twenty
Shares, ten of which went to the Proprietors, and the other
Moiety to the Principal Actors, in such Sub-divisions as their
different Merit might pretend to. These Shares of the Patentees
were promiscuously sold out to Mony-making Persons, call'd
Adventurers,[14] who, tho' utterly ignorant of Theatrical Affairs,
were still admitted to a proportionate Vote in the Management
of them; all particular Encouragements to Actors were by them,
of Consequence, look'd upon as so many Sums deducted from
their private Dividends. While therefore the Theatrical Hive
had so many Drones in it, the labouring Actors, sure, were under
the highest Discouragement, if not a direct State of Oppression.
Their Hardship will at least appear in a much stronger Light,
when compar'd to our later Situation, who with scarce half their
Merit, succeeded to be Sharers under a Patent upon five times
easier Conditions: For as they had but half the Profits divided
among ten, or more of them; we had three fourths of the whole
Profits, divided only among three of us: And as they might be
said to have ten Task-masters over them, we never had but one
Assistant-manager (not an Actor) join'd with us; who, by the

Crown's Indulgence, was sometimes too of our own chusing. Under this heavy Establishment then groan'd this United Company, when I was first admitted into the lowest Rank of it. How they came to be reliev'd by King *William*'s Licence in 1695, how they were again dispers'd, early in Queen *Anne's* Reign; and from what Accidents Fortune took better care of *Us*, their unequal Successors, will be told in its Place: But to prepare you for the opening so large a Scene of their History, methinks I ought, (in Justice to their Memory too) to give you such particular Characters of their Theatrical Merit, as in my plain Judgment they seem'd to deserve. Presuming then, that this Attempt may not be disagreeable to the Curious, or the true Lovers of the Theatre, take it without farther Preface.

In the Year 1690, when I first came into this Company, the principal Actors then at the Head of it were,

Of Men.	Of Women.
Mr. *Betterton*,	Mrs. *Betterton*,
Mr. *Monfort*,	Mrs. *Barry*,
Mr. *Kynaston*,	Mrs. *Leigh*,
Mr. *Sandford*,	Mrs. *Butler*,
Mr. *Nokes*,	Mrs. *Monfort*, and
Mr. *Underhill*, and	Mrs. *Bracegirdle*.
Mr. *Leigh*.	

These Actors, whom I have selected from their Contemporaries, were all original Masters in their different Stile, not meer auricular Imitators of one another, which commonly is the highest Merit of the middle Rank; but Self-judges of nature, from whose various Lights they only took their true Instruction. If in the following Account of them, I may be oblig'd to hint at the Faults of others, I never mean such Observations should extend to those who are now in Possession of the Stage; for as I design not my Memoirs shall come down to their Time, I would not lie under the Imputation of speaking in their Disfavour to the Publick, whose Approbation they must depend upon for Support.[15] But to my Purpose.

Betterton was an Actor, as *Shakespear* was an Author, both without Competitors! form'd for the mutal Assistance, and Illustration of each others Genius! How *Shakepear* wrote, all Men who have a Taste for Nature may read, and know--- but with what higher Rapture would he still be *read*, could they conceive how *Betterton play'd* him! Then might they know, the one was born alone to speak what the other only knew, to write! Pity it is, that the momentary Beauties flowing from an harmonious Elocution, cannot like those of Poetry, be their own Record! That the animated Graces of the Player can live no longer than the instant Breath and Motion that presents them; or at best can but faintly glimmer through the Memory, or imperfect Attestation of a few surviving Spectators. Could *how Betterton* spoke be as easily known as *what* he spoke; then might you see the Muse of *Shakespear* in her Triumph, with all her Beauties in their best Array, rising into real Life, and charming her Beholders. But alas! since all this is so far out of the reach of Description, how shall I shew you *Betterton*? Should I therefore tell you, that all the *Othellos, Hamlets, Hotspurs, Mackbeths,* and *Brutus*'s, whom you may have seen since his time, have fallen far short of him; This still would give you no Idea of his particular Excellence. Let us see then what a particular Comparison may do! whether that may yet draw him nearer to you?

You have seen a *Hamlet* perhaps, who, on the first appearance of his Father's Spirit, has thrown himself into all the straining Vociferation requisite to express Rage and Fury, and the House has thunder'd with Applause; tho' the mis-guided Actor was all the while (as *Shakepear* terms it) tearing a Passion into Rags[16] ---- I am the more bold to offer you this particular Instance, because the late Mr. *Addison*, while I sate by him, to see this Scene acted, made the same Observation, asking me with some Surprize, if I thought *Hamlet* should be in so violent a Passion with the Ghost, which tho' it might have astonish'd, it had not provok'd him? for you may observe that in this beautiful Speech, the Passion never rises beyond an almost breathless Astonishment, or an Impatience, limited by filial Reverence, to enquire into the suspected Wrongs that may have rais'd him from his peaceful Tomb! and a Desire to know what a Spirit so seem-

ingly distrest, might wish or enjoin a sorrowful Son to execute
towards his future Quiet in the Grave? This was the Light into
which *Betterton* threw this Scene; which he open'd with a
Pause of mute Amazement! then rising slowly, to a solemn,
trembling Voice, he made the Ghost equally terrible to the
Spectator, as to himself! and in the descriptive Part of the natural
Emotions which the ghastly Vision gave him, the boldness of his
Expostulation was still govern'd by Decency, manly, but not
braving; his Voice never rising into that seeming Outrage, or
wild Defiance of what he naturally rever'd. But alas! to preserve this Medium, between mouthing, and meaning too little,
to keep the Attention more pleasingly awake, by a temper'd
Spirit, than by mere Vehemence of Voice, is of all the Master-
strokes of an Actor the most difficult to reach. In this none yet
have equall'd *Betterton*. But I am unwilling to shew his Superiority only by recounting the Errors of those, who now cannot
answer to them, let their farther Failings therefore be forgotten!
or rather, shall I in some measure excuse them? For I am not yet
sure, that they might not be as much owing to the false Judgment
of the Spectator, as the Actor. While the Million are so apt to
be transported, when the Drum of their Ear is so roundly rat-
tled; while they take the Life of Elocution to lie in the Strength
of the Lungs, it is no wonder the Actor, whose end is Applause, should be so often tempted, at this easy rate, to excite it.
Shall I go a little farther? and allow that this Extreme is more
pardonable than its opposite Error. I mean that dangerous Affectation of the Monotone, or solemn Sameness of Pronunciation, which to my Ear is insupportable; for of all the Faults
that so frequently pass upon the Vulgar, that of Flatness will
have the fewest Admirers. That this is an Error of ancient standing seems evident by what *Hamlet* says, in his Instructions to
the Players, *viz.*

Be not too tame, neither, &c.[17]

The Actor, doubtless, is as strongly ty'd down to the Rules of
Horace, as the Writer.

Si vis me flere, dolendum est
Primum ipsi tibi ----- [18]

He that feels not himself the Passion he would raise, will talk
to a sleeping Audience: But this never was the Fault of *Betterton;*
and it had often amaz'd me, to see those who soon came after
him, throw out in some Parts of a Character, a just and graceful
Spirit, which *Betterton* himself could not but have applauded.
And yet in the equally shining Passages of the same Character,
have heavily dragg'd the Sentiment along, like a dead Weight;
with a long-ton'd Voice, and absent Eye, as if they had fairly
forgot what they were about: If you have never made this Observation, I am contented you should not know, where to apply
it.[19]

A farther Excellence in *Betterton,* was that he could vary his
Spirit to the different Characters he acted. Those wild impatient
Starts, that fierce and flashing Fire, which he threw into *Hotspur,* never came from the unruffled Temper of his *Brutus* (for I
have, more than once, seen a *Brutus* as warm as *Hotspur*) when
the *Betterton Brutus* was provok'd, in his Dispute with *Cassius,*
his Spirit flew only to his Eye; his steady Look alone supply'd
that Terror, which he disdain'd an Intemperance in his Voice
should rise to. Thus, with a settled Dignity of Contempt, like
an unheeding Rock, he repell'd upon himself the Foam of *Cassius.* Perhaps the very Words of *Shakespear* will better let you
into my Meaning:

> *Must I give way, and room, to your rash Choler?*
> *Shall I be frighted when a Madman stares?*

And a little after,

> *There is no Terror,* Cassius, *in your Looks!* &c.[20]

Not but, in some part of this Scene, where he reproaches *Cas-
sius,* his Temper is not under his Suppression, but opens into that
Warmth which becomes a Man of Virtue; yet this is that *Hasty
Spark* of Anger, which *Brutus* himself endeavours to excuse.

But with whatever strength of Nature we see the Poet shew,
at once, the Philosopher and the Heroe, yet the Image of the
Actor's Excellence will be still imperfect to you, unless Language cou'd put Colours in our Words to paint the Voice with.

Et, si vis similem pingere, pinge sonum,[21] is enjoying an Impossibility. The most that a *Vandyke* can arrive at, is to make his Portraits of great Persons seem to *think;* a *Shakepear* goes farther yet, and tells you *what* his Pictures thought; a *Betterton* steps beyond 'em both, and calls them from the Grave, to breathe, and be themselves again, in Feature, Speech, and Motion. When the skilful Actor shews you all these Powers united, and gratifies at once your Eye, your Ear, your Understanding. To conceive the Pleasure rising from such Harmony, you must have been present at it! 'tis not to be told you!

There cannot be a stronger Proof of the Charms of harmonious Elocution, than the many, even unnatural Scenes and Flights of the false Sublime it has lifted into Applause. In what Raptures have I seen an Audience, at the furious Fustian and turgid Rants in *Nat. Lee's Alexander the Great!* For though I can allow this Play a few great Beauties, yet it is not without its extravagant Blemishes. Every Play of the same Author has more or less of them. Let me give you a Sample from this. *Alexander,* in a full crowd of Courtiers, without being occasionally call'd or provok'd to it, falls into this Rhapsody of Vain-glory.

> *Can none remember? Yes, I know all must!*

And therefore they shall know it agen.

> *When Glory, like the dazzling Eagle, stood*
> *Perch'd on my Beaver, in the Granic Flood,*
> *When Fortune's Self, my Standard trembling bore,*
> *And the pale Fates stood frighted on the Shore,*
> *When the Immortals on the Billows rode,*
> *And I myself appear'd the leading God.*[22]

When these flowing Numbers came from the Mouth of a *Betterton,* the Multitude no more desired Sense to them, than our musical *Connoisseurs* think it essential in the celebrate Airs of an *Italian* Opera. Does not this prove, that there is very near as much Enchantment in the well-govern'd Voice of an Actor, as in the sweet Pipe of an Eunuch? If I tell you, there was no one Tragedy, for many Years, more in favour with the Town than

Alexander, to what must we impute this its command of publick
Admiration? Not to its intrinsick Merit, surely, if it swarms with
Passages like this I have shewn you! If this Passage has Merit,
let us see what Figure it would make upon Canvas, what sort of
Picture would rise from it. If *Le Brun,*[23] who was famous for
painting the Battles of this Heroe, had seen this lofty Description, what one Image could he have possibly taken from it? In
what Colours would he have shewn us *Glory perch'd upon a
Beaver?* How would he have drawn *Fortune trembling?* Or, indeed, what use could he have made of *pale Fates,* or *Immortals*
riding upon *Billows,* with this blustering *God* of his own making
at the *head* of 'em? Where, then, must have lain the Charm, that
once made the Publick so partial to this *Tragedy?* Why plainly,
in the Grace and Harmony of the Actor's Utterance. For the
Actor himself is not accountable for the false Poetry of his
Author; That, the Hearer is to judge of; if it passes upon him,
the Actor can have no Quarrel to it; who, if the Periods given
him are round, smooth, spirited, and high-sounding, even in a
false Passion, must throw out the same Fire and Grace, as may
be required in one justly rising from Nature; where those his
Excellencies will then be only more pleasing, in proportion to the
Taste of his Hearer. And I am of opinion, that to the extraordinary Success of this very Play, we may impute the Corruption
of so many Actors, and Tragick Writers, as were immediately
misled by it. The unskilful Actor, who imagin'd all the Merit
of delivering those blazing Rants, lay only in the Strength, and
strain'd Exertion of the Voice, began to tear his Lungs, upon
every false, or slight Occasion, to arrive at the same Applause.
And it is from hence I date our having seen the same Reason
prevalent, for above fifty Years. Thus equally misguided too,
many a barren-brain'd Author has stream'd into a frothy flowing
Style, pompously rolling into sounding Periods, signifying ----
roundly nothing; of which Number, in some of my former Labours, I am something more than suspicious, that I may myself
have made one. But, to keep a little closer to *Betterton.*

When this favourite Play I am speaking of, from its being too
frequently acted, was worn out, and came to be deserted by the

Town, upon the sudden death of *Monfort*, who had play'd *Alexander* with Success, for several Years, the Part was given to *Betterton*, which, under this great Disadvantage of the Satiety it had given, he immediately reviv'd, with so new a Lustre, that for three Days together it fill'd the House; and had his then declining Strength been equal to the Fatigue the Action gave him, it probably might have doubled its Success; an uncommon Instance of the Power and intrinsick Merit of an Actor. This I mention, not only to prove what irresistable Pleasure may arise from a judicious Elocution, with scarce Sense to assist it; but to shew you too, that tho' *Betterton* never wanted Fire, and Force, when his Character demanded it; yet, where it was not demanded, he never prostituted his Power to the low Ambition of a false Applause. And further, that when, from a too advanced Age, he resign'd that toilsome Part of *Alexander*, the Play, for many Years after, never was able to impose upon the Publick; and I look upon his so particularly supporting the false Fire and Extravagancies of that Character, to be a more surprizing Proof of his Skill, than his being eminent in those of *Shakepear;* because there, Truth and Nature coming to his Assistance, he had not the same Difficulties to combat, and consequently, we must be less amaz'd at his Success, where we are more able to account for it.

Notwithstanding the extraordinary Power he shew'd in blowing *Alexander* once more into a blaze of Admiration, *Betterton* had so just a Sense of what was true, or false Applause, that I have heard him say, he never thought any kind of it equal to an attentive Silence; that there were many ways of deceiving an Audience into a loud one; but to keep them husht and quiet, was an Applause which only Truth and Merit could arrive at: Of which Art, there never was an equal Master to himself. From these various Excellencies, he had so full a Possession of the Esteem and Regard of his Auditors, that upon his Entrance into every Scene, he seem'd to seize upon the Eyes and Ears of the Giddy and Inadvertent! To have talk'd, or look'd another way, would then have been thought Insensibility, or Ignorance. In all his Soliloquies of moment, the strong Intelligence of his

Attitude and Aspect, drew you into such an impatient Gaze, and eager Expectation, that you almost imbib'd the Sentiment with your Eye, before the Ear could reach it.

As *Betterton* is the Centre to which all my Observations upon Action tend, you will give me leave, under his Character, to enlarge upon that Head. In the just Delivery of Poetical Numbers, particularly where the Sentiments are pathetick, it is scarce credible, upon how minute an Article of Sound depends their greatest Beauty or Inaffection. The Voice of a Singer is not more strictly ty'd to Time and Tune, than that of an Actor in Theatrical Elocution: The least Syllable too long, or too slightly dwelt upon, in a Period, depreciates it to nothing; which very Syllable, if rightly touch'd, shall, like the heightening Stroke of Light from a Master's Pencil, give Life and Spirit to the whole. I never heard a Line in Tragedy come from *Betterton*, wherein my Judgment, my Ear, and my Imagination, were not fully satisfy'd; which, since his Time, I cannot equally say of any one Actor whatsoever: Not but it is possible to be much his Inferior, with great Excellencies; which I shall observe in another Place. Had it been practicable to have ty'd down the clattering Hands of all the ill Judges who were commonly the Majority of an Audience, to what amazing Perfection might the *English* Theatre have arriv'd, with so just an Actor as *Betterton* at the Head of it! If what was Truth only, could have been applauded, how many noisy Actors had shook their Plumes with Shame, who, from the injudicious Approbation of the Multitude, have bawl'd and strutted, in the place of Merit? If therefore the bare speaking Voice has such Allurements in it, how much less ought we to wonder, however we may lament, that the sweeter Notes of Vocal Musick should so have captivated even the politer World, into an Apostacy from Sense, to an Idolatry of Sound. Let us enquire from whence this Enchantment rises. I am afraid it may be too naturally accounted for: For when we complain, that the finest Musick, purchas'd at such vast Expence, is so often thrown away upon the most miserable Poetry, we seem not to consider, that when the Movement of the Air, and Tone of the Voice, are exquisitely harmonious, tho' we regard not one *Word* of what we hear, yet the Power of the Melody is so busy in the Heart, that we naturally annex Ideas to it of our own Creation, and, in some sort, become our selves the Poet to the Composer; and what Poet is so dull as not to be charm'd with the Child of his own Fancy? So that there is even a kind of Language in agreeable Sounds, which, like the Aspect of Beauty, without Words, speaks and plays with the Imagination. While this Taste therefore is so naturally prevalent, I doubt, to propose Remedies for it, were but giving Laws to the Winds, or Advice to Inamorato's: And however gravely we may assert, that Profit ought always to be inseparable from the Delight of the Theatre; nay admitting that the Pleasure would be heighten'd by the uniting them; yet, while Instruction is so little the Concern of the Auditor, how can we hope that so choice a Commodity will come to a Market where there is so seldom a Demand for it?

It is not to the Actor therefore, but to the vitiated and low Taste of the Spectator, that the Corruptions of the Stage (of what kind soever) have been owing. If the Publick, by whom they must live, had Spirit enough to discountenance, and declare against all the Trash and Fopperies they have been so frequently fond of, both the Actors, and the Authors, to the best of their Power, must naturally have serv'd their daily Table, with sound and wholesome Diet.--- But I have not yet done with my Article of Elocution.

As we have sometimes great Composers of Musick, who cannot sing, we have as frequently great Writers that cannot read; and tho', without the nicest Ear, no Man can be Master of Poetical Numbers, yet the best Ear in the World will not always enable him to pronounce them. Of this Truth, *Dryden,* our first great Master of Verse and Harmony, was a strong Instance: When he brought his Play of *Amphytrion* to the Stage,[24] I heard him give it his first Reading to the Actors, in which, though it is true, he deliver'd the plain Sense of every Period, yet the whole was in so cold, so flat, and unaffecting a manner, that I am afraid of not being believ'd, when I affirm it.

On the contrary, *Lee,* far his Inferior in Poetry, was so pathe-

tick a Reader of his own Senses, that I have been inform'd by an
Actor, who was present, that while *Lee* was reading to Major
Mohun at a Rehearsal, *Mohun*, in the Warmth of his Admiration, threw down his Part, and said, Unless I were able to *play*
it, as well as you *read* it, to what purpose should I undertake
it? And yet this very Author, whose Elocution rais'd such
Admiration in so capital an Actor, when he attempted to be an
Actor himself, soon quitted the Stage, in an honest Despair of
ever making any profitable Figure there. From all this I would
infer, That let our Conception of what we are to speak, be
ever so just, and the Ear ever so true, yet, when we are to deliver
it to an Audience (I will leave Fear out of the question) there
must go along with the whole, a natural Freedom, and becoming
Grace, which is easier to conceive than to describe: For without
this inexpressible somewhat, the Performance will come out
oddly disguis'd, or somewhere defectively, unsurprizing to the
Hearer. Of this Defect too, I will give you yet a stranger Instance, which you will allow Fear could not be the Occasion of:
If you remember *Estcourt*,[25] you must have known that he was
long enough upon the Stage, not to be under the least Restraint
from Fear, in his Performance: This Man was so amazing and
extraordinary a Mimick, that no Man or Woman, from the
Coquette to the Privy-Counsellor, ever mov'd or spoke before
him, but he could carry their Voice, Look, Mien, and Motion,
instantly into another Company: I have heard him make long
Harangues, and form various Arguments, even in the manner of
thinking, of an eminent Pleader at the Bar, with every the least
Article and Singularity of his Utterance so perfectly imitated,
that he was the very *alter ipse*, scarce to be distinguish'd from his
Original. Yet more; I have seen, upon the Margin of the written
Part of *Falstaff*, which he acted, his own Notes and Observations
upon almost every Speech of it, describing the true Spirit
of the Humour, and with what tone of Voice, look, Gesture,
each of them ought to be delivered. Yet in his Execution upon
the Stage, he seem'd to have lost all those just Ideas he had form'd
of it, and almost thro' the Character, labour'd under a heavy
Load of Flatness: In a word, with all his Skill in Mimickry, and

Knowledge of what ought to be done, he never, upon the Stage, could bring it truly into Practice, but was upon the whole, a languid, unaffecting Actor. After I have shewn you so many necessary Qualifications, not one of which can be spar'd in true Theatrical Elocution, and have at the same time prov'd, that with the Assistance of them all united, the whole may still come forth defective; what Talents shall we say will infallibly form an Actor? This, I confess, is one of Nature's Secrets, too deep for me to dive into; let us content our selves therefore with affirming, That *Genius*, which Nature only gives, only can complete him. This *Genius* then was so strong in *Betterton*, that it shone out in every Speech and Motion of him. Yet Voice, and Person, are such necessary Supports to it, that, by the Multitude, they have been preferr'd to *Genius* itself, or at least often mistaken for it. *Betterton* had a Voice of that kind, which gave more Spirit to Terror, than to the softer Passions; of more Strength than Melody. The Rage and Jealousy of *Othello*, became him better than the Sighs and Tenderness of *Castalio*:[26] For tho' in *Castalio* he only excell'd others, in *Othello* he excell'd himself; which you will easily believe, when you consider, that in spite of hs Complexion, *Othello* has more natural Beauties than the best Actor can find in all the Magazine of Poetry, to animate his Power, and delight his Judgement with.

The Person of this excellent Actor was suitable to his Voice, more manly than sweet, not exceeding the middle Stature, inclining to the corpulent; of a serious and penetrating Aspect; his Limbs nearer the athletick, than the delicate Proportion; yet however form'd, there arose from the Harmony of the whole a commanding Mien of Majesty, which the fairer-fac'd, or (as *Shakpear* calls 'em) the *curled* Darlings of his Time,[27] ever wanted something to be equal Masters of. There was some Years ago, to be had, almost in every Print-shop, a *Metzotinto*, from *Kneller*,[28] extremely like him.

In all I have said of *Betterton*, I confine my self to the Time of his Strength, and the highest Power in Action, that you may make Allowances from what he was able to execute at fifty, to what you might have seen of him at past seventy; for tho' to the last he was without his equal, he might not then be equal to his former self; yet so far was he from being ever overtaken, that for many Years after his decease, I seldom saw any of his Parts, in *Shakepear*, supply'd by others, but it drew from me the Lamentation of *Ophelia* upon *Hamlet's* being unlike, what she had seen him.

------ *Ah! woe is me!*
T' have seen, what I have seen, see what I see![29]

The last Part this great Master of his Profession acted, was *Melantius* in the *Maid's Tragedy*,[30] for his own Benefit; when ing suddenly seiz'd by the Gout, he submitted, by extraordinary Applications, to have his Foot so far reliev'd, that he might be able to walk on the Stage, in a Slipper, rather than wholly disappoint his Auditors. He was observ'd that Day, to have exerted a more than ordinary Spirit, and met with suitable Applause; but the unhappy Consequence of tampering with his Distemper was, that it flew into his Head, and kill'd him in three Days, (I think) in the seventy-fourth Year of his Age.

I once thought to have fill'd up my Work with a select Dissertation upon Theatrical Action, but I find, by the Digressions I have been tempted to make in this Account of *Betterton*, that all I can say upon that Head, will naturally fall in, and possibly be less tedious, if dispers'd among the various Characters of the particular Actors, I have promis'd to treat of; I shall therefore make use of those several Vehicles, which you will find waiting in the next Chapter, to carry you through the rest of the Journey, at your Leisure.

Tho' as I have before observ'd, Women were not admitted to the Stage, 'till the return of King *Charles*, yet it could not be so suddenly supply'd with them, but that there was still a Necessity, for some time, to put the handsomest young Men into Petticoats; which *Kynaston* was then said to have worn, with Success; particularly in the Part of *Evadne*, in the *Maid's Tragedy*, which I have heard him speak of; and which calls to my Mind a ridiculous Distress that arose from these sort of Shifts, which the Stage was then put to--- The King coming a little before his ususal time to a Tragedy, found the Actors not ready to begin, when his Majesty not chusing to have as much Patience as his good Subjects, sent to them, to know the Meaning of it; upon which the Master of the Company came to the Box, and rightly judging, that the best Excuse for their Default, would be the true one, fairly told his Majesty, that the Queen was not *shav'd* yet: The King, whose good Humour lov'd to laugh at a Jest, as well as to make one, accepted the Excuse, which serv'd to divert him, till the male Queen cou'd be effeminated. In a word, *Kynaston*, at that time was so beautiful a Youth, that the Ladies of Quality prided themselves in taking him with them in their Coaches, to *Hyde-Park*, in his Theatrical Habit, after the Play; which in those Days, they might have sufficient time to do, because Plays then, were us'd to begin at four a-Clock; The Hour that People of the same Rank, are now going to Dinner--- Of this Truth, I had the Curiosity to enquire, and had it confirm'd from his own Mouth, in his advanc'd Age: And indeed, to the last of him, his handsomeness was very little abated; ev'n at past sixty, his Teeth were all sound, white, and even, as one would wish to see,

in a reigning Toast of twenty. He had something of a formal
Gravity in his Mien, which was attributed to the stately Step
he had been so early confin'd to, in a female Decency. But
ev'n that, in Characters of Superiority had its proper Graces;
it misbecame him not in the Part of *Leon*, in *Fletcher's Rule a
Wife, &c.*[1] which he executed with a determin'd Manliness, and
honest Authority, well worth the best Actor's Imitation. He had
a piercing Eye, and in the Characters of heroick Life, a quick
imperious Vivacity, in his Tone of Voice, that painted the Tyrant truly terrible. There were two Plays of *Dryden* in which he
shone, with uncommon Lustre; in *Aurenge-Zebe* he play'd *Morat*, and in *Don Sebastian, Muley Moloch;*[2] in both these Parts,
he had a fierce, Lion-like Majesty in his Port and Utterance,
that gave the Spectator a kind of trembling Admiration!

Here I cannot help observing upon a modest Mistake, which
I thought the late Mr. *Booth* commited in his acting the Part of
Morat: There are in this fierce Character so many Sentiments
of avow'd Barbarity, Insolence, and Vain-glory, that they blaze
even to a ludicrous Lustre, and doubtless the Poet intended
those to make his Spectators laugh, while they admir'd them;
but *Booth* thought it depreciated the Dignity of Tragedy to
raise a Smile, in any part of it, and therefore cover'd these kind
of Sentiments with a scrupulous Coldness, and unmov'd Delivery, as if he had fear'd the Audience might take too familiar a
Notice of them. In Mr. *Addison's Cato, Syphax* has some Sentiments of near the same Nature, which I ventur'd to speak, as I
imagin'd *Kynaston* would have done, had he been then living to
have stood in the same Character. Mr. *Addison*, who had something of Mr. *Booth's* Diffidence, at the Rehearsal of his Play,
after it was acted, came into my Opinion, and own'd, that
even Tragedy, on such particular Occasions might admit of a
Laugh of *Approbation*. In *Shakespear* Instances of them are
frequent, as in *Macbeth, Hotspur, Richard* the *Third*, and *Harry
the Eighth*, all which Characters, tho' of a tragical Craft, have
sometimes familiar Strokes in them, so highly natural to each
particular Disposition, that it is impossible not to be transported
into an honest Laughter at them: And these are those happy

Liberties, which tho' few Authors are qualify'd to take, yet when justly taken, may challenge a Place among their greatest Beauties. Now whether *Dryden* in his *Morat, feliciter Audet*[3]---- or may be allow'd the Happiness of having hit this Mark, seems not necessary to be determin'd by the Actor; whose Business, sure, is to make the best of his Author's Intention, as in this Part *Kynaston* did, doubtless not without *Dryden*'s Approbation. For these Reasons then, I thought my good Friend, Mr. *Booth* (who certainly had many Excellencies) carry'd his Reverence for the Buskin too far, in not following the bold Flights of the Author, with that Wantonness of Spirit which the Nature of those Sentiments demanded: For Example! *Morat* having a criminal Passion for *Indamora*, promises, at her Request, for one Day, to spare the Life of her Lover *Aurenge-Zebe:* But not chusing to make known the real Motive of his Mercy, when *Nourmahal* says to him,

'*Twill not be safe to let him live an Hour!*

Morat silences her with this heroical *Rhodomontade,*

I'll do't, to shew my Arbitrary Power.[4]

Risum teneatis?[5] It was impossible not to laugh, and reasonably too, when this Line came out of the Mouth of *Kynaston*, with the stern, and haughty Look, that attended it. But above this tyrannical, tumid Superiority of Character, there is a grave, and rational Majesty in *Shakespear*'s *Harry* the Fourth, which tho' not so glaring to the vulgar Eye, requires thrice the Skill, and Grace to become, and support. Of this real Majesty *Kynaston* was entirely Master; here every Sentiment came from him, as if it had been his own, as if he had himself, that instant, conceiv'd it, as if he had lost the Player, and were the real King he personated! a Perfection so rarely found, that very often, in Actors of good Repute, a certain Vacancy of Look, Inanity of Voice, or superfluous Gesture, shall unmask the Man, to the judicious Spectator; who from the least of those Errors plainly sees, the whole but a Lesson given him, to be got by Heart, from some great Author, whose Sense is deeper than the Repeater's

74

Understanding. This true Majesty *Kynaston* had so entire a
Command of, that when he whisper'd the following plain Line
to *Hotspur*,

Send us your Prisoners, or you'll hear of it![6]

He convey'd a more terrible Menace in it than the loudest
Intemperance of Voice could swell to. But let the bold Imitator
beware, for without the Look, and just Elocution that waited
on it, an Attempt of the same nature may fall to nothing.

But the Dignity of this Character appear'd in *Kynaston* still
more shining, in the private Scene between the King, and Prince
his Son: There you saw Majesty, in that sort of Grief, which
only Majesty could feel! there the paternal Concern, for the
Errors of the Son, made the Monarch more rever'd, and dreaded:
His Reproaches so just, yet so unmixt with Anger (and therefore the more piercing) opening as it were the Arms of Nature,
with a secret Wish, that filial Duty, and Penitence awak'd, might
fall into them with Grace and Honour. In this affecting Scene
I thought *Kynaston* shew'd his most masterly Strokes of Nature;
expressing all the various Motions of the Heart, with the same
Force, Dignity, and Feeling they are written; adding to the
whole, that peculiar, and becoming Grace, which the best
Writer cannot inspire into any Actor, that is not born with it.
What made the Merit of this Actor, and that of *Betterton* more
surprizing, was, that though they both observ'd the Rules of
Truth, and Nature, they were each as different in their manner
of acting, as in their personal Form, and Features. But *Kynaston*
staid too long upon the Stage, till his Memory and Spirit began
to fail him. I shall not therefore say any thing of his Imperfections, which, at that time, were visibly not his own, but the
Effects of decaying Nature.

Monfort, a younger Man by twenty Years, and at this time
in his highest Reputation, was an Actor of a very different
Style: Of Person he was tall, well made, fair, and of an agreeable
Aspect: His Voice clear, full, and melodious: In Tragedy he
was the most affecting Lover within my Memory. His Addresses
had a resistless Recommendation from the very Tone of his

Voice, which gave his Words such Softness, that, as *Dryden*, says,

> -----*Like Flakes of feather'd Snow,*
> *They melted as they fell!* ----[7]

All this he particularly verify'd in that Scene of *Alexander*, where the Heroe throws himself at the Feet of *Statira* for Pardon of his past Infidelities. There we saw the Great, the Tender, the Penitent, the Despairing, the Transported, and the Amiable, in the highest Perfection. In Comedy, he gave the truest Life to what we call the *Fine Gentleman;* his Spirit shone the brighter for being polish'd with Decency: In Scenes of Gaity, he never broke into the Regard, that was due to the Presence of equal, or superior Characters, tho' inferior Actors play'd them; he fill'd the Stage, not by elbowing, and crossing it before others, or disconcerting their Action, but by surpassing them, in true and masterly Touches of Nature. He never laugh'd at his own Jest, unless the Point of his Raillery upon another requir'd it--- He had a particular Talent, in giving Life to *bons Mots* and *Repartees:* The Wit of the Poet seem'd always to come from him *extempore,* and sharpen'd into more Wit, from his brilliant manner of delivering it; he had himself a good Share of it, or what is equal to it, so lively a Pleasantness of Humour, that when either of these fell into his Hands upon the Stage, he wantoned with them, to the highest Delight of his Auditors. The *agreeable* was so natural to him, that ev'en in that dissolute Character of the *Rover*[8] he seem'd to wash off the guilt from Vice, and gave it Charms and Merit. For tho' it may be a Reproach to the Poet, to draw such Characters, not only unpunish'd, but rewarded; the Actor may still be allow'd his due Praise in his excellent Performance. And this is a Distinction which, when this Comedy was acted at *Whitehall*, King *William*'s Queen *Mary* was pleas'd to make in favour of *Monfort*, notwithstanding her Disapprobation of the Play.

He had besides all this, a Variety in his Genius, which few capital Actors have shewn, or perhaps have thought it any Addition to their Merit to arrive at; he could entirely change himself; could at once throw off the Man of Sense, for the brisk, vain, rude, and lively Coxcomb, the false, flashy Pretender to Wit, and the Dupe of his own Sufficiency: Of this he gave a delightful Instance in the Character of *Sparkish* in *Wycherly*'s *Country Wife*. In that of Sir *Courtly Nice*⁹ his Excellence was still greater: There his whole Man, Voice, Mien, and Gesture, was no longer *Monfort*, but another Person. There, the insipid, soft Civility, the elegant, and formal Mien; the drawling delicacy of Voice, the stately Flatness of his Address, and the empty Eminence of his Attitudes were so nicely observ'd and guarded by him, that had he not been an entire Master of Nature, had he not kept his Judgment, as it were, a Centinel upon himself, not to admit the least Likeness of what he us'd to be, to enter into any Part of his Performance, he could not possibly have so completely finish'd it. If, some Years after the Death of *Monfort*, I my self had any Success, in either of these Characters, I must pay the Debt, I owe to his Memory, in confessing the Advantages I receiv'd from the just Idea, and strong Impression he had given me, from his acting them. Had he been remember'd, when I first attempted them, my Defects would have been more easily discover'd, and consequently my favourable Reception in them, must have been very much, and justly abated. If it could be remembered how much he had the Advantage of me, in Voice and Person, I could not, here, be suspected of an affected Modesty, or of over-valuing his Excellence: For he sung a clear Countertenour, and had a melodious, warbling Throat, which could not but set off the last Scene of Sir *Courtly* with an uncommon Happiness; which I, alas! could only struggle thro', with the faint Excuses, and real Confidence of a fine Singer under the Imperfection of a feign'd, and screaming Trebble, which at best could only shew you what I would have done, had Nature been more favourable to me.

This excellent Actor was cut off by a tragical Death, in the 33d Year of his Age, generally lamented by his Friends, and all Lovers of the Theatre. The particular Accidents that attended his Fall, are to be found at large in the Trial of the Lord *Mohun*, printed among those of the State, in *Folio*.¹⁰

Sandford might properly be term'd the *Spagnolet*¹¹ of the

LIFE OF COLLEY CIBBER

Theatre, an excellent Actor in disagreeable Characters: For as
the chief Pieces of that famous Painter were of Human Nature
in Pain and Agony; so *Sandford*, upon the Stage, was generally
as flagitious as a *Creon*, a *Maligni*, an *Iago*, or a *Machiavil*,[12]
could make him. The Painter, 'tis true, from the Fire of his
Genius might think the quiet Objects of Nature too tame for his
Pencil, and therefore chose to indulge it in its full Power, upon
those of Violence and Horror: But poor *Sandford* was not the
Stage-Villain by Choice, but from Necessity; for having a low
and crooked Person, such bodily Defects were too strong to be
admitted into great, or amiable Characters; so that whenever,
in any new or revived Play, there was a hateful or mischievous
Person, *Sandford* was sure to have no Competitor for it: Nor
indeed (as we are not to suppose a Villain, or Traitor can be
shewn for our Imitation, or not for our Abhorrence) can it be
doubted, but the less comely the Actor's Person, the fitter he
may be to perform them. The Spectator too, by not being
misled by a tempting Form, may be less inclin'd to excuse the
wicked or immoral Views or Sentiments of them. And though
the hard Fate of an *Oedipus*, might naturally give the Humanity
of an Audience thrice the Pleasure that could arise from the
wilful Wickedness of the best acted *Creon*; yet who could
say that *Sandford*, in such a Part, was not a Master of as true
and just Action, as the best Tragedian could be, whose happier
Person had recommended him to the virtuous Heroe, or any
other more pleasing Favourite of the Imagination? In this dis-
advantageous Light, then, stood *Sandford*, as an Actor; admir'd
by the Judicious, while the Crowd only prais'd him by their
Prejudice. And so unusual had it been to see *Sandford* an innocent Man in a Play, that whenever he was so, the Spectators
would hardly give him Credit in so gross an Improbability. Let
me give you an odd Instance of it, which I heard *Monfort* say
was a real Fact. A new Play (the Name of it I have forgot) was
brought upon the Stage, wherein *Sandford* happen'd to perform
the Part of an honest Statesman: The Pit, after they had sate
three or four Acts, in a quiet Expectation, that the well-dissem-
bled Honesty of *Sandford* (for such of course they concluded
it) would soon be discover'd, or at least, from its Security, in

volve the Actors in the Play, in some surprizing Distress or Confusion, which might raise, and animate the Scenes to come;
when; at last, finding no such matter, but that the Catastrophe
had taken quite another Turn, and that *Sandford* was really an
honest Man to the end of the Play, they fairly damn'd it, as if the
Author had impos'd upon them the most frontless or incredible
Absurdity.

It is not improbable, but that from *Sandford*'s so masterly
personating Characters of Guilt, the inferior Actors might think
his Success chiefly owing to the Defects of his Person; and
from thence might take occasion, whenever they appear'd as
Bravo's, or Murtherers, to make themselves as frightful and as
inhuman Figures, as possible. In King *Charles*'s time, this low
Skill was carry'd to such an Extravagance, that the King himself,
who was black-brow'd, and of a swarthy Complexion, pass'd
a pleasant Remark, upon his observing the grim Looks of the
Murtherers in *Macbeth;* when, turning to his People, in the
Box about him, *Pray, what is the Meaning,* said he, *that we never
see a Rogue in a Play, but,* Godsfish! *they always clap him on a
black Perriwig? when, it is well known, one of the greatest
Rogues in* England *always wears a fair one?* Now, whether or
no Dr. *Oates,* at that time, wore his own Hair, I cannot be positive: Or, if his Majesty pointed at some greater Man, then out
of Power, I leave those to guess at him, who may yet, remember
the changing Complexion of his Ministers.[13] This Story I had
from *Betterton,* who was a Man of Veracity: And, I confess, I
should have thought the King's Observation a very just one,
though he himself had been as fair as *Adonis.* Nor can I, in this
Question, help voting with the Court; for were it not too gross
a Weakness to employ, in wicked Purposes, Men, whose very
suspected Looks might be enough to betray them? Or are we to
suppose it unnatural, that a Murther should be thoroughly committed out of an old red Coat, and a black Perriwig?

For my own part, I profess myself to have been an Admirer
of *Sandford,* and have often lamented, that his masterly Performance could not be rewarded with that Applause, which I
saw much inferior Actors met with, merely because they stood
in more laudable Characters. For, tho' it may be a Merit in an

Audience, to applaud Sentiments of Virtue and Honour; yet
there seems to be an equal Justice, that no Distinction should be
made, as to the excellence of an Actor, whether in a good or
evil Character; since neither the Vice, nor the Virtue of it, is
his own, but given him by the Poet: Therefore, why is not the
Actor who shines in either, equally commendable?----- No, Sir;
this may be Reason, but that is not always a Rule with us;
the Spectator will tell you, that when Virtue is applauded,
he gives part of it to himself; because his Applause, at the same
time, lets others about him see, that he himself admires it. But
when a wicked Action is going forward; when an *Iago* is meditating Revenge, and Mischief; tho' Art and Nature may be
equally strong in the Actor, the Spectator is shy of his Applause,
lest he should, in some sort, be look'd upon as an Aider or an
Abettor of the Wickedness in view; and therefore rather chuses
to rob the Actor of the Praise he may merit, than give it him in
a Character, which he would have you see his Silence modestly
discourages. From the same fond Principle, many Actors have
made it a Point to be seen in Parts sometimes, even flatly written,
only because they stood in the favourable Light of Honour and
Virtue.

I have formerly known an Actress carry this Theatrical Prud-
ery to such a height, that she was, very near, keeping herself
chaste by it: Her Fondness for Virtue on the Stage, she began
to think, might perswade the World, that it had made an Impression on her private Life; and the Appearances of it actually
went so far, that, in an Epilogue to an obscure Play, the Profits
of which were given to her, and wherein she acted a Part of
impregnable Chastity, she bespoke the Favour of the Ladies, by
a Protestation, that in Honour of their Goodness and Virtue,
she would dedicate her unblemish'd Life to their Example. Part
of this Vestal Vow, I remember, was contain'd in the following
Verse:

Study to live the Character I play.[14]

But alas! how weak are the strongest Works of Art, when
Nature besieges it! for though this good Creature so far held
out her Distaste to Mankind, that they could never reduce her

to marry any one of 'em; yet we must own she grew, like
Caesar, greater by her Fall! Her first heroick Motive, to a Sur-
render, was to save the Life of a Lover, who, in his Despair, had
vow'd to destroy himself, with which Act of Mercy (in a jealous
Dispute once, in my hearing) she was provok'd to reproach him
in these very Words; *Villain! did not I save your Life?* The
generous Lover, in return to that first tender Obligation, gave
Life to her Firstborn, and that pious Offspring has, since, rais'd
to her Memory, several innocent Grand-children.

So that, as we see, it is not the Hood, that makes the Monk,
nor the Veil the Vestal; I am apt to think, that if the personal
Morals of an Actor, were to be weighed by his Appearance on
the Stage, the Advantage and Favour (if any were due to either
side) might rather incline to the Traitor, than the Heroe, to the
Sempronius, than the *Cato;* or to the *Syphax*, than the *Juba:*[15]
Because no Man can naturally desire to cover his Honesty with
a wicked Appearance; but an ill Man might possibly incline to
cover his Guilt with the Appearance of Virtue, which was the
Case of the frail Fair One, now mentioned. But be this Question
decided as it may, *Sandford* always appeared to me the honester
Man, in proportion to the Spirit wherewith he expos'd the
wicked, and immoral Characters he acted: For had his Heart
been unsound, or tainted with the least Guilt of them, his Conscience must, in spite of him, in any too near a Resemblance of
himself, have been a Check upon the Vivacity of his Action.
Sandford, therefore, might be said to have contributed his equal
Share, with the foremost Actors, to the true and laudable Use
of the Stage: And in this Light too, of being so frequently
the Object of common Distaste, we may honestly style him a
Theatrical Martyr, to Poetical Justice: For in making Vice odious, or Virtue amiable, where does the Merit differ? To hate
the one, or love the other, are but leading Steps to the same
Temple of Fame, tho' at different Portals.

This Actor, in his manner of Speaking, varied very much from
those I have already mentioned. His Voice had an acute and
piercing Tone, which struck every Syllable of his Words distinctly upon the Ear. He had likewise a peculiar Skill in his

Look of marking out to an Audience whatever he judg'd worth
their more than ordinary Notice. When he deliver'd a Command, he would sometimes give it more Force, by seeming
to slight the Ornament of Harmony. In *Dryden*'s Plays of
Rhime, he as little as possible glutted the Ear with the Jingle
of it; rather chusing, when the Sense would permit him, to lose
it, than to value it.

Had *Sandford* liv'd in *Shakespear*'s Time, I am confident his
Judgment must have chose him, above all other Actors, to have
play'd his *Richard the Third:* I leave his Person out of the
Question, which, tho' naturally made for it, yet that would
have been the least part of his Recommendation; *Sandford* had
stronger Claims to it; he had sometimes an uncouth Stateliness
in his Motion, a harsh and sullen Pride of Speech, a meditating
Brow, a stern Aspect, occasionally changing into an almost ludicrous Triumph over all Goodness and Virtue: From thence
falling into the most asswasive Gentleness, and soothing Candour
of a designing Heart. Those, I say, must have preffer'd him to
it; these would have been Colours so essentially shining in
that Character, that it will be no Dispraise to that great Author,
to say, *Sandford* must have shewn as many masterly Strokes in
it (had he ever acted it) as are visible in the Writing it.

When I first brought *Richard the Third* (with such Alterations as I thought not improper) to the Stage,[16] *Sandford* was
engag'd in the Company then acting under King *William*'s
Licence in *Lincoln's-Inn Fields;* otherwise you cannot but suppose my Interest must have offer'd him that Part. What encourag'd me, therefore, to attempt it myself at the *Theatre-Royal*,
was, that I imagin'd I knew how *Sandford* would have spoken
every Line of it: If therefore, in any Part of it, I succeeded, let
the Merit be given to him: And how far I succeeded in that
Light, those only can be Judges who remember him. In order,
therefore, to give you a nearer Idea of *Sandford*, you must give
me leave (compell'd as I am to be vain) to tell you, that the
late Sir *John Vanburgh*, who was an Admirer of *Sandford*,
after he had seen me act it, assur'd me, That he never knew
any one Actor so particularly profit by another, as I had done

by *Sandford* in *Richard the Third: You have*, said he, *his very Look, Gesture, Gait, Speech, and every Motion of him, and have borrow'd them all, only to serve you in that Character.* If therefore Sir *John Vanbrugh*'s Observation was just, they who remember me in *Richard the Third*, may have a nearer Conception of *Sandford*, than from all the critical Account I can give of him.

I come now to those other Men Actors, who, at this time, were equally famous in the lower Life of Comedy. But I find myself more at a loss to give you them, in their true and proper Light, than Those I have already set before you. Why the Tragedian warms us into Joy, or Admiration, or sets our Eyes on flow with Pity, we can easily explain to another's Apprehension: But it may sometimes puzzle the gravest Spectator to account for that familiar Violence of Laughter, that shall seize him, at some particular Strokes of a true Comedian. How then shall describe what a better Judge might not be able to express? The Rules to please the Fancy cannot so easily be laid down, as those that ought to govern the Judgment. The Decency too, that must be observ'd in Tragedy, reduces, by the manner of speaking it, one Actor to be much more like another, than they can or need be suppos'd to be in Comedy: There the Laws of Action give them such free, and almost unlimited Liberties, to play and wanton with Nature, that the Voice, Look, and Gesture of a Comedian may be as various, as the Manners and Faces of the whole Mankind are different from one another. These are the Difficulties I lie under. Where I want Words, therefore, to describe what I may commend, I can only hope you will give credit to my Opinion: And this Credit I shall most stand need of, when I tell you, that

Nokes[17] was an Actor of a quite different Genius from any I have ever read, heard of, or seen, since or before his Time; and yet his general Excellence may be comprehended in one Article, *viz.* a plain and palpable Simplicity of Nature, which was so utterly his own, that he was often as unaccountably diverting in his common Speech, as on the Stage. I saw him once, giving an Account of some Table-talk, to another Actor behind the

Scenes, which, a Man of Quality accidentally listening to, was so deceiv'd by his Manner, that he ask'd him, if that was a new Play, he was rehearsing? It seems almost amazing, that this Simplicity, so easy to *Nokes*, should never be caught by any one of his Successors. *Leigh* and *Underhill*[18] have been well copied, though not equall'd by others. But not all the mimical Skill of *Estcourt* (fam'd as he was for it) though he had often seen *Nokes*, could scarce give us an Idea of him. After this, perhaps it would be saying less of him, when I own, that though I have still the Sound of every Line he spoke, in my Ear, (which us'd not to be thought a bad one) yet I have often try'd, by my self, but in vain, to reach the least distant Likeness of the *Vis Comica* of *Nokes*. Though this may seem little to his Praise, it may be negatively saying a good deal to it, because I have never seen any one Actor, except himself, whom I could not, at least, so far imitate, as to give you a more tolerable Notion of his Manner. But *Nokes* was so singular a Species, and was so form'd by Nature, for the Stage, that I question if (beyond the trouble of getting Words by Heart) it ever cost him an Hour's Labour to arrive at that high Reputation he had, and deserved.

The Characters he particularly shone in, were Sir *Martin Marr-al*, *Gomez* in the *Spanish Friar*, Sir *Nicholas Cully* in *Love in a Tub*, *Barnaby Brittle* in the *Wanton Wife*, Sir *Davy Dunce* in the *Soldier's Fortune*, *Sosia* in *Amphytrion*, &c. &c. &c.[19] To tell you how he acted them, is beyond the reach of Criticism: But, to tell you what Effect his Action had upon the Spectator, is not impossible: This then is all you will expect from me, and from hence I must leave you to guess at him.

He scarce ever made his first Entrance in a Play, but he was received with an involuntary Applause, not of Hands only, for those may be, and have often been partially prostituted, and bespoken; but by a General Laughter, which the very sight of him provok'd, and Nature cou'd not resist; yet the louder the Laugh, the graver was his Look upon it; and sure, the ridiculous Solemnity of his Features were enough to have set a whole Bench of Bishops into a Titter, cou'd he have been honour'd (may it be no Offence to suppose it) with such grave, and right reverend Auditors. In the ludicrous Distresses, which by the Laws of Comedy, Folly is often involv'd in; he sunk into such a mixture of piteous Pusillanimity, and a Consternation so rufully ridiculous and inconsolable, that when he had shook you, to a Fatigue of Laughter, it became a moot point, whether you ought not to have pity'd him. When he debated any matter by himself, he would shut up his Mouth with a dumb studious Powt, and roll his full Eye, into such a vacant Amazement, such a palpable Ignorance of what to think of it, that his silent Perplexity (which would sometimes hold him several Minutes) gave your Imagination as full Content, as the most absurd thing he could say upon it. In the Character of Sir *Martin Marrall*, who is always committing Blunders to the Prejudice of his own Interest, when he had brought himself to a Dilemma in his Affairs, by vainly proceeding upon his own Head, and was, afterwards afraid to look his governing Servant, and Counsellor in the Face; what a copious, and distressful Harangue have I seen him make, with his Looks (while the House has been in one continued Roar, for several Minutes) before he could prevail with his Courage to speak a Word to him! Then might you have, at once, read in his face *Vexation* ---- That his own Measures, which he had piqued himself upon, had fail'd. *Envy* --- of his Servant's superior Wit --- *Distress* --- to Retrieve, the Occasion he had lost. *Shame* --- to confess his Folly; and yet a sullen Desire, to be reconcil'd, and better advis'd, for the future! What Tragedy ever shew'd us such a Tumult of Passions, rising, at once, in one Bosom! or what buskin'd Hero standing under the Load of them, could have more effectually, mov'd his Spectators, by the most pathetick Speech, than poor miserable *Nokes* did, by this silent Eloquence, and piteous Plight of his Features.

His Person was of the middle size, his Voice clear, and audible; his natural Countenance grave, and sober; but the Moment he spoke, the settled Seriousness of his Features was utterly discharg'd, and a dry, drolling, or laughing Levity took such full Possession of him, that I can only refer the Idea of him to your Imagination. In some of his low Characters, that became it, he had a shuffling Shamble in his Gait, with so contented an Igno-

rance in his Aspect, and an aukward Absurdity in his Gesture,
that had you not known him, you could not have believ'd,
that naturally he could have had a Grain of common Sense. In a
Word, I am tempted to sum up the Character of *Nokes*, as a
Comedian, in a Parodie of what *Shakespear's Mark Antony* says
of *Brutus*, as a Hero.

> *His Life was Laughter, and the* Ludicrous
> *So mixt, in him, that Nature might stand up,*
> *And say to all the World---- This was an Actor.*[20]

Leigh was of the mecurial kind, and though not so strict an
Observer of Nature, yet never so wanton in his Performance,
as to be wholly out of her Sight. In Humour, he lov'd to take a
full Career, but was careful enough to stop short, when just
upon the Precipice: He had great Variety, in his manner, and
was famous in very different Characters: In the canting, grave
Hypocrisy of the *Spanish* Friar, he stretcht the Veil of Piety
so thinly over him, that in every Look, Word, and Motion, you
saw a palpable, wicked Slyness shine through it---- Here he kept
his Vivacity demurely confin'd, till the pretended Duty of his
Function demanded it; and then he exerted it, with a cholerick
sacerdotal Insolence. But the Friar is a Character of such glaring
Vice, and so strongly drawn, that a very indifferent Actor cannot but hit upon the broad Jests, that are remarkable, in every
Scene of it. Though I have never yet seen any one, that has fill'd
them with half the Truth, and Spirit of *Leigh---- Leigh* rais'd the
Character as much above the Poet's Imagination, as the Character has sometimes rais'd other Actors above themselves! and I
do not doubt, but the Poet's Knowledge of *Leigh's* Genius
help'd him to many a pleasant Stroke of Nature, which without
that Knowledge never might have enter'd into his Conception.
Leigh was so eminent in his Character, that the late Earl of
Dorset (who was equally an Admirer, and a Judge of Theatrical
Merit) had a whole Length of him, in the Friar's Habit, drawn
by *Kneller:* The whole Portrait is highly painted, and extremely
like him. But no wonder *Leigh* arriv'd to such Fame, in what

was so completely written for him; when Characters that would make the Reader yawn, in the Closet, have by the Strength of his Action, been lifted into the lowdest Laughter, on the Stage. Of this kind was the Scrivener's great boobily Son in the *Villain; Ralph*, a stupid, staring, Under-servant, in Sir *Solomon Single*. Quite opposite to those were Sir *Jolly Jumble*, in the *Soldier's Fortune*, and his old *Belfond* in the *Squire* of *Alsatia*.[21] In Sir *Jolly* he was all Life, and laughing Humour; and when *Nokes* acted with him in the same Play, they return'd the Ball so dexterously upon one another, that every Scene between them, seem'd but one continued Rest[22] of Excellence--- But alas! when those Actors were gone, that Comedy, and many others, for the same Reason, were rarely known to stand upon their own Legs; by seeing no more of *Leigh* or *Nokes* in them, the Characters were quite sunk, and alter'd. In his Sir *William Belfond*, *Leigh* shew'd a more spirited Variety, than ever I saw, any Actor, in any one Character come up to: The Poet, 'tis true, had here, exactly chalk'd for him, the Out-lines of Nature; but the high Colouring, the strong Lights and Shades of Humour, that enliven'd the whole, and struck our Admiration, with Surprize and Delight, were wholly owing to the Actor. The easy Reader might, perhaps, have been pleas'd with the Author without discomposing a Feature; but the Spectator must have heartily held his Sides, or the Actor would have heartily made them ach for it.

Now, though I observ'd before, that *Nokes* never was tolerably touch'd by any of his Successors; yet, in this Character, I must own, I have seen *Leigh* extremely well imitated, by my late facetious Friend *Penkethman*,[23] who though far short of what was inimitable, in the Original, yet as to the general Resemblance, was a very valuable Copy of him: And, as I know *Penkethman* cannot yet be out of your Memory, I have chose to mention him here, to give you the nearest Idea I can, of the Excellence of *Leigh* in that particular Light: For *Leigh* had many masterly Variations, which the other cou'd not, nor ever pretended to reach; particularly in the Dotage, and Follies of extreme old Age, in the Characters of *Fumble* in the *Fond*

Husband, and the Toothless Lawyer, in the *City Politicks;*[24] both which Plays liv'd only by the extraordinary Performance of *Nokes* and *Leigh*.

There were two other Characters, of the farcical kind, *Geta* in the *Prophetess*,[25] and *Crack* in Sir *Courtly Nice*, which as they are less confin'd to Nature, the imitation of them was less difficult to *Penkethman;* who, to say the Truth, delighted more in the whimsical, than the natural; therefore, when I say he sometimes resembled *Leigh*, I reserve this Distinction, on his Master's side; that the pleasant Extravagancies of *Leigh* were all the Flowers of his own Fancy, while the less fertile Brain of my Friend was contented to make use of the Stock his Predecessor had left him. What I have said, therefore, is not to detract from honest *Pinky*'s Merit, but to do Justice to his Predecessor--- And though, 'tis true, we as seldom see a good Actor, as a great Poet arise from the bare *Imitation* of another's Genius; yet, if this be a general Rule, *Penkethman* was the nearest to an Exception from it; for with those, who never knew *Leigh*, he might very well have pass'd for a more than common Original. Yet again, as my Partiality for *Penkethman* ought not to lead me from Truth, I must beg leave (though out of its Place) to tell you fairly what was the best of him, that the Superiority of *Leigh* may stand in its due Light---- *Penkethman* had certainly, from Nature, a great deal of comic Power about him; but his Judgment was, by no means equal to it; for he would make frequent Deviations into the Whimsies of an *Harlequin*. By the way, (let me digress a little farther) whatever Allowances are made for the Licence of that Character, I mean of an *Harlequin*, whatever Pretences may be urg'd, from the Practice of the ancient Comedy, for it's being play'd in a Mask, resembling no Part of the Human Species; I am apt to think, the best Excuse a modern Actor can plead for his continuing it, is that the low, senseless, and monstrous things he says, and does in it, no theatrical Assurance could get through, with a bare Face: Let me give you an Instance of even *Penkethman*'s being out of Countenance for want of it: When he first play'd *Harlequin* in the *Emperor of the Moon*,[26] several Gentleman (who inadvertently judg'd by the Rules of Nature) fancy'd that a great deal of the Drollery, and Spirit of his Grimace was lost, by his wearing that useless, unmeaning Masque of a black Cat, and therefore insisted, that the next time of his acting that Part, he should play without it: Their Desire was accordingly comply'd with--- but, alas! in vain--- *Penkethman* could not take to himself the Shame of the Character without being conceal'd--- he was no more *Harle-quin*--- his Humour was quite disconcerted! his Conscience could not, with the same *Effronterie* declare against Nature, without the cover of that unchanging Face, which he was sure would never blush for it! no! it was quite another Case! without that Armour his Courage could not come up to the bold Strokes, that were necessary to get the better of common Sense. Now if this Circumstance will justify the Modesty of *Penkethman*, it, cannot but throw a wholesome Contempt on the low Merit of an *Harlequin*. But how farther necessary the Masque is to that Fool's Coat, we have lately had a stronger Proof, in the Favour, that the *Harlequin Sauvage* met with, at *Paris*, and the ill Fate that follow'd the same *Sauvage*, when he pull'd off his Masque in *London*.[27] So that it seems, what was Wit from an *Harlequin*, was something too extravagant from a human Creature. If there-fore *Penkethman*, in Characters drawn from Nature, might sometimes launch out into a few gamesome Liberties, which would not have been excus'd from a more correct Comedian; yet, in his manner of taking them, he always seem'd to me, in a kind of Consciousness of the Hazard he was running, as if he fairly confess'd, that what he did was only, as well as he *could* do--- That he was willing to take his Chance for Success, but if he did not meet with it, a Rebuke should break no Squares; he would mend it another time, and would take whatever pleas'd his Judges to think of him, in good part; and I have often thought, that a good deal of the Favour he met with, was owing to this seeming humble way of waving all Pretences to Merit, but what the Town would please to allow him. What confirms me in this Opinion is, that when it has been his ill Fortune to meet with a *Disgraccia*, I have known him to say apart to himself, yet loud enough to be heard--- *Odso!* I believe I *am* a *little wrong here!*[28] which once was so well receiv'd, by the Audience, that they turn'd their Reproof into Applause.

Now, the Judgment of *Leigh* always guarded the happier Sallies of his Fancy, from the least Hazard of Disapprobation: he seem'd not to court, but to attack your Applause, and always came off victorious; nor did his highest Assurance amount to any more, than that just Confidence, without which the commendable Spirit of every good Actor must be abated; and of this Spirit *Leigh* was a most perfect Master. He was much admir'd by King *Charles*, who us'd to distinguish him, when spoke of, by the Title of *his Actor*: Which however makes me imagine, that in his Exile that Prince might have receiv'd his first Impression of good Actors from the *French* Stage; for *Leigh* had more of that farcical Vivacity than *Nokes;* but *Nokes* was never languid by his more strict Adherence to Nature, and as far as my Judgment is worth taking, if their intrinsick Merit could be justly weigh'd, *Nokes* must have had the better in the Balance. Upon the unfortunate Death of *Monfort*, *Leigh* fell ill of a Fever, and dy'd within a Week after him, in *December* 1692.

Underhill was a correct, and natural Comedian, his particular Excellence was in Characters, that may be called Still-life, I mean the stiff, the heavy, and the stupid; to these he gave the exactest, and most expressive Colours, and in some of them, look'd, as if it were not in the Power of human Passions to alter a Feature of him. In the solemn Formality of *Obadiah* in the *Committee*, and in the boobily heaviness of *Lolpoop* in the *Squire* of *Alsatia*, he seem'd the immoveable Log he stood for! a Countenance of Wood could not be more fixt than his, when the Blockhead of a Character required it: His Face was full and long; from his Crown to the end of his Nose, was the shorter half of it, so that the Disproportion of his lower Features, when soberly compos'd, with an unwandering Eye hanging over them, threw him into the most lumpish, moping Mortal, that ever made Beholders merry! not but, at other times, he could be wakened into Spirit equally ridiculous---- In the course, rustick Humour of Justice *Clodpate*, in *Epsome Wells*,[29] he was a delightful Brute! and in the blunt Vivacity of Sir *Sampson*, in

Love for *Love*, he shew'd all that true perverse Spirit, that is
commonly seen in much Wit, and ill Nature. This Character
is one of those few so well written, with so much Wit and Humour, that an Actor must be the grossest Dunce, that does not
appear with an unusual Life in it: But it will still shew as great
a Proportion of Skill, to come near *Underhill* in the acting it,
which (not to undervalue those who soon came after him) I
have not yet seen. He was particularly admir'd too, for the
Grave-digger in *Hamlet*. The Author of the *Tatler* recom-
mends him to the Favour of the Town, upon that Play's being
acted for his Benefit,[30] wherein, after his Age had some Years
oblig'd him to leave the Stage, he came on again, for that Day,
to perform his old Part; but, alas! so worn, and disabled, as if
himself was to have lain in the Grave he was digging; when he
could no more excite Laughter, his Infirmities were dismiss'd
with Pity: He dy'd soon after, a super-annuated Pensioner, in
the List of those who, were supported by the joint Sharers,
under the first Patent granted to Sir *Richard Steele*.

The deep Impressions of these excellent Actors, which I
receiv'd in my Youth, I am afraid, may have drawn me into
the common Foible of us old Fellows; which is, a Fondness, and
perhaps, a tedious Partiality for the Pleasures we have formerly
tasted, and think are now fallen off, because we can no longer
enjoy them. If therefore I lie under that Suspicion, tho' I have
related nothing incredible, or out of the reach of a good Judge's
Conception, I must appeal to those Few, who are about my own
Age, for the Truth and Likeness of these Theatrical Portraits.

There were, at this time, several others in some degree of
Favour with the Publick, *Powel*, *Verbruggen*, *Williams*, &c.[31]
But as I cannot think their best Improvements made them, in
any wise, equal to those I have spoke of, I ought not to range
them in the same Class. Neither were *Wilks*, or *Dogget*, yet
come to the Stage; nor was *Booth* initiated till about six Years
after them; or Mrs. *Oldfield* known, 'till the Year 1700. I must
therefore reserve the four last for their proper Period, and proceed to the Actresses, that were famous with *Betterton*, at the
latter end of the last Century.

Mrs. *Barry*[32] was then in possession of almost all the chief Parts in Tragedy: With what Skill she gave Life to them, you will judge from the Words of *Dryden*, in his Preface to *Cleomenes*,[33] where he says,

Mrs. Barry, *always excellent, has in this Tragedy excell'd herself, and gain'd a Reputation, beyond any Woman I have ever seen on the Theatre.*

I very perfectly remember her acting that Part; and however unnecessary it may seem, to give my Judgment after *Dryden*'s, I cannot help saying, I do not only close with his Opinion, but will venture to add, that (tho' *Dryden* has been dead these Thirty Eight Years) the same Compliment, to this Hour, may be due to her Excellence. And tho' she was then, not a little, past her Youth, she was not, till that time, fully arriv'd to her Maturity of Power and Judgment: From whence I would observe, That the short Life of Beauty, is not long enough to form a complete Actress. In Men, the Delicacy of Person is not so absolutely necessary, nor the Decline of it so soon taken notice of. The Fame Mrs. *Barry* arriv'd to, is a particular Proof of the Difficulty there is, in judging with Certainty, from their first Trials, whether young People will ever make any great Figure on a Theatre. There was, it seems, so little Hope of Mrs. *Barry*, at her first setting out, that she was, at the end of the first Year, discharg'd the Company, among others, that were thought to be a useless Expence to it. I take it for granted that the Objection to Mrs. *Barry*, at that time, must have been a defective Ear, or some unskilful Dissonance, in her manner of pronouncing: But where there is a proper Voice, and Person, with the Addition of a good Understanding, Experience tells us, that such Defect is not always invincible; of which, not only Mrs. *Barry*, but the late Mrs. *Oldfield*, are eminent Instances. Mrs. *Oldfield* had been a Year, in the Theatre-Royal, before she was observ'd to give any tolerable Hope of her being an Actress; so unlike, to all manner of Propriety, was her Speaking! How unaccountably, then, does a Genius for the Stage makes its way towards Perfection? For, notwithstanding these equal Disadvantages, both these

Actresses, tho' of different Excellence, made themselves complete Mistresses of their Art, by the prevalence of their Understanding. If this Observation may be of any use, to the Masters
of future Theatres, I shall not then have made it to no purpose.

   Mrs. *Barry*, in Characters of Greatness, had a presence of
elevated Dignity, her Mien and Motion superb, and gracefully
majestick; her Voice full, clear, and strong, so that no Violence
of Passion could be too much for her: And when Distress, or
Tenderness possess'd her, she subsided into the most affecting
Melody, and Softness. In the Art of exciting Pity, she had a
Power beyond all the Actresses I have yet seen, or what your
Imagination can conceive. Of the former of these two great
Excellencies, she gave the most delightful Proofs in almost all
the Heroic Plays of *Dryden* and *Lee;* and of the latter, in the
softer Passions of *Otway*'s *Monimia* and *Belvidera*.³⁴ In Scenes
of Anger, Defiance, or Resentment, while she was impetuous,
and terrible, she pour'd out the Sentiment with an enchanting
Harmony; and it was this particular Excellence, for which
Dryden made her the above-recited Compliment, upon her
acting *Cassandra* in his *Cleomenes.* But here, I am apt to think
his Partiality for that Character, may have tempted his Judgment
to let it pass for her Master-piece; when he could not but know,
there were several other Characters in which her Action might
have given her a fairer Pretence to the Praise he has bestow'd
on her, for *Cassandra;* for, in no Part of that, is there the least
ground for Compassion, as in *Monimia;* nor equal cause for Admiration, as in the nobler Love of *Cleopatra,* or the tempestuous
Jealousy of *Roxana.*³⁵ 'Twas in these Lights, I thought Mrs.
Barry shone with a much brighter Excellence than in *Cassandra.*
She was the first Person whose Merit was distinguish'd, by the
Indulgence of having an annual Benefit-Play,³⁶ which was
granted to her alone, if I mistake not, first in King *James*'s time,
and which became not common to others, 'till the Division of
this Company, after the Death of King *William*'s Queen *Mary.*
This great Actress dy'd of a Fever, towards the latter end of
Queen *Anne;* the Year I have forgot; but perhaps you will

recollect it, by an Expression that fell from her in blank Verse, in her last Hours, when she was delirious, *viz.*

> *Ha, ha! and so they make us Lords, by Dozens!*[37]

Mrs. *Betterton*,[38] tho' far advanc'd in Years, was so great a Mistress of Nature, that even Mrs. *Barry*, who acted the Lady *Macbeth* after her, could not in that Part, with all her superior Strength, and Melody of Voice, throw out those quick and careless Strokes of Terror, from the Disorder of a guilty Mind, which the other gave us, with a Facility in her Manner, that render'd them at once tremendous, and delightful. Time could not impair her Skill, tho' he had brought her Person to decay. She was, to the last, the Admiration of all true Judges of Nature, and Lovers of *Shakespear*, in whose Plays she chiefly excell'd, and without a Rival. When she quitted the Stage, several good Actresses were the better for her Instruction. She was a Woman of an unblemish'd, and sober Life; and had the Honour to teach Queen *Anne*, when Princess, the Part of *Semandra* in *Mithridates*,[39] which she acted at Court in King *Charles*'s time. After the Death of Mr. *Betterton*, her Husband, that Princess, when Queen, order'd her a Pension for Life, but she liv'd not to receive more than the first half Year of it.

Mrs. *Leigh*,[40] the Wife of *Leigh* already mention'd, had a very droll way of dressing the pretty Foibles of superannuated Beauties. She had, in her self, a good deal of Humour, and knew how to infuse it into the affected Mothers, Aunts, and modest stale Maids, that had miss'd their Market; of this sort were the Modish Mother in the *Chances*,[41] affecting to be politely commode, for her own Daughter; the coquette Prude of an Aunt, in Sir *Courtly Nice*, who prides herself in being chaste, and cruel, at Fifty; And the languishing Lady *Wishfort*, in *The Way of the World:* In all these, with many others, she was extremely entertaining, and painted, in a lively manner, the blind Side of Nature.

Mrs. *Butler*,[41a] who had her Christian Name of *Charlotte* given her by King *Charles*, was the Daughter of a decay'd Knight, and had the Honour of that Prince's Recommendation to the Theatre; a provident Restitution, giving to the Stage in kind, what he had sometimes taken from it: The Publick, at least, was oblig'd by it; for she prov'd not only a good Actress, but was allow'd, in those Days, to sing and dance to great Perfection. In the Dramatick Opera's of *Dioclesian*, and that of *King Arthur*,[42] she was a capital, and admired Performer. In speaking too, she had a sweet-ton'd Voice, which, with her naturally genteel Air, and sensible Pronunciation, render'd her wholly Mistress of the Amiable, in many serious Characters. In Parts of Humour too she had a manner of blending her assuasive Softness, even with the Gay, the Lively, and the Alluring. Of this she gave an agreeable Instance, in her Action of the (*Villers*) Duke of *Buckingham*'s second *Constantia* in the *Chances*. In which, if I should say, I have never seen her exceeded, I might still do no wrong to the late Mrs. *Oldfield*'s lively Performance of the same Character. Mrs. *Oldfield*'s Fame may spare Mrs. *Butler*'s Action this Compliment, without the least Diminution, or Dispute of her Superiority, in Characters of more moment.

Here I cannot help observing, when there was but one Theatre in *London*, at what unequal Sallaries, compar'd to those of later Days, the hired Actors were then held, by the absolute Authority of their frugal Masters, the Patentees; for Mrs. *Butler* had then but Forty Shillings a Week, and could she have obtain'd an Addition of Ten Shillings more (which was refus'd her) would never have left their Service; but being offer'd her own Conditions, to go with Mr. *Ashbury*[43] to *Dublin* (who was then raising a Company of Actors for that Theatre, where there had been none since the Revolution) her Discontent, here, prevail'd with her to accept of his Offer, and he found his Account in her Value. Were not those Patentees most sagacious Oeconomists, that could lay hold on so notable an Expedient, to lessen their Charge? How gladly, in my Time of being a Sharer, would we have given four times her Income, to an Actress of equal Merit?

Mrs. *Monfort*,[44] whose second Marriage gave her the Name of *Verbruggen*, was Mistress of more Variety of Humour, than

I knew in any one Woman Actress. This variety too, was attended with an equal Vivacity, which made her excellent in Characters extremely different. As she was naturally a pleasant Mimick, she had the Skill to make that Talent useful on the Stage, a Talent which may be surprising in a Conversation, and yet be lost when brought to the Theatre, which was the Case of *Estcourt* already mention'd: But where the Elocution is round, distinct, voluble, and various, as Mrs. *Monfort*'s was, the Mimick, there, is a great Assistant to the Actor. Nothing, tho' ever so barren, if within the Bounds of Nature, could be flat in her Hands. She gave many heightening Touches to Characters but coldly written, and often made an Author vain of his Work, that in it self had little merit. She was so fond of Humour, in what low Part soever to be found, that she would make no scruple of defacing her fair Form, to come heartily into it; for when she was eminent in several desirable Characters of Wit, and Humour, in higher Life, she would be, in as much Fancy, when descending into the antiquated *Abigail*, of *Fletcher*,[45] as when triumphing in all the Airs, and vain Graces of a fine Lady; a Merit, that few Actresses care for. In a Play of *D'urfey*'s, now forgotten, call'd, *The Western Lass*, which Part she acted, she transform'd her whole Being, Body, Shape, Voice, Language, Look, and Features, into almost another Animal; with a strong *Devonshire* Dialect, a broad laughing Voice, a poking Head, round Shoulders, an unconceiving Eye, and the most be-diz'ning dowdy Dress, that ever covered the untrain'd Limbs of a *Joan Trot*. To have seen her here, you would have thought it impossible the same Creature could ever have been recovered, to what was as easy to her, the Gay, the Lively, and the Desirable. Nor was her Humour limited, to her Sex; for, while her Shape permitted, she was a more adroit pretty Fellow, than is usually seen upon the Stage: Her easy Air, Action, Mien, and Gesture, quite chang'd from the Quoif, to the cock'd Hat, and Cavalier in fashion. People were so fond of seeing her as a Man, that when the Part of *Bays* in the *Rehearsal*, had, for some time, lain dormant, she was desired to take it up, which I have seen her act with all the true, coxcombly

Spirit, and Humour, that the Sufficiency of the Character required.

But what found most Employment for her whole various Excellence at once, was the Part of *Melantha*, in *Marriage-Ala-
mode*.[46] *Melantha* is as finish'd an Impertinent, as ever flutter'd in
a Drawing-Room, and seems to contain the most compleat
System of Female Foppery, that could possibly be crowded
into the tortur'd Form of a Fine Lady. Her Language, Dress,
Motion, Manners, Soul, and Body, are in a continual Hurry to
be something more, than is necessary, or commendable. And
tho' I doubt it will be a vain Labour, to offer you a just Likeness
of Mrs. *Monfort*'s Action, yet the fantastick Impression is still
so strong in my Memory, that I cannot help saying something,
tho' fantastically, about it. The first ridiculous Airs that break
from her, are, upon a Gallant, never seen before, who delivers
her a Letter from her Father, recommending him to her good
Graces, as an honourable Lover. Here now, one would think
she might naturally shew a little of the Sexe's decent Reserve,
though never so slightly cover'd! No, Sir; not a Tittle of it;
Modesty is the Virtue of a poor-soul'd Country Gentlewoman;
she is too much a Court Lady, to be under so vulgar a Confusion; she reads the Letter, therefore, with a careless, dropping
Lip, and an erected Brow, humming it hastily over, as if she
were impatient to outgo her Father's Commands, by making a
complete Conquest of him at once; and, that the Letter might
not embarrass her Attack, crack! she crumbles it at once, into
her Palm, and pours upon him her whole Artillery of Airs,
Eyes, and Motion; down goes her dainty, diving Body, to the
Ground, as if she were sinking under the conscious Load of
her own Attractions; then launches into a Flood of Fine Language, and Compliment, still playing her Chest forward in fifty
Falls and Risings, like a Swan upon waving Water; and, to
complete her Impertinence, she is so rapidly fond of her own
Wit, that she will not give her Lover leave to praise it: Silent
assenting Bows, and vain Endeavours to speak, are all the share
of the Conversation he is admitted to, which, at last, he is reliev'd from, by her Engagement to half a Score Visits, which

she *swims* from him to make, with a Promise to return in a Twinkling.

If this Sketch has Colour enough to give you any near Conception of her, I then need only tell you, that throughout the whole Character, her variety of Humour was every way proportionable; as, indeed, in most Parts, that she thought worth her care, or that had the least Matter for her Fancy to work upon, I may justly say, That no Actress, from her own Conception, could have heighten'd them with more lively Strokes of Nature.

I come now to the last, and only living Person, of all those whose Theatrical Characters I have promis'd you, Mrs. *Bracegirdle;* who, I know, would rather pass her remaining Days forgotten, as an Actress, than to have her Youth recollected in the most favourable Light I am able to place it; yet, as she is essentially necessary to my Theatrical History, and, as I only bring her back to the Company of those, with whom she pass'd the Spring and Summer of her Life, I hope it will excuse the Liberty I take, in commemorating the Delight which the Publick receiv'd from her Appearance, while she was an Ornament to the Theatre.

Mrs. *Bracegirdle* was now, but just blooming to her Maturity; her Reputation, as an Actress, gradually rising with that of her Person; never any Woman was in such general Favour of her Spectators, which, to the last Scene of her Dramatick Life, she maintain'd, by not being unguarded in her private Character. This Discretion contributed, not a little, to make her the *Cara*, the Darling of the Theatre: For it will be no extravagant thing to say, scarce an Audience saw her, that were less than half of them Lovers, without a suspected Favourite among them: And tho' she might be said to have been the Universal Passion, and under the highest Temptations; her Constancy in resisting them, serv'd but to increase the number of her Admirers: And this perhaps you will more easily believe, when I extend not my Encomiums on her Person, beyond a Sincerity that can be suspected; for she had no greater Claim to Beauty, than what the most desirable *Brunette* might pretend to. But her Youth, and lively Aspect, threw out such a Glow of Health, and Chearfulness, that, on the Stage, few Spectators that were not past it, could behold her without Desire. It was even a Fashion among the Gay, and Young, to have a Taste or *Tendre* for Mrs. *Bracegirdle*. She inspired the best Authors to write for her, and two of them,[47] when they gave her a Lover, in a Play, seem'd palpably to plead their own Passions, and make their private Court to her, in ficticious Characters. In all the chief Parts she acted, the desirable was so predominant, that no Judge could be cold enough to consider, from what other particular Excellence she became delightful. To speak critically of an Actress, that was extremely good, were as hazardous, as to be positive in one's Opinion of the best Opera Singer. People often judge by Comparison, where there is no Similitude, in the Performance. So that, in this case, we have only Taste to appeal to, and of Taste there can be no disputing. I shall therefore only say of Mrs. *Bracegirdle*, That the most eminent Authors always chose her for their favourite Character, and shall leave that uncontestable Proof of her Merit to its own Value. Yet let me say, there were two very different Characters, in which she acquitted herself with uncommon Applause: If any thing could excuse that desperate Extravagance of Love, that almost frantick Passion of *Lee's Alexander the Great*, it must have been, when Mrs. *Bracegirdle* was his *Statira*: As when she acted *Millamant*,[48] all the Faults, Follies, and Affectation of that agreeable Tyrant, were venially melted down into so many Charms, and Attractions of a conscious Beauty. In other Characters, where singing was a necessary Part of them, her Voice and Action gave a Pleasure, which good Sense, in those Days, was not asham'd to give Praise to.

She retir'd from the Stage in the Height of her Favour from the Publick, when most of her Contemporaries, whom she had been bred up with, were declining, in the Year 1710, nor could she be perswaded to return to it, under new Masters, upon the most advantageous Terms, that were offer'd her; excepting one Day, about a Year after, to assist her good Friend, Mr. *Betterton*, when she play'd *Angelica*, in *Love for Love*, for his Benefit.[49] She has still the Happiness to retain her usual Chearfulness, and to be, without the transitory Charm of Youth, agreeable.

If, in my Account of these memorable Actors, I have not deviated from Truth, which, in the least Article I am not conscious of, may we not venture to say, They had not their Equals, at any one Time, upon any one Theatre in *Europe?* Or, if we confine the Comparison, to that of *France* alone, I believe no other Stage can be much disparag'd, by being left out of the question; which cannot properly be decided, by the single Merit of any one Actor; whether their *Baron,*[50] or our *Betterton,* might be the Superior, (take which Side you please) that Point reaches, either way, but to a thirteenth part of what I contend for, *viz.* That no Stage, at any one Period, could shew thirteen Actors, standing all in equal Lights of Excellence, in their Profession: And I am the bolder, in this Challenge, to any other Nation, because no Theatre having so extended a variety of natural Characters, as the *English,* can have a Demand for Actors of such various Capacities; why then, where they could not be equally wanted, should we suppose them, at any one time, to have existed?

How imperfect soever this copious Account of them may be, I am not without Hope, at least, it may in some degree shew, what Talents are requisite to make Actors valuable: And if that may any ways inform, or assist the Judgment of future Spectators, it may, as often, be of service to their publick Entertainments; for as their Hearers are, so will Actors be; worse, or better, as the false, or true Taste applauds, or discommends them. Hence only can our Theatres improve, or must degenerate.

There is another Point, relating to the hard Condition of those who write for the Stage, which I would recommend to the Consideration of their Hearers; which is, that the extreme Severity with which they damn a bad Play, seems too terrible a Warning to those whose untried Genius might hereafter give them a good one: Whereas it might be a temptation, to a latent Author, to make the Experiment, could he be sure that, though not approved, his Muse might, at least, be dismiss'd with Decency: But the Vivacity of our modern Criticks is of late grown so riotous, that an unsuccessful Author has no more Mercy shewn him, than a notorious Cheat, in a Pillory; every Fool, the lowest Member of the Mob, becomes a Wit, and will have a fling at him. They come now to a new Play, like Hounds to a Carcass, and are all in a full Cry, sometimes for an Hour together, before the Curtain rises to throw it amongst them. Sure, those Gentlemen cannot but allow, that a Play condemn'd after a fair Hearing, falls with thrice the Ignominy, as when it is refus'd that common Justice.

But when their critical Interruptions grow so loud, and of so long a continuance, that the Attention of quiet People (though not so complete Criticks) is terrify'd, and the Skill of the Actors quite disconcerted by the Tumult, the Play then seems rather to fall by Assassins, than by a lawful Sentence. Is it possible that such Auditors can receive Delight, or think it any Praise to them, to prosecute so injurious, so unmanly a Treatment? And tho' perhaps the Compassionate, on the other side (who know they have as good a Right to clap, and support, as others have to cat-call, damn, and destroy,) may oppose this Oppression; their Good-nature, alas! contributes little to the Redress; for in this sort of Civil War, the unhappy Author, like a good Prince, while his Subjects are at mortal Variance, is sure to be a Loser by a Victory on either Side; for still the Commonwealth, his Play, is, during the Conflict, torn to pieces. While this is the Case, while the Theatre is so turbulent a Sea, and so infested with Pirates, what Poetical Merchant, of any Substance, will venture to trade in it? If these valiant Gentlemen pretend to be Lovers of Plays, why will they deter Gentlemen, from giving them such, as are fit for Gentlemen to see? In a word, this new Race of Criticks seem to me, like the Lion-Whelps in the *Tower*, who are so boisterously gamesome at their Meals, that they dash down the Bowls of Milk, brought for their own Breakfast.

As a good Play is certainly the most rational, and the highest Entertainment, that human Invention can produce, let that be my Apology (if I need any) for having thus freely delivered my Mind, in behalf of those Gentlemen, who, under such ca-

lamitous Hazards, may hereafter be reduc'd to write for the
Stage; whose Case I shall compassionate, from the same Motive,
that prevail'd on *Dido*, to assist the *Trojans* in Distress.

> *Non ignara mali miseris succurrere disco.*[51]   Virg.

Or, as *Dryden* has it,

> *I learn to pity Woes so like my own.*

If those particular Gentlemen have sometimes made me the
humbled Object of their Wit, and Humour, their Triumph
at least has done me this involuntary Service, that it has driven
me a Year or two sooner into a quiet Life, than otherwise, my
own want of Judgment might have led me to:[52] I left the Stage,
before my Strength left me; and tho' I came to it again, for some
few Days, a Year or two after; my Reception there not only
turn'd to my Account, but seem'd a fair Invitation, that I would
make my Visits more frequent: But, to give over a Winner, can
be no very imprudent Resolution.

CHAP. VI.¹

Having given you the State of the Theatre, at my first Admission to it; I am now drawing towards the several Revolutions it suffer'd, in my own Time. But (as you find by the setting out of my History) that I always intended myself the Heroe of it, it may be necessary to let you know me, in my Obscurity, as well as in my higher Light, when I became one of the Theatrical Triumvirat.

The Patentees,² who were now Masters of this united, and only Company of Comedians, seem'd to make it a Rule, that no young Persons, desirous to be Actors, should be admitted into Pay under, at least, half a Year's Probation; wisely knowing, that how early soever they might be approv'd of, there could be no great fear of losing them, while they had, then, no other Market to go to. But, alas! Pay was the least of my Concern; the Joy, and Privilege of every Day seeing Plays, for nothing, I thought was a sufficient Consideration, for the best of my Services. So that it was no Pain to my Patience, that I waited full three Quarters of a Year, before I was taken into a Salary of Ten Shillings *per* Week;³ which, with the Assistance of Food, and Raiment, at my Father's House, I then thought a most plentiful Accession, and myself the happiest of Mortals.

The first Thing that enters into the Head of a young Actor, is that of being a Heroe: In this Ambition I was soon snubb'd, by the Insufficiency of my Voice; to which might be added, an uninform'd meagre Person (tho' then not ill made) with a dismal pale Complexion.⁴ Under these Disadvantages, I had but a melancholy Prospect of ever playing a Lover, with Mrs. *Bracegirdle*, which I had flatter'd my Hopes, that my Youth might one Day, have recommended me to. What was most promising in me, then,

was the Aptness of my Ear; for I was soon allow'd to speak
justly, tho' what was grave and serious, did not equally become
me. The first Part, therefore, in which I appear'd, with any
glimpse of Success, was the Chaplain in the *Orphan* of *Otway*.
There is in this Character (of one Scene only) a decent Pleasantry, and Sense enough to shew an Audience, whether the Actor
has any himself. Here was the first Applause I ever receiv'd,
which, you may be sure, made my Heart leap with a higher Joy,
than may be necessary to describe; and yet my Transport was
not then half so high, as at what *Goodman* (who had now left
the Stage) said of me, the next Day, in my hearing. *Goodman*
often came to a Rehearsal for Amusement, and having sate out
the *Orphan*, the Day before; in a Conversation with some of the
principal Actors, enquir'd what new young Fellow that was,
whom he had seen in the Chaplain? Upon which, *Monfort*
reply'd *That's he, behind you. Goodman* then turning about,
look'd earnestly at me, and, after some pause, clapping me on the
Shoulder, rejoin'd, *If he does not make a good Actor, I'll be
d---'d!* The Surprize of being commended, by one who had
been himself so eminent, on the Stage, and in so positive a manner, was more than I could support; in a Word, it almost took
away my Breath, and (laugh, if you please) fairly drew Tears
from my Eyes! And, tho' it may be as ridiculous, as incredible,
to tell you what a full Vanity, and Content, at that time possess'd
me, I will still make it a Question, whether *Alexander* himself, or
Charles the Twelfth of *Sweden,* when at the Head of their first
victorious Armies, could feel a greater Transport, in their Bos-
oms, than I did then in mine, when but in the Rear of this Troop
of Comedians. You see, to what low Particulars I am forc'd to
descend, to give you a true Resemblance of the early and lively
Follies of my Mind. Let me give you another Instance, of my
Discretion, more desparate, than that, of preferring the Stage,
to any other Views of Life. One might think, that the Madness
of breaking, from the Advice, and Care of Parents, to turn
Player, could not easily be exceeded: But what think you, Sir,
of ---- Matrimony? which, before I was Two-and-twenty, I
actually committed, when I had but Twenty Pounds a Year,

which my Father had assur'd to me, and Twenty Shillings a
Week from my Theatrical Labours, to maintain, as I then
thought, the happiest young Couple, that ever took a Leap in
the Dark![5] If after this, to complete my Fortune, I turn'd Poet
too, this last Folly, indeed, had something a better Excuse ---
Necessity: Had it never been my Lot to have come to the Stage,
'tis probable, I might never have been inclin'd, or reduc'd to have
wrote for it: But having once expos'd my Person there, I thought
it could be no additional Dishonour to let my Parts, whatever
they were, take their Fortune along with it.[6]---- But, to return
to the Progress I made as an Actor.

Queen *Mary* having commanded the *Double Dealer* to be
acted,[7] *Kynaston* happen'd to be so ill, that he could not hope to
be able next Day to perform his Part of the Lord *Touchwood*.
In this Exigence, the Author, Mr. *Congreve*, advis'd that it might
be given to me, if at so short a Warning I could undertake it. The
Flattery of being thus distinguish'd by so celebrated an Author,
and the Honour to act before a Queen, you may be sure, made
me blind to whatever Difficulties might attend it. I accepted the
Part, and was ready in it before I slept; next Day the Queen was
present at the Play, and was receiv'd with a new Prologue from
the Author, spoken by Mrs. *Barry*, humbly acknowledging the
great Honour done to the Stage, and to his Play in particular:
Two Lines of it, which though I have not since read, I still remember.

> *But never were in* Rome, *nor* Athens *seen,*
> *So fair a Circle, or so bright a Queen.*

After the Play, Mr. *Congreve* made me the Compliment of saying, that I had not only answer'd, but had exceeded his Expectations, and that he would shew me he was sincere, by his saying
more of me to the Masters---- He was as good as his Word, and
the next Pay-day, I found my Salary, of fifteen, was then advanc'd to twenty Shillings a Week. But alas! this favourable
Opinion of Mr. *Congreve*, made no farther Impression upon the
Judgment of my good Masters; it only serv'd to heighten my
own Vanity; but could not recommend me to any new Trials of

my Capacity; not a Step farther could I get, 'till the Company
was again divided; when the Desertion of the best Actors left a
clear Stage, for younger Champions to mount, and shew their
best Pretensions to favour. But it is now time to enter upon those
Facts, that immediately preceded this remarkable Revolution of
the Theatre.

You have seen how compleat a Set of Actors were under the
Government of the united Patents in 1690; if their Gains were
not extraordinary, what shall we impute it to, but some extraordinary ill Management? I was then too young to be in their
Secrets, and therefore can only observe upon what I saw, and
have since thought visibly wrong.

Though the Success of the *Prophetess*, and King *Arthur* (two
dramatic Opera's, in which the Patentees had embark'd all their
Hopes) was, in Appearance, very great, yet their whole Receipts
did not so far balance their Expence, as to keep them out of a
large Debt, which it was publickly known was, about this time,
contracted, and which found work for the Court of Chancery
for about twenty Years following, till one side of the Cause grew
weary. But this was not all that was wrong; every Branch of the
Theatrical Trade had been sacrific'd, to the necessary sitting out
those tall Ships of Burthen, that were to bring home the *Indies*.
Plays of course were neglected, Actors held cheap, and slightly
dress'd, while Singers, and Dancers were better paid, and em-
broider'd. These Measures, of course, created Murmurings, on
one side, and ill Humour and Contempt on the other. When it
became necessary therefore to lessen the Charge, a Resolution
was taken to begin with the Sallaries of the Actors; and what
seem'd to make this Resolution more necessary at this time, was
the Loss of *Nokes, Monfort,* and *Leigh,* who all dy'd about the
same Year:[8] No wonder then, if when these great Pillars were
at once remov'd, the Building grew weaker, and the Audiences
very much abated. Now in this Distress, what more natural
Remedy could be found, than to incite and encourage (tho' with
some Hazard) the Industry of the surviving Actors? But the
Patentees, it seems, thought the surer way was to bring down
their Pay, in proportion to the Fall of their Audiences. To make

this Project more feasible, they propos'd to begin at the Head of 'em, rightly judging, that if the Principals acquiesc'd, their Inferiors would murmur in vain. To bring this about with a better Grace, they under Pretence of bringing younger Actors forward, order'd several of *Betterton's*, and Mrs. *Barry's* chief Parts to be given to young *Powel*, and Mrs. *Bracegirdle*. In this they committed two palpable Errors; for while the best Actors are in Health, and still on the Stage, the Publick is always apt to be out of Humour, when those of a lower Class pretend to stand in their Places; or admitting, at this time, they might have been accepted, this Project might very probably have lessen'd, but could not possibly mend an Audience; and was a sure Loss of that Time, in studying, which might have been better employ'd in giving the Auditor Variety, the only Temptation to a pall'd Appetite; and Variety is only to be given by Industry: But Industry will always be lame, when the Actor has Reason to be discontented. This the Patentees did not consider, or pretended not to value, while they thought their Power secure, and uncontroulable: But farther, their first Project did not succeed; for tho' the giddy Head of *Powel*, accepted the Parts of *Betterton;* Mrs. *Bracegirdle* had a different way of thinking, and desir'd to be excus'd, from those of Mrs. *Barry;* her good Sense was not to be misled by the insidious Favour of the Patentees; she knew the Stage was wide enough for her Success, without entring into any such rash, and invidious Competition, with Mrs. *Barry*, and therefore wholly refus'd acting any Part that properly belong'd to her. But this Proceeding, however, was Warning enough to make *Betterton* be upon his Guard, and to alarm others, with Apprehensions of their own Safety, from the Design that was laid against him: *Betterton*, upon this, drew into his Party most of the valuable Actors, who to secure their Unity, enter'd with him into a sort of Association, to stand, or fall together. All this the Patentees for some time slighted, but when Matters drew towards a Crisis, they found it adviseable to take the same Measures, and accordingly open'd an Association on their part; both which were severally sign'd, as the Interest or Inclination of either Side led them.

During these Contentions, which the impolitick Patentees had rais'd against themselves (not only by this I have mentioned, but by many other Grievances, which my Memory retains not) the Actors offer'd a Treaty of Peace; but their Masters imagining no Consequence could shake the Right of their Authority, refus'd all Terms of Accommodation. In the mean time this Dissention was so prejudicial to their daily Affairs, that I remember it was allow'd by both Parties, that before *Christmas*, the Patent had lost the getting of at least a thousand Pounds by it.

My having been a Witness of this unnecessary Rupture, was of great use to me, when many Years after, I came to be a Manager my self. I laid it down as a settled Maxim, that no Company could flourish while the chief Actors, and the Undertakers were at variance. I therefore made it a Point, while it was possible, upon tolerable Terms, to keep the valuable Actors in humour with their Station; and tho' I was as jealous of their Encroachments, as any of my Co-partners could be, I always guarded against the least Warmth, in my Expostulations with them; not but at the same time they might see, I was perhaps more determin'd in the Question, than those that gave a loose to their Resentment, and when they were cool, were as apt to recede.[9] I do not remember that I ever made a promise to any, that I did not keep, and therefore was cautious how I made them. This Coldness, though it might not please, at least left them nothing to reproach me with; and if Temper, and fair Words could prevent a Disobligation, I was sure never to give Offence or receive it. But as I was but one of three, I could not oblige others to observe the same Conduct. However, by this means, I kept many an unreasonable Discontent, from breaking out, and both Sides found their Account in it.

How a contemptuous and overbearing manner of treating Actors had like to have ruin'd us, in our early Prosperity, shall be shewn in its Place: If future Managers should chance to think my way right, I suppose they will follow it; if not, when they find what happen'd to the Patentees (who chose to disagree with their People) perhaps they may think better of it.

The Patentees then, who by their united Powers, had made a Monopoly of the Stage, and consequently presum'd they might impose what Conditions they pleas'd upon their People, did not consider, that they were all this while endeavouring to enslave a Set of Actors, whom the Publick (more arbitrary than themselves) were inclin'd to support; nor did they reflect, that the Spectator naturally wish'd, that the Actor, who gave him Delight, might enjoy the Profits arising from his Labour, without regard of what pretended Damage, or Injustice might fall upon his Owners, whose personal Merit the Publick was not so well acquainted with. From this Consideration, then, several Persons of the highest Distinction espous'd their Cause, and sometimes, in the Circle, entertain'd the King with the State of the Theatre. At length their Grievances were laid before the Earl of *Dorset*, then Lord Chamberlain, who took the most effectual Method for their Relief. The Learned of the Law were advis'd with, and they gave their Opinion, that no Patent for acting Plays, &c. could tie up the Hands of a succeeding Prince, from granting the like Authority, where it might be thought proper to trust it. But while this Affair was in Agitation, Queen Mary dy'd,[10] which of course occasion'd a Cessation of all publick Diversions. In this melancholy Interim, *Betterton*, and his Adherents had more Leisure to sollicit their Redress; and the Patentees now finding, that the Party against them was gathering Strength, were reduc'd to make sure of as good a Company, as the Leavings of *Betterton*'s Interest could form; and these, you may be sure, would not lose this Occasion of setting a Price upon their Merit, equal to their own Opinion of it, which was just double to what they had before. *Powel*, and *Verbruggen*, who had then but forty Shillings a Week, were now rais'd each of them to four Pounds, and others in proportion: As for my self, I was then too insignificant to be taken into their Councils, and consequently stood among those of little Importance, like Cattle in a Market, to be sold to the first Bidder. But the Patentees seeming in the greater Distress for Actors, condescended to purchase me. Thus, without any farther Merit, than that of being

a scarce Commodity, I was advanc'd to thirty Shillings a Week:
Yet our Company was so far from being full, that our Com-
manders were forc'd to beat up for Voluntiers, in several
distant Counties; it was this Occasion that first brought *Johnson*
and *Bullock*[11] to the Service of the Theatre-Royal.

Forces being thus rais'd, and the War declared on both Sides,
Betterton, and his Chiefs had the Honour of an Audience
of the *King,* who consider'd them as the only Subjects, whom
he had not yet deliver'd from arbitrary Power; and graciously
dismiss'd them, with an Assurance of Relief, and Support---
Accordingly a select number of them were impower'd by his
Royal Licence,[12] to act in a separate Theatre, for themselves.
This great Point being obtain'd, many People of Quality came
into a voluntary Subscription of twenty, and some of forty
Guineas a-piece, for the erecting a Theatre within the Walls
of the Tennis-Court, in *Lincolns-Inn-Fields.* But as it requir'd
Time to fit it up, it gave the Patentees more Leisure to muster
their Forces, who notwithstanding were not able to take the
Field till the *Easter-Monday* in *April* following. Their first Attempt was a reviv'd Play, call'd *Abdelazar,* or the *Moor's Revenge,* poorly written, by Mrs. *Behn.*[13] The House was very
full, but whether it was the Play, or the Actors, that were not
approv'd, the next Day's Audience sunk to nothing. However,
we were assur'd, that let the Audiences be never so low, our
Masters would make good all Deficiencies, and so indeed they
did, 'till towards the End of the Season, when Dues to Ballance
came too thick upon 'em. But that I may go gradually on with
my own Fortune, I must take this Occasion to let you know, by
the following Circumstance, how very low my Capacity, as an
Actor, was then rated: It was thought necessary, at our Opening,
that the Town shou'd be address'd in a new Prologue; but to our
great Distress, among several, that were offer'd, not one was
judg'd fit to be spoken. This I thought a favourable Occasion,
to do my self some remarkable Service, if I should have the good
Fortune, to produce one that might be accepted. The next
(memorable) Day my Muse brought forth her first Fruit that

ever made publick; how good, or bad imports not; my Prologue was accepted, and resolv'd on to be spoken. This Point being gain'd, I began to stand upon Terms, you will say, not unreasonable; which were, that if I might speak it my self, I would expect no farther Reward for my Labour: This was judg'd as bad as having no Prologue at all! You may imagine how hard I thought it, that they durst not trust my poor poetical Brat, to my own Care. But since I found it was to be given into other Hands, I insisted that two Guineas should be the Price of my parting with it; which with a Sigh I receiv'd, and *Powel* spoke the Prologue: But every Line, that was applauded, went sorely to my Heart, when I reflected, that the same Praise might have been given to my own speaking it; nor could the Success of the Author compensate the Distress of the Actor. However, in the End, it serv'd, in some sort, to mend our People's Opinion of me; and whatever the Criticks might think of it, one of the Patentees (who, it is true, knew no difference between *Dryden* and *D'urfey*)[14] said, upon the Success of it, that insooth! I was an ingenious young Man. This sober Compliment (though I could have no Reason to be vain upon it) I thought was a fair Promise to my being in favour. But to Matters of more Moment: Now let us reconnoitre the Enemy.

After we had stolen some few Days March upon them, the Forces of *Betterton* came up with us in terrible Order: In about three Weeks following,[15] the new Theatre was open'd against us, with a veteran Company, and a new Train of Artillery; or in plainer *English*, the old Actors, in *Lincolns-Inn-Fields* began, with a new Comedy of Mr. *Congreve*'s, call'd *Love* for *Love;* which ran on with such extraordinary Success, that they had seldom occasion to act any other Play, 'till the End of the Season. This valuable Play had a narrow Escape, from falling into the Hands of the Patentees; for before the Division of the Company, it had been read, and accepted of at the Theatre-Royal: But while the Articles of Agreement for it were preparing, the Rupture, in the Theatrical State, was so far advanc'd, that the Author took Time to pause, before he sign'd them; when finding that all Hopes of Accommodation were impracticable, he thought it adviseable, to let it take its Fortune, with those Actors for whom he had first intended the Parts.

Mr. *Congreve* was then in such high Reputation, as an Author, that besides his Profits, from his Play, they offer'd him a whole Share with them, which he accepted; in Consideration of which he oblig'd himself, if his Health permitted, to give them one new Play every Year. *Dryden*, in King *Charles*'s Time, had the same Share, with the King's Company; but he bound himself to give them two Plays every Season. This you may imagine he could not hold long, and I am apt to think, he might have serv'd them better, with one in a Year, not so hastily written. Mr. *Congreve*, whatever Impediment he met with, was three Years before, in pursuance to his Agreement, he produc'd the *Mourning Bride;* and if I mistake not, the Interval had been much the same, when he gave them the *Way of the World*. But it came out the stronger, for the Time it cost him, and to their better Support, when they sorely wanted it: For though they went on with Success for a Year or two, and even, when their Affairs were declining, stood in much higher Estimation of the Publick, than their Opponents; yet, in the End, both Sides were great Sufferers by their Separation; the natural Consequence of two Houses, which I have already mention'd in a former Chapter.

The first Error this new Colony of Actors fell into, was their inconsiderately parting with *Williams*, and Mrs. *Monfort*,[16] upon a too nice (not to say severe) Punctilio; in not allowing them to be equal Sharers with the rest; which before they had acted one Play, occasion'd their Return to the Service of the Patentees. As I have call'd this an Error, I ought to give my Reasons for it. Though the Industry of *Williams* was not equal to his Capacity; for he lov'd his Bottle better than his Business; and though Mrs. *Monfort* was only excellent in Comedy, yet their Merit was too great, almost on any Scruples, to be added to the Enemy; and, at worst, they were certainly much more above those they would have rank'd them with, than they could possibly be under those, they were not admitted to be equal to. Of this Fact there is a poetical Record, in the Prologue to *Love for Love*, where the Author speaking of the, then, happy State of the Stage, observes,

that if, in Paradise, when two only were there, they both fell;
the Surprize was less, if from so numerous a Body as theirs, there
had been any Deserters.

> Abate the Wonder, and the Fault forgive,
> If, in our larger Family, we grieve
> One falling *Adam*, and one tempted *Eve*.[17]

These Lines alluded to the Revolt of the Persons above mention'd.

Notwithstanding the Acquisition of these two Actors, who
were of more Importance, than any of those, to whose Assistance they came, the Affairs of the Patentees were still, in a very
creeping Condition; they were now, too late, convinc'd of their
Error, in having provok'd their People to this Civil War, of the
Theatre! quite chang'd, and dismal, now, was the Prospect before them! their Houses thin, and the Town crowding into a
new one! Actors at double Sallaries, and not half the usual Audiences, to pay them! and all this brought upon them, by those,
whom their full Security had contemn'd, and who were now in
a fair way of making their Fortunes, upon the ruin'd Interest of
their Oppressors.

Here, tho' at this time, my Fortune depended on the Success
of the Patentees, I cannot help, in regard to Truth, remembering
the rude, and riotous Havock we made of all the late dramatic
Honours of the Theatre! all became at once the Spoil of Ignorance, and Self-conceit! *Shakespear* was defac'd, and tortur'd in
every signal Character---- *Hamlet*, and *Othello*, lost in one Hour
all their good Sense, their Dignity, and Fame. *Brutus* and *Cassius*
became noisy Blusterers, with bold unmeaning Eyes, mistaken
Sentiments, and turgid Elocution! Nothing, sure, could more
painfully regret a judicious Spectator, than to see, at our first
setting out, with what rude Confidence, those Habits, which
Actors of real Merit had left behind them, were worn by giddy
Pretenders that so vulgarly disgrac'd them! Not young Lawyers
in hir'd Robes, and Plumes, at a Masquerade, could be less, what
they would seem, or more aukwardly personate the Characters
they belong'd to.[18] If, in all these Acts of wanton Waste, these

Insults, upon injur'd Nature, you observe, I have not yet charg'd
one of them upon my self; it is not from an imaginary Vanity,
that I could have avoided them; but that I was rather safe, by
being too low, at that time, to be admitted even to my Chance
of falling into the same eminent Errors: So that as none of those
great Parts ever fell to my Share, I could not be accountable
for the Execution of them: Nor indeed could I get one good
Part of any kind, 'till many Months after; unless it were of that
sort, which no body else car'd for, or would venture to expose
themselves in. The first unintended Favour, therefore, of a Part
of any Value, Necessity threw upon me, on the following Occasion.

As it has been always judg'd their natural Interest, where
there are two Theatres, to do one another as much Mischief as
they can; you may imagine it could not be long, before this
hostile Policy shew'd itself, in Action. It happen'd, upon our
having Information on a *Saturday* Morning, that the *Tuesday*
after,[19] *Hamlet* was intended to be acted at the other House,
where it had not yet been seen; our merry menaging Actors (for
they were now in a manner left to govern themselves) resolv'd,
at any rate, to steal a March upon the Enemy, and take Possession
of the same Play the Day before them: Accordingly, *Hamlet*
was given out that Night, to be acted with us on *Monday*. The
Notice of this sudden Enterprize, soon reach'd the other House,
who, in my Opinion, too much regarded it; for they shorten'd
their first Orders, and resolv'd that *Hamlet* should to *Hamlet* be
oppos'd, on the same Day; whereas, had they given notice in
their Bills, that the same Play would have been acted by them
the Day after, the Town would have been in no doubt, which
House they should have reserv'd themselves for; ours must certainly have been empty, and theirs, with more Honour, have
been crowded: Experience, many Years after, in like Cases, has
convinc'd me, that this would have been the more laudable Conduct. But be that as it may; when, in their *Monday*'s Bills, it was
seen that *Hamlet* was up against us, our Consternation was terrible, to find that so hopeful a Project was frustrated. In this Distress, *Powell*, who was our commanding Officer, and whose

enterprising Head wanted nothing but Skill to carry him thro'
the most desperate Attempts; for, like others of his Cast, he had
murder'd many a Hero, only to get into his Cloaths. This *Powell*,
I say, immediately call'd a Council of War; where the Question
was, Whether he should fairly face the Enemy, or make a Retreat, to some other Play of more probable Safety? It was soon
resolv'd that to act *Hamlet* against *Hamlet*, would be certainly
throwing away the Play, and disgracing themselves to little or no
Audience; to conclude, *Powell*, who was vain enough to envy
Betterton, as his Rival, propos'd to change Plays with them, and
that, as they had given out the *Old Batchelor*, and had chang'd it
for *Hamlet*, against us; we should give up our *Hamlet*, and turn
the *Old Batchelor* upon them. This Motion was agreed to, *Nem-
ine contradicente;*[20] but upon Enquiry, it was found, that there
were not two Persons among them, who had ever acted in that
Play: But that Objection, it seems, (though all the Parts were
to be study'd in six Hours) was soon got over; *Powell* had an
Equivalent, *in petto*, that would balance any Deficiency on that
Score; which was, that he would play the *Old Batchelor* himself,
and mimick *Betterton*, throughout the whole Part. This happy
Thought was approv'd with Delight, and Applause, as whatever
can be suppos'd to ridicule Merit, generally gives Joy to those
that want it: Accordingly, the Bills were chang'd, and at the
bottom inserted,

The Part of the *Old Batchelor*, to be perform'd in Imitation
of the Original.

Printed Books of the Play were sent for in haste, and every Actor
had one, to pick out of it the Part he had chosen: Thus, while
they were each of them chewing the Morsel, they had most mind
to, some one happening to cast his Eye over the *Dramatis Per-
sonae*, found that the main Matter was still forgot, that no body
had yet been thought of for the Part of Alderman *Fondlewife*.
Here we were all a-ground agen! nor was it to be conceiv'd
who could make the least tolerable Shift with it. This Character
had been so admirably acted by *Dogget*, that though it is only
seen in the Fourth Act, it may be no Dispraise to the Play, to say,

it probably ow'd the greatest Part of its Success to his Performance. But, as the Case was now desperate, any Resource was
better than none, Somebody must swallow the bitter Pill, or the
Play must die. At last it was recollected, that I had been heard
to say, in my wild way of talking, what a vast mind I had to
play *Nykin,* by which Name the Character was more frequently
call'd. Notwithstanding they were thus distress'd about the Disposal of this Part, most of 'em shook their Heads, at my being
mention'd for it; yet *Powell,* who was resolv'd, at all Hazards, to
fall upon *Betterton,* and having no concern for what might become of any one, that serv'd his Ends or Purpose, order'd me to
be sent for; and, as he naturally lov'd to set other People wrong,
honestly said, before I came, *If the Fool has a mind to blow himself up, at once, let us ev'n give him a clear Stage for it.* Accordingly, the Part was put into my Hands, between Eleven and
Twelve that Morning, which I durst not refuse, because others
were as much straitned in time, for Study, as myself. But I had
this casual Advantage of most of them; that having so constantly
observ'd *Dogget*'s Performance, I wanted but little Trouble, to
make me perfect in the Words; so that when it came to my
turn to rehearse, while others read their Parts, from their Books,
I had put mine in my Pocket, and went thro' the first Scene
without it; and though I was more abash'd to rehearse so remarkable a Part before the Actors (which is natural to most young
People) than to act before an Audience, yet some of the better-
natur'd encourag'd me so far, as to say, they did not think I
should make an ill Figure in it: To conclude, the Curiosity to see
Betterton mimick'd, drew us a pretty good Andience, and *Powell* (as far as Applause is a Proof of it) was allow'd to have
burlesqu'd him very well. As I have question'd the certain Value
of Applause, I hope I may venture, with less Vanity, to say how
particular a Share I had of it, in the same Play. At my first
Appearance, one might have imagin'd, by the various Murmurs
of the Audience, that they were in doubt whether *Dogget* himself were not return'd, or that they could not conceive what
strange Face it could be, that so nearly resembled him; for I had
laid the Tint of Forty Years, more than my real Age, upon my

Features, and, to the most minute placing of a Hair, was dress'd
exactly like him: When I spoke, the Surprize was still greater, as
if I had not only borrow'd his Cloaths, but his Voice too. But
tho' that was the least difficult Part of him, to be imitated, they
seem'd to allow, I had so much of him, in every other Requisite,
that my Applause was, perhaps, more than proportionable: For,
whether I had done so much, where so little was expected, or that
the Generosity of my Hearers were more than usually zealous,
upon so unexpected an Occasion, or from what other Motive
such Favour might be pour'd upon me, I cannot say; but, in plain
and honest Truth, upon my going off from the first Scene, a
much better Actor might have been proud of the Applause,
that follow'd me; after one loud *Plaudit* was ended, and sunk into
a general Whisper, that seem'd still to continue their private
Approbation, it reviv'd to a second, and again to a third, still
louder than the former, If, to all this, I add that *Dogget* himself
was, in the Pit, at the same time, it would be too rank Affectation, if I should not confess, that, to see him there a Witness of
my Reception, was, to me, as consummate a triumph, as the
Heart of Vanity could be indulg'd with. But whatever Vanity
I might set upon my self, from this unexpected Success, I found
that was no Rule to other People's Judgment of me. There were
few or no Parts, of the same kind, to be had; nor could they conceive, from what I had done in this, what other sort of Characters
I could be fit for. If I sollicited for any thing of a different Nature, I was answer'd, *That was not in my Way*. And what *was* in
my Way, it seems, was not, as yet, resolv'd upon. And though I
reply'd, *that I thought any thing, naturally written, ought to be
in every one's Way that pretended to be an Actor;* this was
look'd upon as a vain, impracticable Conceit of my own. Yet it
is a Conceit, that, in forty Years farther Experience, I have not
yet given up; I still think, that a Painter, who can draw but one
sort of Object, or an Actor that shines, but in one Light, can
neither of them boast of that ample Genius, which is necessary to
form a thorough Master of his Art: For tho' Genius may have a
particular Inclination, yet a good History-Painter, or a good
Actor, will, without being at a loss, give you, upon Demand, a

proper Likeness of whatever Nature produces. If he cannot do this, he is only an Actor, as the Shoemaker was allow'd a limited Judge of *Appelles's*[21] Painting; but *not beyond his Last*. Now, tho' to do any one thing well, may have more Merit, than we often meet with; and may be enough, to procure a Man the Name of a good Actor, from the Publick; yet, in my Opinion, it is but still the Name, without the Substance. If his Talent is in such narrow Bounds, that he dares not step out of them, to look upon the Singularities of Mankind, and cannot catch them, in whatever Form they present themselves; if he is not Master of the *Quicquid agunt homines*, &c.[22] in any Shape, that Human Nature is fit to be seen in; if he cannot change himself into several distinct Persons, so as to vary his whole Tone of Voice, his Motion, his Look, and Gesture, whether in high, or lower Life, and, at the same time, keep close to those Variations, without leaving the Character they singly belong to; if his best Skill, falls short of this Capacity, what Pretence have we to call him a complete Master of his Art? And tho' I do not insist, that he ought always to shew himself, in these various Lights, yet, before we compliment him with that Title, he ought, at least, by some few Proofs, to let us see, that he has them all, in his Power. If I am ask'd, who, ever, arriv'd at this imaginary Excellence, I confess, the Instances are very few; but I will venture to name *Monfort*, as one of them, whose theatrical Character I have given, in my last Chapter: For, in his Youth, he had acted Low Humour, with great Success, even down to *Tallboy* in the *Jovial Crew;*[23] and when he was in great Esteem, as a tragedian, he was, in Comedy, the most complete Gentleman that I ever saw upon the Stage. Let me add too, that *Betterton*, in his declining Age, was as eminent, in Sir *John Falstaff*, as in the Vigour of it, in his *Othello*.

While I thus measure the Value of an Actor, by the Variety of Shapes he is able to throw himself into, you may naturally suspect, that I am all this while, leading my own Theatrical Character into your Favour: Why, really, to speak as an honest Man, I cannot wholly deny it: But in this, I shall endeavour to be no farther partial to myself, than known Facts will make me; from the good, or bad Evidence or which, your better Judg-

ment will condemn, or acquit me. And to shew you, that I will
conceal no Truth, that is against me, I frankly own, that had I
been always left, to my own choice of Characters, I am doubtful
whether I might ever have deserv'd an equal Share of that Estimation, which the Publick seem'd to have held me in: Nor am I
sure, that it was not Vanity in me, often to have suspected, that
I was kept out of the Parts, I had most mind to, by the Jealousy,
or Prejudice of my Cotemporaries; some Instances of which, I
could give you, were they not too slight, to be remember'd: In
the mean time, be pleas'd to observe, how slowly, in my younger
Days, my Good-fortune came forward.

My early Success in the *Old Batchelor*, of which I have given
so full an Account, having open'd no farther way to my Advancement, was enough, perhaps, to have made a young Fellow
of more Modesty despair; but being of a Temper not easily dis-
hearten'd, I resolv'd to leave nothing unattempted, that might
shew me, in some new Rank of Distinction. Having then no
other Resource, I was at last reduc'd to write a Character for
myself; but as that was not finish'd till about a Year after, I could
not, in the Interim, procure any one Part, that gave me the least
Inclination to act it; and consequently, such as I got, I perform'd
with a proportionable Negligence. But this Misfortune, if it
were one, you are not to wonder at; for the same Fate attended
me, more, or less, to the last Days of my remaining on the Stage.
What Defect in me, this may have been owing to, I have not yet
had Sense enough to find out, but I soon found out as good a
thing, which was, never to be mortify'd at it: Though I am
afraid this seeming Philosophy was rather owing to my Inclination to Pleasure, than Business. But to my Point. The next Year[24]
I produc'd the Comedy of *Love's last Shift;* yet the Difficulty
of getting it to the Stage, was not easily surmounted; for, at that
time, as little was expected from me, as an Author, as had been
from my Pretensions to be an Actor. However, Mr. *Southern*,
the Author of *Oroonoko*, having had the Patience to hear me
read it, to him, happened to like it so well, that he immediately
recommended it to the Patentees, and it was accordingly acted
in *January* 1695.[25] In this Play, I gave myself the Part of Sir

Novelty,[26] which was thought, a good Portrait of the Foppery then in fashion. Here too, Mr. *Southern*,[27] though he had approv'd my Play, came into the common Diffidence of me, as an Actor: For, when on the first Day of it, I was standing, myself, to prompt the *Prologue*, he took me by the Hand, and said, Young Man! *I pronounce thy Play a good one; I will answer for its Success, if thou dost not spoil it by thy own Action.* Though this might be a fair *Salvo*, for his favourable Judgment of the Play; yet if it were his real Opinion of me, as an Actor, I had the good Fortune to deceive him: I succeeded so well, in both, that People seem'd at a Loss, which they should give the Preference to. But (now let me shew a little more Vanity, and my Apology for it, shall come after) the Compliment which my Lord *Dorset* (then Lord Chamberlain) made me upon it, is, I own, what I had rather not suppress, *viz.* That it was the best, First Play, that any Author in his Memory, had produc'd; and that for a young Fellow, to shew himself such an Actor, and such a Writer, in one Day, was something extraordinary. But as this noble Lord has been celebrated for his Good-nature, I am contented, that as much of this Compliment should be suppos'd to exceed my Deserts, as may be imagin'd to have been heighten'd, by his generous Inclination to encourage a young Beginner. If this Excuse cannot soften the Vanity of telling a Truth so much, in my own Favour, I must lie, at the Mercy of my Reader.[28] But there was a still higher Compliment pass'd upon me, which I may publish without Vanity, because it was not a design'd one, and apparently came from my Enemies, *viz.* That, to their certain Knowledge *it was not my own:* This Report is taken notice of in my Dedication to the Play. If they spoke Truth, if they knew what other Person it really belong'd to, I will, at least allow them true to their Trust; for above forty Years have since past, and they have not yet reveal'd the Secret.[29]

The new Light, in which the Character of Sir *Novelty* had shewn me, one might have thought, were enough, to have dissipated the Doubts, of what I might now, be possibly good for. But to whatever Chance, my Ill-fortune was due; whether I had still, but little Merit, or that the Menagers, if I had any, were not competent Judges of it; or whether I was not generally elbow'd, by other Actors (which I am most inclin'd to think the true Cause) when any fresh Parts were to be dispos'd of, not one Part of any consequence was I preferr'd to, 'till the Year following: then, indeed, from Sir *John Vanbrugh's* favourable Opinion of me, I began, with others, to have a better of myself: For he not only did me Honour, as an Author, by writing his *Relapse*, as a Sequel, or Second Part, to *Love's last Shift;*[30] but as an Actor too, by preferring me, to the chief Character in his own Play; (which from Sir Novelty) he had enobled by the Style of Baron of *Foppington*. This Play (the *Relapse*) from its new, and easy Turn of Wit, had great Success, and gave me, as a Comedian, a second Flight of Reputation along with it.

As the Matter I write must be very flat, or impertinent, to those, who have no Taste, or Concern for the Stage; and may to those, who delight in it too, be equally tedious, when I talk of no body but myself; I shall endeavour to relieve your Patience, by a Word or two more of this Gentleman, so far as he lent his Pen to the Support of the Theatre.

Though the *Relapse* was the first Play this agreeable Author produc'd, yet it was not, it seems, the first he had written; for he had at that time, by him, (more than) all the Scenes, that were acted of the *Provok'd Wife;*[31] but being then doubtful, whether he should ever trust them to the Stage, he thought no more of it: But after the Success of the *Relapse*, he was more strongly importun'd, than able, to refuse it to the Publick. Why the last written Play was first acted, and for what Reason they were given to different Stages, what follows, will explain.

In his first Step, into publick Life, when he was but an Ensign, and had a Heart above his Income, he happen'd somewhere, at his Winter-Quarters, upon a very slender Acquaintance with Sir *Thomas Skipwith*, to receive a particular Obligation from him, which he had not forgot at the Time I am speaking of: When Sir *Thomas's* Interest, in the Theatrical Patent (for he had a large Share in it, though he little concern'd himself in the Conduct of it) was rising but very slowly, he thought, that to give it a Lift, by a new Comedy, if it succeeded, might be the handsomest Return he could make to those his former Favours; and having observ'd, that in *Love's last Shift*, most of the Actors had acquitted themselves, beyond what was expected of them; he took a sudden Hint from what he lik'd, in that Play, and in less than three Months, in the beginning of *April* following, brought us the *Relapse* finish'd; but the Season being then too far advanc'd, it was not acted 'till the succeeding Winter. Upon the Success of the *Relapse*, the late Lord *Hallifax*, who was a great Favourer of *Betterton*'s Company, having formerly, by way of Family-Amusement, heard the *Provok'd Wife* read to him, in its looser Sheets, engag'd Sir John *Vanburgh* to revise it, and give it to the theatre in *Lincolns-Inn Fields*. This was a Request not to be refus'd to so eminent a Patron of the Muses, as the Lord *Hallifax*, who was equally a Friend and Admirer of Sir *John* himself. Nor was Sir *Thomas Skipwith*, in the least disobliged, by so reasonable a Compliance: After which, Sir *John* was agen at liberty, to repeat his Civilities to his Friend, Sir *Thomas;* and about the same time, or not long after, gave us the Comedy of *Aesop;*[32] for his Inclination always led him to serve Sir *Thomas*. Besides, our Company, about this time, began to be look'd upon, in another Light; the late Contempt we had lain under, was now wearing off, and from the Success of two or three new Plays, our Actors, by being originals in a few good Parts, where they had not the Disadvantage of Comparison against them, sometimes found new Favour, in those old Plays, where others had exceeded them.

Of this Good-fortune, perhaps, I had more than my Share, from the two very different chief Characters, I had succeeded in; for I was equally approv'd in *Aesop*, as the *Lord Foppington*, allowing the Difference, to be no less, than as Wisdom, in a Person deform'd, may be less entertaining to the general Taste, then Folly and Foppery, finely drest: For the Character that delivers Precepts of Wisdom, is, in some sort, severe upon the Auditor, by shewing him one wiser than himself. But when Folly is his Object, he applauds himself, for being wiser than the Coxcomb he laughs at: And who is not more pleas'd with an Occasion to commend, than accuse himself?

Though, to write much, in a little time, is no Excuse for writing ill; yet Sir *John Vanbrugh*'s Pen, is not to be a little admir'd, for its Spirit, Ease, and Readiness, in producing Plays so fast, upon the Neck of one another; for, notwithstanding this quick Dispatch, there is a clear and lively Simplicity in his Wit, that neither wants the Ornament of Learning, nor has the least Smell of the Lamp in it. As the Face of a fine Woman, with only her Locks loose, about her, may be then it its greatest Beauty; such were his Productions, only adorn'd by Nature. There is something so catching to the Ear, so easy to the Memory, in all he writ, that it has been observ'd, by all the Actors of my Time, that the Style of no Author whatsoever, gave their Memory less trouble, than that of Sir *John Vanbrugh;* which I myself, who have been charg'd with several of his strongest Characters, can confirm by a pleasing Experience. And indeed his Wit, and Humour, was so little laboured, that his most entertaining Scenes seem'd to be no more, than his common Conversation committed to Paper. Here, I confess my Judgment at a Loss, whether, in this, I give him more, or less, than his due Praise? For may it not be more laudable, to raise an Estate (whether in Wealth, or Fame) by Pains, and honest Industry, than to be born to it? Yet, if his Scenes really were, as to me they always seem'd, delightful, are they not, thus, expeditiously written, the more surprising? let the Wit, and Merit of them, then, be weigh'd by wiser Criticks, than I pretend to be: But no wonder, while his Conceptions were so full of Life, and Humour, his Muse should be sometimes too warm, to wait the slow Pace of Judgment, or to endure the Drudgery, of forming a regular Fable to them: Yet we see the *Relapse,* however imperfect, in the Conduct, by the mere Force of its agreeable Wit, ran away with the Hearts of its Hearers; while *Love's last Shift,* which (as Mr. *Congreve* justly said of it) had only in it, a great many things, that were *like* Wit, that in reality were *not* Wit. And what is still less pardonable (as I say of it myself) has a great deal of Puerility, and frothy Stage-Language in it, yet by the mere moral Delight receiv'd from its Fable, it has been, with the other,

in a continued, and equal Possession of the Stage, for more than
forty Years.[33]

As I have already promis'd you, to refer your Judgment of
me, as an Actor, rather to known Facts, than my own Opinion,
(which, I could not be sure, would keep clear of Self-partiality)
I must a little farther risque my being tedious, to be as good as
my Word. I have elsewhere allow'd, that my want of a strong
and full Voice, soon cut short my Hopes of making any valuable
Figure, in Tragedy; and I have been many Years since, con-
vinced, that whatever Opinion I might have of my own Judgment, or Capacity to amend the palpable Errors, that I saw our
Tragedians, most in favour, commit; yet in the Auditors, who
would have been sensible of any such Amendments (could I
have made them) were so very few, that my best Endeavour
would have been but an unavailing Labour, or, what is yet worse,
might have appeared both to our Actors, and to many Auditors,
the vain Mistake of my own Self-Conceit: For so strong, so very
near indispensible, is that one Article of Voice, in the forming
a good Tragedian, that an Actor may want any other Qualification whatsoever, and yet have a better Chance for Applause,
than he will ever have, with all the Skill, in the World, if his
Voice is not equal to it. Mistake me not; I say, for *Applause* only
---- but Applause does not always stay for, nor always follow
intrinsick Merit; Applause will frequently open, like a young
Hound, upon a wrong Scent; and the Majority of Auditors, you
know, are generally composed of Babblers, that are profuse of
their Voices, before there is any thing on foot, that calls for
them: Not but, I grant, to lead, or mislead the Many, will always
stand in some Rank of a necessary Merit; yet when I say a good
Tragedian, I mean one, in Opinion of whose *real* Merit, the best
Judges would agree.

Having so far given up my Pretensions to the Buskin, I ought
now to account for my having been, notwithstanding, so often
seen, in some particular Characters in Tragedy, as *Iago, Wolsey,
Syphax, Richard* the *Third*, &c. If, in any of this kind I have succeeded, perhaps it has been a Merit dearly purchas'd; for, from

the Delight I seem'd to take in my performing them, half my Auditors have been persuaded, that a great Share of the Wickedness of them, must have been in my own Nature: If this is true, as true I fear (I had almost said hope) it is, I look upon it rather as a Praise, than a Censure of my Performance. Aversion there is an involuntary Commendation, where we are only hated, for being like the thing, we *ought* to be like; a sort of Praise however, which few Actors besides my self could endure: Had it been equal to the usual Praise given to Vertue, my Cotemporaries would have thought themselves injur'd, if I had pretended to any Share of it: So that you see, it has been, as much the Dislike others had to them, as Choice, that has thrown me sometimes into these Characters. But it may be farther observ'd, that in the Characters I have nam'd, where there is so much close meditated Mischief, Deceit, Pride, Insolence, or Cruelty, they cannot have the least Cast, or Profer of the Amiable in them; consequently, there can be no great Demand for that harmonious Sound, or pleasing, round Melody of Voice, which in the softer Sentiments of Love, the Wailings of distressful Vertue, or in the Throws and Swellings of Honour, and Ambition, may be needful to recommend them to our Pity, or Admiration: So that again my want of that requisite Voice might less disqualify me for the vicious, than the virtuous Character, This too may have been a more favourable Reason for my having been chosen for them--- a yet farther Consideration, that inclin'd me to them, was that they are generally better written, thicker sown, with sensible Reflections, and come by so much nearer to common Life, and Nature, than Characters of Admiration, as Vice is more the Practice of Mankind than Virtue: Nor could I sometimes help smiling, at those dainty Actors, that were too squeamish to swallow them! as if they were one Jot the better Men, for acting a good Man well, or another Man the worse, for doing equal Justice to a bad one! 'Tis not, sure, *what* we act, but *how* we act what is allotted us, that speaks our intrinsick Value! as in real Life, the wise Man, or the Fool, be he Prince, or Peasant, will, in either State, be equally the Fool, or the wise Man--- but alas! in personated Life, this is no Rule to the Vulgar! they are apt to think all before them real, and rate the Actor according to his borrow'd Vice, or Virtue.

If then I had always too careless a Concern for false, or vulgar Applause, I ought not to complain, if I have had less of it, than others of my Time, or not less of it, than I desir'd: Yet I will venture to say, that from the common, weak Appetite of false Applause, many Actors have run into more Errors, and Absurdities, than their greatest Ignorance could otherwise have committed: If this Charge is true, it will lie chiefly upon the better Judgment of the Spectator to reform it.

But not to make too great a Merit of my avoiding this common Road to Applause, perhaps I was vain enough to think, I had more ways, than one, to come at it. That, in the Variety of Characters I acted, the Chances to win it, were the stronger on my Side--- That, if the Multitude were not in a Roar, to see me, in *Cardinal Wolsey*, I could be sure of them in Alderman *Fondlewife*. If they hated me in *Iago*, in Sir *Fopling* they took me for a fine Gentleman; if they were silent at *Syphax*, no *Italian* Eunuch was more applauded than when I sung in Sir *Courtly*. If the Morals of *Aesop* were too grave for them, Justice *Shallow* was as simple, and as merry an old Rake, as the wisest of our young ones could wish me. And though the Terror and Detestation rais'd by King *Richard*, might be too severe a delight for them, yet the more gentle and modern Vanities of a Poet *Bays*, or the well-bred Vices of a Lord *Foppington*, were not at all, more than their merry Hearts, or nicer Morals could bear.[34]

These few Instances out of fifty more I could give you, may serve to explain, what sort of Merit, I at most pretended to; which was, that I supply'd, with Variety, whatever I might want of that particular Skill, wherein others went before me. How this Variety was executed (for by that only is its value to be rated) you who have so often been my Spectator, are the proper Judge: If you pronounce my Performance to have been defective, I am condemn'd by my own Evidence; if you acquit me, these Out-lines may serve for a Sketch of my Theatrical Character.

The *Lincolns-Inn-Fields* Company were, now in 1693,[2] a Common-wealth, like that of *Holland*, divided from the Tyranny of *Spain:* But the Similitude goes very little farther; short was the Duration of the Theatrical Power! for though Success pour'd in so fast upon them, at their first Opening, that every thing seem'd to support it self; yet Experience, in a Year or two shew'd them, that they had never been worse govern'd, then when they govern'd themselves! many of them began to make their particular Interest more their Point, then that of the general: and though some Deference might be had to the Measures, and Advice of *Betterton*, several of them wanted to govern, in their Turn; and were often out of Humour, that their Opinion was not equally regarded--- But have we not seen the same Infirmity in Senates? The Tragedians seem'd to think their Rank as much above the Comedians, as in the Characters they severally acted; when the first were in their Finery, the latter were impatient, at the Expence; and look'd upon it, as rather laid out, upon the real, than the fictitious Person of the Actor; nay, I have known, in our own Company, this ridiculous sort of Regret carry'd so far, that the Tragedian has thought himself injur'd, when the *Comedian* pretended to wear a fine Coat! I remember *Powel*, upon surveying my first Dress, in the *Relapse*, was out of all temper, and reproach'd our Master in very rude Terms, that he had not so good a Suit to play *Caesar Borgia*[3] in! tho' he knew, at the same time, my Lord *Foppington* fill'd the House, when his bouncing *Borgia* would do little more than pay Fiddles, and Candles to it: And though a Character of Vanity, might be suppos'd more expensive in Dress, than possibly one of Ambition; yet the high Heart of this heroical Actor could not bear, that a

Comedian should ever pretend to be as well dress'd as himself. Thus again on the contrary, when *Betterton* propos'd to set off a Tragedy, the Comedians were sure to murmur at the Charge of it: And the late Reputation which *Dogget* had acquir'd from acting his *Ben*, in *Love* for *Love*, made him a more declar'd Male-content on such Occasions; he over-valu'd Comedy for its being nearer to Nature, than Tragedy; which is allow'd to say many fine things, that Nature never spoke, in the same Words; and supposing his Opinion were just, yet he should have consider'd, that the Publick had a Taste, as well as himself; which, in Policy, he ought to have comply'd with. *Dogget* however could not, with Patience, look upon the costly Trains and Plumes of Tragedy, in which knowing himself to be useless, he thought were all a vain Extravagance: And when he found his Singularity could no longer oppose that Expence, he so obstinately adhered to his own Opinion, that he left the Society of his old Friends, and came over to us at the *Theatre-Royal:* And yet this Actor always set up for a Theatrical Patriot. This happen'd in the Winter following the first Division of the (only) Company. He came time enough to the *Theatre-Royal*, to act the Part of *Lory*, in the *Relapse*, an arch Valet, quite after the *French* cast, pert, and familiar. But it suited so ill with *Dogget*'s dry, and closely-natural manner of acting, that upon the second Day he desir'd it might be dispos'd of to another; which the Author complying with, gave it to *Penkethman;* who though, in other Lights, much his Inferior, yet this Part he seem'd better to become. *Dogget* was so immoveable in his Opinion of whatever he thought was right, or wrong, that he could never be easy, under any kind of Theatrical Government; and was generally so warm, in pursuit of his Interest, that he often out-ran it; I remember him three times, for some Years, unemploy'd in any Theatre,[4] from his not being able to bear, in common with others, the disagreeable Accidents, that in such Societies are unavoidable. But whatever Pretences he had form'd for this first deserting, from *Lincolns-Inn-Fields*, I always thought his best Reason for it, was, that he look'd upon it as a sinking Ship;[5] not only from the melancholy Abatement of their Profits, but likewise from the Neglect, and

Disorder in their Government: He plainly saw, that their extraordinary Success at first, had made them too confident of its Duration, and from thence had slacken'd their Industry--- by which he observ'd, at the same time, the old House, where there was scarce any other Merit than Industry, began to flourish. And indeed they seem'd not enough to consider, that the Appetite of the Publick, like that of a fine Gentleman, could only be kept warm, by Variety; that let their Merit be never so high, yet the Taste of a Town was not always constant, nor infallible: That it was dangerous to hold their Rivals in too much Contempt; for they found, that a young industrious Company were soon a Match, for the best Actors, when too securely negligent: And negligent they certainly were, and fondly fancy'd, that had each of their different Schemes been follow'd, their Audiences would not so suddenly have fallen off.

But alas! the Vanity of applauded Actors, when they are not crowded to, as they may have been, makes them naturally impute the Change to any Cause, rather than the true one, Satiety: They are mighty loath, to think a Town, once so fond of them, could ever be tired; and yet, at one time, or other, more or less, thin Houses have been the certain Fate of the most prosperous Actors, ever since I remember the Stage! But against this Evil, the provident Patentees had found out a Relief, which the new House were not yet Masters of, *viz.* Never to pay their People, when the Mony did not come in; nor then neither, but in such Proportions, as suited their Conveniency. I my self was one of the many, who for six acting Weeks together, never receiv'd one Day's Pay; and for some Years after, seldom had above half our nominal Sallaries: But to the best of my Memory, the Finances of the other House, held it not above one Season more, before they were reduc'd to the same Expedient of making the like scanty Payments.

Such was the Distress, and Fortune of both these Companies, since their Division, from the *Theatre-Royal;* either working at half Wages, or by the alternate Successes, intercepting the Bread from one another's Mouths; irreconcileable Enemies, yet without Hope of Relief, from a Victory on either side; sometimes both Parties reduc'd, and yet each supporting their Spirits, by seeing the other under the same Calamity.

During this State of the Stage, it was, that the lowest Expedient was made use of, to ingratiate our Company, in the Publick Favour: Our Master, who had some time practic'd the Law, and therefore lov'd a Storm, better than fair Weather (for it was his own Conduct chiefly, that had brought the Patent into these Dangers) took nothing so much to Heart, as that Partiality, wherewith he imagin'd the People of Quality had preferr'd the Actors of the other House, to those of his own: To ballance this Misfortune, he was resolv'd, at least, to be well with their Domesticks, and therefore cunningly open'd the upper Gallery to them *gratis:* For before this time no Footman[6] was ever admitted, or had presum'd to come into it, till after the fourth Act was ended: This additional Privilege (the greatest Plague that ever Playhouse had to complain of) he conceiv'd would not only incline them, to give us a good Word, in the respective Families they belong'd to, but would naturally incite them, to come all Hands aloft, in the Crack of our Applauses: And indeed it so far succeeded, that it often thunder'd from the full Gallery above, while our thin Pit, and Boxes below, were in the utmost Serenity. this riotous Privilege, so craftily given, and which from Custom, was at last ripen'd into Right, became the most disgraceful Nusance, that ever depreciated the Theatre. How often have the most polite Audiences, in the most affecting Scenes of the best Plays, been distrub'd and insulted, by the Noise and Clamour of these savage Spectators? From the same narrow way of thinking too, were so many ordinary People, and unlick'd Cubs of Condition, admitted behind our Scenes, for Money, and sometimes without it: the Plagues, and Inconveniences of which Custom, we found so intollerable, when we afterwards had the Stage in our Hands, that at the Hazard of our Lives, we were forc'd to get rid of them; our only Expedient was, by refusing Money from all Persons, without distinction, at the Stage Door; by this means we preserv'd to our selves the Right and Liberty of chusing our own Company there: And by a strict Observance of this Order, we brought what had been before debas'd into all the Licenses of a Lobby, into the Decencies of a Drawing-Room.

About the distressful Time I was speaking of, in the Year 1696,[7] *Wilks*, who now had been five Years in great Esteem on the *Dublin* Theatre, return'd to that of *Drury-Lane;* in which last he had first set out, and had continued to act some small Parts, for one Winter only. The considerable Figure which he so lately made upon the Stage in *London*, makes me imagine that a particular Account of his first commencing Actor may not be unacceptable, to the Curious; I shall, therefore, give it them, as I had it, from his own Mouth.

In King *James*'s Reign he had some time employ'd in the Secretary's Office in *Ireland* (his native Country) and remain'd in it, till after the Battle of the *Boyn*, which completed the Revolution. Upon that happy, and unexpected Deliverance, the People of *Dublin*, among the various Expressions of their Joy, had a Mind to have a Play; but the Actors being dispers'd, during the War, some private Persons agreed, in the best manner they were able, to give one, to the Publick, *gratis*, at the *Theatre*. The Play was *Othello*, in which *Wilks* acted the *Moor;* and the Applause he receiv'd in it, warm'd him to so strong an Inclination for the Stage, that he immediately prefer'd it to all his other Views in Life: For he quitted his Post, and with the first fair Occasion came over, to try his Fortune, in the (then only) Company of Actors in *London*. The Person, who supply'd his Post, in *Dublin*, he told me, rais'd to himself, from thence, a Fortune of fifty thousand Pounds. Here you have a much stronger Instance of an extravagant Passion for the Stage, than that, which I have elsewhere shewn in my self; I only quitted my *Hopes* of being preferr'd to the like Post, for it; but *Wilks* quitted his actual *Possession*, for the imaginary Happiness, which the Life of an Actor presented to him. And, though possibly, we might both have better'd our Fortunes, in a more honourable Station, yet whether better Fortunes might have equally gratify'd our Vanity (the universal Passion of Mankind) may admit of a Question.

Upon his being formerly receiv'd into the *Theatre-Royal* (which was in the Winter after I had been initiated) his Station there was much upon the same Class, with my own; our Parts were generally of an equal Insignificancy, not of consequence enough to give either a Preference: But *Wilks* being more impatient of his low Condition, than I was, (and, indeed, the Company was then so well stock'd with good Actors, that there was very little hope of getting forward) laid hold of a more expeditious way for his Advancement, and return'd agen to *Dublin*, with Mr. *Ashbury*, the Patentee of that Theatre, to act in his new Company there: There went with him, at the same time, Mrs. *Butler*, whose Character I have already given, and *Estcourt*, who had not appear'd upon any Stage, and was yet only known as an excellent Mimick: *Wilks* having no Competitor in *Dublin*, was immediately preferr'd to whatever Parts his Inclination led him, and his early Reputation on that Stage, as soon rais'd, in him, an Ambition to shew himself on a better. And I have heard him say (in Raillery of the Vanity, which young Actors are liable to) that when the News of *Monfort*'s Death came to *Ireland*, he from that time thought his Fortune was made, and took a Resolution to return a second time to *England*, with the first Opportunity; but as his Engagements to the Stage, where he was, were too strong to be suddenly broke from, he return'd not to the *Theatre-Royal*, 'till the Year 1696.

Upon his first Arrival, *Powel*, who was now in possession of all the chief Parts of *Monfort*, and the only actor that stood in *Wilks*'s way; in seeming Civility, offer'd him his choice of whatever he thought fit, to make his first Appearance in; tho', in reality, the Favour was intended to hurt him. But *Wilks* rightly judg'd it more modest, to accept only a Part of *Powel*'s, and which *Monfort* had never acted, that of *Palamede* in *Dryden*'s *Marriage Alamode*. Here too, he had the Advantage of having the Ball play'd into his Hand, by the inimitable Mrs. *Monfort*, who was then his *Melantha* in the same Play: Whatever Fame *Wilks* had brought with him, from *Ireland*, he as yet appear'd but a very raw Actor, to what he was afterwards allow'd to be: His Faults however, I shall rather leave to the Judgments of those, who then may remember him, than to take upon me the disagreeable Office of being patricular upon them, farther than by saying, that in this Part of *Palamede*, he was short of *Powel*, and miss'd a good deal of the loose Humour of the Character, which the other more happily hit. But however, he was young, erect, of a pleasing Aspect, and, in the whole, gave the Town, and the Stage sufficient Hopes of him. I ought to make some Allowances too, for the Restraint he must naturally have been under, from his first Appearance upon a new Stage. But from that he soon recovered, and grew daily, more in Favour not only of the Town, but likewise of the Patentee, whom *Powel*, before *Wilks*'s Arrival, had treated, in almost what manner he pleas'd.

Upon this visible Success of *Wilks*, the pretended Contempt, which *Powel* had held him in, began to sour into an open Jealousy; he, now, plainly saw, he was a formidable Rival, and (which more hurt him) saw too, that other People saw it; and therefore found it high time, to oppose, and be troublesome to him. But *Wilks* happening to be as jealous of his Fame, as the other, you may imagine such clashing Candidates could not be long without a Rupture: In short, a Challenge, I very well remember, came from *Powel*, when he was hotheaded; but the next Morning he was cool enough, to let it end, in favour of *Wilks*. Yet however the Magnanimity, on either Part, might subside, the Animosity was as deep in the Heart, as ever, tho' it was not afterwards so openly avow'd: For when *Powel* found that intimidating would not carry his Point; but that *Wilks*, when provok'd, would really give Battle, he (*Powel*) grew so out of Humour, that he cock'd his Hat, and in his Passion walk'd off, to the Service of the Company, in *Lincoln's-Inn Fields*. But there, finding more Competitors, and that he made a worse Figure among them, than in the Company he came from, he staid but one Winter with them, before he return'd to his old Quarters, in *Drury-Lane;* where, after these unsuccessful Pushes of his Ambition, he, at last became a Matyr to Negligence, and quietly submitted to the Advantages, and Superiority, which (during his his late Desertion) *Wilks* had more easily got over him.

However trifling these Theatrical Anecdotes may seem, to a sensible Reader, yet, as the different Conduct of these rival Actors may be of use, to others of the same Profession, and from thence may contribute to the Pleasure of the Publick; let that be my Excuse, for pursuing them. I must, therefore, let it be known, that though, in Voice, and Ear, Nature had been more kind to *Powel*, yet he so often lost the Value of them, by an unheedful Confidence, that the constant wakeful Care, and Decency, of *Wilks*, left the other far behind, in the publick Esteem, and Approbation. Nor was his Memory less tenacious than that of *Wilks;* but *Powel* put too much Trust in it, and idly deferr'd the Studying of his Parts, as School-boys do their Exercise, to the last Day; which commonly brings them out proportionably defective. But *Wilks* never lost an Hour of precious Time, and was, in all his Parts, perfect, to such an Exactitude, that I question, if in forty Years, he ever five times chang'd or misplac'd an Article, in any one of them. To be Master of this uncommon Diligence, is adding, to the Gift of Nature, all that is in an Actor's Power; and this Duty of Studying perfect, whatever Actor is remiss in, he will proportionably find, that Nature may have been kind to him, in vain: For though *Powel* had an Assurance, that cover'd this Neglect much better, than a Man of more Modesty might have done; yet with all his Intrepidity, very often the Diffidence, and Concern for what he was to *say*, made him lose the Look of what he was to *be:* While, therefore, *Powel* presided, his idle Example made this Fault so common to others, that I cannot but confess, in the general Infection, I had my Share of it; nor was my too critical Excuse for it, a good one, *viz.* That scarce one Part, in five, that fell to my Lot, was worth the Labour. But to shew Respect to an Audience, is worth the best Actor's Labour, and, his Business considered, he must be a very impudent one, that comes before them, with a conscious Negligence of what he is about. But *Wilks* was never known, to make any of these venial Distinctions; nor however barren his Part might be, could bear even the Self-Reproach of favouring his Memory: And I have been astonished, to see him swallow a Volume of Froth, and Insipidity, in a new Play, that we were sure could not live above three Days, tho' favoured, and recommended to the Stage, by some good Person of Quality. Upon such Occasions, in compassion to his fruitless Toil, and Labour, I have sometimes cry'd out with *Cato* ---- *Painful Praeemi-*

nence![8] So insupportable, in my Sense, was the Task, when the bare Praise, of not having been negligent, was sure to be the only Reward of it. But so indefatigable was the Diligence of *Wilks*, that he seem'd to love it, as a good Man does Virtue, for its own sake; of which the following Instance will give you an extraordinary Proof.

In some new Comedy, he happen'd to complain of a crabbed Speech in his Part, which, he said, gave him more trouble to study, than all the rest of it had done; upon which, he apply'd to the Author, either to soften, or shorten it. The Author, that he might make the matter quite easy to him, fairly cut it all out. But when he got home, from the Rehearsal, *Wilks* thought it such an Indignity to his Memory, that any thing should be thought too hard for it, that he actually made himself perfect in that Speech, though he knew it was never to be made use of. From this singular Act of Supererogation, you may judge, how indefatigable the Labour of his Memory must have been, when his Profit, and Honour, were more concern'd to make use of it.

But besides this indispensable Quality of Diligence, *Wilks* had the Advantage of a sober Character, in private Life, which *Powel* not having the least Regard to, labour'd under the unhappy Disfavour, not to say, Contempt, of the Publick, to whom his licentious Courses were no Secret: Even when he did well, that natural Prejudice pursu'd him; neither the Heroe, nor the Gentleman; the young *Ammon*, nor the *Dorimant*,[9] could conceal, from the conscious Spectator, the true *George Powel*. And this sort of Disesteem, or Favour, every Actor, will feel, and more, or less, have his Share of, as he *has*, or has *not*, a due Regard to his private Life, and Reputation. Nay, even false Reports shall affect him, and become the Cause, or Pretence at least, of undervaluing, or treating him injuriously. Let me give a known Instance of it, and, at the same time, a Justification of myself, from an Imputation, that was laid upon me, not many Years, before I quitted the Theatre, of which you will see the Consequence.[10]

After the vast Success of that new Species of Dramatick Poetry, the *Beggars Opera*:[11] The Year following, I was so stu-

pid, as to attempt something of the same Kind, upon a quite dif-
erent Foundation, that of recommending Virtue, and Innocence;
which I ignorantly thought, might not have a less Pretence to
Favour, than setting Greatness, and Authority, in a contemptible, and the most vulgar Vice, and Wickedness, in an amiable
Light. But behold how fondly I was mistaken! *Love in a Riddle*[12]
(for so my newfangled Performance was call'd) was as vilely
damn'd, and hooted at, as so vain a Presumption, in the idle Cause
of Virtue, could deserve. Yet this is not what I complain of; I
will allow my Poetry, to have been as much below the other, as
Taste, or Criticism, can sink it: I will grant likewise, that the applauded Author of the *Beggars Opera* (whom I knew to be an
honest good-natur'd Man, and who, when he had descended to
write more like one in the Cause of Virtue, had been as unfortunate, as others of that Class;) I will grant, I say, that in his *Beggars
Opera*, he had more skilfully gratify'd the Publick Taste, than
all the brightest Authors that ever writ before him; and I
have sometimes thought, from the Modesty of his Motto, *Nos'
haec novimus esse nihil*,[13] that he gave them that Performance, as
a Satyr upon the Depravity of their Judgment (as *Ben. Johnson*,
of old, was said to have given his *Bartholomew-Fair*, in Ridicule
of the vulgar Taste, which had dislik'd his *Sejanus*)[14] and that,
by artfully seducing them, to be the Champions of the Immoralities he himself detested, he should be amply reveng'd on their
former Severity, and Ignorance. This were indeed a Triumph!
which, even the Author of *Cato*, might have envy'd! *Cato*,
'tis true, succeeded, but reach'd not, by full forty Days, the
Progresss, and Applauses, of the *Beggars Opera*. Will it, however, admit of a Question, which of the two Compositions a
good Writer, would rather wish to have been the Author of?
Yet, on the other side, must we not allow, that to have taken a
whole Nation, High, and Low, into a general Applause, has
shewn a Power in Poetry, which, tho' often attempted in the
same kind, none but this one Author, could ever yet arrive
at? By what Rule, then, are we to judge of our true National
Taste? But, to keep a little closer to my Point,

The same Author, the next Year, had, according to the Laws of

the Land, transported his Heroe to the *West-Indies*, in a Second
Part to the *Beggars* Opera;[15] but so it happen'd, to the Surprize
of the Publick, this Second Part was forbid to come upon the
Stage! Various were the Speculations, upon this Act of Power:
Some thought that the Author, others that the Town, was hardly
dealt with; a third sort, who perhaps had envy'd him the Success
of his First Part, affirm'd, when it was printed, that whatever the
Intention might be, the Fact was in his Favour, that he had been a
greater Gainer, by Subscriptions to his Copy, than he could have
been by a bare Theatrical Presentation. Whether any Part of
these Opinions were true, I am not concern'd to determine, or
consider. But how they affected me, I am going to tell you. Soon
after this Prohibition, my Performance was to come upon the
Stage, at a time, when many People were out of Humour, at the
late Disappointment, and seem'd willing to lay hold of any Pretence of making a Reprizal. Great Umbrage was taken, that I
was permitted, to have the whole Town to my self, by this absolute Forbiddance of what, they had more mind to have been
entertain'd with. And, some few Days before my Bawble was
acted, I was inform'd, that a strong Party would be made against
it: This Report I slighted, as not conceiving why it should be
true; and when I was afterwards told, what was the pretended
Provocation of this Party, I slighted it, still more, as having less
Reason to suppose, any Persons could believe me capable (had I
had the Power) of giving such a Provocation. The Report, it
seems, that had run against me, was this: That, to make way for
the Success of my own Play, I had privately found means, or
made Interest, that the Second Part of the *Beggars Opera*, might
be suppress'd. What an involuntary Compliment did the Report-
ers of this Falshood make me? to suppose me of Consideration
enough, to influence a great Officer of State, to gratify the Spleen,
or Envy, of a Comedian, so far, as to rob the Publick of an innocent Diversion (if it were such) that none, but that cunning
Comedian, might be suffered to give it them. This is so very gross
a Supposition, that it needs only its own senseless Face, to confound it; let that alone, then, be my Defence against it. But
against blind Malice, and staring Inhumanity, whatever is upon

the Stage, has no Defence! There, they knew, I stood helpless, and expos'd, to whatever they might please to load, or asperse me with. I had not considered, poor Devil! that, from the Security of a full Pit, Dunces, might be Criticks, Cowards valiant, and 'Prentices Gentlemen! Whether any such were concerne'd in the Murder of my Play, I am not certain; For I never endeavour'd, to discover any one of its Assassins; I cannot afford them a milder Name, from their unmannerly manner of destroying it. Had it been heard, they might have left me nothing to say to them: 'Tis true, it faintly held up its wounded Head, a second Day, and would have spoke for Mercy, but was not suffer'd. Not even the Presence of a Royal Heir apparent, could protect it. But then I was reduc'd to be serious with them; their Clamour, then, became an Insolence, which I thought it my Duty, by the Sacrifice of any Interest of my own, to put an end to. I therefore quitted the Actor, for the Author, and, stepping forward to the Pit, told them, *That since I found they were not inclin'd, that this Play should go forward, I gave them my Word, that after this Night, it should never be acted agen: But that, in the mean time, I hop'd, they would consider, in whose Presence they were, and for that Reason, at least, would suspend what further Marks of their Displeasure, they might imagine I had deserved.* At this there was a dead Silence; and, after some little Pause, a few civiliz'd Hands, signify'd their Approbation. When the Play went on, I observ'd about a Dozen Persons, of no extraordinary Appearance, sullenly walk'd out of the Pit. After which, every Scene of it, while uninterrupted, met with more Applause, than my best Hopes had expected. But it came too late: Peace to its *Manes!*[16] I had given my Word it should fall, and I kept it, by giving out another Play, for the next Day, though I knew the Boxes were all lett, for the same again. Such, then, was the Treatment I met with: How much of it, the Errors of the Play might deserve, I refer to the Judgment of those, who may have Curiosity, and idle Time enough to read it. But if I had no occasion to complain of the Reception it met with, from its *quieted* Audience, sure it can be no great Vanity, to impute its Disgraces chiefly, to that severe Resentment, which a groundless Report

of me had inflam'd: Yet those Disgraces have left me something
to boast of, an Honour preferable, even to the Applause of my
Enemies: A noble Lord came behind the Scenes, and told me,
from the Box, where he was in waiting, *That what I said, to quiet*
the Audience, was extremely well taken there; and that I had
been commended for it, in a very obliging manner. Now, though
this was the only Tumult, that I have known to have been so effectually appeas'd, these fifty Years, by any thing that could be
said to an Audience, in the same Humour, I will not take any
great Merit to myself upon it; because when, like me, you will
but humbly submit to their doing you all the Mischief they can,
they will, at any time, be satisfy'd.

I have mention'd this particular Fact, to inforce what I before
observ'd, That the private Character of an Actor, will always,
more or less, affect his Publick Performance. And if I suffer'd so
much, from the bare *Suspicion* of my having been guilty of a
base Action; what should not an Actor expect, that is hardy
enough, to think his whole private Character of no consequence?
I could offer many more, tho' less severe Instances, of the same
Nature. I have seen the most tender Sentiment of Love, in Tragedy, create Laughter, instead of Compassion, when it has been
applicable to the real Engagements of the Person, that utter'd it.
I have known good Parts thrown up, from an humble Consciousness, that something in them, might put an Audience in mind of
--- what was rather wish'd might be forgotten: Those remarkable Words of *Evadne*, in the *Maid's Tragedy* ------ *A Maiden-*
head, Amintor, *at my Years?* --- have sometimes been a much
stronger Jest, for being a true one. But these Reproaches, which,
in all Nations, the Theatre must have been us'd to, unless we
could suppose Actors something more, than Human Creatures,
void of Faults, or Frailties. 'Tis a Misfortune, at least, not limited
to the *English* Stage. I have seen the better-bred Audience, in
Paris, made merry, even with a modest Expression, when it has
come from the Mouth of an Actress, whose private Character it
seem'd not to belong to. The Apprehension of these kind of
Fleers,[16a] from the Witlings of a Pit, has been carry'd so far, in
our own Country that a late valuable Actress[17] (who was con-

scious her Beauty was not her greatest Merit) desired the Warmth
of some Lines might be abated, when they have made her too remarkably handsome: But in this Discretion she was alone, few
others were afraid of undeserving the finest things, that could be
said, to them. But to consider this Matter seriously, I cannot but
think, at a Play, a sensible Auditor would contribute all he could,
to his being well deceiv'd, and not suffer his Imagination, so far
to wander, from the well-acted Character before him, as to
gratify a frivolous Spleen, by Mocks, or personal Sneers, on the
Performer, at the Expence of his better Entertainment. But I
must now take up *Wilks*, and *Powel*, again, where I left them.

Though the Contention for Superiority, between them, seem'd
about this time, to end in favour of the former, yet the Distress
of the Patentee (in having his Servant his Master, as *Powel* had
lately been) was not much reliev'd by the Victory; he had only
chang'd the Man, but not the Malady: For *Wilks*, by being in
Possession of so many good Parts, fell into the common Error
of most Actors, that of over-rating their Merit, or never thinking
it is so thoroughly consider'd, as it ought to be; which generally
makes them proportionably troublesome to the Master; who,
they might consider, only pays them, to profit by them. The
Patentee therefore, found it as difficult to satisfy the continual
Demands of *Wilks*, as it was dangerous to refuse them; very few
were made, that were not granted, and as few were granted, as
were not grudg'd him: Not but our good Master, was as sly a
Tyrant, as ever was at the Head of a Theatre; for he gave the
Actors more Liberty, and fewer Days Pay, than any of his Predecessors: He could laugh with them over a Bottle, and bite
them,[18] in their Bargains: He kept them poor, that they might
not be able to rebel; and sometimes merry, that they might not
think of it: All their Articles of Agreement had a Clause in them,
that he was sure to creep out at, *viz.* Their respective Sallaries,
were to be paid, in such manner, and proportion, as others of
the same Company were paid; which in effect, made them all,
when he pleas'd, but limited Sharers of Loss, and himself sole
Proprietor of Profits; and this Loss, or Profit, they only had such
verbal Accounts of, as he thought proper to give them. 'Tis true,

he would sometimes advance them Money (but not more, than he knew at most could be due to them) upon their Bonds; upon which, whenever they were mutinous, he would threaten to sue them. This was the Net we danc'd in for several Years: But no Wonder we were Dupes, while our Master was a Lawyer. This Grievance, however, *Wilks* was resolv'd for himself, at least, to remedy at any rate; and grew daily more intractable, for every Day his Redress was delay'd. Here our Master found himself under a Difficulty, he knew not well how to get out of: For as he was a close subtle Man, he seldom made use of a Confident, in his Schemes of Government: But here the old Expedient of Delay, would stand him in no longer stead; *Wilks* must instantly be comply'd with, or *Powel* come again into Power! In a Word, he was push'd so home, that he was reduc'd even to take my Opinion into his Assistance: For he knew I was a Rival to neither of them; perhaps too, he had fancy'd, that from the Success of my first Play, I might know as much of the Stage, and what made an Actor valuable, as either of them: He saw too, that tho' they had each of them five good Parts to my one; yet the Applause which in my few, I had met with, was given me by better Judges, than, as yet, had approv'd of the best They had done. They generally measur'd the goodness of a Part, by the Quantity, or Length of it: I thought none bad for being short, that were closely-natural; nor any the better, for being long, without that valuable Quality. But, in this, I doubt, as to their Interest, they judg'd better, than my self; for I have generally observ'd, that those, who do a great deal not ill, have been preferr'd to those, who do but little, though never so masterly. And therefore I allow, that while there were so few good Parts, and as few good Judges of them, it ought to have been no Wonder to me, that, as an Actor, I was less valued, by the Master, or the common People, than either of them: All the Advantage I had of them, was, that by not being troublesome, I had more of our Master's personal Inclination, than any Actor of the male Sex;[19] and so much of it, that I was almost the only one, whom at that time, he us'd to take into his Parties of Pleasure; very often *tete à tete*, and sometimes, in a *Partie quarrèe*. These then were the Qualifications, however

good, or bad, to which may be imputed our Master's having
made Choice of me, to assist him, in the Difficulty, under which
he now labour'd. He was himself sometimes inclin'd to set up
Powel again, as a Check upon the over-bearing Temper of
Wilks: Tho' to say Truth, he lik'd neither of them; but was still
under a Necessity, that one of them should preside; tho' he scarce
knew which of the two Evils to chuse. This Question, when I
happen'd to be alone with him, was often debated in our Evening Conversation; nor indeed, did I find it an easy matter to
know which Party I ought to recommend to his Election. I
knew they were neither of them Well-wishers to me, as in common they were Enemies to most Actors, in proportion to the
Merit, that seem'd to be rising, in them. But as I had the Prosperity of the Stage more at Heart, than any other Consideration,
I could not be long undetermin'd, in my Opinion, and therefore
gave it to our Master, at once, in favour of *Wilks*. I, with all the
Force I could muster, insisted, "That if *Powel* were preferr'd,
the ill Example of his Negligence, and abandon'd Character
(whatever his Merit on the Stage might be) would reduce our
Company to Contempt, and Beggary; observing at the same
time, in how much better Order our Affairs went forward, since
Wilks came among us, of which I recounted several Instances,
that are not so necessary to tire my Reader with. All this, though
he allow'd to be true; yet *Powel*, he said, was a better Actor
than *Wilks*, when he minded his Business (that is to say, when he
was, what he seldom was, sober) But *Powel*, it seems, had a still
greater Merit to him, which was, (as he observ'd) that when
Affairs were in his Hands, he had kept the Actors quiet, without
one Day's Pay, for six Weeks together, and it was not every
body could do that; for you see, said he, *Wilks* will never be easy,
unless I give him his whole Pay, when others have it not, and
what an Injustice would that be to the rest, if I were to comply
with him? How do I know, but then they may be all, in a Mutiny and *mayhap* (that was his Expression) with *Powel* at the
Head of 'em?" By this Specimen of our Debate, it may be judg'd,
under how particular, and merry a Government, the Theatre
then labour'd. To conclude, this Matter ended in a Resolution, to

sign a new Agreement, with *Wilks*, which entitled him, to his full Pay of four Pounds a Week, without any conditional Deductions. How far soever my Advice might have contributed to our Master's settling his Affairs upon this Foot, I never durst make the least Merit of it to *Wilks*, well knowing that his great Heart would have taken it as a mortal Affront, had I (tho' never so distantly) hinted, that his Demands had needed any Assistance, but the Justice of them. From this Time, then, *Wilks* became first Minister, or Bustle-master-general of the Company.[20] He, now, seem'd to take new Delight, in keeping the Actors close to their Business; and got every Play reviv'd with Care, in which he had acted the chief Part, in *Dublin:* 'Tis true, this might be done with a particular View of setting off himself to advantage; but if, at the same time, it serv'd the Company, he ought not to want our Commendation: Now, tho' my own Conduct, neither had the Appearance of his Merit, nor the Reward that follow'd his Industry; I cannot help observing, that it shew'd me, to the best of my Power, a more cordial Common-wealth's Man: His first Views, in serving himself, made his Service to the whole but an incidental Merit; whereas, by my prosecuting the Means, to make him easy, in his Pay, unknown to him, or without asking any Favour for my self, at the same time, I gave a more unquestionable Proof of my preferring the Publick, to my private Interest: From the same Principle I never murmur'd at whatever little Parts fell to my Share, and tho' I knew it would not recommend me to the Favour of the common People, I often submitted to play wicked Characters, rather than they should be worse done by weaker Actors than my self: But perhaps, in all this Patience under my Situation, I supported my Spirits, by a conscious Vanity: For I fancy'd I had more Reason to value my self, upon being sometimes the Confident, and Companion of our Master, than *Wilks* had, in all the more publick Favours he had extorted from him. I imagin'd too, there was sometimes as much Skill to be shewn, in a short Part, as in the most voluminous, which he generally made choice of; that even the coxcombly Follies of a Sir *John Daw*, might as well distinguish the Capacity of an Actor, as all the dry Enterprizes, and busy Conduct of a *Truewit*.[21] Nor could I have any Reason to repine at the Superiority he enjoy'd, when I consider'd at how dear a Rate it was purchas'd, at the continual Expence of a restless Jealousy, and fretful Impatience ---- These were the Passions, that, in the height of his Successes, kept him lean to his last Hour, while what I wanted in Rank, or Glory, was amply made up to me, in Ease and Chearfulness. But let not this Observation either lessen his Merit, or lift up my own; since our different Tempers were not, in our Choice, but equally natural, to both of us. To be employ'd on the Stage was the Delight of his Life; to be justly excus'd from it, was the Joy of mine: I lov'd Ease, and he Pre-eminence: In that, he might be more commendable. Tho' he often disturb'd me, he seldom could do it, without more disordering himself: In our Disputes, his Warmth could less bear Truth, than I could support manifest Injuries: He would hazard our Undoing, to gratify his Passions, tho' otherwise an honest Man; and I rather chose to give up my Reason, or not see my Wrong, than ruin our Community by an equal Rashness. By this opposite Conduct, our Accounts at the End of our Labours, stood thus: While he liv'd, he was the elder Man, when he dy'd, he was not so old as I am: He never left the Stage, till he left the World: I never so well enjoy'd the World, as when I left the Stage: He dy'd in Possession of his Wishes; and I, by having had a less cholerick Ambition, am still tasting mine, in Health, and Liberty. But, as he in a great measure wore out the Organs of Life, in his incessant Labours, to gratify the Publick, the many whom he gave Pleasure to, will always owe his Memory a favourable Report--- Some Facts, that will vouch for the Truth of this Account, will be found in the Sequel of these Memoirs. If I have spoke with more Freedom of his quondam Competitor *Powel,* let my good Intentions to future Actors, in shewing what will so much concern them to avoid, be my Excuse for it: For though *Powel* had from Nature, much more than *Wilks;* in Voice, and Ear, in Elocution, in Tragedy, and Humour in Comedy, greatly the Advantage of him; yet, as I have observ'd, from the Neglect, and Abuse of those valuable Gifts, he suffer'd *Wilks,* to be of thrice the Service to our Society. Let me give another Instance of the Reward, and Favour, which in a Theatre, Diligence, and Sobriety seldom fail of: *Mills*[22] the elder grew into the Friendship of *Wilks*, with not a great deal more, than those useful Qualities to recommend him: He was an honest, quiet, careful Man, of as few Faults, as Excellencies, and *Wilks* rather chose him for his second, in many Plays, than an Actor of perhaps greater Skill, that was not so labouriously diligent. And from this constant Assiduity, *Mills* with making to himself a Friend in *Wilks*, was advanc'd to a larger Sallary, than any Man-Actor had enjoy'd, during my time, on the Stage. I have yet to offer a more happy Recommendation of Temperance, which a late celebrated Actor was warn'd into, by the misconduct of *Powel*. About the Year, that *Wilks* return'd from *Dublin*, *Booth*, who had commenc'd Actor, upon that Theatre, came over to the Company, in *Lincolns-Inn-Fields:*[23] He was, then, but an Under-graduate of the Buskin, and as he told me himself, had been for some time too frank a Lover of the Bottle; but having had the Happiness to observe, into what Contempt, and Distresses *Powel* had plung'd himself by the same Vice, he was so struck with the Terror of his Example, that he fix'd a Resolution (which from that time, to the end of his Days, he strictly observ'd) of utterly reforming it; an uncommon Act of Philosophy in a young Man! of which in his Fame, and Fortune, he afterwards enjoy'd the Reward and Benefit. These Observations I have not meerly thrown together as a Moralist, but to prove, that the briskest loose Liver, or intemperate Man (though Morality were out of the Question) can never arrive at the necessary Excellencies of a good, or useful Actor.

Though the Master of our Theatre had no Conception himself of Theatrical Merit, either in Authors, or Actors; yet his Judgment was govern'd by a saving Rule, in both: He look'd into his Receipts for the Value of a Play, and from common Fame he judg'd of his Actors. But by whatever Rule he was govern'd, while he had prudently reserv'd to himself a Power of not paying them more than their Merit could get, he could not be much deceiv'd by their being over, or under-valued. In a Word, he had, with great Skill, inverted the Constitution of the Stage, and quite chang'd the Channel of Profits arising from it: Formerly (when there was but one Company) the Proprietors punctually paid the Actors, their appointed Sallaries, and took to themselves only the clear Profits: But our wiser Proprietor, took first out of every Day's Receipts, Two Shillings in the Pound to himself; and left their Sallaries to be paid, only, as the less, or greater Deficiencies of Acting (according to his own Accounts) would permit. What seem'd most extraordinary in these Measures, was, that at the same time, he had persuaded us to be contented with our Condition, upon his assuring us, That as fast as Mony would come in, we should all be paid our Arrears: And, that we might not have it always in our Power to say he had never intended to keep his Word; I remember, in a few Years after this Time, he once paid us Nine Days, in one Week: This happen'd, when the *Funeral*, or *Grief Alamode*[2] was first acted, with more than expected Success. Whether this well-tim'd Bounty was only allow'd us, to save Appearances, I will not say; but if that was his real Motive for it, it was too costly a Frolick to be repeated. and was at least, the only Grimace of its Kind he vouchsafed us; we never having received one Day more of those Arrears in above Fifteen Years Service.

While the Actors were in this Condition, I think I may very well be excus'd, in my presuming to write Plays; which I was forc'd to do, for the Support of my increasing Family, my precarious Income, as an Actor, being then too scanty, to supply it, with even the Necessaries of Life.

It may be observable too, that my Muse, and my Spouse, were equally prolifick; that the one was seldom the Mother of a Child, but, in the same Year, the other made me the Father of a Play: I think we had about a Dozen of each sort between us; of both which Kinds, some dy'd in their Infancy, and near an equal number of each were alive, when I quitted the Theatre. But it is no wonder, when a Muse is only call'd upon, by Family-Duty, she should not always rejoice, in the Fruit of her Labour. To this Necessity of Writing, then, I attribute the Defects of my second Play, which coming out too hastily, the Year after my first, turn'd to very little Account. But having got as much, by my First, as I ought to have expected, from the Success of them Both, I had no great Reason to complain: Not but, I confess, so bad was my Second, that I do not chuse to tell you the Name of it;[3] and, that it might be peaceably forgotten, I have not given it a Place, in the Two Volumes of those I publish'd in *Quarto*, in the Year 1721. And whenever I took upon me, to make some dormant Play of an old Author, to the best of my Judgment, fitter for the Stage, it was, honestly, not to be idle, that set me to work; as a good Housewife will mend old Linnen, when she has not better Employment. But when I was more warmly engag'd, by a Subject entirely new, I only thought it a good Subject, when it seem'd worthy of an abler Pen, than my own, and might prove as useful to the Hearer, as profitable, to myself: Therefore, whatever any of my Productions, might want of Skill, Learning, Wit, or Humour; or however unqualify'd I might be, to instruct others, who so ill govern'd my self: Yet such Plays (entirely my own) were not wanting, at least, in what our most admired Writers seem'd to neglect, and without which, I cannot allow the most taking Play, to be intrinsically Good, or to be a Work, upon which a Man of Sense and Probity should value himself: I mean, when they do not, as well *prodesse*, as *delectare*, give Profit with Delight. The *Utile dulci*[4] was, of old, equally the Point; and has always been in my Aim, however wide of the Mark, I may have shot my Arrow. It has often given me Amazement, that our best Authors of that Time, could think the Wit, and Spirit of their Scenes, could be an Excuse for making the Looseness of them publick. The many Instances of their Talents so abus'd, are too glaring, to need a closer Comment, and are sometimes too gross to be recited. If then, to have avoided this Imputation, or rather to have had the Interest, and Honour of Virtue, always in view, can give Merit, to a Play; I am contented, that my Readers should think such Merit, the All, that mine have to boast of. Libertines, of mere Wit, and Pleasure, may laugh at these grave Laws, that would limit a lively Genius; but every sensible honest Man, conscious of their Truth, and Use, will give these Ralliers Smile for Smile, and shew a due Contempt, for their Merriment.

But while our Authors took these extraordinary Liberties with their Wit, I remember, the Ladies were then observ'd, to be decently afraid of venturing bare-fac'd to a new Comedy, 'till they had been assur'd they might do it, without the Risque of an Insult, to their Modesty; or, if their Curiosity were too strong, for their Patience, they took care, at least, to save Appearances, and rarely came upon the first Days of Acting, but in Masks (then daily worn, and admitted, in the Pit, the Side-Boxes, and Gallery) which Custom, however, had so many ill Consequences attending it, that it has been abolish'd these many Years.[5]

These Immoralities of the Stage, had, by an avow'd Indulgence, been creeping into it, ever since King *Charles* his Time: Nothing that was loose, could then be too low for it: The *London Cuckolds*,[6] the most rank Play that ever succeeded, was then in the highest Court-Favour. In this almost general Corruption, *Dryden*, whose Plays were more fam'd for their Wit, than their Chastity, led the way, which he fairly confesses, and endeavours to excuse in his Epilogue to the *Pilgrim*, reviv'd in 1700, for his

Benefit,[7] in his declining Age, and Fortune. The following Lines
of it, will make good my Observation.

> Perhaps the Parson[8] stretch'd a Point too far,
> When, with our Theatres, he wag'd a War.
> He tells you, that this very moral Age
> Receiv'd the first Infection from the Stage.
> But sure, a banish'd Court, with Lewdness fraught,
> The Seeds of open Vice returning brought.
> Thus lodg'd (as Vice by great Example thrives)
> It first debauch'd the Daughters, and the Wives.
> *London*, a fruitful Soil, yet never bore
> So plentiful a Crop of Horns before.
> The Poets, who must live by Courts, or starve,
> Were proud, so good a Government to serve;
> And mixing with Buffoons, and Pimps profane,
> Tainted the Stage, for some small Snip of Gain:
> For they, like Harlots under Bawds profest,
> Took all the' ungodly Pains, and got the least.
> Thus did the thriving Malady prevail,
> The Court, it's Head, the Poets but the Tail.
> The Sin was of our Native Growth, 'tis true,
> The Scandal of the Sin was wholly new.
> Misses there were but modestly conceal'd;
> *Whitehall* the naked *Venus* first reveal'd.
> Where standing, as at *Cyprus*, in her Shrine,
> The Strumpet was ador'd with Rites Divine, &c.

This Epilogue, and the Prologue, to the same Play, written by
Dryden, I spoke myself, which not being usually done by the
same Person, I have a mind, while I think of it, to let you know
on what Occasion they both fell to my Share, and how other
Actors were affected by it.

Sir *John Vanbrugh*, who had given some light Touches of his
Pen to the *Pilgrim*, to assist the Benefit-Day of *Dryden*, had the
Disposal of the Parts; and I being then, as an Actor, in some Favour with him, he read the Play first, with me alone, and was
pleas'd to offer me my choice of what I might like best for

myself, in it. But as the chief Characters were not (according to my Taste) the most shining, it was no great Self-denial in me, that I desired, he would first take care of those, who were more difficult to be pleas'd; I therefore only chose, for my self, two short incidental Parts, that of the *Stuttering Cook*, and the *Mad Englishman;* in which homely Characters, I saw more Matter for Delight, than those that might have a better Pretence to the Amiable: And when the Play came to be acted, I was not deceiv'd, in my Choice. Sir *John*, upon my being contented with so little a Share in the Entertainment, gave me the Epilogue to make up my Mess, which being written so much above the Strain of common Authors, I confess, I was not a little pleas'd with it. And *Dryden*, upon his hearing me repeat it, to him, made me a further Compliment of trusting me with the Prologue. This so particular Distinction, was so look'd upon, by the Actors, as something too extraordinary. But no one was so impatiently ruffled at it, as *Wilks*, who seldom chose soft Words, when he spoke of any thing he did not like. The most gentle thing he said of it was, That he did not understand such Treatment; that, for his part, he look'd upon it, as an Affront to all the rest of the Company, that there should be but One, out of the Whole, judg'd fit to speak either a Prologue, or an Epilogue. To quiet him, I offer'd to decline either in his Favour, or both, if it were equally easy to the Author: But he was too much concern'd, to accept of an Offer, that had been made to another, in preference to himself; and which he seem'd to think his best way of resenting, was to contemn. But from that time, however, he was resolv'd, to the best of his Power, never to let the first Offer of a Prologue escape him: Which little Ambition, sometimes, made him pay too dear, for his Success; the Flatness of the many miserable Prologues, that by this means fell to his Lot, seem'd wofully unequal, to the few good ones, he might have reason to triumph in.

I have given you this Fact, only as a Sample of those frequent Rubs, and Impediments I met with, when any Step was made to my being distinguish'd as an Actor; and from this Incident too, you may partly see what occasion'd so many Prologues, after the Death of *Betterton*, to fall into the Hands of one Speaker:

But it is not every Successor, to a vacant Post, that brings into it, the Talents equal to those of a Predecessor. To speak a good Prologue well, is, in my Opinion, one of the hardest Parts, and strongest Proofs of sound Elocution; of which, I confess, I never thought, that any of the several who attempted it, shew'd themselves, by far, equal Masters to *Betterton*. *Betterton*, in the Delivery of a good Prologue, had a natural Gravity, that gave Strength to good Sense; a temper'd Spirit, that gave Life to Wit; and a dry Reserve, in his Smile, that threw Ridicule into its brightest Colours; of these Qualities, in the speaking of a Prologue, *Booth* only had the first, but attain'd not to the other two: *Wilks* had Spirit, but gave too loose a Rein to it, and it was seldom he could speak a grave and weighty Verse, harmoniously: His Accents were frequently too sharp, and violent, which sometimes occasion'd his eagerly cutting off half the Sound of Syllables, that ought to have been gently melted into the Melody of Metre. In Verses of Humour too, he would sometimes carry the Mimickry farther than the Hint would bear, even to a trifling Light, as if himself were pleas'd to see it so glittering. In the Truth of this Criticism, I have been confirm'd by those, whose Judgment I dare more confidently rely on, than my own. *Wilks* had many Excellencies; but if we leave Prologue-speaking out of the Number, he will still have enough to have made him a valuable Actor. And I only make this Exception from them, to caution others from imitating, what, in his Time, they might have too implicitly admired. But I have a Word or two more to say concerning the Immoralities of the Stage. Our Theatrical Writers were not only accus'd of Immorality, but Prophaneness; many flagrant Instances of which were collected, and publish'd by a Non-juring Clergyman, *Jeremy Collier*, in his *View of the Stage*, &c. about the Year 1697.[9] However just his Charge against the Authors, that then wrote for it, might be, I cannot but think his Sentence, against the Stage itself, is unequal; Reformation, he thinks, too mild a Treatment for it, and is therefore for laying his Ax to the Root of it. If there were to be a Rule of Judgment, for Offenses of the same Nature, what might become of the Pulpit, where many a seditious and corrupted Teacher, has been

known, to cover the most pernicious Doctrine with the Mask of
Religion? This puts me in mind of what the noted *Jo. Hains*,[10]
the Comedian, a Fellow of a wicked Wit, said upon this Occasion; who being ask'd, What could transport Mr. *Collier* into so
blind a Zeal, for a general Suppression of the Stage, when only
some particular Authors had abus'd it; whereas the Stage, he
could not but know, was generally allow'd, when rightly conducted, to be a delightful Method of mending our Morals? For
that Reason, (*reply'd* Hains:) *Collier* is, by Profession, a Moral-
mender himself, and two of Trade, you know, can never agree.

The Authors of the *Old Batchelor*, and of the *Relapse*,[11] were
those, whom *Collier* most labour'd to convict of Immorality; to
which they severally publish'd their Reply. The first seem'd
too much hurt, to be able to defend himself; and the other felt
him so little, that his Wit only laugh'd at his Lashes.

My first Play, of the *Fool in Fashion*, too, being then in a
course of Success; perhaps for that Reason, only, this severe
Author thought himself oblig'd to attack it; in which, I hope,
he has shewn more Zeal, than Justice. His greatest Charge against
it is, That it sometimes uses the Word, *Faith!* as an Oath, in the
Dialogue: But if *Faith* may as well signify our given Word, or
Credit, as our religious Belief, why might not his Charity have
taken it, in the less criminal Sense? Nevertheless, Mr. *Collier*'s
Book, was, upon the whole, thought so laudable a Work, that
King *William*, soon after it was publish'd, granted him a *Nolo
prosequi*,[12] when he stood answerable to the Law, for his having
absolv'd two Criminals, just before they were executed for High
Treason.[13] And it must be farther granted, that his calling our
Dramatick Writers to this strict Account, had a very wholesom Effect, upon those, who writ after this Time. They were,
now, a great deal more upon their Guard; Indecencies were no
longer Wit; and, by degrees, the Fair Sex came again to fill the
Boxes, on the first Day of a new Comedy, without Fear or Censure. But the Master of the Revels,[14] who then, licens'd all the
Plays, for the Stage, assisted this Reformation, with a more zealous Severity, than ever. He would strike out whole Scenes of a
vicious, or immoral Character, tho' it were visibly shewn to be

reform'd, or punish'd. A severe Instance of this Kind falling upon my self, may be an Excuse for my relating it. When *Richard the Third* (as I alter'd it from *Shakepear*) came from his Hands, to the Stage, he expung'd the whole First Act, without sparing a Line of it.[15] This extraordinary Stroke of a *Sic volo*,[16] occasioned my applying to him, for the small Indulgence of a Speech, or two, that the other four Acts might limp on, with a little less Absurdity. No, he had not Leisure to consider what might be separately inoffensive. He had an Objection to the whole Act, and the Reason he gave for it was, that the Distresses of King *Henry the Sixth*, who is kill'd by *Richard* in the first Act, would put weak People too much in mind of King *James*, then living in *France;* a notable Proof of his Zeal for the Government! Those who have read, either the Play, or the History, I dare say, will think he strain'd hard for the Parallel. In a word, we were forc'd, for some few Years, to let the Play take its Fate, with only four Acts divided into five; by the Loss of so considerable a Limb, may one not modestly suppose, it was robb'd of, at least, a fifth part of that Favour, it afterwards met with? For tho' this first Act was at last recovered, and made the Play whole agen; yet the Relief came too late, to repay me for the Pains I had taken in it. Nor did I ever hear that this zealous Severity of the Master of the Revels, was afterwards thought justifiable. But my Good-fortune, in process of Time, gave me an Opportunity to talk with my Oppressor, in my Turn.

The Patent[17] granted by his late Majesty, King *George* I. to Sir *Richard Steele*, and his Assigns, of which I was one, made us sole Judges of what Plays might be proper for the Stage, without submitting them, to the Approbation, or License of any other particular Person. Notwithstanding which, the Master of the Revels demanded his Fee of Forty Shillings, upon our acting a new One, tho' we had spar'd him the Trouble of perusing it. This occasion'd my being deputed to him, to enquire into the Right of his Demand, and to make an amicable End of our Dispute. I confess, I did not dislike the Office; and told him, according to my Instructions, That I came not to defend, even our own Right, in prejudice to his; that if our Patent, had inadvertently superseded the Grant of any former Power, or Warrant, whereon he might ground his Pretensions, we would not insist upon our Broad Seal, but would readily answer his Demands upon sight of such his Warrant, any thing in our Patent to the contrary notwithstanding. This I had reason to think he could not do; and, when I found he made no direct Reply to my Question, I repeated it with greater Civilities, and offers of Compliance, 'till I was forc'd in the end to conclude, with telling him, That as his Pretensions were not back'd with any visible Instrument of Right, and as his strongest Plea was Custom, we could not so far extend our Complaisance, as to continue his Fees upon so slender a Claim to them: And from that Time, neither our Plays, or his Fees, gave either of us any farther trouble. In this Negotiation, I am the bolder to think Justice was on our Side, because the Law lately pass'd, by which the Power of Licensing Plays, &c. is given to a proper Person, is a strong Presumption, that no Law had ever given that Power to any such Person before.

My having mentioned this Law, which so immediately affected the Stage, inclines me to throw out a few Observations upon it: But I must first lead you gradually thro' the Facts, and natural Causes, that made such a Law necessary.

Although it had been taken for granted, from Time immemorial, that no Company of Comedians, could act Plays, &c. without the Royal License, or Protection of some legal Authority; a Theatre was, notwithstanding, erected in *Goodman's-Fields*, about seven Years ago,[18] where Plays, without any such License, were acted for some time, unmolested, and with Impunity. After a Year or two, this Playhouse was thought a Nusance too near the City: Upon which the Lord-Mayor, and Aldermen, petition'd the Crown to suppress it: What Steps were taken, in Favour of that Petition, I know not, but common Fame seem'd to allow from what had, or had not been done in it, that acting Plays in the said Theatre was not evidently unlawful. However, this Question of Acting without a License, a little time after, came to a nearer Decision in *Westminster-Hall;* the Occasion of bringing it thither was this: It happened that the Purchasers

of the Patent, to whom Mr. *Booth* and Myself had sold our
Shares, were at variance with the Comedians, that were then left
to their Government, and the Variance ended, in the chief of
those Comedians deserting, and setting up for themselves in the
little House in the *Hay-Market*, in 1733, by which Desertion the
Patentees were very much distressed, and considerable Losers.
Their Affairs being in this desparate Condition, they were advis'd, to put the Act of the Twelfth of Queen *Anne*, against
Vagabonds, in force, against these Deserters, then acting in the
Hay-Market without License. Accordingly, one of their chief
Performers[19] was taken from the Stage, by a Justice of Peace his
Warrant, and committed to *Bridewell* as one within the Penalty
of the said Act. When the Legality of this Commitment was
disputed in *Westminster-Hall*, by all I could observe, from the
learned Pleadings on both Sides (for I had the Curiosity to hear
them) it did not appear to me, that the Comedian, so committed, was within the Description of the said Act, he being a
House-keeper, and having a Vote for the *Westminster* Members of Parliament. He was discharged accordingly, and conducted through the Hall, with the Congratulations of the
Crowds that attended, and wish'd well to his Cause.

The Issue of this Trial threw me, at that time, into a very odd
Reflexion, viz. That if acting Plays, without License, did not
make the Performers Vagabonds, unless they wandered from
their Habitations so to do, how particular was the Case of Us
three late Menaging Actors, at the *Theatre-Royal*, who in
twenty Years before had paid, upon an Averidge, at least Twenty
Thousand Pounds, to be protected (as Actors) from a Law, that
has not since appeared to be against us. Now, whether we might
certainly have acted without any License at all, I shall not pretend to determine; but this I have, of my own Knowledge, to
say, That in Queen *Anne*'s Reign, the Stage was in such Confusion, and its Affairs in such Distress, that Sir *John Vanbrugh*,
and Mr. *Congreve*, after they had held it about one Year, threw
up the Menagement of it, as an unprofitable Post, after which,
a License for Acting was not thought worth any Gentleman's

asking for, and almost seem'd to go a begging, till some time after, by the Care, Application, and Industry of three Actors, it became so prosperous, and the Profits so considerable, that it created a new Place, and a *Sine-cure* of a Thousand Pounds a Year, which the Labour of those Actors constantly paid, to such Persons as had from time to time, Merit or Interest enough, to get their Names inserted as Fourth Menagers in a License with them, for acting Plays, *&c.* a Preferment, that many a Sir *Francis Wronghead*[20] would have jump'd at. But to go on with my Story. This Endeavour of the Patentees, to suppress the Comedians acting in the *Hay-Market*, proving ineffectual, and no Hopes of a Reunion then appearing, the Remains of the Company left in *Drury-Lane*, were reduced to a very Low Condition. At this time a third Purchaser, *Charles Fleetwood*, Esq; stept in; who judging the best Time to buy was, when the Stock was at the lowest Price, struck up a Bargain at once, for Five Parts in Six of the Patent; and, at the same time, gave the revolted Comedians their own Terms to return, and come under his Government in *Drury-Lane*, where they now continue to act, at very ample Sallaries, as I am informed, in 1738. But (as I have observ'd) the late Cause of the prosecuted Comedian having gone so strongly in his Favour, and the House in *Goodman's-Fields* too, continuing to act with as little Authority, unmolested; these so tollerated Companies gave Encouragement to a broken Wit,[21] to collect a fourth Company, who, for some time acted Plays in the *Hay-Market*, which House the united *Drury-Lane* Comedians had lately quitted: This enterprising Person, I say (whom I do not chuse to name, unless it could be to his Advantage, or that it were of Importance) had Sense enough to know, that the best Plays, with bad Actors, would turn but to a very poor Account; and therefore found it necessary to give the Publick some Pieces of an extraordinary Kind, the Poetry of which he conceiv'd ought to be so strong, that the greatest Dunce of an Actor could not spoil it: He knew too, that as he was in haste to get Mony, it would take up less Time to be intrepidly abusive, than decently entertaining; that, to draw the Mob after

him, he must rake the Channel, and pelt their Superiors; that, to
shew himself somebody, he must come up to *Juvenal*'s Advice,
and stand the Consequences:

> *Aude aliquid brevibus Gyaris, et carcere dignum*
> *Si vis esse aliquis* ----[22]	Juv. Sat. I.

Such then, was the mettlesome Modesty he set out with; upon
this Principle he produc'd several frank, and free Farces, that
seem'd to knock all Distinctions of Mankind on the Head: Religion, Laws, Government, Priests, Judges, and Ministers, were
all laid flat, at the Feet of this *Herculean* Satyrist! This *Drawcansir*[23] in Wit, that spared neither Friend nor Foe! who, to
make his Poetical Fame immortal, like another *Erostratus*,[24] set
Fire to his Stage, by writing up to an Act of Parliament to demolish it. I shall not give the particular Strokes of his Ingenuity a
Chance to be remembred, by reciting them; it may be enough to
say, in general Terms, they were so openly flagrant, that the
Wisdom of the Legislature thought it high time, to take a proper
Notice of them.

Having now shewn, by what means there came to be four
Theatres, besides a fifth for Operas, in *London*, all open at the
same time, and that while they were so numerous, it was evident some of them must have starv'd, unless they fed upon the
Trash and Filth of Buffoonery, and Licentiousness; I now come,
as I promis'd, to speak of that necessary Law, which has reduced
their Number, and prevents the Repetition of such Abuses, in
those that remain open, for the Publick Recreation.

When this Law was in Debate, a lively Spirit, and uncommon
Eloquence was employ'd against it.[25] It was urg'd, That *one* of
the greatest Goods we can enjoy, is *Liberty*. (This we may
grant to be an incontestable Truth, without its being the least
Objection to this Law.) It was said too, That to bring the Stage
under the Restraint of a Licenser, was leading the way to an Attack, upon the Liberty of the Press. This amounts but to a
Jealousy at best, which I hope, and believe all honest *Englishmen*
have as much Reason to think a groundless, as to fear, it is a just
Jealousy: For the Stage, and the Press, I shall endeavour to

shew, are very different Weapons to wound with. If a great Man could be no more injured, by being personally ridicul'd, or made contemptible, in a Play, than by the same Matter only printed, and read against him, in a Pamphlet, or the strongest Verse; then indeed the Stage, and the Press might pretend, to be upon an equal Foot of Liberty: But when the wide Difference between these two Liberties comes to be explain'd, and consider'd, I dare say we shall find the Injuries from one, capable of being ten times more severe, and formidable, than from the other: Let us see, at least, if the Case will not be vastly alter'd. Read what Mr. *Collier*, in his *Defence* of his *Short View of the Stage*, &c. Page 25, says to this Point; he sets this Difference, in a clear Light. These are his Words:

"The Satyr of a Comedian, and another Poet have a different effect upon Reputation: A Character of Disadvantage, upon the Stage, makes a stronger Impression, than elsewhere: Reading is but Hearing at secondhand; now Hearing, at best, is a more languid Conveyance, than Sight. For as *Horace* observes,

> *Segnius irritant animum, aemissa per aurem,*
> *Quam quae sunt oculis subjecta fidelibus.*[26]

The Eye is much more affecting, and strikes deeper into the Memory, than the Ear: Besides, upon the Stage, both the Senses are in Conjunction. The Life of the Actor fortifies the Object, and awakens the Mind to take hold of it--- Thus a dramatic Abuse is rivetted, in the Audience; a Jest is improv'd into Argument, and Rallying grows up into Reason: Thus a Character of Scandal becomes almost indelible; a Man goes for a Blockhead, upon *Content*, and he that is made a Fool in a Play, is often made one for his Life. 'Tis true, he passes for such only among the prejudic'd, and unthinking; but these are no inconsiderable Division of Mankind. For these Reasons, I humbly conceive, the Stage stands in need of a great deal of Discipline, and Restraint: To give them an unlimited Range, is in effect to make them Masters of all moral Distinctions, and to lay Honour and Religion, at their Mercy. To shew Greatness ridiculous, is the way to lose the Use, and abate the Value of the Quality. Things made

little in jest, will soon be so in earnest; for Laughing, and Esteem,
are seldom bestow'd on the same Object."

If this was Truth, and Reason (as sure it was) forty Years
ago; will it not carry the same Conviction with it to these Days,
when there came to be a much stronger Call for a Reformation
of the Stage, than when this Author wrote against it, or perhaps than was ever known, since the *English* Stage had a Being?
And now let us ask another Question! Does not the general
Opinion of Mankind suppose, that the Honour, and Reputation
of a Minister is, or ought to be, as dear to him, as his Life? Yet
when the Law, in Queen *Anne*'s Time, had made even an unsuccessful Attempt upon the Life of a Minister, capital, could any
Reason be found, that the Fame, and Honour of his Character
should not be under equal Protection? Was the Wound that
Guiscard gave to the late Lord *Oxford*,[27] when a Minister, a
greater Injury, than the Theatrical Insult which was offer'd to
a later Minister, in a more valuable Part, his Character? Was it
not as high time, then, to make this dangerous Weapon of mimical Insolence, and Defamation out of the Hands of a mad Poet,
as to wrest the Knife from the lifted Hand of a Murderer? And
is not that Law of a milder Nature, which *prevents* a Crime, than
that which *punishes* it, after it is committed? May not one think
it amazing, that the Liberty of defaming lawful Power and
Dignity, should have been so eloquently contended for? or especially that this Liberty ought to triumph in a Theatre, where
the most able, the most innocent, and most upright Person,
must himself be, while the Wound is given, defenceless? How
long must a Man so injur'd, lie bleeding, before the Pain and
Anguish of his Fame (if it suffers wrongfully) can be dispell'd? or say, he has deserv'd Reproof, and publick Accusa-
tion, yet the Weight and Greatness of his Office, never can
deserve it from a publick Stage, where the lowest Malice by
sawcy Parallels and abusive Inuendoes, may do every thing
but name him: But alas! Liberty is so tender, so chaste a Vir-
gin, that, it seems, not to suffer her to do irreparable Injuries,
with Impunity, is a Violation of her! It cannot sure be a
principle of Liberty, that would turn the Stage into a Court

of Enquiry, that would let the partial Applauses of a vulgar
Audience give Sentence upon the Conduct of Authority, and
put Impeachments into the Mouth of a *Harlequin?* Will not
every impartial Man think, that Malice, Envy, Faction, or Mis-
rule, might have too much Advantage over lawful Power, if the
Range of such a Stage-liberty were unlimited, and insisted on
to be enroll'd among the glorious Rights of an *English* Subject?

I remember much such another ancient Liberty, which many
of the good People of *England* were once extremely fond of;
I mean that of throwing Squibs, and Crackers, at all Spectators
without distinction, upon a Lord-Mayor's Day; but about forty
Years ago a certain Nobleman happening to have one of his
Eyes burnt out by this mischievous Merriment, it occasion'd a
penal Law, to prevent those Sorts of Jests, from being laugh'd
at for the future: Yet I have never heard, that the most zealous
Patriot ever thought such a Law was the least Restraint upon
our Liberty.

If I am ask'd, why I am so voluntary a Champion for the
Honour of this Law, that has limited the Number of Play-
Houses, and which now can no longer concern me, as a Professor
of the Stage? I reply, that it being a Law, so nearly relating to the
Theatre, it seems not at all foreign to my History, to have taken
notice of it; and as I have farther promis'd, to give the Publick a
true Portrait of my Mind, I ought fairly to let them see how far
I am, or am not a Blockhead, when I pretend to talk of serious
Matters, that may be judg'd so far above my Capacity: Nor will
it in the least discompose me, whether my Observations are contemn'd, or applauded. A Blockhead is not always an unhappy
Fellow, and if the World will not flatter us, we can flatter our
selves; perhaps too it will be as difficult to convince us, we are in
the wrong, as that you wiser Gentlemen are one Tittle the better
for your Knowledge. It is yet a Question, with me, whether we
weak Heads have not as much Pleasure too, in giving our shallow
Reason a little Exercise, as those clearer Brains have, that are
allow'd to dive into the deepest Doubts and Mysteries; to reflect,
or form a Judgment upon remarkable things *past*, is as delightful to me, as it is to the gravest Politician to penetrate into what

is *present*, or to enter, into Speculations upon what is, or is not likely to come. Why are Histories written, if all Men are not to judge of them? Therefore, if my Reader has no more to do, than I have, I have a Chance for his being as willing to have a little more upon the same Subject, as I am to give it him.

When direct Arguments against this Bill were found too weak, Recourse was had to dissuasive ones: It was said, that this Restraint upon the Stage, would not remedy the Evil complain'd of: That a Play refus'd to be licens'd, would still be printed, with double Advantage, when it should be insinuated, that it was refus'd, for some Strokes of Wit, &c. and would be more likely then, to have its Effect, among the People. However natural this Consequence may seem, I doubt it will be very difficult, to give a *printed* Satyr, or Libel, half the Force, or Credit of an *acted* one. The most artful, or notorious Lye, or strain'd Allusion that ever slander'd a great Man, may be read, by some People, with a Smile of Contempt, or at worst, it can impose but on one Person, at once: But when the Words of the same plausible Stuff, shall be repeated on a Theatre, the Wit of it among a Crowd of Hearers, is liable to be over-valu'd, and may unite, and warm a whole Body of the Malicious, or Ignorant, into a Plaudit; nay, the partial Claps of only *twenty* ill-minded Persons, among several hundreds of silent Hearers, shall, and often have been, mistaken for a general Approbation, and frequently draw into their Party the Indifferent, or Inapprehensive, who rather, than be thought not to understand the Conceit, will laugh, with the Laughers, and join in the Triumph! But alas! the *quiet* Reader of the same ingenious Matter, can only like for *himself*; and the Poison has a much slower Operation, upon the Body of a People, when it is so retail'd out, than when sold to a full Audience by wholesale. The *single* Reader too may happen to be a sensible, or unprejudic'd Person; and then the merry Dose meeting with the Antidote of a sound Judgment, perhaps may have no Operation at all: With such a one, the Wit of the most ingenious Satyr, will only, by its intrinsick Truth, or Value, gain upon his Approbation; or if it be worth an Answer, a printed Falshood, may possibly be confounded by printed Proofs against it.

But against Contempt, and Scandal heighten'd, and colour'd by
the Skill of an *Actor*, ludicrously infusing it into a Multitude,
there is no immediate Defence to be made, or equal Reparation to
be had for it; for it would be but a poor Satisfaction, at last, after
lying long patient, under the Injury, that Time only is to shew
(which would probably be the Case) that the Author of it was
a desparate Indigent, that did it for Bread. How much less dangerous, or offensive, then, is the *written*, than the *acted* Scandal?
The Impression the Comedian gives to it, is a kind of double
Stamp upon the Poet's Paper, that raises it to ten times the intrinsick Value. Might we not strengthen this Argument too, even
by the Eloquence, that seem'd to have oppos'd this Law? I will
say for my self, at least, that when I came to read the printed
Arguments against it, I could scarce believe they were the
same, that had amaz'd, and rais'd such Admiration, in me, when
they had the Advantage of a lively Elocution, and of that Grace
and Spirit, which gave Strength and Lustre to them, in the Delivery!

Upon the whole; if the Stage ought ever to have been reform'd; if to place a Power *somewhere* of restraining its Immoralities, was not inconsistent, with the Liberties of a civiliz'd
People (neither of which, sure any moral Man of Sense can dispute) might it not have shewn a Spirit too poorly prejudic'd, to
have rejected so rational a Law, only because, the Honour, and
Office of a Minister might happen, in some small Measure, to
be protected by it.

But however little Weight there may be, in the Observations
I have made upon it, I shall for my own Part always think them
just; unless I should live to see (which I do not expect) some
future Set of upright Ministers use their utmost Endeavours to
repeal it.

And now, we have seen the Consequence of what many People
are apt to contend for, Variety of Play-houses! How was it possible so many could honestly subsist, on what was fit to be seen?
Their extraordinary Number, of Course, reduc'd them to live
upon the Gratification of such Hearers, as they knew would be
best pleas'd with publick Offence; and publick Offence, of what

kind soever, will always be a good Reason for making Laws, to restrain it.

To conclude, let us now consider this Law, in a quite different Light; let us leave the political Part of it quite out of the Question; what Advantage could either the Spectators of Plays, or the Masters of Play-houses have gain'd, by its having never been made? How could the same Stock of Plays supply four Theatres, which (without such additional Entertainments, as a Nation of common Sense ought to be asham'd of) could not well support two? Satiety must have been the natural Consequence, of the same Plays being twice as often repeated, as now they need be; and Satiety puts an end to all Tastes, that the Mind of Man can delight in. Had therefore, this Law been made seven Years ago, I should not have parted with my Share in the Patent, under a thousand Pounds more, than I receiv'd for it---[28] So that as far as I am able to judge, both the Publick, as Spectators, and the Patentees, as Undertakers, are, or might be, in a way of being better entertain'd, and more considerable Gainers by it.

I now return to the State of the Stage, where I left it, about the Year 1697, from whence this Pursuit of its Immoralities, has led me farther, than I first design'd to have follow'd it.

I now begin to doubt, that the *Gayetè du Coeur*, in which I first undertook this Work, may have drawn me, into a more laborious Amusement, than I shall know how to away with: For though I cannot say, I have yet jaded my Vanity, it is not impossible but, by this time, the most candid of my Readers may want a little Breath; especially, when they consider, that all this Load, I have heap'd upon their Patience, contains but seven Years of the forty three I pass'd upon the Stage; the History of which Period I have enjoyn'd my self to transmit to the Judgment (or Oblivion) of Posterity. However, even my Dulness will find somebody to do it right; if my Reader is an ill-natur'd one, he will be as much pleas'd to find me a Dunce in my old Age, as possibly he may have been, to prove me a brisk Blockhead, in my Youth: But if he has no Gall to gratify, and would (for his simple Amusement) as well know, how the Play-houses went on some forty Years ago, as how they do now, I will honestly tell him the rest of my Story, as well as I can. Lest therefore, the frequent Digressions, that have broke in, upon it, may have entangled his Memory, I must beg leave, just to throw together the Heads of what I have already given him, that he may again recover the Clue of my Discourse.

Let him, then, remember, from the Year 1660 to 1684,[2] the various Fortune of the (then) King's, and Duke's, two famous Companies; their being reduc'd to one united; the distinct Characters I have given of thirteen Actors, which in the Year 1690 were the most famous, then, remaining of them; the Cause of their being again divided in 1695, and the Consequences of that Division, 'till 1697; from whence I shall lead them to our Second Union in ---- Hold! let me see ---- ay, it was in that memorable

Year, when the two Kingdoms of *England* and *Scotland* were made one. And I remember a Particular, that confirms me I am right in my Chronology; for the Play of *Hamlet* being acted soon after, *Estcourt*, who then took upon him to say any thing, added a fourth Line to *Shakespear*'s Prologue to the Play, in that Play, which originally consisted but of three, but *Estcourt* made it run thus:

> For Us, and for our Tragedy,
> Thus stooping to your Clemency,
> [*This being a Year of Unity*,]
> We beg your Hearing patiently.

This new Chronological Line coming unexpectedly upon the Audience, was receiv'd with Applause, tho' several grave Faces look'd a little out of Humour at it. However, by this Fact, it is plain our Theatrical Union happen'd in 1708.[3] But to speak of it, in its Place, I must go a little back again.

From 1697, to this Union, both Companies went on, without any memorable Change in their Affairs, unless it were that *Betterton*'s People (however good in their Kind) were most of them too far advanc'd in Years to mend; and tho' we, in *Drury-Lane*, were too young to be excellent, we were not too old to be better. But what will not Satiety depreciate? For though I must own, and avow, that in our highest Prosperity, I always thought we were greatly their Inferiors; yet, by our good Fortune of being seen in quite new Lights, which several new-written Plays had shewn us in, we now began to make a considerable Stand against them. One good new Play, to a rising Company, is of inconceivable Value. In *Oroonoko* (and why may I not name another, tho' it be my own?) in *Love's last Shift*, and in Sequel of it, the *Relapse;* several of our People shew'd themselves in a new Style of Acting,[4] in which Nature had not as yet been seen. I cannot here forget a Misfortune that befel our Society, about this time, by the Loss of a young Actor, *Hildebrand Horden*,[5] who was kill'd at the Bar of the *Rose-Tavern*, in a frivolous, rash, accidental Quarrel; for which a late Resident at *Venice*, Colonel *Burgess*, and several other Persons of Distinction, took their Trials, and were acquitted. This young Man had almost every natural Gift, that could promise an excellent Actor; he had besides, a good deal of Table-wit, and Humour, with a handsome Person, and was every Day rising into publick Favour. Before he was bury'd, it was observable, that two or three Days together, several of the Fair Sex, well dress'd, came in Masks (then frequently worn) and some in their own Coaches, to visit this Theatrical Heroe, in his Shrowd. He was the elder Son of Dr. *Horden*, Minister of *Twickenham*, in *Middlesex*. But this Misfortune was soon repair'd, by the Return of *Wilks*, from *Dublin* (who upon this young Man's Death, was sent for over) and liv'd long enough among us to enjoy that Approbation, from which the other was so unhappily cut off. The Winter following, *Estcourt*, the famous Mimick, of whom I have already spoken, had the same Invitation from *Ireland*, where he had commenc'd Actor:[6] His first Part here, at the *Theatre-Royal*, was the *Spanish Friar*, in which, tho' he had remembred every Look, and Motion of the late *Tony Leigh*, so far as to put the Spectator very much in mind of him; yet it was visible through the whole, notwithstanding his Exactness in the Out-lines, the true Spirit, that was to fill up the Figure, was not the same, but unskilfully dawb'd on, like a Child's Painting upon the Face of a *Metzo-tinto:* It was too plain to the judicious, that the Conception was not his own, but imprinted in his Memory, by another, of whom he only presented a dead Likeness. But these were Defects, not so obvious to common Spectators; no wonder, therefore, if by his being much sought after, in private Companies, he met with a sort of Indulgence, not to say Partiality, for what he sometimes did upon the Stage.

In the Year 1699, Mrs. *Oldfield* was first taken into the House, where she remain'd about a Twelvemonth almost a Mute, and unheeded, 'till Sir *John Vanbrugh*, who first recommended her, gave her the Part of *Alinda*, in the *Pilgrim* revis'd. This gentle Character, happily became that want of Confidence, which is inseparable from young Beginners, who without it, seldom arrive to any Excellence: Notwithstanding, I own I was, then, so far deceiv'd in my Opinion of her, that I thought, she had little more than her Person, that appear'd necessary to the forming a good Actress; for she set out with so extraordinary a Diffidence, that it kept her too despondingly down, to a formal, plain (not to say) flat manner of speaking. Nor could the silver Tone of her Voice, 'till after some time, incline my Ear to any Hope, in her favour. But Publick Approbation is the warm Weather of a Theatrical Plant, which will soon bring it forward, to whatever Perfection Nature has design'd it. However Mrs. *Oldfield* (perhaps for want of fresh Parts) seem'd to come but slowly forward, 'till the Year 1703. Our Company, that Summer, acted at the *Bath*, during the Residence of Queen *Anne* at that Place. At this time it happen'd, that Mrs. *Verbruggen*, by reason of her last Sickness (of which she some few Months after, dyd'd) was left in *London;* and though most of her Parts were, of course, to be dispos'd of, yet so earnest was the Female Scramble for them, that only one of them fell to the Share of Mrs. *Oldfield*, that of *Leonora*, in Sir *Courtly Nice;* a Character of good plain Sense, but not over elegantly written. It was in this Part Mrs. *Oldfield* surpris'd me into an Opinion of her having all the innate Powers of a good Actress, though they were yet, but in the Bloom of what they promis'd. Before she had acted this Part, I had so cold an Expectation from her Abilities, that she could scarce prevail with me, to rehearse with her the Scenes, she was chiefly concern'd in, with Sir *Courtly*, which I then acted. However, we ran them over, with a mutual Inadvertency of one another. I seem'd careless, as concluding, that any Assistance I could give her, would be to little, or no purpose; and she mutter'd out her Words in a sort of mifty manner, at my low Opinion of her. But when the Play came to be acted, she had a just Occasion to triumph over the Error of my Judgment, by the (almost) Amazement, that her unexpected Performance awak'd me to; so forward, and a sudden Step into Nature, I had never seen; and what made her Performance more valuable, was, that I knew it all proceeded from her own Understanding, untaught, and unassisted by any one more experienc'd Actor. Perhaps it may not be unacceptable, if I enlarge a little more upon the Theatrical Character of so memorable an Actress.

Though this Part of *Leonora*, in itself, was of so little value, that when she grew more into Esteem, it was one of the several she gave away, to inferior Actresses; yet it was the first (as I have observ'd) that corrected my Judgment of her, and confirm'd me, in a strong Belief, that she could not fail, in very little time, of being what she was afterwards allow'd to be, the foremost Ornament of our Theatre. Upon this unexpected Sally, then, of the Power, and Disposition, of so unforeseen an Actress, it was, that I again took up the two first Acts of the *Careless Husband*, which I had written the Summer before, and had thrown aside, in despair of having Justice done to the Character of Lady *Betty Modish*, by any one Woman then among us; Mrs. *Verbruggen* being now in a very declining state of Health, and Mrs. *Bracegirdle* out of my Reach, and engag'd in another Company: But, as I have said, Mrs. *Oldfield* having thrown out such new Proffers of a Genius, I was no longer at a loss for Support; my Doubts were dispell'd, and I had now a new Call to finish it: Accordingly, the *Careless Husband* took its Fate upon the Stage, the Winter following, in 1704.[7] Whatever favourable Reception, this Comedy has met with from the Publick; it would be unjust in me, not to place a large Share of it to the Account of Mrs. *Oldfield;* not only from the uncommon Excellence of her Action; but even from her personal manner of Conversing. There are many Sentiments in the Character of Lady *Betty Modish*, that I may almost say, were originally her own, or only dress'd with a little more Care, than when they negligently fell, from her lively Humour: Had her Birth plac'd her in a higher Rank of Life, she had certainly appear'd, in reality, what in this Play she only, excellently, acted, an agreeably gay Woman of Quality, a little too conscious of her natural Attractions. I have often seen her, in private Societies, where Women of the best Rank might have borrow'd some part of her Behaviour, without the least Diminution of their Sense, or Dignity. And this very Morning, where I am now writing at the *Bath*, *November* 11, 1738, the same Words were said of her, by a Lady of Condition, whose better Judgment of her Personal Merit, in that Light, has embolden'd me to repeat them. After her Success, in this Character of higher Life; all that Nature had given her of the Actress, seem'd to have risen to its full Perfection: But the Variety of her Power could not be known, 'till she was seen, in variety of Characters; which, as fast as they fell to her, she equally excell'd in. Authors had much more, from her Performance, than they had reason to hope for, from what they had written for her; and none had less than another, but as their Genius in the Parts they allotted her, was more or less elevated.

In the Wearing of her Person, she was particularly fortunate; her Figure was always improving, to her Thirty-sixth Year; but her Excellence in acting was never at a stand: And the last new Character she shone in (*Lady Townly*)[8] was a Proof that she was still able to do more, if more could have been done for *her*. She had one Mark of good Sense, rarely known, in any Actor of either Sex, but herself. I have observ'd several, with promising Dispositions, very desirous of Instruction at their first setting out; but no sooner had they found their least Account, in it, than they were, as desirous of being left to their own Capacity, which they, then, thought should be disgrac'd, by their seeming to want any farther Assistance. But this was not Mrs. *Oldfield*'s way of thinking; for to the last Year of her Life, she never undertook any Part she lik'd, without being importunately desirous of having all the Helps in it, that another could possibly give her. By knowing so much herself, she found how much more there was of Nature, yet needful to be known. Yet it was a hard matter to give her any Hint, that she was not able to take, or improve. With all this Merit, she was tractable, and less presuming, in her Station, than several, that had not half her Pretensions to be troublesome: But she lost nothing by her easy Conduct; she had every thing she ask'd, which she took care should always be reasonable, because she hated as much to be *grudg'd*, as *deny'd* a Civility. Upon her extraordinary Action in the *Provok'd Husband*, the Menagers made her a Present of Fifty Guineas more than her Agreement, which never was more than a Verbal one;

for they knew she was above deserting them, to engage upon
any other Stage, and she was conscious, they would never think
it their Interest, to give her cause of Complaint. In the last two
Months of her Illness, when she was no longer able to assist them,
she declin'd receiving her Sallary, tho' by her Agreement, she
was entitled to it. Upon the whole, she was, to the last Scene she
acted, the Delight of her Spectators: Why then may we not
close her Character, with the same Indulgence with which *Horace* speaks of a commendable Poem:

> *Ubi plura nitent --- non ego paucis
> Offendor maculis -----*[9]

> *Where in the whole, such various Beauties shine,*
> 'Twere idle, upon Errors, to refine.

What more might be said of her as an Actress, may be found in
the Preface to the *Provok'd Husband*,[10] to which I refer the
Reader.

   With the Acquisition, then, of so advanc'd a Comedian as
Mrs. *Oldfield*, and the Addition of one so much in Favour as
Wilks, and by the visible Improvement of our other Actors, as
Penkethman, Johnson, Bullock, and I think I may venture to
name myself in the Number (but, in what Rank, I leave to the
Judgment of those who have been my Spectators) the Reputation of our Company began to get ground; Mrs. *Oldfield*, and
Wilks, by their frequently playing against one another, in our
best Comedies, very happily supported that Humour, and Vivacity, which is so peculiar to our *English* Stage. The *French*, our
only modern Competitors, seldom give us their Lovers, in such
various Lights: In their Comedies (however lively a People
they are by nature) their Lovers are generally constant, simple
Sighers, both of a Mind, and equally distress'd, about the
Difficulties of their coming together; which naturally makes
their Conversation so serious, that they are seldom good Company to their Auditors: And tho' I allow them many other
Beauties, of which we are too negligent; yet our Variety
of Humour has Excellencies that all their valuable Observance

of Rules have never yet attain'd to. By these Advantages, then, we began to have an equal Share of the politer sort of Spectators, who, for several Years, could not allow our Company to stand in any comparison, with the other. But Theatrical Favour, like Publick Commerce, will sometimes deceive the best Judgments, by an unaccountable change of its Channel; the best Commodities are not always known to meet with the best Markets. To this Decline of the Old Company, many Accidents might contribute; as the too distant Situation of their Theatre; or their want of a better, for it was not, then, in the condition it now is; but small, and poorly fitted up, within the Walls of a Tennis *Quaree* Court, which is of the lesser sort. *Booth*, who was then a young Actor, among them, has often told me of the Difficulties *Betterton*, then labour'd under, and complain'd of: How impracticable he found it, to keep their Body to that common Order, which was necessary for their Support; of their relying too much upon their intrinsick Merit; and though but few of them were young, even when they first became their own Masters, yet they were all now, ten Years older, and consequently more liable to fall into an inactive Negligence, or were only separately diligent, for themselves, in the sole Regard of their Benefit-Plays; which several of their Principals knew, at worst, would raise them Contributions, that would more than tolerably subsist them, for the current Year. But as these were too precarious Expedients, to be always depended upon, and brought in nothing, to the general Support of the Numbers, who were at Sallaries under them; they were reduc'd to have recourse to foreign Novelties; *L'Abbeè*, *Balon*, and Mademoiselle *Subligny*, three of the, then, most famous Dancers of the *French* Opera, were, at several times, brought over at extraordinary Rates, to revive that sickly Appetite, which plain Sense, and Nature had satiated. But alas! there was no recovering to a sound Constitution, by those most costly Cordials; the Novelty of a Dance, was but of a short Duration, and perhaps hurtful, in its consequence; for it made a Play, without a Dance, less endur'd, than it had been before, when such Dancing was not to be had. But perhaps, their exhibiting these Novelties,

might be owing to the Success we had met with, in our more
barbarous introducing of *French* Mimicks, and Tumblers the
Year before; of which Mr. *Rowe*, thus complains in his Prologue
to one of his first Plays:

> *Must* Shakespear, Fletcher, *and laborious* Ben,
> *Be left for* Scaramouch, *and* Harlequin? [11]

While the Crowd, therefore, so fluctuated, from one House,
to another, as their Eyes were more, or less regaled, than their
Ears, it could not be a Question much in Debate, which had the
better Actors; the Merit of either, seem'd to be of little moment;
and the Complaint in the foregoing Lines, tho' it might be just,
for a time, could not be a just one for ever; because the best Play
that ever was writ, may tire by being too often repeated, a Misfortune naturally attending the Obligation, to play every Day;
not that whenever such Satiety commences, it will be any Proof
of the Play's being a bad one, or of its being ill acted. In a Word,
Satiety is, seldom, enough consider'd, by either Critics, Spectators, or Actors, as the true, not to say just, Cause of declining
Audiences, to the most rational Entertainments: And tho' I
cannot say, I never saw a good new Play, not attended with due
Encouragement, yet to keep a Theatre daily open, without sometimes giving the Publick a bad old one, is more than, I doubt,
the Wit of human Writers, or Excellence of Actors, will ever be
able to accomplish. And, as both Authors, and Comedians, may
have often succeeded, where a sound Judgement would have
condemn'd them, it might puzzle the nicest Critick living, to
prove in what sort of Excellence, the true Value of either consisted: For, if their Merit were to be measur'd by the full Houses,
they may have brought; if the Judgment of the Crowd were
infallible; I am afraid we shall be reduc'd to allow, that the *Beggars Opera* was the best-written Play, and Sir *Harry Wildair*[12]
(as *Wilks* play'd it) was the best acted Part, that ever our *English* Theatre had to boast of. That Critick indeed, must be rigid,
to a Folly, that would deny either of them, their due Praise,
when they severally drew such Numbers after them; all their
Hearers could not be mistaken; and yet, if they were all, in the

right, what sort of Fame will remain to those celebrated Authors,
and Actors, that had so long, and deservedly been admired,
before these were in Being. The only Distinction I shall make
between them is, That to write, or act, like the Authors, or
Actors, of the latter end of the last century, I am of Opinion,
will be found a far better Pretence to Success, than to imitate
these who have been so crowded to, in the beginning of this.
All I would infer from this Explanation, is, that though we had,
then, the better Audiences, and might have more of the young
World on our Side; yet this was no sure Proof, that the other
Company were not, in the Truth of Action, greatly our Superiors. These elder Actors, then besides the Disadvantages I
have mention'd, having only the fewer, true Judges to admire
them, naturally wanted the Support of the Crowd, whose Taste
was to be pleas'd at a cheaper Rate, and with coarser Fare. To
recover them therefore, to their due Estimation, a new Project
was form'd, to building them a stately Theatre, in the *Hay-
Market*, by Sir *John Vanbrugh*, for which he rais'd a Subscription of thirty Persons of Quality, at one hundred Pounds each,
in Consideration whereof every Subscriber, for his own Life,
was to be admitted, to whatever Entertainments should be publickly perform'd there, without farther Payment for his Entrance. Of this Theatre, I saw the first Stone laid, on which was
inscrib'd *The little Whig*, in Honour to a Lady of extraordinary Beauty, then the celebrated Toast, and Pride of that Party.

    In the Year 1706,[13] when this House was finish'd, *Betterton*,
and his Co-partners dissolv'd their own Agreement, and threw
themselves under the Direction of Sir *John Vanbrugh*, and Mr.
Congreve; imagining, perhaps, that the Conduct of two such
eminent Authors, might give a more prosperous Turn to their
Condition; that the Plays, it would, now, be their Interest, to
write for them, would soon recover the Town to a true Taste,
and be an Advantage, that no other Company could hope for;
that in the Interim till such Plays could be written, the Grandeur
of their House, as it was a new Spectacle, might allure the Crowd
to support them: But if these were their Views, we shall see,
that their Dependence upon them, was too sanguine. As to their

Prospect of new Plays, I doubt it was not enough consider'd, that good ones were Plants of a slow Growth; and though, Sir *John Vanbrugh* had a very quick Pen, yet Mr. *Congreve* was too judicious a Writer, to let any thing come hastily out of his Hands: As to their other Dependence, the House, they had not yet discover'd, that almost every proper Quality, and Convenience of a good Theatre had been sacrific'd, or neglected, to shew the Spectator a vast, triumphal Piece of Architecture! And that the best Play, for the Reasons I am going to offer, could not but be under greater Disadvantages, and be less capable of delighting the Auditor, here, than it could have been in the plain Theatre they came from. For what could their vast Columns, their guilded Cornices, their immoderate high Roofs avail, when scarce one Word in ten, could be distinctly heard in it? Nor had it, then, the Form, it now stands in, which Necessity, two or three Years after reduc'd it to: At the first opening it, the flat Cieling, that is now over the Orchestre, was then a Semi-oval Arch, that sprung fifteen Feet higher from above the Cornice: The Cieling over the Pit too, was still more rais'd, being one level Line from the highest back part of the upper Gallery, to the Front of the Stage: The Front-boxes were a continued Semicircle, to the bare Walls of the House on each Side: This extraordinary, and superfluous Space occasion'd such an Undulation, from the Voice of every Actor, that generally what they said sounded like the Gabbling of so many People, in the lofty Isles in a Cathedral--- The Tone of a Trumpet, or the Swell of an Eunuch's holding Note, 'tis true, might be sweeten'd by it; but the articulate Sounds of a speaking Voice were drown'd, by the hollow Reverberations of one Word upon another. To this Inconvenience, why may we not add that of its Situation; for at that time it had not the Advantage of almost a large City, which has since been built, in its Neighbourhood: Those costly Spaces of *Hanover, Grosvenor,* and *Cavendish* Squares, with the many, and great adjacent Streets about them, were then all but so many green Fields of Pasture, from whence they could draw little, or no Sustenance, unless it were that of a Milk-Diet. The City, the Inns of Court,

and the middle Part of the Town, which were the most constant
Support of a Theatre, and chiefly to be rely'd on, were now too
far, out of the Reach of an easy Walk; and Coach-hire is often
too hard a Tax, upon the Pit, and Gallery. But from the vast
Increase of the Buildings I have mention'd, the Situation of that
Theatre has since that Time receiv'd considerable Advantages;
a new World of People of Condition are nearer to it, than formerly, and I am of Opinion, that if the auditory Part were a little
more reduc'd to the Model of that in *Drury-Lane*, an excellent
Company of Actors would, now, find a better Account in it,
than in any other House is this populous City: Let me not be
mistaken, I say, an excellent Company, and such as might be able
to do Justice to the best of Plays, and throw out those latent
Beauties in them, which only excellent Actors can discover, and
give Life to. If such a Company were now there, they would
meet with a quite different Set of Auditors, than other Theatres
have lately been us'd to: Polite Hearers would be content with
polite Entertainments; and I remember the time, when Plays,
without the Aid of Farce, or Pantomine, were as decently attended as Opera's, or private Assemblies, where a noisy Sloven
would have past his time as uneasily, in a Front-box, as in a
Drawing-room; when a Hat upon a Man's Head there would
have been look'd upon, as a sure Mark of a Brute, or a Booby: But
of all this I have seen too, the Reverse, where in the Presence
of Ladies, at a Play, common Civility has been set at defiance,
and the Privilege of being a rude Clown, even to a Nusance, has,
in a manner been demanded, as one of the Rights of *English*
Liberty: Now, though I grant, that Liberty is so precious a
Jewel, that we ought not to suffer the least Ray of its Lustre,
to be diminish'd; yet methinks the Liberty of seeing a Play, in
quiet, has as laudable a Claim to Protection, as the Privilege of
not suffering you to do it, has to Impunity. But since we are
so happy, as not to have a certain Power among us, which, in
another Country is call'd the *Police*, let us rather bear this Insult,
than buy its Remedy at too dear a Rate; and let it be the Punish-
ment of such wrong-headed Savages, that they never will, or
can know the true Value of that Liberty, which they so stupidly

abuse: Such vulgar Minds possess their Liberty, as profligate Husbands do fine Wives, only to disgrace them. In a Word, when Liberty boils over, such is the Scum of it. But to our new erected Theatre.

Not long before this time, the *Italian* Opera began first to steal into *England;* but in as rude a Disguise, and unlike it self, as possible; in a lame, hobling Translation, into our own Language, with false Quantities, or metre out of Measure, to its original Notes, sung by our own unskilful Voices, with Graces misapply'd to almost every Sentiment, and with Action, lifeless and unmeaning, through every Character: The first *Italian* Performer, that made any distinguish'd Figure in it, was *Valentini*, a true sensible Singer, at that time, but of a Throat too weak, to sustain those melodious Warblings, for which the fairer Sex have since idoliz'd his Successors. However, this Defect was so well supply'd by his Action, that his Hearers bore with the Absurdity of his Singing his first Part of *Turnus* in *Camilla*, all in *Italian*, while every other Character was sung and recited to him in *English*. This I have mention'd to shew not only our Tramontane Taste, but that the crowded Audiences, which follow'd it to *Drury-Lane*, might be another Occasion of their growing thinner in *Lincolns-Inn-Fields*.

To strike in, therefore, with this prevailing Novelty, Sir *John Vanbrugh*, and Mr. *Congreve*, open'd their new *Hay-Market Theatre*, with a translated Opera, to *Italian* Musick, call'd the *Triumph of Love*, but this not having in it, the Charms of *Camilla*, either from the Inequality of the Musick, or Voices, had but a cold Reception, being perform'd but three Days, and those not crowded. Immediately, upon the Failure of this *Opera*, Sir *John Vanbrugh* produc'd his Comedy call'd the *Confederacy*,[14] taken (but greatly improv'd) from the *Bourgeois à la mode* of *Dancour:* Though the Fate of this Play was something better, yet I thought, it was not equal to its Merit: For it is written with an uncommon Vein of Wit and Humour; which confirms me, in my former Observation, that the difficulty of hearing distinctly in that, then wide Theatre, was no small Impediment to the Applause, that might have follow'd the same Actors in it, upon any other Stage; and indeed every Play acted there, before the House was alter'd, seem'd to suffer, from the same Inconvenience: In a Word, the Prospect of Profits, from this Theatre was so very barren, that Mr. *Congreve*, in a few Months gave up his Share, and Interest in the Government of it, wholly to Sir *John Vanbrugh*. But Sir *John* being sole Proprietor of the House, was at all Events, oblig'd to do his utmost to support it. As he had a happier Talent of throwing the *English* Spirit, into his Translation of *French* Plays, than any former Author, who had borrow'd from them, he, in the same Season, gave the Publick three more of that kind, call'd the *Cuckold in Conceit;* from the *Cocu imaginaire* of *Moliere; Squire Trelooby*, from his *Monsier de Pourceaugnac*, and the *Mistake*, from the *D'epit Amoureux* of the same Author.[15] Yet all these, however well executed, came to the Ear in the same undistinguish'd Utterance, by which almost all their Plays had equally suffer'd: For what few could plainly hear, it was not likely a great many could applaud.

It must farther be consider'd too, that this Company were, not now, what they had been, when they first revolted from the Patentees in *Drury-Lane*, and became their own Masters, in *Lincolns-Inn-Fields*. Several of them, excellent, in their different Talents, were now dead; as *Smith*, *Kynaston*, *Sandford*, and *Leigh:* Mrs. *Betterton*, and *Underhill* being, at this time, also superannuated Pensioners, whose Places were generally but ill supply'd: Nor could it be expected that *Betterton* himself, at past seventy, could retain his former Force, and Spirit; though he was yet far distant from any Competitor. Thus then were these Remains of the best Set of Actors, that I believe were ever known, at once, in *England*, by Time, Death, and the Satiety of their Hearers mould'ring to decay.

It was, now, the Town-talk, that nothing but a Union of the two Companies could recover the Stage, to its former Reputation, which Opinion was certainly true: One could have thought too, that the Patentee of *Drury-Lane* could not have fail'd to close with it, he being, then, on the prosperous Side of the Question, having no Relief to ask for himself, and little more to do in the matter, than to consider what he might safely grant: But it seems this was not his way of counting; he had other Persons, who had great Claims to Shares, in the Profits of this Stage, which Profits, by a Union, he foresaw would be too visible, to be doubted of, and might raise up a new Spirit, in those Adventurers, to revive their Suits at Law with him; for he had led them a Chace in Chancery several Years, and when they had driven him, into a Contempt of that Court, he con-jur'd up a Spirit, in the Shape of Six and eight Pence a-day, that constantly struck the Tip-staff blind, whenever he came near him: He knew the intrinsick Value of Delay, and was resolv'd to stick to it, as the surest way to give the Plantiffs enough on't. And by this Expedient our good Master had long walk'd about, at his Leisure, cool, and contented, as a Fox, when the Hounds were drawn off, and gone home from him. But whether I am right, or not, in my Conjectures, certain it is, that this close Master of *Drury-Lane*, had no Inclination to a Union, as will appear by the Sequel.

Sir *John Vanbrugh* knew too, that to make a Union worth his while, he must not seem too hasty for it; he therefore found himself under a Necessity, in the mean time of letting his whole Theatrical Farm to some industrious Tenant, that might put it into better Condition. This is that Crisis, as I observ'd, in the Eighth Chapter, when the Royal License, for acting Plays, &c. was judged of so little Value, as not to have one Suitor for it. At this time then, the Master of *Drury-Lane* happen'd to have a sort of primier Agent in his Stage-Affairs, that seem'd in Appear-ance as much to govern the Master, as the Master himself did to govern his Actors: But this Person was under no Stipulation, or Sallary, for the Service he render'd; but had gradually wrought himself into the Master's extraordinary Confidence, and Trust, from an habitual Intimacy, a cheerful Humour, and an inde-fatigable Zeal for his Interest. If I should farther say, that this Person has been well known in almost every Metropolis, in *Eu-rope;* that few private Men have, with so little Reproach, run through more various Turns of Fortune; that, on the wrong side of Three-score, he has yet the open Spirit of a hale young

Fellow of five and twenty; that though he still chuses to speak
what he thinks, to his best Friends, with an undisguis'd Freedom,
he is, notwithstanding acceptable to many Persons of the first
Rank, and Condition; that any one of them (provided he likes
them) may now send him, for their Service, to *Constantinople*, at
half a Day's Warning; that Time has, not yet, been able to make
a visible Change, in any Part of him, but the Colour of his Hair,
from a fierce coal-black, to that of a milder milk-white: When
I have taken this Liberty with him, methinks it cannot be taking
a much greater, if I at once should tell you, that this Person was
Mr. *Owen Swiney*,[16] and that it was to him Sir *John Vanbrugh*,
in this Exigence of his Theatrical Affairs, made an Offer of his
Actors, under such Agreements of Sallary, as might be made
with them; and of his House, Cloaths, and Scenes, with the
Queen's License to employ them, upon Payment of only the
casual Rent of five Pounds, upon every acting Day, and not
to exceed 700£. in the Year. Of this Proposal, Mr. *Swiney* desir'd a Day, or two to consider; for however he might like
it, he would not meddle in any sort, without the Consent,
and Approbation of his Friend, and Patron, the Master of *Drury-
Lane*. Having given the Reasons why this Patentee was averse
to a Union, it may now seem less a Wonder, why he immediately consented that *Swiney* should take the *Hay-Market* House,
&c. and continue that Company to act against him; but the
real Truth was, that he had a mind both Companies should
be clandestinely under one, and the same Interest; and yet in
so loose a manner, that he might declare his Verbal Agreement with *Swiney* good, or null, and void, as he might best
find his Account in either. What flatter'd him, that he had
this wholesome Project, and *Swiney* to execute it, both in his
Power, was, that at this time, *Swiney* happen'd to stand in
his Books, Debtor to Cash, upwards of Two Hundred Pounds:
But here, we shall find, he over-rated his Security. However,
Swiney as yet follow'd his Orders; he took the *Hay-Market*
Theatre, and had farther, the private Consent of the Patentee,
to take such of his Actors from *Drury-Lane*, as either from Inclination, or Discontent, might be willing to come over to him,

in the *Hay-Market*. The only one he made an Exception of, was myself: For tho' he chiefly depended upon his Singers, and Dancers, he said, it would be necessary to keep some one tolerable Actor with him, that might enable him to set those Machines a going. Under this Limitation, of not entertaining me, *Swiney* seem'd to acquiesce, 'till after he had open'd, with the so recruited Company, in the *Hay-Market:* The Actors that came to him from *Drury-Lane*, were *Wilks, Estcoart, Mills, Keen,*[17] *Johnson, Bullock,* Mrs. *Oldfield,* Mrs. *Rogers,* and some few others of less note: But I must here let you know, that this Project was form'd, and put in Execution, all in very few Days, in the Summer-Season, when no Theatre was open. To all which I was entirely a Stranger, being at this time at a Gentleman's House in *Gloucestershire,*[18] scribbling, if I mistake not, the *Wife's Resentment.*

The first Word I heard of this Transaction, was by a Letter from *Swiney,* inviting me to make One in the *Hay-Market* Company, whom he hop'd I could not but now think the stronger Party. But, I confess, I was not a little alarm'd, at this Revolution: For I consider'd, that I knew of no visible Fund to support these Actors, but their own Industry; that all his Recruits from *Drury-Lane* would want new Cloathing; and that the warmest Industry would be always labouring up Hill, under so necessary an Expence, so bad a Situation, and so inconvenient a Theatre. I was always of opinion too, that in changing Sides, in most Conditions, there generally were discovered more unforeseen Inconveniencies, than visible Advantages; and that at worst, there would always some sort of Merit remain with Fidelity, tho' unsuccessful. Upon these Considerations, I was only thankful for the Offers made me, from the *Hay-Market,* without accepting them; and soon after came to Town towards the usual time of their beginning to act, to offer my Service to our old Master. But I found our Company so thinn'd, that it was almost impracticable, to bring any one tolerable Play upon the Stage.[19] When I ask'd him, where were his Actors, and in what manner he intended to proceed? he reply'd, *Don't you trouble yourself, come along, and I'll shew you.* He then led me about all the By-places in the

House, and shew'd me fifty little Back-doors, dark Closets, and
narrow Passages, in Alterations and Contrivances of which kind
he had busied his Head, most part of the Vacation; for he was
scarce ever, without some notable Joyner, or a Bricklayer extraordinary, in pay, for twenty Years. And there are so many
odd obscure Places about a Theatre, that his Genius in Nook-
building was never out of Employment; nor could the most vain-
headed Author, be more deaf to an Interruption in reciting his
Works, than our wise Master was, while entertaining me with
the Improvements he had made in his invisible Architecture; all
which, without thinking any one Part of it necessary; tho' I
seem'd to approve, I could not help, now and then, breaking in,
upon his Delight, with the impertinent Question of--- *But, Master, where are your Actors?* But it seems I had taken a wrong
time for this sort of Enquiry; his Head was full of Matters of
more moment (and, as you find) I was to come another time for
an Answer: A very hopeful condition I found myself in, under
the Conduct of so profound a Vertuoso, and so considerate a
Master! But, to speak of him seriously, and to account for this
Disregard to his Actors, his Notion was, that Singing, and Dancing, or any sort of Exotick Entertainments, would make an ordinary Company of Actors too hard, for the best Set, who had
only plain Plays to subsist on. Now, tho' I am afraid too much
might be said, in favour of this Opinion, yet I thought he laid
more Stress upon that sort of Merit, than it would bear; as I
therefore found myself of so little Value with him, I could not
help setting a little more upon myself, and was resolv'd to come
to a short Explanation with him. I told him, I came to serve him,
at a time, when many of his best Actors had deserted him; that
he might now have the Refusal of me; but I could not afford to
carry the Compliment so far, as to lessen my Income by it; that I
therefore expected, either my casual Pay to be advanced, or
the Payment of my former Sallary made certain, for, as many
Days, as we had acted the Year before.--- No, he was not willing
to alter his former Method; but I might chuse whatever Parts
I had a mind to act, of theirs who had left him. When I found
him, as I thought, so insensible, or impregnable, I look'd gravely

LIFE OF COLLEY CIBBER

in his Face, and told him--- He knew upon what Terms, I was willing to serve him; and took my leave. By this time, the *Hay-Market* Company had begun acting, to Audiences something better than usual, and were all paid their full Sallaries, a Blessing they had not felt, in some Years, in either House before. Upon this Success, *Swiney* press'd the Patentee to execute the Articles they had as yet only verbally agreed on, which were in Substance, That *Swiney* should take the *Hay-Market* House in his own Name, and have what Actors he thought necessary from *Drury-Lane*, after all Payments punctually made, the Profits should be equally divided between these two Undertakers. But soft, and fair! Rashness was a Fault, that had never yet been imputed to the Patentee; certain Payments were Methods he had not of a long, long time been us'd to; that Point still wanted time for Consideration. But *Swiney* was as hasty, as the other was slow, and was resolv'd to know what he had to trust to, before they parted; and to keep him the closer, to his Bargain, he stood upon his Right of having *Me* added to that Company, if I was willing to come into it. But this was a Point as absolutely refus'd on one side, as insisted on, on the other. In this Contest, high Words were exchang'd on both sides, 'till, in the end, this their last private Meeting came to an open Rupture: But before it was publickly known, *Swiney*, by fairly letting me into the whole Transaction, took effectual means to secure me in his Interest. When the Mystery of the Patentee's Indifference to me was unfolded, and that his slighting me, was owing, to the Security he rely'd on, of *Swiney*'s not daring to engage me, I could have no further Debate with myself, which side of the Question I should adhere to. To conclude, I agreed, in two Words, to act with *Swiney*;[20] and from this time, every Change that happen'd in the Theatrical Government, was a nearer Step to that twenty Years of Prosperity, which Actors, under the Menagement of Actors, not long afterwards, enjoy'd. What was the immediate Consequence of this last Desertion from *Drury-Lane*, shall be the Subject of another Chapter.

Having shewn the particular Conduct of the Patentee, in refus-ing so fair an Opportunity of securing to himself both Companies, under his sole Power, and Interest; I shall now lead the Reader, after a short View of what pass'd in this new Establishment of the *Hay-Market* Theatre, to the Accidents, that the Year following, compell'd the same Patentee, to receive both Companies, united, into the *Drury-Lane* Theatre, notwithstanding his Disinclination to it.

It may, now, be imagin'd, that such a Detachment of Actors, from *Drury-Lane*, could not but give a new Spirit to those in the *Hay-Market;* not only by enabling them to act each others Plays to better Advantage; but by an emulous Industry, which had lain too long inactive among them, and without which they plainly saw, they could not be sure of Subsistance. Plays, by this means began to recover a good Share of their former Esteem, and Favour; and the Profits of them, in about a Month, enabled our new Menager to discharge his Debt (of something more than Two Hundred Pounds) to his old Friend, the Patentee; who had now left him, and his Troop, in trust, to fight their own Battles. The greatest Inconvenience they still labour'd under, was the immoderate Wideness of their House; in which, as I have observ'd, the Difficulty of Hearing, may be said to have bury'd half the Auditors Entertainment. This Defect seem'd evident, from the much better Reception several new Plays (first acted there) met with when they afterwards came to be play'd by the same Actors, in *Drury-Lane:* Of this Number were the *Stratagem*, and the *Wife's Resentment*; to which I may add, the *Double Gallant*. This last, was a Play made up of what little was tolerable, in two, or three others,[2] that had no Success, and were laid aside, as so much Poetical Lumber; but by collecting and adapting the best Parts of 'em all, into one Play, the *Double Gallant* has had a Place, every Winter, amongst the Publick Entertainments, these Thirty Years. As I was only the Compiler of this Piece, I did not publish it in my own Name;[3] but as my having but a Hand in it, could not be long a Secret, I have been often treated as a Plagiary on that Account: Not that I think I have any Right to complain, of whatever would detract from the Merit of that sort of Labour; yet, a Cobler may be allow'd to be useful, though he is not famous: And I hope a Man is not blameable for doing a little Good, tho' he cannot do as much as another? But so it is --- Twopenny Criticks must live, as well as Eighteenpenny Authors.

While the Stage was thus recovering its former Strength, a more honourable Mark of Favour was shewn to it, than it was ever known before, or since, to have receiv'd. The, then, Lord *Hallifax*, was not only the Patron of the Men of Genius of this Time, but had likewise a generous Concern for the Reputation, and Prosperity of the Theatre, from whence the most elegant Dramatick Labours of the Learned, he knew, had often shone in their brightest Lustre. A Proposal therefore was drawn up, and address'd to that noble Lord for his Approbation, and Assistance, to raise a publick Subscription for Reviving Three Plays of the best Authors, with the full Strength of the Company; every Subscriber to have Three Tickets, for the first Day of each Play, for his single Payment of Three Guineas. This Subscription his Lordship so zealously encourag'd, that from his Recommendation chiefly, in a very little time, it was compleated. The Plays were *Julius Caesar* of *Shakespear;* the *King and no King* of *Fletcher;* and the Comic Scenes of *Dryden's Marriage à la mode*, and of his *Maiden Queen*[4] put together, for it was judg'd that as these comic Episodes were utterly independent of the serious Scenes, they were originally written to, they might on this Occasion be as well Episodes either to the other, and so make up five livelier Acts between them: At least the Project so well succeeded, that those comic Parts have never since been replac'd, but were continu'd to be jointly acted, as one Play, several Years after.

By the Aid of this Subscription, which happen'd in 1707, and by the additional Strength, and Industry of this Company, not only the Actors, (several of which were handsomely advanc'd, in their Sallaries) were duly paid, but the Menager himself too, at the Foot of his Account stood a considerable Gainer.

At the same time, the Patentee of *Drury-Lane* went on in his usual Method of paying extraordinary Prices to Singers, Dancers, and other exotick Performers, which were as constantly deducted out of the sinking Sallaries of his Actors: 'Tis true, his Actors, perhaps, might not deserve much more, than he gave them; yet, by what I have related, it is plain he chose not to be troubled, with such, as visibly had deserv'd more: For it seems he had not purchas'd his Share of the Patent, to mend the Stage, but to make Mony of it: And to say Truth, his Sense of every thing to be shewn there, was much upon a Level, with the Taste of the Multitude, whose Opinion, and whose Mony weigh'd with him full as much, as that of the best Judges. His Point was to please the Majority, who, could more easily comprehend any thing they *saw*, than the daintiest things, that could be said to them. But in this Notion he kept no medium; for in my Memory, he carry'd it so far, that he was (some few Years before this time) actually dealing for an extraordinary large Elephant, at a certain Sum, for every Day he might think fit to shew the tractable Genius of that vast quiet Creature, in any Play, or Farce, in the Theatre (then standing) in *Dorset-Garden*. But from the Jealousy, which so formidable a Rival had rais'd in his Dancers, and by his Bricklayer's assuring him, that if the Walls were to be open'd wide enough for its Entrance, it might endanger the Fall of the House, he gave up his Project, and with it, so hopeful a Prospect of making the Receipts of the Stage run higher than all the Wit, and Force of the best Writers had ever yet rais'd them to.

About the same time of his being under this Disappointment, he put in Practice another Project of as new, though not of so bold a Nature; which was his introducing a Set of Rope-dancers, into the same Theatre; for the first Day of whose Performance, he had given out some Play, in which, I had a material Part: But I was hardy enough to go into the Pit, and acquainted the Spectators near me, that I hop'd, they would not think it a Mark of my Disrespect to them, if I declin'd acting upon any Stage, that was brought to so low a Disgrace, as ours was like to be by that Day's Entertainment. My Excuse was so well taken, that I never after found any ill Consequences, or heard of the least Disapprobation of it: And the whole Body of Actors too, protesting against such an Abuse of their Profession, our cautious Master was too much alarm'd, and intimidated to repeat it.

After what I have said, it will be no Wonder, that all due Regards to the original Use, and Institution of the Stage should be utterly lost, or neglected: Nor was the Conduct of this Menager easily to be alter'd, while he had found the Secret of making Mony, out of Disorder and Confusion: for however strange it may seem, I have often observ'd him inclin'd to be cheerful, in the Distresses of his Theatrical Affairs, and equally reserv'd and pensive, when they went smoothly forward with a visible Profit. Upon a Run of good Audiences, he was more frighted to be thought a Gainer, which might make him accountable to others, than he was dejected with bad Houses, which at worst, he knew would make others accountable to him: And as, upon a moderate Computation, it cannot be suppos'd, that the contested Accounts of a twenty Years Wear, and Tear, in a Play-house, could be fairly adjusted by a Master in Chancery, under four-score Years more, it will be no Surprize, that by the Neglect, or rather the Discretion of other Proprietors, in not throwing away good Money after bad, this Hero of a Menager, who alone supported the War, should in time so fortify himself by Delay, and so tire his Enemies, that he became sole Monarch of his Theatrical Empire, and left the quiet Possession of it, to his Successors.

If these Facts seem too trivial for the Attention of a sensible Reader, let it be consider'd, that they are not chosen Fictions, to *entertain*, but Truths necessary to *inform* him, under what low Shifts, and Disgraces, what Disorders and Revolutions the Stage labour'd, before it could recover that Strength, and Repu-

tation, wherewith it began to flourish, towards the latter End of
Queen *Anne's* Reign; and which it continu'd to enjoy, for a
Course of twenty Years following. But let us resume our Ac-
count of the new Settlement, in the *Hay-Market*.

It may be a natural Question, why the Actors, whom *Swiney*
brought over to his Undertaking, in the *Hay-Market*, would tie
themselves down to limited Sallaries? for though he, as their
Menager was oblig'd to make them certain Payments, it was not
certain that the Receipts would enable him to do it; and since
their own Industry was the only visible Fund they had to depend upon, why would they not, for that Reason, insist upon
their being Sharers as well of possible Profits, as Losses? How
far in this Point, they acted right, or wrong, will appear from
the following State of their Case.

It must first be consider'd, that this Scheme of their Desertion,
was all concerted, and put in execution in a Week's Time, which
short Warning might make them overlook that Circumstance,
and the sudden Prospect of being deliver'd from having seldom
more, than half their Pay, was a Contentment that had bounded
all their farther Views. Besides, as there could be no room to
doubt of their receiving their full Pay, previous to any Profits,
that might be reap'd by their Labour, and as they had no great
Reason to apprehend those Profits could exceed their respective
Sallaries, so far as to make them repine at them, they might think
it but reasonable, to let the Chance of any extraordinary Gain be
on the Side of their Leader, and Director. But farther, as this
Scheme had the Approbation of the Court, these Actors, in reality, had it not, in their Power to alter any Part of it: And what
induc'd the Court to encourage it, was, that by having the
Theatre, and its Menager more immediately dependent on the
Power of the Lord Chamberlain, it was not doubted but the
Stage would be recover'd into such a Reputation, as might now
do Honour, to that absolute Command, which the Court, or its
Officers seem'd always fond of having over it.

Here, to set the Constitution of the Stage in a clearer Light,
it may not be amiss, to look back a little on the Power of a Lord
Chamberlain, which, as may have been observ'd, in all Changes

of the Theatrical Government, has been the main Spring without which no Scheme, of what kind soever, could be set in Motion. My Intent is not to enquire how far, by Law, this Power has been limited, or extended; but meerly as an Historian, to relate Facts, to gratify the Curious, and then leave them to their own Reflections: This, too, I am the more inclin'd to, because there is no one Circumstance, which has affected the Stage, wherein so many Spectators, from those of the highest Rank, to the Vulgar, have seem'd more positively knowing, or less inform'd in.

Though in all the Letters Patent, for acting Plays, &c. since King *Charles* the *First*'s Time, there has been no mention of the Lord Chamberlain, or of any Subordination to his Command, or Authority--- yet it was still taken for granted, that no Letters Patent, by the bare Omission of such a great Officer's Name, could have superseded, or taken out of his Hands, that Power, which Time out of Mind, he always had exercis'd over the Theatre. The common Opinions then abroad were, that if the Profession of Actors was unlawful, it was not in the Power of the Crown to license it; and, if it were not unlawful, it ought to be free, and independent, as other Professions; and that a Patent to exercise it, was only an honorary Favour, from the Crown, to give it a better Grace of Recommendation to the Publick. But as the Truth of this Question seem'd to be wrapt in a great deal of Obscurity, in the old Laws made in former Reigns, relating to Players, &c. it may be no Wonder, that the best Companies of Actors should be desirous of taking Shelter under the visible Power of a Lord Chamberlain, who they knew had, at his Pleasure, favour'd, and protected, or born hard upon them: But be all this as it may, a Lord Chamberlain (from whencesoever his Power might be deriv'd) had, till of later Years, had always an implicit Obedience paid to it: I shall now give some few Instances, in what manner it was exercis'd.

What appear'd to be most reasonably, under his Cognizance was the licensing, or refusing new Plays, or striking out what might be thought offensive, in them: Which Province had been, for many Years, assign'd to his inferior Officer, the Master of the

Revels; yet was not this License irrevocable; for several Plays, though acted, by that Permission, had been silenc'd afterwards. The first Instance of this kind, that common Fame has delivered down to us, is that of the *Maid's Tragedy* of *Beaumont* and *Fletcher*, which was forbid in King *Charles* the *Second's* time, by an Order from the Lord Chamberlain. For what Reason this Interdiction was laid upon it, the Politicks of those Days, have only left us to guess. Some said, that the killing of the King, in that Play, while the tragical Death of King *Charles* the *First*, was then so fresh, in People's Memory, was an Object too horribly impious, for a publick Entertainment. What makes this Conjecture seem to have some Foundation, is that the celebrated *Waller*, in Compliment to that Court, alter'd the last Act of this Play (which is printed at the End of his Works) and gave it a new Catastrophe, wherein the Life of the King is loyally sav'd, and the Lady's Matter made up, with a less terrible Reparation. Others have given out, that a repenting Mistress, in a romantick Revenge of her Dishonour, killing the King, in the very Bed he expected her to come into, was shewing a too dangerous Example to other *Evadnes*, then shining at Court, in the same Rank of royal Distinction; who, if ever their Consciences should have run equally mad, might have had frequent Opportunities of putting the Expiation of their Frailty, into the like Execution. But this I doubt is too keep a Speculation, or too ludicrous a Reason, to be rely'd on; it being well known, that the Ladies, then in favour, were not so nice, in their Notions, as to think their Preferment their Dishonour, or their Lover a Tyrant: Besides, that easy Monarch lov'd his Roses, without Thorns; nor do we hear, that he much chose, to be himself the first Gatherer of them.

The *Lucius Junius Brutus* of *Nat. Lee*, was, in the same Reign, silenc'd after the third Day of acting it; it being objected, that the Plan, and Sentiments of it had too boldly vindicated, and might enflame Republican Principles.

A Prologue (by *Dryden*) to the *Prophetess*, was forbid by the Lord *Dorset*, after the first Day of its being spoken. This happen'd when King *William* was prosecuting the War, in *Ire-*

land. It must be confess'd, that this Prologue had some familiar, metaphorical Sneers, at the Revolution itself; and as the Poetry of it was good, the Offence of it was less pardonable.

The Tragedy of *Mary* Queen of *Scotland*, had been offer'd to the Stage twenty Years before it was acted: But from the profound Penetration of the Master of the Revels, who saw political Spectres in it, that never appear'd in the Presentation, it had lain, so long upon the Hands of the Author; who had at last, the good Fortune to prevail with a Nobleman, to favour his Petition to Queen *Anne*, for Permission to have it acted: The Queen had the Goodness to refer the Merit of his Play, to the Opinion of that noble Person, although he was not her Majesty's Lord Chamberlain; upon whose Report of its being, every way, an innocent Piece, it was soon after acted with Success.[5]

Reader, by your Leave--- I will but just speak a Word, or two to any Author, that has not yet writ one Line of his next Play, and then I will come to my Point again--- What I would say to him, is this--- Sir, before you set Pen to Paper, think well, and principally of your Design, or chief Action, towards which every Line you write ought to be drawn, as to its Centre: If we can say of your finest Sentiments, This, or That might be left out, without maiming the Story you would tell us, depend upon it, that fine thing is said in a wrong Place; and though you may urge, that a bright Thought is not to be resisted, you will not be able to deny, that those very fine Lines would be much finer, if you could find a proper Occasion for them: Otherwise you will be thought to take less Advice from *Aristotle*, or *Horace*, than from the Poet *Bays* in the *Rehearsal*, who very smartly says--- *What the Devil is the Plot good for, but to bring in fine things?* Compliment the Taste of your Hearers, as much as you please with them, provided they belong to your Subject, but don't like a dainty Preacher, who has his Eye more upon this World, than the next, leave your Text for them. When your Fable is good, every Part of it will cost you much less Labour, to keep your Narration alive, than you will be forced to bestow upon those elegant Discourses, that are not absolutely conducive to your Catastrophe, or main Purpose: Scenes of that kind, shew but at best, the unprofitable, or injudicious Spirit of a Genius. It is but a melancholy Commendation of a fine Thought, to say, when we have heard it, *Well! but what's all this to the Purpose?* Take therefore, in some part, Example by the Author last mention'd! There are three Plays of his, The *Earl* of *Essex, Anna Bullen,* and *Mary Queen of Scots,*[6] which tho' they are all written in the most barren, barbarous Stile, that was ever able to keep Possession of the Stage, have all interested the Hearts of his Auditors. To what then could this Success be owing, but to the intrinsick, and naked Value of the well-conducted Tales, he has simply told us? There is something so happy in the Disposition of all his Fables; all his chief Characters are thrown into such natural Circumstances of Distress, that their Misery, or Affliction wants very little Assistance from the Ornaments of Stile, or Words to speak them. When a skilful Actor is so situated, his bare plaintive Tone of Voice, the Cast of Sorrow from his Eye, his slowly graceful Gesture, his humble Sighs of Resignation under his Calamities: All these, I say, are sometimes without a Tongue, equal to the strongest Eloquence. At such a time, the attentive Auditor supplies from his own Heart, whatever the Poet's Language may fall short of, in Expression, and melts himself into every Pang of Humanity, which the like Misfortunes in real Life could have inspir'd.

After what I have observ'd, whenever I see a Tragedy defective in its Fable, let there be never so many fine Lines in it; I hope I shall be forgiven, if I impute that Defect, to the Idleness, the weak Judgment, or barren Invention of the Author.

If I should be ask'd, why I have not always, my self, follow'd the Rules I would impose upon others; I can only answer, that whenever I have not, I lie equally open to the same critical Censure. But having often observ'd a better than ordinary Stile thrown away, upon the loose, and wandering Scenes of an ill-chosen Story, I imagin'd these Observations might convince some future Author, of how great Advantage a Fable well plann'd must be to a Man of any tolerable Genius.

All this, I own, is leading my Reader out of the way; but if he has as much Time upon his Hands, as I have, (provided we are neither of us tir'd) it may be equally to the Purpose, what he reads, or what I write of. But as I have no Objection to Method, when it is not troublesome, I return to my Subject.

Hitherto we have seen no very unreasonable Instance of this absolute Power of a Lord Chamberlain, though we were to admit, that no one knew of any real Law, or Construction of Law, by which this Power was given him. I shall now offer some Facts relating to it of a more extraordinary Nature, which I leave my Reader to give a Name to.

About the middle of King *William*'s Reign, an Order of the Lord Chamberlain was, then, subsisting, that no Actor of either Company, should presume to go from one, to the other, without a Discharge from their respective Menagers, and the Permission of the Lord Chamberlain. Notwithstanding such Order, *Powel* being uneasy, at the Favour, *Wilks*, was then rising into, had without such Discharge, left the *Drury-Lane* Theatre, and engag'd himself to that of *Lincolns-Inn-Fields:* But by what follows, it will appear, that this Order was not so much intended, to do both of them *good*, as to do, that which the Court chiefly favour'd (*Lincolns-Inn-Fields*) no harm. For when *Powel* grew dissatisfy'd at his Station there too, he return'd to *Drury-Lane* (as he had before gone from it) without a Discharge: But halt a little! here, on this Side of the Question, the Order was to stand, in force, and the same Offence against it now, was not to be equally pass'd over. He was the next Day taken up by a Messenger, and confin'd to the Porter's-Lodge, where, to the best of my Remembrance, he remain'd about two Days; when the Menagers of *Lincolns-Inn-Fields*, not thinking an Actor of his loose Character worth their farther Trouble, gave him up; though perhaps he was releas'd, for some better Reason. Upon this occasion, the next Day, behind the Scenes, at *Drury-Lane*, a Person of great Quality, in my hearing, enquiring of *Powel*, into the Nature of his Offence, after he had heard it, told him, That if he had had Patience, or Spirit enough, to have staid in his Confinement, till he had given him Notice of it, he would have found him a handsomer way of coming out of it.

Another Time the same Actor, *Powel*, was provok'd at *Will*'s

Coffeehouse, in a Dispute about the Play-house Affairs, to strike
a Gentleman, whose Family had been sometimes Masters of
it; a Complaint of this Insolence was, in the Absence of the Lord
Chamberlain, immediatly made to the Vice-Chamberlain, who
so highly resented it, that he thought himself bound in Honour,
to carry his Power of redressing it, as far as it could possibly go:
For *Powel* having a Part in the Play, that was acted the Day after;
the Vice-Chamberlain sent an Order to silence the whole Company, for having suffer'd *Powel* to appear upon the Stage, before he had made that Gentleman Satisfaction, although the
Masters of the Theatre had had no Notice of *Powel*'s Misbe-
haviour: However, this Order was obey'd, and remain'd in force
for two or three Days, till the same Authority was pleas'd, or
advis'd, to revoke it. From the Measures this injur'd Gentleman
took for his Redress, it may be judg'd how far it was taken for
granted, that a Lord Chamberlain had an absolute Power over
the Theatre.[7]

I shall now give an Instance of an Actor, who had the Resolution to stand upon the Defence of his Liberty, against the
same Authority, and was reliev'd by it.

In the same King's Reign, *Dogget*, who though, from a severe
Exactness in his Nature, he could be seldom long easy in any
Theatre, where Irregularity, not to say Injustice, too often prevail'd, yet in the private Conduct of his Affairs, he was a prudent,
honest Man. He therefore took an unusual Care, when he return'd to act under the Patent, in *Drury-Lane,* to have his Articles drawn firm and binding: But having some Reason to think
the Patentee had not dealt fairly with him, he quitted the Stage,
and would act no more, rather chusing to lose his whatever un-
satisfy'd, Demands, than go through the chargeable, and tedious
Course of the Law to recover it. But the Patentee, who (from
other People's Judgment) knew the Value of him, and who
wanted too, to have him sooner back, than the Law could possibly bring him, thought the surer way would be, to desire a
shorter Redress from the Authority of the Lord Chamberlain.
Accordingly upon his Complaint, a Messenger was immediately
dispatch'd to *Norwich,* where *Dogget* then was, to bring him

up, in Custody: But doughty *Dogget*, who had Mony in his Pocket, and the Cause of Liberty at his Heart, was not, in the least intimidated, by this formidable Summons. He was observ'd to obey it, with a particular Chearfulness, entertaining his fellow Traveller, the Messenger, all the way in the Coach (for he had protested against riding) with as much Humour, as a Man of his Business might be capable of tasting. And as he found his Charges were to be defray'd, he, at every Inn, call'd for the best Dainties the Country could afford, or a pretended weak Appetite could digest. At this Rate they jollily roll'd on, more with the Air of a Jaunt, than a Journey, or a Party of Pleasure, than of a poor Devil in durance. Upon his Arrival in Town, he immediately apply'd to the Lord Chief Justice *Holt*, for his *Habeas Corpus*. As his Case was something particular, that eminent, and learned Minister of the Law took a particular Notice of it: For *Dogget* was not only discharg'd, but the Process of his Confinement (according to common Fame) had a Censure pass'd upon it, in Court, which I doubt, I am not Lawyer enough to repeat! To conclude, the officious Agents in this Affair finding, that, in *Dogget*, they had mistaken their Man, were mollify'd into milder Proceedings, and (as he afterwards told me) whisper'd something, in his Ear, that took away *Dogget*'s farther Uneasiness about it.

By these Instances we see how naturally Power only founded on Custom, is apt, where the Law is silent, to run into Excesses, and while it laudably pretends to govern others, how hard it is to govern itself. But since the Law has lately open'd its Mouth, and has said plainly, that some Part of this Power to govern the Theatre shall be, and is plac'd in a proper Person; and as it is evident, that the Power of that white Staff, ever since it has been in the noble Hand, that now holds it, has been us'd with the utmost Lenity, I would beg Leave of the murmuring Multitude, who frequent the Theatre, to offer them a simple Question or two, *viz.* Pray Gentlemen, how came you, or rather your Forefathers never to be mutinous, upon any of the occasional Facts I have related? And why have you been so often tumultuous, upon a Law's being made, that only confirms a less Power, than was formerly exercis'd, without any Law to support it? You cannot sure, say, such Discontent is either just, or natural, unless you allow it a Maxim in your Politicks, that Power exercis'd *without* Law, is a less Grievance, than the same Power exercis'd *according* to law!

Having thus given the clearest View I was able, of the usual Regard paid to the Power of a Lord Chamberlain, the Reader will more easily conceive, what Influence, and Operation that Power must naturally have, in all Theatrical Revolutions; and particularly in the complete Re-union of both Companies, which happen'd in the Year following.

From the Time, that the Company of Actors, in the *Hay-Market*, was recruited with those from *Drury-Lane*, and came into the Hands of their new Director, *Swiney*, the Theatre, for three or four Years following, suffer'd so many Convulsions, and was thrown every other Winter under such different Interests, and Menagement, before it came to a firm and lasting Settlement, that I am doubtful, if the most candid Reader will have Patience, to go through a full, and fair Account of it: And yet I would fain flatter my self, that those, who are not too wise, to frequent the Theatre (or have Wit enough to distinguish what sort of Sights there, either do Honour, or Disgrace to it) may think their national Diversion no contemptible Subject, for a more able Historian, than I pretend to be: If I have any particular Qualification, for the Task, more than another, it is that I have been an ocular Witness of the several Facts, that are to fill up the rest of my Volume; and am, perhaps, the only Person living (however unworthy) from whom the same Materials can be collected; but let them come from whom they may, whether, at best, they will be worth reading; perhaps a Judgment may be better form'd after a patient Perusal of the following Digression.

In whatever cold Esteem, the Stage may be, among the wise, and powerful; it is not so much a Reproach, to those, who contentedly enjoy it in its lowest Condition, as that Condition of it, is to those, who (though they cannot but know, to how valuable a publick Use, a Theatre, well establish'd, might be rais'd) yet in so many civiliz'd Nations, have neglected it. This perhaps will be call'd thinking my own wiser, than all the wise Heads, in *Europe*. But I hope a more humble Sense will be given to it;

at least I only mean, that if so many Governments have their Reasons, for their Disregard of their Theatres, those Reasons may be deeper, than my Capacity has yet been able to dive into: If therefore my simple Opinion is a wrong one, let the Singularity of it expose me: And though I am only building a Theatre in the Air, it is there, however, at so little Expence, and in so much better a Taste, than any I have yet seen, that I cannot help saying of it, as a wiser Man did (it may be) upon a wiser Occasion:

> ----Si quid novisti rectius istis,
> Candidus imperti; si non ----[2]   Hor.

Give me leave to play, with my Project, in Fancy.

I say then, that as I allow nothing is more liable to debase, and corrupt the Minds of a People, than a licentious Theatre; so under a just, and proper Establishment, it were possible to make it, as apparently the School of Manners, and of Virtue. Were I to collect all the Arguments, that might be given for my Opinion, or to inforce it by exemplary Proofs, it might swell this short Digression to a Volume; I shall therefore trust the Validity of what I have laid down, to a single Fact, that may be still fresh, in the Memory of many living Spectators. When the Tragedy of *Cato* was first acted, let us call to mind the noble Spirit of Patriotism, which that Play then infus'd into the Breasts of a free People, that crowded to it; with what affecting Force, was that most elevated of Human Virtues recommended? Even the false Pretenders to it felt an unwilling Conviction, and made it a Point of Honour to be foremost, in their Approbation; and this too at a time, when the fermented Nation had their different Views of Government. Yet the sublime Sentiments of Liberty, in that venerable Character, rais'd, in every sensible Hearer such conscious Admiration, such compell'd Assent to the Conduct of a suffering Virtue, as even *demanded* two almost irreconcileable Parties to embrace, and join in their equal Applauses of it. Now, not to take from the Merit of the Writer, had that Play never come to the Stage, how much of this valuable Effect of it must have been lost? It then could have had no

more immediate weight with the Publick, than our poring upon
the many ancient Authors, through whose Works the same
Sentiments have been, perhaps, less profitably dispers'd, tho'
amongst Millions of Readers; but by bringing such Sentiments
to the Theatre, and into Action, what a superior Lustre did
they shine with? There, *Cato* breath'd again, in Life; and
tho' he perish'd in the Cause of Liberty, his Virtue was victorious, and left the Triumph of it in the Heart of every melting
Spectator. If Effects, like these, are laudable; if the Representa-
tion of such Plays can carry Conviction with so much Pleasure,
to the Understanding, have they not vastly the Advantage of
any other Human Helps to Eloquence? What equal Method can
be found to lead, or stimulate the Mind, to a quicker Sense of
Truth, and Virtue, or warm a People into the Love, and Practice
of such Principles, as might be at once a Defence, and Honour
to their Country? In what Shape could we listen to Virtue with
equal Delight, or Appetite of Instruction? The Mind of Man is
naturally free, and when he is compell'd, or menac'd, into any
Opinion that he does not readily conceive, he is more apt to
doubt the Truth of it, than when his Capacity is led by Delight,
into Evidence and Reason. To preserve a Theatre in this Strength
and Purity of Morals, is, I grant, what the wisest Nations, have
not been able to perpetuate, or to transmit long to their Posterity: But this Difficulty will rather heighten, than take from the
Honour of the Theatre: The greatest Empires have decay'd,
for want of proper Heads to guide them, and the Ruins of them
sometimes have been the Subject of Theatres, that could not be,
themselves exempt, from as various Revolutions: Yet may not
the most natural Inference from all this be, That the Talents
requisite to form good Actors, great Writers, and true Judges,
were like those of wise and memorable Ministers, as well the
Gifts of Fortune, as of Nature, and not always to be found, in
all Climes or Ages. Or can there be a stronger modern Evidence
of the Value of Dramatick Performances, than that in many
Countries, where the Papal Religion prevails, the Holy Policy
(though it allows not to an Actor Christian Burial) is so conscious of the Usefulness of his Art, that it will frequently take in

the Assistance of the Theatre, to give even Sacred History, in a Tragedy, a Recommendation to the more pathetick Regard of their People. How can such Principles, in the Face of the World, refuse the Bones of a Wretch the lowest Benefit of Christian Charity, after having admitted his Profession (for which they deprive him of that Charity) to serve the solemn Purposes of Religion? How far then is this Religious Inhumanity short of that famous Painter's, who, to make his *Crucifix* a Master-piece of Nature, stabb'd the innocent Hireling, from whose Body he drew it; and having heighten'd the holy Portrait, with his last Agonies of Life, then sent it to be the consecrated Ornament of an Altar? Though we have only the Authority of common Fame, for this Story, yet be it true, or false, the Comparison will still be just. Or let me ask another Question more humanly political.

How came the *Athenians* to lay out an Hundred Thousand Pounds, upon the Decorations of one single Tragedy of *Sophocles?* Not sure, as it was merely a Spectacle for Idleness, or Vacancy of Thought to gape at, but because it was the most rational, most instructive, and delightful Composition, that human Wit had yet arriv'd at; and consequently the most worthy to be the Entertainment of a wise, and warlike Nation: And it may be still a Question, whether the *Sophocles* inspir'd this Publick Spirit, or this Publick Spirit inspir'd the *Sophocles?*

But alas! as the Power of giving, or receiving such Inspirations, from either of these Causes, seems pretty well at an End; now I have shot my Bolt, I shall descend to talk more like a Man of the Age, I live in: For, indeed, what is all this to a common *English* Reader? Why truly, as *Shakespear* terms it---- *Caviare to the Multitude!*[3] Honest *John Trott* will tell you, that if he were to believe what I have said of the *Athenians*, he is at most, but astonish'd at it; but that if the twentieth Part of the Sum I have mention'd were to be apply'd, out of our Publick Money, to the Setting off the best Tragedy, the nicest Noddle in the Nation could produce, it would probably raise the Passions higher in those that did *Not* like it, than in those that did; it might as likely meet with an Insurrection, as the Applause of the

People, and so, mayhap, be fitter for the Subject of a Tragedy, than for a Publick Fund to support it.---- Truly, Mr. *Trott*, I cannot but own, that I am very much of your Opinion: I am only concern'd, that the Theatre has not a better Pretence to the Care and further Consideration of those Governments, where it is tolerated; but as what I have said will not probably do it any great Harm, I hope I have not put you out of Patience, by throwing a few good Wishes after an old Acquaintance.

To conclude this Digression. If, for the Support of the Stage, what is generally shewn there, must be lower'd to the Taste of common Spectators; or if it is inconsistent with Liberty, to mend that vulgar Taste, by making the Multitude less merry there; or by abolishing every low, and senseless Jollity, in which the Understanding can have no Share; whenever, I say, such is the State of the Stage, it will be as often liable, to unanswerable Censure, and manifest Disgraces. Yet there *was* a Time, not yet, out of many People's Memory, when it subsisted upon its own rational Labours; when even Success attended an Attempt to reduce it to Decency; and when Actors themselves were hardy enough to hazard their Interest, in pursuit of so dangerous a Reformation. And this Crisis, I am myself as impatient, as any tir'd Reader can be, to arrive at. I shall therefore endeavour to lead him the shortest way to it. But as I am a little jealous of the badness of the Road, I must reserve to myself the Liberty of calling upon any Master, in my Way, for a little Refreshment to whatever Company may have the Curiosity, or Goodness, to go along with me.

When the sole menaging Patentee at *Drury-Lane*, for several Years could never be persuaded or driven to any Account with the Adventurers; Sir *Thomas Skipwith* (who, if I am rightly inform'd, had an equal Share with him) grew so weary of the Affair, that he actually made a Present of his entire Interest in it, upon the following Occasion.

Sir *Thomas* happen'd, in the Summer preceding the Re-union of the Companies, to make a Visit to an intimate Friend of his, Colonel *Brett*, of *Sandywell*, in *Gloucestershire;* where the Pleasantness of the Place, and the agreeable manner of passing his

Time there, had rais'd him to such a Gallantry of Heart, that, in
return to the Civilities of his Friend the Colonel, he made him
an Offer of his whole Right in the Patent; but not to over-rate
the Value of his Present, told him, he himself had made nothing
of it, these ten Years: But the Colonel (he said) being a greater
Favourite of the People in Power, and (as he believ'd) among
the Actors too, than himself was, might think of some Scheme,
to turn it to Advantage, and in that Light, if he lik'd it, it was at
his Service. After a great deal of Raillery on both sides, of what
Sir *Thomas* had *not* made of it, and the particular Advantages
the Colonel was likely to make of it; they came to a laughing
Resolution, That an Instrument should be drawn the next
Morning, of an absolute Conveyance of the Premises. A Gentleman of the Law, well known to them both, happening to be a
Guest there, at the same time, the next Day produc'd the Deed,
according to his Instructions, in the Presence of whom, and of
others, it was sign'd, seal'd, and deliver'd, to the Purposes therein
contain'd.[4]

This Transaction may be another Instance (as I have elsewhere observ'd) at how low a Value, the Interests, in a Theatrical License were then held; tho' it was visible, from the Success
of *Swiney* in that very Year, that with tolerable Menagement,
they could, at no time have fail'd of being a profitable Purchase.

The next Thing to be consider'd was, what the Colonel should
do with his new Theatrical Commission, which, in another's Possession, had been of so little Importance. Here it may be necessary to premise, that this Gentleman was the first of any
Consideration, since my coming to the Stage, with whom I had
contracted a Personal Intimacy; which might be the Reason,
why, in this Debate, my Opinion had some weight with him: Of
this Intimacy too, I am the more tempted to talk, from the natural
Pleasure of calling back, in Age, the Pursuits, and happy Ardours
of Youth long past, which, like the Ideas of a delightful Spring,
in a Winter's Rumination, are sometimes equal to the former
Enjoyment of them. I shall therefore, rather chuse, in this Place
to gratify myself, than my Reader, by setting the fairest Side
of this Gentleman in view, and by indulging a little conscious

Vanity, in shewing how early in Life, I fell into the Possession
of so agreeable a Companion: Whatever Failings he might have
to others, he had none to me; nor was he, where he had them,
without his valuable Qualities to balance or soften them. Let,
then, what was not, to be commended in him, rest with his Ashes,
never to be rak'd into: But the friendly Favours I receiv'd from
him, while living, give me still a Pleasure, in paying this only
Mite of my Acknowledgment, in my Power, to his Memory.
And if my taking this Liberty, may find Pardon from several
of his fair Relations, still living, for whom I profess the utmost
Respect, it will give me but little Concern, tho' my critical
Readers should think it all Impertinence.

This Gentleman, then, *Henry*, was the eldest Son of *Henry
Brett*, Esq; of *Cowley*, in *Gloucestershire*, who coming early to
his Estate of about Two Thousand a Year, by the usual Negli-
gences of young Heirs, had, before this his eldest Son came of
age, sunk it to about half that Value, and that not wholly free
from Incumbrances. Mr. *Brett*, whom I am speaking of, had his
Education, and I might say ended it, at the University of *Oxford;*
for tho' he was settled some time after at the *Temple*, he so little
followed the Law there, that his Neglect of it, made the Law
(like some of his fair and frail Admirers) very often follow
him. As he had an uncommon Share of Social Wit, and a handsom Person, with a sanguine Bloom in his Complexion, no
wonder they persuaded him, that he might have a better Chance
of Fortune, by throwing such Accomplishments, into the gayer
World, than by shutting them up, in a Study. The first View,
that fires the Head of a young Gentleman of this modish Ambition, just broke loose, from Business, is to cut a Figure (as they
call it) in a Side-box, at the Play, from whence their next Step
is, to the *Green Room* behind the Scenes, sometimes their *Non
ultra*. Hither, at last then, in this hopeful Quest of his Fortune,
came this Gentleman-Errant, not doubting but the fickle Dame,
while he was thus qualify'd to receive her, might be tempted to
fall into his Lap. And though, possibly, the Charms of our Theatrical Nymphs might have their Share, in drawing him thither;
yet in my Observation, the most visible Cause of his first coming,

was a more sincere Passion he had conceiv'd for a fair full-bottom'd Perriwig, which I then wore in my first Play of the *Fool in Fashion*, in the Year 1695.[5] For it is to be noted, that, the *Beaux* of those Days, were of a quite different Cast, from the modern Stamp, and had more of the Stateliness of the Peacock in their Mien, than (which now seems to be their highest Emulation) the pert Air of a Lapwing. Now whatever Contempt Philosophers may have, for a fine Perriwig; my Friend, who was not to despise the World, but to live in it, knew very well, that so material an Article of Dress, upon the Head of a Man of Sense, if it became him, could never fail of drawing to him a more partial Regard, and Benevolence, than could possibly be hop'd for, in an ill-made one. This perhaps may soften the grave Censure, which so youthful a Purchase might otherwise, have laid upon him: In a word, he made his Attack upon this Perriwig, as your young Fellows generally do upon a Lady of Pleasure; first, by a few, familiar Praises of her Person, and then, a civil Enquiry, into the Price of it. But upon his observing me a little surpriz'd at the Levity of his Question, about a Fop's Perriwig, he began to railly himself, with so much Wit, and Humour, upon the Folly of his Fondness for it, that he struck me, with an equal Desire of granting any thing, in my Power, to oblige so facetious a Customer. This singular Beginning of our Conversation, and the mutual Laughs that ensued upon it, ended in an Agreement, to finish our Bargain that Night, over a Bottle.

If it were possible, the Relation of the happy Indiscretions which pass'd between us that Night, could give the tenth Part of Pleasure, I then receiv'd from them, I could still repeat them with Delight: But as it may be doubtful, whether the Patience of a Reader may be quite so strong, as the Vanity of an Author, I shall cut it short, by only saying, That single Bottle was the Sire of many a jolly Dozen, that for some Years following, like orderly Children, whenever they were call'd for came into the same Company. Nor indeed, did I think from that time, whenever he was to be had, any Evening could be agreeably enjoy'd without him. But the long continuance of our Intimacy, perhaps, may be thus accounted for.

He who can taste Wit in another, may, in some sort, be said to have it himself: Now, as I always had, and (I bless myself for the Folly) still have a quick Relish of whatever did, or can give me Delight: This Gentleman could not but see the youthful Joy, I was generally rais'd to, whenever I had the Happiness of a *Tête à tête* with him; and it may be a moot Point, whether Wit is not as often inspir'd, by a proper Attention, as by the brightest Reply, to it. Therefore as he had Wit enough for any two People, and I had Attention enough for any four, there could not well be wanting a sociable Delight, on either side. And tho' it may be true, that a Man of a handsom Person is apt to draw a partial Ear to every thing he says; yet this Gentleman seldom said any thing, that might not have made a Man of the plainest Person agreeable. Such a continual Desire to please, it may be imagin'd, could not but, sometimes lead him into a little venial Flattery, rather than not succeed in it. And I, perhaps, might be one of those Flies, that was caught in this Honey. As I was, then, a young successful Author, and an Actor, in some unexpected Favour, whether deservedly, or not, imports not; yet such Appearances, at least were plausible Pretences enough, for an amicable Adulation to enlarge upon; and the Sallies of it a less Vanity, than mine might not have been able to resist. Whatever this Weakness on my side might be, I was not alone in it; for I have heard a Gentleman of Condition say, who knew the World as well, as most Men, that live in it, that let his Discretion be ever so much upon its guard, he never fell into Mr. *Brett*'s Company, without being loth to leave it, or carrying away a better Opinion of himself, from it. If his Conversation had this Effect among the Men; what must we suppose to have been the Consequences, when he gave it, a yet softer turn among the Fair Sex? Here now, a *French* Novellist would tell you fifty pretty Lies of him; but as I chuse to be tender of Secrets of that sort, I shall only borrow the good Breeding of that Language, and tell you, in a Word, that I knew several Instances of his being *un Homme a bonne Fortune*. But though his frequent Successes might generally keep him, from the usual Disquiets of a Lover, he knew this was a Life too liquorish to last; and therefore had Reflexion enough, to be govern'd

by the Advice of his Friends, to turn these his Advantages of
Nature to a better use.

Among the many Men of Condition, with whom, his Conversation had recommended him, to an Intimacy; Sir *Thomas Skipwith* had taken a particular Inclination to him; and as he had the
Advancement of his Fortune, at Heart, introduc'd him, where
there was a Lady,[6] who had enough, in her Power, to disencum-
ber him of the World, and make him every way, easy, for Life.

While he was in pursuit of this Affair, which no time was to
be lost in (for the Lady was to be in Town but for three Weeks)
I one Day found him idling behind the Scenes, before the Play
was begun. Upon sight of him, I took the usual Freedom he
allow'd me, to rate him roundly, for the Madness of not improving every Moment, in his Power, in what was of such consequence to him. Why are you not (said I) where you know you
only should be? If your Design should once get Wind, in the
Town, the Ill-will of your Enemies, or the Sincerity of the
Lady's Friends, may soon blow up your Hopes, which, in your
Circumstances of Life, cannot be long supported, by the bare
Appearance of a Gentleman. --- Yet, as it might not be so trivial
in its Effect, as I fear it may be in the Narration, and is a Mark of
that Intimacy, which is necessary should be known, had been
between us, I will honestly make bold with my Scruples, and
let the plain Truth of my Story take its Chance for Contempt,
or Approbation.

After twenty Excuses, to clear himself of the Neglect, I had
so warmly charg'd him with, he concluded them, with telling
me, he had been out all the Morning, upon Business, and that his
Linnen was too much soil'd, to be seen in Company. Oh, ho! said
I, is that all? Come along with me, we will soon get over that
dainty Difficulty: Upon which I had haul'd him, by the Sleeve,
into my Shifting-Room, he either staring, laughing, or hanging
back all the way. There, when I had lock'd him in, I began to
strip off my upper Cloaths, and bad him do the same; still he
either did not, or would not, seem to understand me, and continuing his Laugh, cry'd What! is the Puppy mad? No no, only
positive, said I; for look you, in short, the Play is ready to begin,

and the Parts that you, and I, are to act to Day, are not of equal
consequence; mine of young *Reveller* (in *Greenwich-Park*)[7] is
but a Rake; but whatever you may be, you are not to appear so;
therefore take my Shirt, and give me yours; for depend upon't,
stay here you shall not, and so go about your Business. To conclude, we fairly chang'd Linnen, nor could his Mother's have
wrap'd him up more fortunately; for in about ten Days he
marry'd the Lady. In a Year or two after his Marriage, he was
chosen a Member of that Parliament, which was sitting, when
King *William* dy'd. And, upon the raising of some new Regi-
ments, was made Lieutenant-Colonel, to that of Sir *Charles
Hotham*. But as his Ambition extended not beyond the Bounds
of a Park Wall, and a pleasant Retreat in the Corner of it, which,
with too much Expence he had just finish'd, he, within another
Year, had leave to resign his Company to a younger Brother.

This was the Figure, in Life, he made, when Sir *Thomas Skipwith* thought him the most proper Person, to oblige (if it could
be an Obligation) with the Present of his Interest in the Patent.
And from these Anecdotes of my Intimacy with him, it may be
less a Surprise, when he came to Town invested with this new
Theatrical Power, that I should be the first Person, to whom he
took any Notice of it. And notwithstanding he knew I was then
engag'd, in another Interest, at the *Hay-Market*, he desired we
might consider together, of the best Use he could make of it,
assuring me, at the same time, he should think it of none to
himself, unless it could in some Shape be turn'd to my Advantage. This friendly Declaration, though it might be generous in
him to make, was not needful, to incline me, in whatever might
be honestly in my Power, whether by Interest or Negotiation,
to serve him. My first Advice, therefore, was, That he should
produce his Deed to the other Menaging Patentee of *Drury-
Lane*, and demand immediate Entrance to a joint Possession of
all Effects, and Powers, to which that Deed had given him an
equal Title. After which, if he met with no Opposition, to this
Demand (as upon sight of it he did not) that he should be watch-
ful against any Contradiction, from his Collegue, in whatever
he might propose, in carrying on the Affair, but to let him see,

that he was determin'd in all his Measures. Yet to heighten that Resolution, with an Ease and Temper in his manner, as if he took it for granted, there could be no Opposition made, to whatever he had a mind to. For that this Method, added to his natural Talent of Persuading, would imperceptibely lead his Collegue, into a Reliance on his superior Understanding, That however little he car'd for Business, he should give himself the Air at least, of Enquiry into what *had* been done, that what he intended to do, might be thought more considerable, and be the readier comply'd with: For if he once suffer'd his Collegue to seem wiser than himself, there would be no end of his perplexing him with absurd, and dilatory Measures; direct, and plain Dealing being a Quality his natural Diffidence would never suffer him to be Master of; of which, his not complying with his Verbal Agreement with *Swiney*, when the *Hay-Market* House was taken for both their Uses, was an Evidence. And though some People thought it Depth, and Policy in him, to keep things often in Confusion, it was ever my Opinion they over-rated his Skill, and that, in reality his Parts were too weak, for his Post, in which he had always acted, to the best of his Knowledge. That his late Collegue, Sir *Thomas Skipwith*, had trusted too much to his Capacity, for this sort of Business; and was treated by him accordingly, without ever receiving any Profits from it, for several Years: Insomuch that when he found his Interest in such desperate Hands, he thought the best thing he could do with it was, (as he saw) to give it away. Therefore if he (Mr. *Brett*) could once fix himself, as I had advis'd, upon a different Foot with this, hitherto untractable Menager, the Business would soon run through whatever Channel, he might have a mind to lead it. And though I allow'd the greatest Difficulty he would meet with, would be in getting his Consent to a Union of the two Companies, which was the only Scheme, that could raise the Patent to its former Value, and which, I knew, this close Menager would secretly lay all possible Rubs in the way to; yet it was visible, there was a way of reducing him to Compliance: For though, it was true his Caution would never part with a Straw, by way of Concession, yet to a high Hand, he would give up any thing, provided he was suffer'd to keep his Title to it: If his Hat were taken from his Head, in the Street, he would make no farther Resistance, than to say, *I am not willing to part with it.* Much less would he have the Resolution, openly to oppose any just Measures, when he should find one, who with an equal Right, to his, and with a known Interest to bring them about, was resolv'd to go through with them.

Now though I knew my Friend was as thoroughly acquainted with his Patentee's Temper, as myself, yet I thought it not amiss to quicken and support his Resolution, by confirming to him, the little Trouble he would meet with, in pursuit of the Union I had advis'd him to; for it must be known, that on our side, Trouble was a sort of Physick we did not much care to take: But as the Fatigue of this Affair was likely to be lower'd by a good deal of Entertainment, and Humour, which would naturally engage him, in his dealing with so exotick a Partner; I knew that this softening the Business, into a Diversion, would lessen every Difficulty, that lay in our way to it.

However copiously I may have indulg'd my self in this Commemoration of a Gentleman, with whom I had pass'd so many of my younger Days, with Pleasure, yet the Reader may by this Insight into his Character, and by that of the other Patentee, be better able to judge of the secret Springs, that gave Motion to, or obstructed so considerable an Event, as that of the Re-union of the two Companies of Actors in 1708. In Histories of more weight, for want of such Particulars, we are often deceiv'd in the true Causes of Fact, that most concern us, to be let into; which sometimes makes us ascribe to Policy, or false Appearances of Wisdom, what perhaps, in reality, was the mere Effect of Chance, or Humour.

Immediately after Mr. *Brett* was admitted as a joint Patentee, he made use of the Intimacy he had with the Vice-Chamberlain to assist his Scheme of this intended Union, in which he so far prevail'd, that it was soon after left to the particular Care of the same Vice-Chamberlain, to give him all the Aid, and Power, necessary to the bringing what he desired, to Perfection. The Scheme was, to have but one Theatre for Plays, and another

for Operas, under separate Interests. And this the generality of
Spectators, as well as the most approv'd Actors, had been sometimes calling for, as the only Expedient to recover the Credit
of the Stage, and the valuable Interests of its Menagers.

As the Condition of the Comedians at this time, is taken notice
of in my *Dedication* of the *Wife's Resentment,* to the Marquis
(now Duke) of *Kent,* and then Lord-Chamberlain, which was
publish'd above thirty Years ago,[8] when I had no thought of
ever troubling the World, with this Theatrical History, I see no
Reason, why it may not pass, as a Voucher of the Facts I am now
speaking of; I shall therefore give them, in the very Light I then
saw them. After some Acknowledgement for his Lordship's
Protection of our (*Hay-Market*) Theatre, it is further said ---

"The Stage has, for many Years, 'till of late, groan'd under
the greatest Discouragements, which have been very much, if
not wholly owing to the Mismenagement of those, that have
aukwardly govern'd it. Great Sums have been ventur'd upon
empty Projects, and Hopes of immoderate Gains; and when
those Hopes have fail'd, the Loss has been tyrannically deducted
out of the Actors Sallary. And if your Lordship had not re-
deem'd them --- *This is meant of our being suffer'd to come over
to* Swiney --- they were very near being wholly laid aside, or, at
least, the Use of their Labour was to be swallow'd up, in the pretended Merit of Singing, and Dancing."

What follows relates to the Difficulties in dealing with the
then impracticable Menager, *viz.*

"--- And though your Lordship's Tenderness of oppressing, is
so very just, that you have rather staid to convince a Man of
your good Intentions to him, than to do him even a Service
against his Will; yet since your Lordship has so happily begun
the Establishment of the separate Diversions, we live in hope,
that the same Justice, and Resolution, will still persuade you, to
go as successfully through with it. But while any Man is suffer'd
to confound the Industry, and Use of them, by acting publickly,
in opposition, to your Lordship's equal Intentions, under a false,
and inticate Pretence of not being able to comply with them;
the Town is likely to be more entertain'd with the private Dis-

sensions, than the publick Performance of either, and the Actors, in a perpetual Fear, and Necessity of petitioning your Lordship every Season, for new Relief."

Such was the State of the Stage, immediately preceding the time of Mr. *Brett*'s being admitted a joint Patentee, who, as he saw, with clearer Eyes, what was its evident Interest, left no proper Measures unattempted, to make this, so long despair'd-of, Union practicable. The most apparent Difficulty to be got over, in this Affair, was, what could be done for *Swiney*, in consideration of his being oblig'd to give up those Actors, whom the Power and Choice of the Lord-Chamberlain, had the Year before, set at the Head of, and by whole Menagement, those Actors had found themselves, in a prosperous Condition. But an Accident, at this time, happily contributed to make that Master Easy. The Inclination of our People of Quality for foreign Operas, had now reach'd the Ears of *Italy*, and the Credit of their Taste had drawn over from thence, without any more particular Invitation, one of their capital Singers, the famous Signior *Cavalero Nicolini*:[9] From whose Arrival, and the Impatience of the Town, to hear him, it was concluded, that Operas being, now, so completely provided, and could not fail of Success; and that, by making *Swiney* sole Director of them, the Profits must be an ample Compensation, for his Resignation of the Actors. This matter being thus adjusted, by *Swiney*'s Acceptance of the Opera only to be perform'd at the *Hay-Market* House; the Actors were all order'd to return to *Drury-Lane*, there to remain (under the Patentees) her Majesty's only Company of Comedians.

Plays, and Operas, being thus establish'd, upon separate Interests, they were now left, to make the best of their way, into Favour, by their different Merit. Although the Opera is not a Plant of our Native Growth, nor what our plainer Appetites are fond of, and is of so delicate a Nature, that without excessive Charge, it cannot live long among us; especially while the nicest *Connoisseurs* in Musick fall into such various Heresies in Taste, every Sect pretending to be the true one: Yet, as it was call'd a Theatrical Entertainment, and by its Alliance, or Neutrality, has more, or less affected our Domestick Theatre, a short View of its Progress may be allow'd a Place in our History.

After this new Regulation, the first Opera that appear'd, was *Pyrrhus*.[2] Subscriptions, at that time were not extended, as of late, to the whole Season, but were limited to the first Six Days only of a new Opera. The chief Performers, in this, were *Nicolini*, *Valentini*, and Mrs. *Tofts;*[3] and for the inferior Parts, the best that were then to be found. Whatever Praises may have been given to the most famous Voices, that have been heard since *Nicolini;* upon the whole, I cannot but come into the Opinion, that still prevails among several Persons of Condition, who are able to give a Reason for their liking, that no Singer, since his Time, has so justly, and gracefully acquitted himself, in whatever Character he appear'd, as *Nicolini*. At most, the Difference between him, and the greatest Favourite of the Ladies, *Farinelli*,[4] amounted but to this, that he might sometimes more exquisitely surprize us, but *Nicolini* (by pleasing the Eye, as well as the Ear) fill'd us with a more various, and *rational* Delight. Whether in this Excellence, he has since had any Competitor, perhaps, will be better judg'd, by what the Critical Censor of *Great Brit-ain* says of him in his 115th *Tatler*,[5] *viz.*

"*Nicolini* sets off the Character he bears in an Opera, by his Action, as much as he does the Words of it, by his Voice; every Limb, and Finger, contributes to the Part he acts, inso-much that a deaf Man might go along with him in the Sense of it. There is scarce a beautiful Posture, in an old Statue, which he does not plant himself in, as the different Circumstances of the Story give occasion for it---- He performs the most ordinary Action, in a manner suitable to the Greatness of his Character, and shews the Prince, even in the giving of a Letter, or dispatch-ing of a Message, *&c.*"

His Voice at this first Time of being among us, (for he made us a second Visit when it was impair'd) had all that strong, clear, Sweetness of Tone, so lately admir'd in *Senesino*. A blind Man could scarce have distinguish'd them; but in Volubility of Throat, the former had much the Superority. This so excellent Performer's Agreement was Eight Hundred Guineas for the Year, which is but an eighth Part more, than half the Sum, that has since been given to several, that could never totally surpass him: The Consequence of which is, that the Losses by Operas, for several Seasons, to the End of the Year 1738, have been so great, that those Gentlemen of Quality, who last undertook the Direction of them, found it ridiculous any longer to entertain the Publick, at so extravagant an Expence, while no one particu-lar Person thought himself oblig'd by it.

Mrs. *Tofts*, who took her first Grounds of Musick here in her own Country, before the *Italian* Taste had so highly prevail'd, was then but an Adept at it: Yet, whatever Defect the fashion-ably Skilful might find in her manner, she had, in the general Sense of her Spectators, Charms that few of the most learned Singers ever arrive at. The Beauty of her fine proportion'd Figure, and the exquisitely sweet, silver Tone of her Voice, with that peculiar, rapid Swiftness of her Throat, were Perfections not to be imitated by Art, or Labour. *Valentini* I have already mention'd, therefore need only say farther of him, that though he was every way inferior to *Nicolini*, yet as he had the Advan-

tage of giving us our first Impression of a good Opera Singer, he
had still his Admirers, and was of great Service, in being so skilful
a Second to his Superior.

Three such excellent Performers, in the same kind of Entertainment at once, *England* till this Time had never seen: Without any farther Comparison, then, with the much dearer bought,
who have succeeded them; their Novelty, at least, was a Charm
that drew vast Audiences of the fine World after them. *Swiney*
their sole Director was prosperous, and in one Winter, a Gainer
by them, of a moderate younger Brother's Fortune. But as Musick, by so profuse a Dispensation of her Beauties, could not
always supply our dainty Appetites, with equal Variety, nor
for ever please us with the same Objects; the Opera, after one
luxurious Season like the fine Wife of a roving Husband, began
to lose its Charms, and every Day discovered to our Satiety, Imperfections, which our former Fondness had been blind to: But
of this I shall observe more in its Place; in the mean time, let
us enquire into the Productions of our native Theatre.

It may be easily conceiv'd, that by this entire Re-union of the
two Companies, Plays must generally have been perform'd, to
a more than usual Advantage, and Exactness: For now every
chief Actor, according to his particular Capacity, piqued himself upon rectifying those Errors, which during their divided
State, were almost unavoidable. Such a Choice of Actors added
a Richness to every good Play, as it was, then, serv'd up, to the
publick Entertainment: The common People crowded to them,
with a more joyous Expectation, and those of the higher Taste
return'd to them, as to old Acquaintances, with new Desires,
after a long Absence. In a Word, all Parties seem'd better pleas'd,
but he, who one might imagine had most Reason to be so, the
(lately) sole menaging Patentee. He, indeed saw his Power daily
mould'ring from his own Hands, into those of Mr. *Brett;* whose
Gentlemanly manner of making every one's Business easy to
him, threw their old Master under a Disregard, which he had
not been us'd to, nor could with all his happy Change of Affairs,
support. Although this grave Theatrical Minister, of whom I
have been oblig'd to make such frequent mention, had acquitted

the Reputation of a most profound Politician, by being often incomprehensible, yet I am not sure, that his Conduct at this Juncture, gave us not an evident Proof, that he was, like other frail Mortals, more a Slave to his Passions, than his Interest; for no Creature ever seem'd more fond of Power, that so little knew how to use it, to his Profit and Reputation; otherwise he could not possibly have been so discontented, in his secure, and prosperous State of the Theatre, as to resolve, at all Hazards, to destroy it. We shall now see what infallible Measures he took, to bring this laudable Scheme to Perfection.

He plainly saw, that as this disagreeable Prosperity was chiefly owing to the Conduct of Mr. *Brett*, there could be no hope of recovering the Stage to its former Confusion, but by finding some effectual Means to make Mr. *Brett* weary of his Charge: The most probable he could, for the present, think of, in this Distress, was to call in the Adventurers (whom for many Years, by his Defence in Law, he had kept out) now to take care of their visibly improving Interests. This fair Appearance of Equity, being known to be his own Proposal, he rightly guess'd would incline these Adventurers to form a Majority of Votes on his Side, in all Theatrical Questions; and consequently become a Check upon the Power of Mr. *Brett*, who had so visibly alienated the Hearts of his Theatrical Subjects, and now began to govern without him. When the Adventurers, therefore, were re-admitted to their old Government; after having recommended himself to them, by proposing to make some small Dividend of the Profits (though he did not design that Jest should be repeated) he took care that the Creditors of the Patent, who were, then, no inconsiderable Body, should carry off the every Weeks clear Profits, in proportion to their several Dues and Demands. This Conduct, so speciously just, he had Hopes would let Mr. *Brett* see, that his Share, in the Patent, was not so valuable an Acquisition as, perhaps, he might think it; and probably might make a Man of his Turn to Pleasure, soon weary of the little Profit, and great Plague it gave him. Now, though these might be all notable Expedients, yet I cannot say they would have wholly contributed to Mr. *Brett*'s quitting his Post, had not a Matter of much stronger Moment, an unexpected Dispute between him, and Sir *Thomas Skipwith*, prevail'd with him to lay it down: For in the midst of this flourshing State of the Patent, Mr. *Brett* was surpriz'd with a Subpoena into Chancery, from Sir *Thomas Skipwith*, who alleg'd, in his Bill, that the Conveyance he had made of his Interest, in the Patent, to Mr. *Brett*, was only intended in Trust. (Whatever the Intent might be, the Deed it self, which I then read, made no mention of any Trust whatever.) But whether Mr. *Brett*, as Sir *Thomas* farther asserted, had previously, or after the Deed was sign'd, given his Word of Honour, that if he should ever make the Stage turn to any Account, or Profit, he would certainly restore it: That indeed, I can say nothing to; but be the Deed valid, or void, the Facts that apparently follow'd were, that tho' Mr. *Brett*, in his Answer to this Bill, absolutely deny'd his receiving this Assignment, either in Trust, or upon any limited Condition, of what kind soever; yet he made no farther Defence, in the Cause. But since he found Sir *Thomas* had thought fit, on any Account to sue for the Restitution of it; and Mr. *Brett* being himself conscious, that, as the World knew, he had paid no Consideration for it; his keeping it might be misconstrued, or not favourably spoken of; or perhaps finding, tho' the Profits were great, they were constantly swallow'd up (as has been observ'd) by the previous Satisfaction of old Debts, he grew so tir'd of the Plague, and Trouble, the whole Affair had given him, and was likely still to engage him in, that in a few Weeks after, he withdrew himself, from all Concern with the Theatre, and quietly left Sir *Thomas* to find his better Account in it. And thus stood this undecided Right, till upon the Demise of Sir *Thomas*, Mr. *Brett* being allow'd the Charges he had been at, in his Attendance, and Prosecution of the Union, reconvey'd this Share of the Patent to Sir *George Skipwith*, the Son, and Heir of Sir *Thomas*.

Our Politician, the old Patentee, having thus fortunately got rid of Mr. *Brett*,[7] who had so rashly brought the Patent once more to a profitable Tenure, was now again at liberty, to chuse rather to lose all, than not to have it all to himself.

I have, elsewhere, observ'd that nothing can so effectually se-

cure the Strength, or contribute to the Prosperity of a good
Company, as the Directors of it having always, as near as possible,
an amicable Understanding, with three or four of their best
Actors, whose good, or ill-will, must naturally make a wide
Difference, in their profitable, or useless manner of serving them:
While the Principal are kept reasonably easy, the lower Class
can never be troublesome, without hurting themselves: But when
a valuable Actor is hardly treated, the Master must be a very
cunning Man, that finds his Account in it. We shall now see
how far Experience will verify this Observation.

The Patentees thinking themselves secure, in being restor'd
to their former absolute Power, over this, now, only Company,
chose rather to govern it by the Reverse of the Method I
have recommended: For tho' the daily Charge of their united
company amounted not, by a good deal, to what either of the
two Companies, now in *Drury-Lane*, or *Covent-Garden*, singly,
arises; they notwithstanding fell into their former Politicks, of
thinking every Shilling taken from a hir'd Actor, so much clear
Gain to the Proprietor: Many of their People, therefore, were
actually, if not injudiciously, reduc'd in their Pay, and others
given to understand, the same Fate was design'd them, of which
last Number I, my self was one, which occurs to my Memory,
by the Answer I made to one of the Adventurers; who, in Justification of their intended Proceeding, told me, that my Sallary,
tho' it should be less, than it was, by ten Shillings a Week, would
still be more than ever *Goodman* had, who was a better Actor,
than I could pretend to be: To which I reply'd, This may
be true, but then you know, Sir, it is as true, that *Goodman*
was forc'd to go upon the High-way for a Livelihood. As this
was a known Fact of *Goodman*, my mentioning it, on that Occasion, I believe, was of Service to me; at least my Sallary was
not reduc'd after it. To say a Word or two more of *Goodman*,
so celebrated an Actor, in his Time, perhaps may set the Conduct
of the Patentees in a clearer Light. Tho' *Goodman* had left the
Stage, before I came to it, I had some slight Acquaintance with
him. About the Time of his being expected to be an Evidence
against Sir *John Fenwick*, in the Assassination Plot, in 1696, I

happen'd to meet him at Dinner, at Sir *Thomas Skipwith*'s, who
as he was an agreeable Companion himself, liked *Goodman* for
the same Quality. Here it was, that *Goodman*, without Disguise,
or sparing himself, fell into a laughing Account of several loose
Passages of *his* younger Life; as his being expell'd the University
of *Cambridge*, for being one of the hot-headed Sparks, who were
concern'd in the cutting, and defacing the Duke of *Mon-
mouth*'s Picture, then Chancellor of that Place. But this Disgrace,
it seems, had not disqualify'd him for the Stage; which, like the
Sea-Service, refuses no Man, for his Morals, that is able-body'd:
There, as an Actor, he soon grew into a different Reputation;
but whatever his Merit might be, the Pay of a hired Hero, in
those Days, was so very low, that he was forc'd, it seems, to take
the Air (as he call'd it) and borrow what Mony the first Man
he met, had about him. But this being his first Exploit of that
kind, which the Scantiness of his Theatrical Fortune had reduc'd him to, King *James* was prevail'd upon, to pardon him:
Which *Goodman* said, was doing him so particular an Honour,
that no Man could wonder, if his Acknowledgment had carry'd
him, a little farther, than ordinary, into the Interest of that
Prince: But as he had, lately, been out of Luck, in backing his
old Master, he had now no way to get home the Life he was out,
upon his account, but by being under the same Obligations to
King *William*.

Another Anecdote of him, tho' not quite so dishonourably
enterprizing, which I had from his own Mouth, at a different
time, will equally shew, to what low Shifts in Life, the poor
Provision for good Actors, under the early Government of the
Patent, reduc'd them. In the younger Days of their Heroism,
Captain *Griffin*, and *Goodman*, were confin'd by their moderate Sallaries, to the Oeconomy of lying together, in the same
Bed, and having but one whole Shirt between them: One of
them being under the Obligation of a Rendezvous, with a fair
Lady, insisted upon his wearing it, out of his Turn, which occasion'd so high a Dispute, that the Combat was immediately
demanded, and accordingly their Pretensions to it, were decided

by a fair Tilt upon the Spot, in the Room, where they lay: But whether *Clytus*, or *Alexander*[8] was oblig'd to see no Company, till a worse could be wash'd for him, seems not to be a material Point, in their History, or to my Purpose.

By this Rate of *Goodman*, who, till the Time of his quitting the Stage, never had more, than what is call'd forty Shillings a Week, it may be judg'd, how cheap the Labour of Actors had been formerly; and the Patentees thought it a Folly to continue the higher Price, (which their Divisions had since rais'd them to) now there was but one Market for them; but alas! they had forgot their former fatal Mistake of squabbling with their Actors, in 1695; nor did they make any Allowance for the Changes and Operations of Time, or enough consider the Interest the Actors had in the Lord Chamberlain, on whose Protection they might always rely, and whose Decrees had been less restrain'd by Precedent, than those of a Lord Chancellor.

In this mistaken View of their Interest, the Patentees, by treating their Actors as Enemies, really made them so: And when once the Masters of a hired Company think not their Actors Hearts as necessary, as their Hands, they cannot be said to have agreed for above half the Work, they are able to do in a Day: Or, if an unexpected Success should, notwithstanding, make the Profits, in any gross Disproportion, greater, than the Wages; the Wages will always have something worse, than a Murmur, at the Head of them, that will not only measure the Merit of the Actor, by the Gains of the Proprietor, but will never naturally be quiet, till every Scheme of getting into Property has been try'd, to make the Servant his own Master: And this, as far as Experience can make me judge, will always be, in either of these Cases, the State of our *English* Theatre. What Truth there may be, in this Observation, we are now coming to a Proof of.

To enumerate all the particular Acts of Power, in which the Patentees daily bore hard, upon this, now only Company of Actors, might be as tedious, as unnecessary; I shall therefore come, at once, to their most material Grievance, upon which they grounded their Complaint to the Lord-Chamberlain, who in the Year following, 1709, took effectual Measures for their Relief.

The Patentees observing that the Benefit-Plays of the Actors, towards the latter end of the Season, brought the most crowded Audiences in the Year; began to think their own Interests too much neglected, by these partial Favours of the Town, to their Actors; and therefore judg'd, it would not be impolitick, in such wholesom annual Profits, to have a Fellow-feeling with them. Accordingly, an *Indulto*[9] was laid of one Third, out of the Profits of every Benefit, for the proper Use, and Behoof of the Patent. But, that a clear Judgment may be form'd of the Equity, or Hardship of this Imposition it will be necessary to shew from whence, and from what Causes, the Actors Claim to Benefits originally proceeded.

During the Reign of King *Charles*, an Actor's Benefit had never been heard of. The first Indulgence of this Kind, was given to Mrs. *Barry* (as has been formerly observed) in King *James*'s Time, in consideration of the extraordinary Applause, that had followed her Performance: But there this Favour rested, to her alone, 'till after the Division of the only Company in 1695, at which time the Patentees were soon reduc'd to pay their Actors, half in good Words, and half in ready Mony. In this precarious Condition, some particular Actors (however binding their Agreements might be) were too poor, or too wise to go to Law with a Lawyer; and therefore rather chose to compound their Arrears, for their being admitted to the Chance of having them made up, by the Profits of a Benefit Play. This Expedient had this Consequence; That the Patentees, tho' their daily Audiences, might, and did sometimes mend, still kept the short Subsistance of their Actors, at a stand, and grew more steady in their Resolution so to keep them, as they found them less apt to mutiny, while their Hopes of being clear'd off, by a Benefit, were depending. In a Year, or two, these Benefits grew so advantageous, that they became, at last, the chief Article, in every Actor's Agreement.

Now though the Agreements of these united Actors, I am

speaking of in 1708, were as yet, only Verbal; yet that made no difference in the honest Obligation, to keep them: But, as Honour at that time happen'd to have but a loose hold of their Consciences, the Patentees rather chose to give it the slip, and went on with their Work without it. No Actor, therefore, could have his Benefit fix'd, 'till he had first sign'd a Paper, signifying his voluntary Acceptance of it, upon the, above, Conditions, any Claims from Custom, to the contrary notwithstanding. Several at first refus'd to sign this Paper; upon which the next in Rank were offer'd on the same Conditions, to come before the Refusers; this smart Expedient got some few of the fearful the Preference to their Seniors; who at last, seeing the time was too short for a present Remedy, and that they must either come into the Boat, or lose their Tide, were forc'd to comply, with what, they, as yet, silently, resented as the severest Injury. In this Situation, therefore, they chose to let the principal Benefits be over, that their Grievances might swell into some bulk, before they made any Application for Redress to the Lord-Chamberlain; who, upon hearing their general Complaint, order'd the Patentees to shew cause, why their Benefits had been diminish'd one Third, contrary to the common Usage? The Patentees pleaded the sign'd Agreement, and the Actors Receipts of the other two Thirds, in full Satisfaction. But these were prov'd to have been exacted from them, by the Methods already mentioned. They notwithstanding insist upon them as lawful. But as Law, and Equity do not always agree, they were look'd upon as unjust, and arbitrary. Whereupon the Patentees were warn'd[10] at their Peril, to refuse the Actors full Satisfaction. But here it was thought necessary, that Judgment should be for some time respited, 'till the Actors, who had leave so to do, could form a Body strong enough to make the Inclination of the Lord-Chamberlain to relieve them, practicable.

Accordingly *Swiney* (who was then sole Director of the Opera only) had Permission to enter into a private Treaty, with such of the united Actors in *Drury-Lane*, as might be thought fit to head a Company, under their own Management, and to be Sharers with him in the *Hay-Market*. The Actors chosen for

this Charge, were *Wilks*, *Dogget*, Mrs. *Oldfield*, and Myself.
But, before I proceed, lest it should seem surprizing, that neither
Betterton, Mrs. *Barry*, Mrs. *Bracegirdle*, or *Booth*, were Parties
in this Treaty; it must be observ'd that *Betterton* was now
Seventy-three, and rather chose, with the Infirmitites of Age
upon him, to rely on such Sallary, as might be appointed him,
than to involve himself, in the Cares, and Hurry, that must un-
avoidably attend the Regulation of a new Company. As to the
two celebrated Actresses I have named, this has been my first
proper Occasion of making it known, that they had both quitted
the Stage the Year before this Transaction was thought of.[11]
And *Booth*, as yet, was scarce out of his Minority as an Actor,
or only in the Promise of that Reputation, which in about four
or five Years after, he happily arriv'd at. However, at this Juncture, he was not so far overlook'd, as not to be offer'd a valuable
Addition to his Sallary: But this he declin'd, being, while the
Patentees were under this Distress, as much, if not more, in
favour, with their chief Manager, as a Schematist, than as an
Actor: And indeed he appear'd, to my Judgment, more inclin'd
to risque his Fortune in *Drury-Lane*, where he should have no
Rival in Parts, or Power, than on any Terms to embark in the
Hay-Market; where he was sure to meet with Opponents in
both. However this his Separation from our Interest, when our
All was at stake, afterwards kept his Advancement, to a Share
with us, in our more successful Days, longer postpon'd, than
otherwise it probably might have been.

When Mrs. *Oldfield* was nominated as a joint Sharer, in our
new Agreement to be made with *Swiney; Dogget*, who had no
Objection to her Merit, insisted that our Affairs could never be
upon a secure Foundation, if there was more, than one Sex
admitted to the Management of them. He therefore hop'd, that
if we offer'd Mrs. *Oldfield* a *Carte Blanche*, instead of a Share,
she would not think herself slighted. This was instantly agreed
to, and Mrs. *Oldfield* receiv'd it rather as a Favour, than a
Disobligation: Her Demands therefore were Two Hundred
Pounds a Year certain, and a Benefit clear of all Charges; which
were readily sign'd to. Her Easiness on this Occasion, some

Years after, when our Establishment was in Prosperity, made us, with less Reluctancy, advance her Two Hundred Pounds, to Three Hundred Guineas *per Annum*, with her usual Benefit, which upon an Average for several Years at least, doubled that Sum.

When a sufficient number of Actors were engag'd, under our Confederacy with *Swiney*, it was then judg'd a proper time, for the Lord-Chamberlain's Power, to operate, which, by lying above a Month dormant, had so far recover'd the Patentees, from any Apprehensions of what might fall upon them, from their late Usurpations on the Benefits of the Actors, that they began to set their Marks, upon those who had distinguish'd themselves, in the Application for Redress. Several little Disgraces were put upon them; particularly in the Disposal of Parts, in Plays to be reviv'd, and as visible a Partiality was shewn in the Promotion of those in their Interest, though their Endeavours to serve them could be of no extraordinary use. How often does History shew us, in the same State of Courts, the same Politicks have been practis'd? All this while, the other Party was passively silent; 'till one Day, the Actor who particularly solicited their Cause, at the Lord-Chamberlain's Office, being shewn there the Order sign'd, for absolutely silencing the Patentees, and ready to be serv'd, flew back with the News to his Companions, then at a Rehearsal, in which he had been wanted; when being call'd to his Part, and something hastily question'd by the Patentee, for his Neglect of Business: This Actor, I say, with an erected Look, and a Theatrical Spirit, at once threw off the Mask, and roundly told him ---- *Sir, I have now no more Business Here, than you have; in half an Hour, you will neither have Actors to command, nor Authority, to employ them.* ---- The Patentee, who though he could not readily comprehend his mysterious manner of Speaking, had just a Glimpse of Terror enough from the Words, to soften his Reproof into a cold formal Declaration, That *if he would not do his Work, he should not be paid.* — But now, to complete the Catastrophe of these Theatrical Commotions, enters the Messenger, with the Order of Silence in his Hand, whom the same Actor officiously introduc'd, telling the Patentee, that the Gentleman wanted to speak with him, from the Lord-Chamberlain. When the Messenger had delivered the Order, the Actor throwing his Head over his shoulder, towards the Patentee, in the manner of *Shakespear*'s *Harry the Eighth* to Cardinal *Wolsey* cry'd *Read o'er that! and now—to Breakfast, with what Appetite you may*.[12] Though these Words might be spoken, in too vindictive, and insulting a manner, to be commended; yet from the Fulness of a Heart injuriously treated, and now reliev'd by that instant Occasion, why might they not be pardon'd?

The Authority of the Patent now no longer subsisting, all the confederated Actors immediately walk'd out of the House, to which they never return'd, 'till they became themselves the Tenants, and Masters of it.

Here agen, we see an higher Instance of the Authority of a Lord-Chamberlain, than any of those I have elsewhere mentioned: From whence that Power might be deriv'd, as I have already said, I am not Lawyer enough to know; however it is evident that a Lawyer obey'd it, though to his Cost; which might incline one, to think, that the Law was not clearly against it: Be that as it may, since the Law has lately made it no longer a Question, let us drop the Enquiry, and proceed to the Facts, which follow'd this Order, that silenc'd the Patent.[13]

From this last injudicious Disagreement of the Patentees with their principal Actors, and from what they had suffered on the same Occasion, in the Division of their only Company in 1695, might we not imagine there was something of Infatuation, in their Management? For though I allow Actors, in general, when they are too much indulg'd, or govern'd by an unsteady Head, to be as unruly a Multitude as Power can be plagued with; yet there is a Medium, which, if cautiously observed by a candid use of Power, making them always know, without feeling their Superior, neither suffering their Encroachments, nor invading their Rights, with an immoveable Adherence to the accepted Laws, they are to walk by; such a Regulation, I say, has never fail'd, in my Observation, to have made them a tractable, and profitable Society. If the Government of a well-establish'd

Theatre were to be compar'd to that of a Nation; there is no one Act of Policy, or Misconduct in the one, or the other, in which the Manager might not, in some parallel Case (laugh, if you please) be equally applauded, or condemned with the Statesman. Perhaps this will not be found so wild a Conceit, if you look into the 193d *Tatler*, Vol. 4, where the Affairs of the State, and those of the very Stage, which I am now treating of, are in a Letter from *Downs* the Prompter, compar'd, and with a great deal of Wit, and Humour, set upon an equal Foot of Policy.[14] The Letter is suppos'd to have been written, in the last Change of the Ministry in Queen *Anne*'s Time: I will therefore venture, upon the Authority of that Author's Imagination, to carry the Comparison as high, as it can possibly go, and say, That as I remember one of our Princes, in the last Century, to have lost his Crown, by too arbitrary a Use of his Power, though he knew how fatal the same Measures had been to his unhappy Father before him; why should we wonder, that the same Passions taking Possession of Men, in lower Life, by an equally impolitick Usage of their Theatrical Subjects, should have involved the Patentees, in proportionable Calamities.

During the Vacation, which immediately follow'd the Silence of the Patent, both Parties were at leisure to form their Schemes for the Winter: For the Patentee would still hold out, notwithstanding his being so miserably maim'd, or over-match'd: He had no more Regard to Blows, than a blind Cock of the Game; he might be beaten, but would never yield, the Patent was still in his Possession, and the Broad-Seal to it visibly as fresh as ever: Besides, he had yet some Actors in his Service,[15] at a much cheaper Rate than those who had left him, the Sallaries of which last now they would not work for him, he was not oblig'd to pay. In this way of thinking, he still kept together such, as had not been invited over to the *Hay-Market*, or had been influenc'd by *Booth*, to follow his Fortune in *Drury-Lane*.

By the Patentee's keeping these Remains of his broken Forces together, it is plain, that he imagin'd this Order of Silence, like others of the same Kind, would be recall'd of course, after a reasonable time of Obedience had been paid to it: But it seems,

he had rely'd too much upon former Precedents; nor had his
Politicks yet div'd, into the Secret, that the Court Power, with
which the Patent had been so long, and often at variance, had
now a mind to take the publick Diversions more absolutely into
their own Hands: Not that I have any stronger Reasons for this
Conjecture, than that the Patent, never after this Order of
Silence, got leave to play during the Queen's Reign. But upon
the Accession of his late Majesty, Power having then a different
Aspect, the Patent found no Difficulty in being permitted to exercise its former Authority for acting Plays, &c. which, however from this time of their lying still, in 1709, did not happen
'till 1714, and which the old Patentee never liv'd to see: For
he dy'd about six Weeks before the new-built Theatre in
Lincoln's-Inn Fields was open'd,[16] where the first Play acted was
the *Recruiting Officer*, under the Management of his Heirs, and
Successors. But of that Theatre, it is not yet time to give any
further Account.

The first Point resolv'd on, by the Comedians now re-estab-
lish'd in the *Hay-Market*, was to alter the Auditory Part of their
Theatre; the Inconveniencies of which have been fully enlarg'd
upon in a former Chapter. What embarrass'd them most in
this Design, was, their want of Time to do it in a more complete
manner, than it now remains in, otherwise they had brought it,
to the original Model of that in *Drury-Lane*, only in a larger
Proportion, as the wider Walls of it would require; as there are
not many Spectators, who may remember what Form the
Drury-Lane Theatre stood in, about forty Years ago, before
the old Patentee, to make it hold more Mony, took it in his
Head to alter it, it were but Justice to lay the original Figure,
which Sir *Christopher Wren* first gave it, and the Alterations of
it, now standing, in a fair Light; that equal Spectators may see,
if they were at their choice, which of the Structures would incline them to a Preference.[16a] But in this Appeal, I only speak to
such Spectators as allow a good Play, well acted, to be the most
valuable Entertainment of the Stage. Whether such Plays (leaving the Skill of the dead, or living Actors equally out of the
Question) have been more, or less, recommended in their Presen-

tation, by either of these different Forms of that Theatre, is our present Matter of Enquiry.

It must be observ'd then, that the Area, or Platform of the old Stage, projected about four Foot forwarder, in a Semi-oval Figure, parallel to the Benches of the Pit; and that the former, lower Doors of Entrance for the Actors, were brought down between the two foremost (and then only) Pilasters; in the Place of which Doors, now the two Stage-Boxes are fixt. That where the Doors of Entrance now are, there formerly stood two additional Side-Wings, in front to a ful Set of Scenes, which had then almost a double Effect, in their Loftiness, and Magnificence.

By this original Form, the usual Station of the Actors, in almost every Scene, was advanc'd at least ten Foot nearer to the Audience, than they now can be; because, not only from the Stage's being shorten'd, in front, but likewise from the additional Interposition of those Stage-Boxes, the Actors (in respect to the Spectators, that fill them) are kept so much more backward from the main Audience, than they us'd to be: But when the Actors were in Possession of that forwarder Space, to advance upon, the Voice was then more in the Centre of the House, so that the most distant Ear had scarce the least Doubt, or Difficulty inhearing what fell from the weakest Utterance: All Objects were thus drawn nearer to the Sense; every painted Scene was stronger; every Grand Scene and Dance more extended; every rich, or fine-coloured Habit had a more lively Lustre: Nor was the minutest Motion of a Feature (properly changing with the Passion, or Humour it suited) ever lost, as they frequently must be in the Obscurity of too great a Distance: And how valuable in Advantage the Facility of hearing distinctly, is to every well-acted Scene, every common Spectator is a Judge. A Voice scarce rais'd above the Tone of a Whisper, either in Tenderness, Resignation, innocent Distress, or Jealousy, suppress'd, often have as much concern with the Heart, as the most clamorous Passions; and when on any of these Occasions, such affecting Speeches are plainly heard, or lost, how wide is the Difference, from the great or little Satisfaction received from

them? To all this a Master of a Company may say, I now receive
Ten Pounds more, than could have been taken formerly, in every
full House! Not unlikely. But might not his House be oftner full,
if the Auditors were oftner pleas'd? Might not every bad House
too, by a Possibility of being made every Day better, add as
much to one side of his Account, as it could take from the other?
If what I have said, carries any Truth in it, why might not the
original Form of this Theatre be restor'd?[16b] But let this Digression avail what it may, the Actors now return'd to the *Hay-*
Market, as I have observ'd, wanted nothing but length of time
to have govern'd their Alteration of that Theatre, by this original Model of *Drury-Lane*, which I have recommended. As
their time therefore was short, they made their best use of it;
they did something to it: They contracted its Wideness, by
three Ranges of Boxes on each Side, and brought down its enormous high Cieling, within so proportionable a Compass, that
it effectually cured those hollow Undulations of the Voice formerly complain'd of. The Remedy had its Effect; their Audiences exceeded their Expectation. There was now no other
Theatre open against them;[17] they had the Town to themselves;
they were their own Masters, and the Profits of their Industry
came into their own Pockets.

Yet with all this fair Weather, the Season of their uninterrupted Prosperity was not yet arriv'd; for the great Expence,
and thinner Audiences of the Opera (of which they then were
equally Directors) was a constant Drawback upon their Gains,
yet not so far, but that their Income this Year, was better than
in their late Station, at *Drury-Lane*. But by the short Experience
we had then had of Operas; by the high Reputation they
seem'd to have been arriv'd at, the Year before; by their Power
of drawing the whole Body of Nobility, as by Enchantment, to
their Solemnities; by that Prodigality of Expence, at which they
were so willing to support them; and from the late extraordinary
Profits *Swiney* had made of them; what Mountains did we not
hope from this Mole-hill? But alas! the fairy Vision was vanish'd,
this bridal Beauty was grown familiar to the general Taste, and
Satiety began to make Excuses for its want of Appetite: Or
what is still stronger, its late Admirers now as much valued their

Judgment, in being able to find out the Faults of the Performers, as they had before, in discovering their Excellencies. The Truth is, that this kind of Entertainment being so intirely sensual, it had no Possibility of getting the better of our Reason, but by its Novelty; and that Novelty could never be supported but by an annual Change of the best Voices, which like the finest Flowers, bloom but for a Season, and when that is over, are only dead Nose-gays. From this Natural Cause, we have seen within these two Years, even *Farinelli* singing to an Audience of five and thirty Pounds; and yet, if common Fame may be credited, the same Voice, so neglected in one Country, has in another had Charms sufficient to make the Crown fit easy, on the Head of a Monarch, which the Jealousy of Politicians (who had their Views, in his keeping it) fear'd without some such extraordinary Amusement, his Satiety of Empire might tempt him, a second time, to resign.[18]

There is too, in the very Species of an *Italian* Singer, such an innate, fantastical Pride, and Caprice, that the Government of them (here at least) is almost impracticable. This Distemper, as we were not sufficiently warn'd, or appriz'd of, threw our musical Affairs into Perplexities, we knew not easily how to get out of. There is scarce a sensible Auditor, in the Kingdom, that has not, since that Time, had Occasion to laugh at the several Instances of it: But what is still more ridiculous, these costly Canary-Birds have sometimes infested the whole Body of our dignified Lovers of Musick, with the same childish Animosities: Ladies have been known to decline their Visits, upon account of their being of a different musical Party. *Caesar*, and *Pompey* made not a warmer Division, in the *Roman* Republick, than those Heroines, their Country Women, the *Faustina* and *Cuzzoni*[19] blew up in our Common-wealth, of Academical Musick, by their implacable Pretensions to Superiority! And while this Greatness of Soul is their unalterable Virtue, it will never be practicable to make two capital Singer of the same Sex, do as they should do, in one Opera, at the same Time! no, not tho' *England* were to double the Sums it has already thrown after them: For even in their own Country, where an extraordinary Occasion, has called a greater Number of their best, to sing together, the Mischief they have made has been proportionable; an Instance of which, if I am rightly inform'd, happen'd at *Parma*, where upon the Celebration of the Marriage of that Duke, a Collection was made of the most eminent Voices, that Expence, or Interest could Purchase, to give as complete an Opera, as the whole vocal Power of *Italy* could form. But when it came to the Proof of this musical Project, behold! what woeful Work they made of it! Every Performer would be a *Caesar*, or nothing; their several Pretensions to Preference were not to be limited within the Laws of Harmony; they would all chuse their own Songs, but not more to set off themselves, than to oppose, or deprive another of an Occasion to shine: Yet any one would sing a bad Song, provided no body else had a good one, till at last, they were thrown together like so many feather'd Warriors, for a Battle-royal, in a Cock-pit, where every one was oblig'd to kill another, to save himself! What Pity it was these froward Misses, and Masters of Musick had not been engag'd to entertain the Court of some King of *Morocco*, that could have known a good Opera, from a bad one! and how much Ease would such a Director have brought them to better Order? But alas! as it has been said of greater Things,

> *Suis et ipsa Roma viribus ruit.*[20]   Hor.

Imperial *Rome* fell, by the too great Strength of its own Citizens! So fell this mighty Opera, ruin'd by the too great Excellency of its Singers! For, upon the whole, it prov'd to be as barbarously bad, as if Malice it self had compos'd it.

Now though something of this kind, equally provoking, has generally embarrass'd the State of Operas, these thirty Years; yet it was the Misfortune of the menaging Actors, at the *Hay-Market*, to have felt the first Effects of it: The Honour of the Singer, and the Interest of the Undertaker were so often at Variance, that the latter began to have but a bad Bargain of it. But not to impute more to the Caprice of those Performers, than was really true, there were two different Accidents, that drew Numbers from our Audiences, before the Season was ended; which were another Company permitted to act in *Drury-Lane*, and the long Trial of Doctor *Sacheverel*, in *Westminster-*

Hall:[21] By the way, it must be observ'd, that this Company was not under the Direction of the Patent (which continued still silenc'd) but was set up by a third Interest, with a License from Court.[22] The Person to whom this new License was granted, was *William Collier*, Esq; a Lawyer of an enterprizing Head, and a jovial Heart; what sort of Favour he was in, with the People, then, in Power, may be judg'd, from his being often admitted to partake with them those detach'd Hours of Life, when Business was to give way to Pleasure: But this was not all his Merit, he was, at the same time, a Member of Parliament for *Truro* in *Cornwall*, and we cannot suppose a Person so qualified could be refus'd such a Trifle, as a License to head a broken Company of Actors. This sagacious Lawyer, then, who had a Lawyer to deal with, observing that his Antagonist kept Possession of a Theatre, without making use of it, and for which he was not oblig'd to pay Rent, unless he actually *did* use it, wisely conceiv'd it might be the Interest of the joint Landlords, since their Tenement was in so precarious a Condition, to grant a Lease to one, who had an undisputed Authority, to be liable, by acting Plays in it, to pay the Rent of it; especially when he tempted them with an Offer of raising it from three, to four Pounds *per Diem.* His Project succeeded, the Lease was sign'd; but the Means of getting into Possession were to be left to his own Cost, and Discretion. This took him up but little Time, he immediately laid Siege to it, with a sufficient Number of Forces, whether lawless, or lawful, I forget but they were such as oblig'd the old Governor to give it up; who, notwithstanding had got Intelligence of his Approaches, and Design, time enough to carry off every thing, that was worth moving, except a great Number of old Scenes, and new Actors, that could not easily follow him.

A ludicrous Account of this Transaction under fictitious Names, may be found in the 99th *Tatler*, Vol 2,[23] which this Explanation may now render more intelligible, to the Readers of that agreeable Author.

This other new License being now in Possession of the *Drury-Lane* Theatre; those Actors, whom the Patentee, ever since the Order of Silence, had retain'd in a State of Inaction,

all to a Man came over to the Service of *Collier*. Of these, *Booth*
was then the chief. The Merit of the rest had as yet made no
considerable Appearance, and as the Patentee had not left a Rag
of their Cloathing behind him, they were but poorly equip'd
for a publick Review; consequently at their first Opening, they
were very little able to annoy us. But during the Trial of *Sacheverel*, our Audiences were extremely weaken'd, by the better
Rank of People's daily attending it: While, at the same time, the
lower Sort, who were not equally admitted to that grand Spectacle, as eagerly crowded into *Drury-Lane*, to a new Comedy,
called *The fair Quaker of Deal.*[24] This Play, having some low
Strokes of natural Humour in it, was rightly calculated, for
the Capacity of the Actors, who play'd it, and to the Taste
of the Multitude, who were now, more dispos'd, and at leisure
to see it: But the most happy Incident, in its Fortune, was the
Charm of the fair Quaker, which was acted by Miss *Santlow*,[25]
(afterwards Mrs. *Booth*) whose Person was then in the full
Bloom of what Beauty she might pretend to: Before this, she
had only been admired as the most excellent Dancer; which,
perhaps, might not a little contribute to the favourable Reception, she now met with as an Actress, in this Character, which so
happily suited her Figure, and Capacity: The gentle Softness of
her Voice, the compos'd Innocence of her Aspect, the Modesty
of her Dress, the reserv'd Decency of her Gesture, and the Simplicity of the Sentiments, that naturally fell from her, made her
seem the amiable Maid she represented: In a Word, not the
enthusiastick Maid of *Orleans*, was more serviceable of old, to
the *French* Army, when the *English* had distress'd them, than
this fair Quaker was, at the Head of that dramatick Attempt,
upon which the Support of their weak Society depended.

But when the Trial, I have mention'd, and the Run of this
Play was over, the Tide of the Town beginning to turn again
in our Favour, *Collier* was reduc'd to give his Theatrical Affairs
a different Scheme; which advanc'd the Stage another Step
towards that Settlement, which, in my Time, was of the longest
Duration.

As coarse Mothers may have comely Children; so Anarchy has been the Parent of many a good Government; and by a Parity of possible Consequences we shall find, that from the frequent Convulsions of the Stage, arose, at last, its longest Settlement, and Prosperity; which many of my Readers (or if I should happen to have but few of them, many of my Spectators, at least) who, I hope, have not yet liv'd half their Time, will be able to remember.

Though the Patent had been often under Distresses, it had never felt any Blow, equal to this unrevoked Order of Silence; which it is not easy to conceive could have fallen upon any other Person's Conduct, than that of the old Patentee: For if he was conscious, of his being under the Subjection of that Power, which had silenc'd him, why would he incur the Danger of a Suspension, by his so obstinate, and impolitick Treatment of his Actors? If he thought such Power over him illegal, how came he to obey it now, more than before, when he slighted a former Order, that injoin'd him to give his Actors their Benefits, on their usual Condition? But to do him Justice, the same Obstinacy, that involv'd him, in these Difficulties, at last, preserv'd to his Heirs the Property of the Patent, in its full Force, and Value; yet to suppose that he foresaw a milder use of Power, in some future Prince's Reign, might be more favourable to him, is begging at best but a cold Question. But whether he knew that this broken Condition of the Patent would not make his troublesome Friends, the Adventurers, fly from it as from a falling House, seems not so difficult a Question. However, let the Reader form his own Judgment of them, from the Facts, that follow'd: It must therefore be observ'd, that the Adventurers

seldom came near the House, but when there was some visible
Appearance of a Dividend: But I could never hear, that upon an
ill Run of Audiences, they had ever returned, or brought in a
single Shilling, to make good the Deficiencies of their daily Receipts. Therefore, as the Patentee, in Possession, had alone, for
several Years, supported, and stood against this Uncertainty of
Fortune, it may be imagin'd, that his Accounts were under so
voluminous a Perplexity, that few of those Adventurers would
have Leisure, or Capacity enough to unravel them: And as they
had formerly thrown away their Time, and Mony at Law, in
a fruitless Enquiry into them, they now seem'd to have intirely
given up their Right and Interest: And, according to my best
Information, notwithstanding the subsequent Gains of the Patent have been sometimes extraordinary, the farther Demands,
or Claims of Right, of the Adventurers have lain dormant, above
these five and twenty Years.

Having shewn by what means *Collier* had dispossess'd this
Patentee, not only of the *Drury-Lane* House, but likewise of
those few Actors, which he had kept, for some time unemploy'd
in it; we are now led to consider another Project of the same
Patentee, which, if we are to judge of by the Event, has shewn
him more a Wise, than a Weak Man; which I confess, at the
time he put it in Execution, seem'd not so clear a Point: For notwithstanding he now saw the Authority, and Power of his
Patent was superseded, or was at best but precarious, and that he
had not one Actor left, in his Service; yet under all these Dilem-
mas, and Distresses, he resolv'd upon rebuilding the New Theatre in *Lincoln's-Inn Fields*, of which he had taken a Lease, at a
low Rent, ever since *Betterton*'s Company had first left it. This
Conduct seem'd too deep for my Comprehension! What are we
to think of his taking this Lease, in the height of his Prosperity,
when he could have no Occasion for it? Was he a Prophet?
Could he then foresee, he should, one time or other, be turn'd
out of *Drury-Lane?* Or did his mere Appetite of Architecture
urge him to build a House, while he could not be sure, he should
ever have leave to make use of it? But of all this, we may think
as we please; whatever was his Motive, he, at his own Expence,
in this Interval of his having nothing else to do, rebuilt that

Theatre from the Ground, as it is now standing. As for the Order of Silence, he seem'd little concern'd at it, while it gave him so much uninterrupted Leisure to supervise a Work, which he naturally took Delight in.

After this Defeat of the Patentee, the Theatrical Forces of *Collier* in *Drury-Lane*, notwithstanding their having drawn the Multitude after them, for about three Weeks, during the Trial of *Sacheverel*, had made but an indifferent Campaign, at the end of the Season. *Collier*, at least, found so little Account in it, that it oblig'd him to push his Court-Interest (which, wherever the Stage was concern'd, was not inconsiderable) to support him in another Scheme; which was, that in consideration of his giving up the *Drury-Lane*, Cloathes, Scenes, and Actors, to *Swiney*, and his joint Sharers, in the *Hay-Market*, he (*Collier*) might be put into an equal Possession of the *Hay-Market* Theatre, with all the Singers, &c. and be made sole Director of the Opera. Accordingly, by Permission of the Lord-Chamberlain, a Treaty was enter'd into, and in a few Days ratified by all Parties,[2] conformable to the said Preliminaries. This was that happy Crisis of Theatrical Liberty, which the labouring Comedians had long sigh'd for; and which, for above twenty Years following, was so memorably fortunate to them.

However, there were two hard Articles, in this Treaty, which though it might be Policy in the Actors to comply with, yet the Imposition of them seem'd little less despotick, than a Tax upon the Poor, when a Government did not want it.

The first of these Articles was, That whereas the sole License for acting Plays, was presum'd to be a more profitable Authority, than that for acting Operas only; that therefore Two Hundred Pounds a Year should be paid to *Collier*, while Master of the Opera, by the Comedians; to whom a Verbal Assurance was given by the *Plenipo*'s on the Court-side, that while such Payment subsisted, no other Company should be permitted to act Plays, against them, within the Liberties, &c. The other Article was, That on every *Wednesday*, whereon an Opera could be perform'd, the Plays should, *toties quoties*,[3] be silent at *Drury-Lane*, to give the Opera a fairer Chance, for a full House.

This last Article, however partial, in the Intention, was in its

Effect, of great Advantage to the sharing Actors: For in all publick Entertainments, a Day's Abstinence naturally increases the Appetite to them: Our every *Thursday*'s Audience, therefore, was visibly the better, by thus making the Day before it a Fast. But as this was not a Favour design'd us, this Prohibition of a Day, methinks, deserves a little farther Notice; because it evidently took a sixth Part of their Income, from all the hired Actors, who were only paid, in proportion to the Number of acting Days. This extraordinary Regard to Operas, was in effect making the Day-labouring Actors the principal Subscribers to them, and the shutting out People from the Play every *Wednesday*, many murmured at, as an Abridgment of their usual Liberty. And tho' I was one of those, who profited by that Order, it ought not to bribe me, into a Concealment of what was then said and thought of it. I remember a Nobleman of the first Rank, then in a high Post, and not out of Court-Favour, said openly behind the Scenes --- *It was shameful to take part of the Actors Bread from them to support the silly Diversion of People of Quality*. But alas! what was all this Grievance, when weighed against the Qualifications of so grave, and stanch a Senator, as *Collier*? Such visible Merit, it seems, was to be made easy, tho' at the Expence of the --- I had almost said, *Honour* of the Court, whose gracious Intention for the Theatrical Common-wealth, might have shone with thrice the Lustre, if such a paltry Price had not been paid for it. But as the Government of the Stage, is but that of the World in Miniature, we ought not to have wondered, that *Collier* had Interest enough to quarter the Weakness of the Opera, upon the Strength of the Comedy. General good Intentions are not always practicable to a Perfection. The most necessary Law can hardly pass, but a Tenderness to some private Interest, shall often hang such Exceptions upon particular Clauses, 'till at last it comes out lame, and lifeless, with the Loss of half its Force, Purpose, and Dignity. As for instance; how many fruitless Motions have been made in Parliaments, to moderate the enormous Exactions, in the Practice of the Law? And what sort of Justice must that be call'd, which, when a Man has not a mind to pay you a Debt of Ten Pounds,

it shall cost you Fifty, before you can get it? How long too, has
the Publick been labouring for a Bridge at *Westminster?* But
the Wonder, that it was not built a Hundred Years ago ceases,
when we are told, That the Fear of making one End of *London*,
as rich, as the other, has been, so long, an Obstruction to it: And
tho' it might seem a still greater Wonder, when a new Law for
building one had at last got over that Apprehension, that it
should meet with any farther Delay; yet Experience has shewn
us, that the Structure of this useful Ornament to our Metropolis
has been so clogg'd by private Jobs, that were to be pick'd out
of the Undertaking, and the Progress of the Work so disconcerted by a tedious Contention of Private Interests, and Endeavours to impose upon the Publick abominable Bargains, that a
whole Year was lost, before a single Stone could be laid to its
Foundation. But Posterity will owe its Praises, to the Zeal, and
Resolution of a truly Noble Commissioner,[4] whose distinguish'd
Impatience has broke thro' those narrow Artifices, those false
and frivolous Objections, that delay'd it, and has already began
to raise, above the Tide, that future Monument of his Publick
Spirit.

How far all this may be allow'd applicable to the State of the
Stage, is not of so great Importance, nor so much my Concern,
as that what is observ'd upon it should always remain a memorable Truth, to the Honour of that Nobleman. But now I go
on: *Collier* being thus possess'd of his Musical Government,
thought his best way would be to farm it out to a Gentleman,
Aaron Hill,[5] Esq; (who, he had reason to suppose, knew something more of Theatrical Matters, than himself) at a Rent, if I
mistake not, of Six Hundred Pounds *per Annum:* But before
the Season was ended (upon what occasion, if I could remember,
it might not be material to say) took it into his Hands again: But
all his Skill, and Interest, could not raise the Direction of the
Opera, to so good a Post, as he thought due to a Person of his
Consideration: He therefore, the Year following, enter'd upon
another high-handed Scheme, which, 'till the Demise of the
Queen, turn'd to his better Account.

After the Comedians were in Possession of *Drury-Lane*, from

whence, during my time upon the Stage, they never departed;
their Swarm of Audiences exceeded all that had been seen, in
thirty Years before; which, however, I do not impute so much
to the Excellence of their Acting, as to their indefatigable Industry, and good Management; for as I have often said, I never
thought, in the general, that we stood in any Place of Comparison with the eminent Actors before us; perhaps too, by there
being now an End of the frequent Divisions, and Disorders, that
had from time to time broke in upon, and frustrated their Labours, not a little might be contributed to their Success.

Collier, then, like a true liquorish Courtier, observing the
Prosperity of a Theatre, which he, the Year before had parted
with for a worse, began to meditate an Exchange of Theatrical
Posts with *Swiney*, who had visibly very fair Pretensions to that
he was in, by his being first chosen, by the Court, to regulate,
and rescue the Stage from the Disorders it had suffer'd, under
its former Menagers: Yet *Collier* knew that sort of Merit could
stand in no Competition, with his being a Member of Parliament:
He therefore had Recourse to his Court-Interest (where meer
Will, and Pleasure, at that time, was the only Law, that dispos'd
of all Theatrical Rights) to oblige *Swiney* to let him be off,
from his bad Bargain, for a better. To this, it may be imagin'd
Swiney demurr'd, and as he had Reason, strongly remonstrated
against it: But as *Collier* has lifted his Conscience under the Command of Interest, he kept it to strict Duty, and was immoveable; insomuch that Sir *John Vanbrugh*, who was a Friend to
Swiney, and who by his Intimacy with the People in Power,
better knew the Motive of their Actions, advis'd *Swiney* rather
to accept of the Change, than by a Non-compliance to hazard
his being exluded from any Post, or Concern in either of the
Theatres: To conclude, it was not long before *Collier* had pro-
cured a new License for acting Plays, &c. for himself, *Wilks*,
Dogget, and *Cibber*, exclusive of *Swiney*, who by this new Regulation was reduc'd to his *Hobson*'s Choice of the Opera.

Swiney being thus transferr'd to the Opera, in the sinking
Condition *Collier* had left it, found the Receipts of it, in the
Winter following 1711, so far short of the Expences, that he was

driven to attend his Fortune in some more favourable Climate,
where he remain'd twenty Years an Exile, from his Friends,
and Country; tho' there has been scarce an *English* Gentleman,
who in his *Tour of France,* or *Italy,* has not renew'd, or created
an Acquaintance with him. As this is a Circumstance, that many
People may have forgot, I cannot remember it, without that Regard, and Concern it deserves from all that know him: Yet it is
some Mitigation of his Misfortune, that since his Return to
England, his grey Hairs, and cheerful Disposition have still
found a general Welcome among his foreign, and former domestick Acquaintance.[6]

Collier being now, first-commission'd Menager with the Comedians, drove them too, to the last Inch of a hard Bargain (the
natural Consequence of all Treaties between Power, and Necessity) He not only demanded six hundred a Year, neat Mony,
the Price at which he had farm'd out his Opera, and to make
the Business a *sine Cure* to him; but likewise insisted, upon a
Moiety of the two hundred, that had been levied upon us the
Year before, in Aid of the Operas; in all 700 £. These large,
and ample Conditions, considering in what Hands we were, we
resolv'd to swallow without wry Faces; rather chusing to run
any Hazard, than contend with a formidable Power, against
which we had no Remedy: But so it happen'd, that Fortune
took better Care of our Interest, than we ourselves had like to
have done: For had *Collier* accepted of our first Offer, of an
equal Share with us, he had got three hundred Pounds a Year
more, by complying with it, than by the Sum he imposed upon
us; our Shares being never less, than a thousand annually, to
each of us, till the End of the Queen's Reign, in 1714. After
which *Collier's* Commission was superseded; his Theatrical Post,
upon the Accession of his late Majesty, being given to Sir *Richard Steele*.

From these various Revolutions, in the Government of the
Theatre, all owing to the Patentees mistaken Principle of increasing their Profits, by too far enslaving their People, and keeping
down the Price of good Actors (and I could almost insist, that
giving large Sallaries to bad Ones, could not have had a worse

Consequence) I say, when it is consider'd, that the Authority for acting Plays, &c. was thought of so little worth, that (as has been observ'd) Sir *Thomas Skipwith* gave away his Share of it, and the Adventurers had fled from it; that Mr. *Congreve*, at another time, had voluntarily resign'd it; and Sir *John Vanbrugh* (meerly to get the Rent of his new House paid) had, by Leave of the Court, farm'd out his License, to *Swiney*, who not without some Hesitation had ventur'd upon it; let me say again, out of this low Condition of the Theatre, was it not owing to the Industry of three, or four Comedians, that a new Place was not created for the Crown to give away, without any Expence attending it, well worth the Acceptance of any Gentleman, whose Merit, or Services had no higher Claim to Preferment, and which *Collier*, and Sir *Richard Steele*, in the two last Reigns, successively enjoy'd? Though, I believe, I may have said something like this, in a former Chapter, I am not unwilling it should be twice taken notice of.

We are now come to that firm Establishment of the Theatre, which except the Admittance of *Booth* into a Share, and *Dogget*'s retiring from it, met with no Change, or Alteration, for above twenty Years after.

Collier, as has been said, having accepted of a certain Appointment of seven hundred *per Annum; Wilks, Dogget*, and Myself were now the only acting Menagers, under the Queen's License; which being a Grant, but during Pleasure, oblig'd us to a Conduct that might not undeserve that Favour. At this Time we were All in the Vigour of our Capacities as Actors; and our Prosperity enabled us, to pay, at least, double the Sallaries, to what the same Actors had usually receiv'd, or could have hoped for under the Government of the Patentees. *Dogget*, who was naturally an Oeconomist, kept our Expences, and Accounts to the best of his Power, within regulated Bounds, and Moderation. *Wilks*, who had a stronger Passion, for Glory, than Lucre, was a little apt to be lavish, in what was not always as necessary for the Profit, as the Honour of the Theatre: For Example, at the Beginning of almost every Season, he would order two, or three Suits to be made, or refresh'd, for Actors of moderate

Consequence, that his having constantly a new one for himself, might seem less particular, tho' he had, as yet, no new Part for it. This expeditious Care of doing us good, without waiting for our Consent to it, *Dogget* always look'd upon, with the Eye of a Man, in Pain: But I, who hated Pain, (tho' I as little liked the Favour, as *Dogget* himself) rather chose to laugh at the Circumstance, than complain of what I knew was not to be cured, but by a Remedy, worse than the Evil. Upon these Occasions, therefore, whenever I saw him, and his Followers so prettily dress'd out, for an old Play, I only commended his Fancy; or at most but whisper'd him not to give himself so much Trouble, about others, upon whose Performance it would but be thrown away: To which, with a smiling Air of Triumph, over my want of Penetration, he has reply'd--- Why, now, that was what I really did it for! to shew others, that I love to take Care of them, as well as of myself. Thus whenever he made himself easy, he had not the least Conception, let the Expence be what it would, that we could possibly dislike it. And from the same Principle, provided a thinner Audience were liberal of their Applause, he gave himself little Concern about the Receipt of it. As in these different Tempers of my Brother-Menagers, there might be equally something right, and wrong, it was equally my Business to keep well with them both: And tho' of the two, I was rather inclin'd to *Dogget*'s way of thinking, yet I was always under the disagreeable Restraint of not letting *Wilks* see it: Therefore, when in any material Point of Menagement, they were ready to come to a Rupture, I found it adviseable to think neither of them, absolutely in the wrong; but by giving to one as much of the Right, in his Opinion this way, as I took from the other in that; their Differences were sometimes soften'd into Concessions, that I have Reason to think prevented many ill Consequences, in our Affairs, that otherwise might have attended them. But this was always to be done with a very gentle Hand; for as *Wilks* was apt to be easily hurt, by Opposition, so when he felt it he was as apt to be insupportable. However, there were some Points, in which we were always unanimous. In the twenty Years, while we were our own

Directors, we never had a Creditor that had Occasion to come
twice for his Bill; every *Monday* Morning discharged us of all
Demands, before we took a Shilling for our own Use. And
from this Time, we neither ask'd any Actor, nor were desired
by them, to sign any written Agreement (to the best of my
Memory) whatsoever: The Rate of their respective Sallaries
were only enter'd in our daily Pay-Roll; which plain Record
every one look'd upon, as good as City-Security: For where an
honest Meaning is mutual, the mutual Confidence will be Bond
enough, in Conscience, on both sides: But that I may not ascribe
more to our Conduct than was really its Due, I ought to give
Fortune her Share of the Commendation; for had not our Success exceeded our Expectation, it might not have been in our
Power, so throughly to have observ'd those laudable Rules of
Oeconomy, Justice, and Lenity, which so happily supported us:
But the Severities, and Oppression we had suffer'd under our
former Masters, made us incapable of imposing them upon
others; which gave our whole Society the cheerful Looks of a
rescued People. But notwithstanding this general Cause of Content, it was not above a Year or two before the Imperfection
of human Nature began to shew itself in contrary Symptoms.
The Merit of the Hazards which the Menagers had run, and
the Difficulties they had combated, in bringing to Perfection,
that Revolution, by which they had all so amply profited, in the
Amendment of their general Income, began now to be forgotten; their Acknowledgments, and thankful Promises of Fidelity,
were no more repeated, or scarce thought obligatory: Ease
and Plenty, by an habitual Employment, had lost their Novelty,
and the Largeness of their Sallaries, seem'd rather lessen'd than
advanc'd, by the extraordinary Gains of the Undertakers; for
that is the Scale, in which the hired Actor will always weigh
his Performance; but whatever Reason there may seem to be,
in his Case, yet as he is frequently apt to throw a little Self-
partiality into the Balance, that Consideration may a good deal
alter the Justness of it. While the Actors, therefore, had this way
of thinking, happy was it, for the Menagers, that their united
Interest was so inseparably the same, and that their Skill and

Power in Acting, stood in a Rank so far above the rest, that if
the whole Body of private Men had deserted them, it would yet
have been an easier Matter, for the Menagers to have pick'd
up Recruits, than for the Deserters to have found proper Officers
to head them. Here, then, in this Distinction lay our Security:
Our being Actors ourselves, was an Advantage to our Government, which all former Menagers, who were only idle Gentlemen, wanted: Nor was our Establishment easily to be broken,
while our Health, and Limbs enabled us, to be Joint-labourers
in the Work we were Masters of.

The only Actor, who, in the Opinion of the Publick, seem'd
to have had a Pretence of being advanc'd to a Share with us,
was certainly *Booth:* But when it is consider'd, how strongly
he had oppos'd the Measures, that had made us Menagers, by
setting himself (as has been observ'd) at the Head of an opposite Interest, he could not as yet, have much to complain of:
Beside, if the Court had thought him, now, an equal Object of
Favour, it could not have been in our Power, to have oppos'd
his Preferment: This I mention, not to take from his Merit,
but to shew, from what Cause it was not, as yet, better provided for. Therefore it may be no Vanity to say, our having at
that Time, no visible Competitors on the Stage, was the only
Interest, that rais'd us to be the Menagers of it.

But here, let me rest a while, and since, at my time of Day, our
best Possessions are but Ease, and Quiet, I must be content, if
I will have Sallies of Pleasure, to take up with those only, that
are to be found in Imagination. When I look back, therefore,
on the Storms of the Stage, we had been toss'd in; when I consider, that various Vicissitude of Hopes and Fears, we had for
twenty Years struggled with, and found our selves, at last, thus
safely set on Shore, to enjoy the Produce of our own Labours;
and to have rais'd those Labours by our Skill, and Industry,
to a much fairer Profit, than our Task-masters, by all their
severe, and griping Government had ever reap'd from them, a
good-natured Reader, that is not offended at the Comparison
of great things, with small, will allow was a Triumph, in proportion, equal to those, that have attended the most heroick

Enterprizes for Liberty! What Transport could the first *Brutus* feel, upon his Expulsion of the *Tarquins*, greater than that which now danc'd in the Heart of a poor Actor, who from an injur'd Labourer, unpaid his Hire, had made himself, without Guilt, a legal Menager of his own Fortune? Let the Grave, and Great contemn, or yawn at these low Conceits, but let me be happy, in the Enjoyment of them! To this Hour my Memory runs o'er that pleasing Prospect of Life past, with little less Delight, than when I was first, in the real Possession of it. This is the natural Temper of my Mind, which my Acquaintance are frequently Witnesses of: And as this, was all the Ambition, Providence had made my obscure Condition capable of, I am thankful, that Means were given me to enjoy the Fruits of it.

--------- *Hoc est*
Vivere bìs, vitâ posse priore frui.[7]

Something like the Meaning of this, the less learned Reader may find in my Title Page.

Notwithstanding the Menaging Actors were, now, in a happier Situation, than their utmost Pretensions could have expected; yet it is not to be suppos'd, but wiser Men have mended it. As we could not all govern our selves, there were Seasons, when we were not all fit to govern others. Our Passions, and our Interest drew not always the same way. *Self*, had a great Sway in our Debates: We had our Partialities; our Prejudices; our Favourites of less Merit; and our Jealousies of those who came too near us; Frailties, which Societies of higher Consideration, while they are compos'd of Men, will not always be free from. To have been constantly capable of Unanimity, had been a Blessing too great for our Station: One Mind, among three People, were to have had three Masters, to one Servant; but when that one Servant is called three different ways, at the same time, whose Business is to be done first? For my own Part, I was forced, almost all my Life, to give up my Share of him. And if I could, by Art, or Persuasion, hinder others from making, what I thought, a wrong use of their Power, it was the all, and utmost I desired. Yet whatever might be our Personal Errors, I shall think I have no Right to speak of them farther, than where the Publick Entertainment was affected by them. If therefore, among so many, some particular Actors were remarkable in any part of their private Lives, that might sometimes make the World merry without Doors; I hope my laughing Friends will excuse me, if I do not so far comply, with their Desires, or Curiosity, as to give them a Place, in my History. I can only recommend such Anecdotes to the Amusement, of a Noble Person, who (in case I conceal them) does me the flattering Honour, to threaten my Work, with a Supplement.[2] 'Tis enough for me, that such Actors had their Merits, to the Publick: Let those recites their Imperfections, who are themselves without them: It is my Misfortune not to have that Qualification. Let us see, then (whatever was amiss in it) how our Administration went forward.

When we were first invested, with this Power; the Joy of our so unexpectedly coming into it, kept us, for some time, in Amity, and Good-humour, with one another: And the Pleasure of reforming the many false Measures, Absurdities, and Abuses, that like Weeds, have suck'd up the due Nourishment from the Fruits of the Theatre, gave us, as yet, no leisure, for private Dissentions. Our daily Receipts exceeded our Imagination: And we seldom met, as a Board, to settle our weekly Accounts, without the Satisfaction of Joint-Heirs, just in Possession of an unexpected Estate, that had been distantly in-tail'd upon them. Such a sudden change of our Condition, it may be imagined, could not but throw out of us a new Spirit, in almost every Play we appear'd in: Nor did we ever sink into that common Negligence, which is apt to follow Good-fortune: Industry, we knew, was the Life of our Business; that it not only conceal'd Faults, but was of equal Value to greater Talents without it; which the Decadence once of *Betterton*'s Company in *Lincoln's-Inn Fields*, has lately shewn us a Proof of.

This then was that happy Period, when both Actors and Menagers were in their highest Enjoyment of general Content, and Prosperity. Now it was that the politer World too, by their decent Attention, their sensible Taste, and their generous Encouragements to Authors, and Actors, once more saw, that the Stage, under a due Regulation, was capable of being what the wisest Ages thought it *might* be, The most rational Scheme, that Human Wit could form, to dissipate, with Innocence, the Cares of Life; to allure even the Turbulent, or Ill-disposed from worse Meditations, and to give the leisure Hours of Business, and Virtue, an instructive Recreation.

If this grave Assertion is less recommended, by falling from the Pen of a Comedian; I must appeal, for the truth of it, to the

Tragedy of *Cato*, which was first acted in 1712.[3] I submit to the Judgment of those, who were then the sensible Spectators of it, if the Success, and Merit of that Play, was not an Evidence of every Article of that Value, which I have given to a decent Theatre? But (as I was observing) it could not be expected the Summer-Days, I am speaking of, could be the constant Weather of the Year; we had our clouded Hours, as well as our sun-shine, and were not always in the same Good-Humour with one another: Fire, Air, and Water, could not be more vexatiously opposite, than the different Tempers of the Three Menagers, though they might equally have their useful, as well as their destructive Qualities. How variously these Elements, in our several Dispositions, operated, may be judg'd from the following single Instance, as well as from a thousand others; which, if they were all to be told, might possibly make my Reader wish I had forgot them.

Much about this time, then, there came over from the *Dublin* Theatre two uncelebrated Actors,[4] to pick up a few Pence among us, in the Winter, as *Wilks* had a Year, or two before, done on their side the Water, in the Summer. But it was not so clear to *Dogget*, and myself, that it was in their Power, to do us the same Service in *Drury-Lane*, as *Wilks* might have done them, in *Dublin*. However *Wilks* was so much a Man of Honour, that he scorn'd to be outdone in the least Point of it, let the Cost be what it would, to his Fellow-Menagers, who had no particular Accounts of Honour open with them. To acquit himself therefore with a better Grace, *Wilks* so order'd it, that his *Hibernian* Friends were got upon our Stage, before any other Menager had well heard of their Arrival. This so generous Dispatch of their Affair, gave *Wilks* a very good Chance of convincing his Friends, that Himself was sole Master of the Masters of the Company. Here now, the different Elements in our Tempers began to work with us. While *Wilks* was only animated by a grateful Hospitality to his Friends, *Dogget* was ruffled into a Storm, and look'd upon this Generosity, as so much Insult, and Injustice upon himself, and the Fraternity. During this Disorder, I stood by, a seeming quiet

Passenger, and since talking to the Winds, I knew could be to
no great Purpose, (whatever Weakness it might be call'd)
could not help smiling, to observe with what officious Ease,
and Delight, *Wilks* was treating his Friends at our Expence,
who were scarce acquainted with them: For, it seems, all this
was to end in their having a Benefit-Play, in the Height of the
Season, for the unprofitable Service they had done us, without our Consent, or Desire to employ them. Upon this *Dogget* bounc'd, and grew almost as untractable as *Wilks* himself.
Here, again, I was forc'd to clap my Patience to the Helm, to
weather this difficult Point between them: Applying myself
therefore to the Person, I imagin'd was most likely to hear me, I
desired *Dogget*, "to consider, that I must naturally, be as much
hurt, by this vain, and over-bearing Behavior of *Wilks*, as he
could be; and that tho' it was true, these Actors, had no Pretence, to the Favour design'd them; yet we could not say they
had done us any farther Harm, than letting the Town see, the
Parts they had been shewn in, had been better done by those,
to whom they properly belong'd: Yet as we had greatly
profited, by the extraordinary Labour of *Wilks*, who acted
long Parts almost every Day, and at least twice to *Dogget*'s
once, and that I granted it might not be so much his Consideration of our common Interest, as his Fondness for Applause, that set him to work; yet even that Vanity, if he
supposed it such, had its Merit to us; and as we had found our
Account in it, it would be Folly upon a Punctilio, to tempt
the Rashness of a Man, who was capable to undo all he had
done, by any Act of Extravagance, that might fly, into his
Head: That admitting this Benefit might be some little Loss
to us, yet to break with him upon it, could not but be ten times
of worse consequence, than our over-looking his disagreeable
manner of making the Demand upon us."

   Tho', I found, this had made *Dogget* drop the Severity of
his Features, yet he endeavour'd still to seem uneasy, by his
starting a new Objection, which was, That we could not be
sure even of the Charge, they were to pay for it: For *Wilks*,
said he, you know will go any Lengths, to make it a good Day,

to them, and may whisper the Door-keepers, to give them the
Ready-mony taken, and return the Account, in such Tickets
only, as these Actors, have not themselves dispos'd of. To make
this easy too, I gave him my Word, to be answerable for the
Charge, myself. Upon this he acceded, and accordingly they
had the Benefit-Play. But so it happen'd (whether as *Dogget*
had suspected, or not, I cannot say) the Ready-Mony receiv'd
fell Ten Pounds short of the Sum, they had agreed to pay for
it. Upon the *Saturday* following, (the Day on which we constantly made up our Accounts) I went early to the Office, and
inquired, if the Ten Pounds had yet been paid in; but not
hearing that one Shilling of it had found its way thither, I
immediately supply'd the Sum out of my own Pocket, and
directed the Treasurer to charge it receiv'd from me, in the
deficient Receipt of the Benefit-Day. Here, now, it might be
imagined, all this silly Matter was accommodated, and that no
one could so properly say, he was aggrieved, as myself: But
let us observe what the Consequence says --- why, the Effect
of my insolent interposing, honesty prov'd to be this: That
the Party most oblig'd, was the most offended; and the Offence was imputed to me, who had been Ten Pounds out of
Pocket, to be able to commit it: For when *Wilks* found, in
the Account, how spitefully the Ten Pounds had been paid in,
he took me aside into the adjacent Stone-Passage, and with
some Warmth ask'd me, What I meant by pretending to pay
in this Ten Pounds? and that, for his part, he did not understand such Treatment. To which I reply'd, That tho' I was
amazed, at his thinking himself ill-treated, I would give him a
plain, justifiable Answer. --- That I had given my Word to
Dogget, the Charge of the Benefit should be fully paid, and
since his Friends had neglected it, I found myself bound to
make it good. Upon which he told me, I was mistaken, if I
thought, he did not see into the bottom of all This --- That
Dogget, and I, were always endeavouring to thwart, and make
him uneasy; but he was able to stand upon his own Legs, and
we should find he would not be us'd so: That he took this
Payment of the Ten Pounds, as an Insult upon him, and a

Slight to his Friends; but rather than suffer it, he would tear the whole Business to pieces: That I knew it was in his Power to do it; and if he could not do a civil thing to a Friend, without all this senseless Rout about it, he could be receiv'd in *Ireland* upon his own Terms, and could as easily mend a Company there, as he had done here: That if he were gone, *Dogget* and I would not be able to keep the Doors open a Week, and, by G---, he would not be a Drudge for nothing. As I knew all this was but the Foam of the high Value he had set upon himself, I thought it not amiss, to seem a little silently concern'd, for the helpless Condition, to which his Resentment of the Injury I have related, was going to reduce us: For I knew I had a Friend, in his Heart, that, if I gave him a little time to cool, would soon bring him to Reason: The sweet Morsel of a Thousand Pounds a Year, was not to be met with at every Table, and might tempt a nicer Palate than his own, to swallow it, when he was not out of Humour. This I knew would always be of weight with him, when the best Arguments I could use, would be of none. I therefore gave him no farther Provocation, than by gravely telling him, We All had it in our Power to do one another a Mischief; but I believ'd none of us much cared to hurt ourselves; that if he was not of my Opinion, it would not be in my Power, to hinder whatever new Scheme, he might resolve upon; that *London* would always have a Playhouse, and I should have some Chance in it, tho' it might not be so good as it had been; that he might be sure, if I had thought my paying in the Ten Pounds could have been so ill receiv'd; I should have been glad to have sav'd it. Upon this he seem'd to mutter something to himself, and walk'd off, as if he had a mind to be alone. I took the Occasion, and return'd to *Dogget*, to finish our Accounts. In about six Minutes *Wilks* came in, to us; not in the best Humour, it may be imagin'd; yet not in so ill a one, but that he took his Share of the Ten Pounds, without shewing the least Contempt of it; which, had he been proud enough to have refus'd, or to have paid in himself, I might have thought, he intended to make good his Menaces, and that the Injury I have done him would never have been forgiven; but, it seems we had different ways of thinking.

Of this kind, more or less delightful, was the Life I led, with this impatient Man, for full twenty Years. *Dogget*, as we shall find, could not hold it so long; but as he had more Mony than I, he had not occasion for so much Philosophy. And thus were our Theatrical Affairs frequently disconcerted, by this irascible Commander, this *Achilles* of our Confederacy; who, I may be bold to say, came very little short of the Spirit Horace gives to that Hero in his ---

Impiger, iracundus, inexorabilis, acer.[5]

This, then, is one of those Personal Anecdotes of our Variances, which, as our publick Performances were affected by it, could not with regard to Truth, and Justice, be omitted.

From this time, to the Year 1712, my Memory (from which Repository alone, every Article of what I write is collected) has nothing worth mentioning, 'till the first acting of the Tragedy of *Cato*.[5a] As to the Play itself, it might be enough to say, That the Author, and the Actors had their different Hopes of Fame, and Profit, amply answer'd by the Performance; but as its Success was attended with remarkable Consequences, it may not be amiss to trace it, from its several Years Concealment, in the Closet, to the Stage.

In 1703, nine Years before it was acted, I had the Pleasure of reading the first four Acts (which was all of it then written) privately with Sir *Richard Steele:* It may be needless, to say it was impossible to lay them out of my Hand, 'till I had gone thro' them; or to dwell upon the Delight, his Friendship to the Author receiv'd, upon my being so warmly pleas'd with them: But my Satisfaction was as highly disappointed, when he told me, Whatever Spirit Mr. *Addison* had shewn, in his writing it, he doubted, he would never have Courage enough, to let his *Cato* stand the Censure of an *English* Audience; that it had only been the Amusement of his leisure Hours in *Italy*, and was never intended, for the Stage. This Poetical Diffidence Sir *Richard* himself spoke of with some Concern, and in the Transport of his Imagination, could not help saying, *Good God! what a Part would* Betterton *make of* Cato! But this was seven Years before *Betterton* died, and when *Booth* (who afterwards made his Fortune by acting it) was in his Theatrical Minority. In the latter end of Queen *Anne*'s Reign, when our National Politicks had changed Hands; the Friends of Mr. *Addison*, then thought it a proper time to animate the Publick with the Sentiments of *Cato;* in a word, their Importunities were too warm, to be resisted; and it was no sooner finish'd, than hurried to the Stage, in *April* 1712, at a time when three Days a Week were usually appointed for the Benefit Plays of particular Actors: But a Work of that critical Importance, was to make its way, through all private Considerations; nor could it possibly give place to a Custom, which the Breach of could very little prejudice the Benefits, that on so unavoidable an Occasion, were (in part, tho' not wholly) postpon'd; it was therefore (*Mondays* excepted) acted every Day for a Month, to constantly crowded Houses. As the Author had made us a Present of whatever Profits he might have claim'd from it, we thought our selves oblig'd, to spare no Cost, in the proper Decorations of it. Its coming so late in the Season, to the Stage, prov'd of particular Advantage, to the sharing Actors; because the Harvest of our annual Gains was generally over, before the middle of *March;* many select Audiences being then, usually reserv'd, in favour to the Benefits of private Actors; which fixt Engagements naturally abated the Receipts of the Days, before and after them: But this unexpected After-crop of *Cato*, largely supplied to us, those Deficiencies; and was almost equal to two fruitful Seasons, in the same Year; at the Close of which, the three menaging Actors found themselves, each a Gainer of thirteen hundred, and fifty Pounds: But to return to the first Reception of this Play from the Publick.

Although *Cato* seems plainly written upon what are called *Whig* Principles; yet the *Torys* of that time had Sense enough not to take it, as the least Reflection, upon their Administration; but on the contrary, they seem'd to brandish, and vaunt their Approbation of every Sentiment in favour of Liberty, which by a publick Act of their Generosity, was carried so high, that one Day, while the Play was acting, they collected fifty Guineas in the Boxes, and made a Present of them to *Booth*,

with this Compliment --- *For his honest Opposition to a per-*
petual Dictator; and his dying so bravely, in the Cause of Lib-
erty: What was insinuated, by any Part of these Words, is
not my Affair; but so publick a Reward had the Appearance of
a laudable Spirit, which only such a Play, as *Cato* could have
inspired; nor could *Booth* be blam'd, if upon so particular a
Distinction of his Merit, he began himself to set more Value
upon it: How far he might carry it, in making use of the
Favour he stood in, with a certain Nobleman,[6] then in Power,
at Court, was not difficult to penetrate; and indeed, ought always to have been expected by the menaging Actors: For
which of them (making the Case every way his own) could
with such Advantages, have contented himself, in the humble
Station of an hired Actor? But let us see how the Menagers
stood severally affected, upon this Occasion.

    Dogget, who, expected, though he fear'd not, the Attempt
of what after happen'd, imagin'd he had thought of an Expedient to prevent it: And to cover his Design with all the Art of
a Statesman, he insinuated to us (for he was a staunch *Whig*)
that this Present of fifty Guineas, was a sort of a *Tory* Triumph,
which they had no Pretence to; and that for his Part, he could
not bear, that so redoubted a Champion for Liberty, as *Cato*,
should be bought off, to the Cause of a contrary Party: He
therefore, in the seeming Zeal of his Heart, proposed, that
the Menagers themselves should make the same Present to
Booth, which had been made him, from the Boxes, the Day
before. This, he said, would recommend the Equality, and
liberal Spirit of our Menagement, to the Town, and might be a
Means, to secure *Booth* more firmly in our Interest; it never
having been known, that the Skill of the best Actor had receiv'd
so round a Reward, or Gratuity, in one Day, before. *Wilks*,
who wanted nothing but Abilities to be as cunning, as *Dogget*,
was so charm'd with the Proposal, that he long'd, that Moment,
to make *Booth* the Present, with his own Hands; and though
he knew he had no Right to do it, without my Consent, had
not Patience to ask it; upon which I turn'd to *Dogget*, with a
cold Smile, and told him, that if *Booth* could be purchas'd at so

cheap a Rate, it would be one of the best Proofs of his Oeconomy, we had ever been beholden to: I therefore desired we
might have a little Patience; that our doing it too hastily might
be only making sure of an Occasion, to throw the fifty Guineas away; for if we should be oblig'd to do better for him,
we could never expect, that *Booth* would think himself bound,
in Honour, to refund them. This seem'd so absurd an Argument to *Wilks*, that he began with his usual Freedom of Speech,
to treat it, as a pitiful Evasion of their intended Generosity: But *Dogget*, who was not so wide of my Meaning, clapping his Hand upon mine, said, with an Air of Security, O!
don't trouble your self! there must be two Words to that
Bargain; let me alone, to menage that Matter. *Wilks*, upon
this dark Discourse, grew uneasy, as if there were some Secret
between us, that he was to be left out of. Therefore to avoid
the Shock of his Intemperance, I was reduc'd to tell him, that
it was my Opinion, that *Booth* would never be made easy, by
any thing we could do for him, till he had a Share, in the
Profits, and Menagement; and that, as he did not want Friends
to assist him, whatever his Merit might be before, every one
would think, since his acting of *Cato*, he had now enough to
back his Pretensions to it. To which *Dogget* reply'd, that
nobody could think his Merit was slighted, by so handsome a
Present, as fifty Guineas; and that for his farther Pretensions,
whatever the License might avail, our Property of House,
Scenes, and Cloaths were our own, and not in the Power of
the Crown to dispose of. To conclude, my Objections, that the
Mony would be only thrown away, *&c.* were overrul'd, and the
same Night *Booth* had the fifty Guineas, which he receiv'd
with a Thankfulness, that made *Wilks*, and *Dogget* perfectly
easy; insomuch that they seem'd, for some time to triumph in
their Conduct, and often endeavour'd to laugh my Jealousy
out of Countenance: But in the following Winter, the Game
happen'd to take a different Turn; and then, if it had been a
laughing Matter, I had as strong an Occasion to smile at their
former Security. But before I make an End of this Matter, I
cannot pass over the good Fortune of the Company, that

follow'd us, to the Act at *Oxford,* which was held in the inter-
vening Summer: Perhaps too, a short View of the Stage, in
that different Situation, may not be unacceptable to the Curious.

After the Restoration of King *Charles,* before the *Cavalier,*
and *Roundhead* Parties, under their new Denomination of
Whig, and *Tory,* began again to be politically troublesome,
publick Acts at *Oxford* (as I find by the Date of several
Prologues written by *Dryden,* for *Hart* on those Occasions)
had been more frequently held, than in later Reigns. Whether
the same Party Dissentions may have occasion'd the Discon-
tinuance of them, is a Speculation, not necessary to be enter'd
into. But these Academical Jubilees have usually been look'd
upon as a kind of congratulatory Compliment, to the Accession of every new Prince, to the Throne, and generally, as
such have attended them. King *James,* notwithstanding his
Religion, had the Honour of it; at which the Players, as usual,
assisted. This I have only mention'd, to give the Reader a
Theatrical Anecdote of a Liberty, which *Tony Leigh* the
Comedian took with the Character of the well known *Obadiah
Walker,* then Head of *University Colledge,* who, in that Prince's
Reign, had turn'd *Roman Catholick:* The Circumstance is this.

In the latter End of the Comedy call'd the *Committee,*[7]
Leigh, who acted the Part of *Teague,* hauling in *Obadiah,*
with an Halter about his Neck, whom, according to his written
Part, he was to threaten to hang, for no better Reason than his
refusing to drink the King's Health, (but here *Leigh*) to
justify his Purpose, with a stronger Provocation, put himself
into a more, than ordinary Heat, with his Captive *Obadiah,*
which having heightened his Master's Curiosity, to know what
Obadiah had done to deserve such Usage, *Leigh,* folding his
Arms, with a ridiculous Stare of Astonishment, reply'd----
Upon my Shoule, he has shange his Religion. As the Merit of this
Jest lay chiefly in the Auditors sudden Application of it, to the
Obadiah of *Oxford,* it was receiv'd with all the Triumph of
Applause, which the Zeal of a different Religion could inspire.
But *Leigh* was given to understand, that the King was highly
displeas'd at it, inasmuch, as it had shewn him, that the Uni-

versity was in a Temper to make a Jest of his Proselyte. But to
return to the Conduct of our own Affairs there, in 1712.[8]

It had been a Custom for the Comedians, while at *Oxford*,
to act twice a Day; the first Play ending every Morning, before the College Hours of dining, and the other never to break
into the Time of shutting their Gates in the Evening. This
extraordinary Labour gave all the hired Actors a Title to
double Pay, which, at the Act, in King *William*'s Time, I had
myself accordingly receiv'd there. But the present Menagers
considering, that by acting only once a Day, their Spirits
might be fresher for every single Performance, and that by
this Means, they might be able to fill up the Term of their
Residence, without the Repetition of their best, and strongest
Plays; and as their Theatre was contriv'd to hold a full third
more, than the usual Form of it had done, one House well-
fill'd, might answer the Profits of two but moderately taken up:
Being enabled too, by their late Success, at *London*, to make
the Journey pleasant, and profitable, to the rest of their Society,
they resolv'd to continue to them, their double Pay, notwithstanding this new Abatement of half their Labour. This Conduct of the Menagers more than answer'd their Intention,
which was rather to get nothing themselves, than not let their
Fraternity be the better for the Expedition. Thus they laid an
Obligation, upon their Company, and were themselves consid-
erably, though unexpected, Gainers by it. But my chief Reason
for bringing the Reader to *Oxford*, was to shew the different
Taste of Plays there, from that which prevail'd at *London*.
A great deal of that false, flashy Wit, and forc'd Humour,
which had been the Delight of our Metropolitan Multitude, was
only rated there at its bare, intrinsick Value; Applause was
not to be purchas'd there, but by the true Sterling, the *Sal
Atticum*[9] of a Genius; unless where the Skill of the Actor pass'd
it upon them, with some extraordinary Strokes of Nature.
Shakespear, and *Johnson* had, there, a sort of classical Authority; for whose masterly Scenes they seem'd to have as implicit a Reverence, as formerly, for the Ethicks of *Aristotle*;
and were as incapable of allowing Moderns to be their Com-

petitors, as of changing their Academical Habits for gaudy
Colours, or Embroidery. Whatever Merit, therefore, some few
of our more politely-written Comedies might pretend to, they
had not the same Effect upon the Imagination there, nor were
receiv'd with that extraordinary Applause, they had met with,
from the People of Mode, and Pleasure, in *London;* whose
vain Accomplishments did not dislike themselves, in the Glass,
that was held to them: The elegant Follies of higher Life,
were not, at *Oxford,* among their Acquaintance, and consequently might not be so good Company, to a learned Audience, as Nature, in her plain Dress, and unornamented, in her
Pursuits and Inclinations, seem'd to be.

The only distinguish'd Merit, allow'd to any modern Writer,
was to the Author of *Cato,* which Play being the Flower of a
Plant, rais'd in that learned Garden, (for there Mr. *Addison*
had his Education) what Favour may we not suppose was due
to him, from an Audience of Brethren, who from that local
Relation to him, might naturally have a warmer Pleasure, in
their Benevolence to his Fame? But not to give more Weight to
this imaginary Circumstance, than it may bear, the Fact was,
that on our first Day of acting it, our House was, in a manner,
invested; and Entrance demanded by twelve a Clock at Noon,
and before one, it was not wide enough for many, who came
too late for Places. The same Crowds continued for three
Days together, (an uncommon Curiosity in that Place) and
the Death of *Cato* triumph'd over the Injuries of *Caesar* every
where. To conclude, our Reception at *Oxford,* whatever our
Merit might be, exceeded our Expectation. At our taking
Leave, we had the Thanks of the Vice-Chancellor, for the
Decency, and Order, observ'd by our whole Society; an Honour which had not always been paid, upon the same Occasions; for at the Act, in King *William*'s Time, I remember
some Pranks of a different Nature had been complain'd of.
Our Receipts had not only enabled us (as I have observ'd) to
double the Pay of every Actor, but to afford out of them,
towards the Repair of St. *Mary*'s Church, the Contribution of
fifty Pounds: Besides which, each of the three Menagers had to

his respective Share, clear of all Charges, one hundred and fifty more, for his one and twenty Day's Labour; which being added to his thirteen hundred, and fifty, shared in the Winter preceding, amounted, in the whole, to fifteen hundred; the greatest Sum ever known to have been shared, in one Year, to that Time: And to the Honour of our Auditors, here, and elsewhere be it spoken, all this was rais'd, without the Aid of those barbarous Entertainments, with which, some few Years after (upon the Re-establishment of two contending Companies) we were forc'd to disgrace the Stage, to support it.

This, therefore, is that remarkable Period, when the Stage, during my Time upon it, was the least reprochable: And it may be worth the publick Observation (if any thing I have said of it can be so) that *One* Stage may, as I have prov'd it has done, very laudably support it self, by such Spectacles only, as are fit to delight a sensible People; but the equal Prosperity of *Two* Stages has always been of a very short Duration. If therefore the Publick should ever recover, into the true Taste of that Time, and stick to it; the Stage must come into it, or *starve;* as whenever the general Taste is vulgar, the Stage must come down to it, to *live*---- But I ask Pardon of the Multitude, who, in all Regulations of the Stage, may expect, to be a little indulg'd, in what they like: If therefore they *will* have a Maypole, why, the Players must *give* them a Maypole; but I only speak, in case they should keep an old Custom of changing their Minds; and by their Privilege of being in the *wrong*, should take a Fancy, by way of Variety, of being in the *right*--- Then, in such a Case, what I have said may appear to have been no intended Design, against their Liberty of judging, for themselves.

After our Return, from *Oxford, Booth* was at full Leisure, to sollicit his Admission, to a Share, in the Menagement; in which he succeeded, about the Beginning of the following Winter: Accordingly a new License (recalling all former Licenses) was issued, wherein *Booth*'s Name was added, to those of the other Menagers.[10] But still, there was a Difficulty, in his Qualification, to be adjusted; what Consideration he

should allow, for an equal Title to our Stock of Cloaths,
Scenes, &c. without which, the License was of no more use,
than the Stock was without the License; or, at least, if there
were any Difference, the former Menagers seem'd to have the
Advantage, in it; the Stock being intirely theirs, and three
Parts in four of the License; for *Collier,* though now but a fifth
Menager, still insisted on his former Appointment of 700 £.
a Year; which, in Equity ought certainly to have been propor-
tionately abated: But Court-Favour was not always measur'd
by *that* Yard; *Collier*'s Matter was soon out of the Question;
his Pretensions were too visible, to be contested; but the Affair
of *Booth* was not so clear a Point: The Lord Chamberlain,
therefore, only recommended it, to be adjusted, among our
selves; which, to say the Truth, at that Time, was a greater
Indulgence than I expected. Let us see, then, how this critical
Case was handled.

  *Wilk*s was of Opinion, that to set a good round Value
upon our Stock, was the only way, to come near an Equivalent, for the Dimunition of our Shares, which the Admission of
Booth must occasion: But *Dogget* insisted, that he had no Mind
to dispose of any Part of his Property, and therefore would set
no Price upon it at all. Though I allow'd, that Both these Opinions might be grounded, on a good deal of Equity, yet I was
not sure that either of them was practicable; and therefore
told them, that when they could Both agree, which of them
could be made so, they might rely on my Consent, in any
Shape. In the mean time, I desired they would consider, that
as our License subsisted only during Pleasure, we could not
pretend, that the Queen might not recall, or alter it: But that
to speak out, without mincing the Matter on either Side,
the Truth was plainly this: That *Booth* had a manifest Merit,
as an Actor; and as he was not supposed to be a *Whig*, it was
as evident, that a good deal for that Reason, a Secretary of
State had taken him into his Protection, which I was afraid
the weak Pretence of our invaded Property, would not be
able to contend with: That his having signaliz'd himself, in
the Character of *Cato* (whose Principles the *Tories* had af-

fected to have taken, into their own Possession) was a very
popular Pretence of making him free of the Stage, by advancing him, to the Profits of it. And, as we had seen, that the
Stage was frequently treated, as if it was not suppos'd, to have
any Property at all; this Favour intended to *Booth* was thought
a right Occasion, to avow that Opinion, by disposing of its
Property, at Pleasure: But be that, as it might, I own'd, it
was not so much my Apprehensions of what the *Court* might
do, that sway'd me, into an Accomodation with *Booth*, as
what the *Town*, (in whose Favour he now apparently stood)
might think *ought* to be done: That, there might be more
danger in contesting their arbitrary Will, and Pleasure, than in
disputing this less terrible Strain of the Prerogative. That if
Booth were only impos'd upon us, from his Merit to the Court,
we were then, in the Condition of other Subjects: Then, indeed, Law, Right, and Possession, might have a tolerable Tug,
for our Property: But as the Town would always look upon his
Merit to *them*, in a stronger Light, and be Judges of it themselves, it would be a weak, and idle Endeavour, in us, not to
sail with the Stream, when we might possibly make a Merit
of our cheerfully admitting him: That though his former
Opposition to our Interest, might, between Man and Man, a
good deal justify our not making an earlier Friend of him;
yet that was a Disobligation, out of the Town's Regard, and
consequently would be of no weight, against so approv'd an
Actor's being preferr'd. But all this, notwithstanding, if they
could both agree, in a different Opinion, I would, at the Hazard
of any Consequence, be guided by it.

Here, now, will be shewn another Instance of our different
Tempers: *Dogget* (who in all Matters, that concern'd our
common Weal, and Interest, little regarded our Opinion, and
even to an Obstinacy, walked by his own) look'd only out
of Humour, at what I had said, and without thinking himself
oblig'd to give any Reason for it, declar'd, he would maintain
his Property. *Wilks*, (who, upon the same Occasions, was as
remarkably ductile, as when his Superiority on the Stage, was
in question, he was assuming, and intractable, said, for his

Part, provided our Business of acting was not interrupted, he did not care what we did: But, in short, he was for playing on, come what would of it. This last Part of his Declaration I did not dislike, and therefore I desir'd, we might all enter into an immediate Treaty with *Booth*, upon the Terms of his Admission. Dogget still sullenly reply'd, that he had no Occasion, to enter into any Treaty. *Wilks* then, to soften him, propos'd, that, if I liked it, *Dogget* might undertake it himself. I agreed. No! he would not be concern'd in it. I then offer'd the same Trust to *Wilks*, if *Dogget* approv'd of it. *Wilks* said, he was not good at making of Bargains, but if I was willing, he would rather leave it to me. *Dogget*, at this, rose up, and said, we might both do as we pleas'd, but that nothing but the Law, should make him part with his Property--- and so went out of the Room. After which he never came among us more, either as an Actor, or Menager.

By his having, in this abrupt manner, abdicated his Post, in our Government; what he left of it, naturally devolv'd, upon *Wilks*, and myself. However, this did not so much distress our Affair, as I have Reason to believe *Dogget* thought it would: For though, by our Indentures tripartite, we could not dispose of his Property, without his Consent: Yet those Indentures could not oblige us to fast, because he had no Appetite; and if the Mill did not grind, we could have no Bread: We therefore determin'd, at any Hazard, to keep our Business still going, and that our fastest way would be, to make the best Bargain we could with *Booth;* one Article of which was to be, That *Booth* should stand equally answerable with us, to *Dogget*, for the Consequence: To which *Booth* made no Objection, and the rest of his Agreement, was to allow us Six Hundred Pounds for his Share, in our Property, which was to be paid by such Sums as should arise from half his Profits of Acting, 'till the whole was discharg'd: Yet so cautious were we in this Affair, that this Agreement was only Verbal on our Part, tho' written, and sign'd by *Booth*, as what intirely contented him: However, Bond and Judgment, could not have made it more secure, to him; for he had his Share, and was able to discharge the Incumbrance upon it, by his Income of that Year only. Let us see what *Dogget* did in this Affair, after he had left us.

Might it not be imagin'd, that *Wilks*, and Myself, by having made this Matter easy to *Booth*, should have deserv'd the Approbation at least, if not the Favour of the Court, that had exerted so much Power to prefer him? But shall I be believed, when I affirm, that *Dogget*, who had so strongly oppos'd the Court, in his Admission to a Share, was very near getting the better of us both, upon that Account, and for some time appeared to have more Favour there, than either of us? Let me tell out my Story, and then think what you please of it.

Dogget, who was equally oblig'd, with us, to act, upon the Stage, as to assist, in the Menagement of it, tho' he had refus'd to do either, still demanded of us his whole Share of the Profits, without considering what Part of them *Booth* might pretend to, from our late Concessions. After many fruitless Endeavours to bring him back, to us; *Booth* join'd with us, in making him an Offer of half a Share, if he had a mind totally to quit the Stage, and make it a *Sine cure*. No! he wanted the Whole, and to sit still himself, while we (if we pleased) might work for him, or let it alone, and none of us all, neither he, nor we, be the better for it. What we imagin'd encourag'd him to hold us at this short Defiance, was, that he had laid up enough to live upon, without the Stage (for he was one of those close Oeconomists, whom Prodigals call a Miser) and therefore partly from an Inclination, as an invincible *Whig*, to signalize himself in defence of his Property, and as much presuming that our Necessities would oblige us to come to his own Terms, he was determin'd (even against the Opinion of his Friends) to make no other Peace, with us. But not being able, by this inflexible Perseverance, to have his wicked Will of us, he was resolv'd to go to the Fountain-head of his own Distress, and try, if from thence, he could turn the Current against us. He appeal'd to the Vice-Chamberlain, to whose Direction, the adjusting of all these Theatrical Difficulties, was then committed: But there, I dare say, the Reader does not expect he should meet with much Favour: However, be that, as it may; for whether any regard was had, to his having some Thousands, in his Pocket; or that he was consider'd, as a Man, who would, or could make more Noise, in the Matter, than Courtiers might care for: Or what Charms, Spells, or Conjurations he might make use of, is all Darkness to me; yet so it was, he one way or other, play'd his Part so well, that, in a few Days after, we received an Order, from the Vice-Chamberlain,[11] positively commanding us, to pay *Dogget* his whole Share, notwithstanding, we had complain'd before of his having withdrawn himself from acting on the Stage, and from the Menagement of it. This I thought was a dainty Distinction, indeed! that *Dogget*'s Defiance of the Commands in favour of *Booth,* should be rewarded with so ample a *Sine cure;* and that we, for our Obedience, should be condemn'd to dig in the Mine, to pay it him! This bitter Pill, I confess, was more than I could down with, and therefore soon determin'd, at all Events, never to take it. But, as I had a Man in Power to deal with, it was not my business to speak *out* to him, or to set forth our Treatment, in its proper Colours. My only Doubt was, Whether I could bring *Wilks* into the same Sentiments (for he never car'd to litigate any thing, that did not affect his Figure upon the Stage.) But I had the good Fortune to lay our Condition, in so precarious, and disagreeable a Light to him, if we submitted to this Order, that he fir'd, before I could get thro' half the Consequences of it; and I began now to find it more difficult, to keep him within Bounds, than I had before to alarm him. I then propos'd to him this Expedient: That we should draw up a Remonstrance, neither seeming to refuse, or comply with this Order; but to start such Objections, and perplexing Difficulties, that should make the whole impracticable: That under such Distractions, as this would raise in our Affairs, we could not be answerable to keep open our Doors, which consequently would destroy the Fruit of the Favour lately granted to *Booth,* as well as of This intended to *Dogget* himself. To this Remonstrance we receiv'd an Answer in Writing, which varied something, in the Measures, to accomodate

Matters with *Dogget*. This was all I desired, when I found the
Style of *Sic jubeo*[12] was alter'd, when this formidable Power
began to *parley* with us, we knew there could not be much,
to be fear'd, from it: For I would have remonstrated, 'till I
had died, rather than have yielded to the roughest, or smoothest
Persuasion, that could intimidate, or deceive us. By this Conduct, we made the Affair, at last, too troublesome for the Ease
of a Courtier to go thro' with. For when it was consider'd,
that the principal Point, the Admission of *Booth* was got
over, *Dogget* was fairly left to the Law, for Relief.

Upon this Disappointment, *Dogget* accordingly preferred a
Bill in *Chancery* against us. *Wilks*, who hated all Business, but
that of entertaining the Publick, left the Conduct of our Cause
to me; in which we had, at our first setting out, this Advantage of *Dogget*, that we had Three Pockets to support our
Expence, where he had but One. My first Direction to our
Solicitor was, to use all possible Delay, that the Law would
admit of; a Direction, that Lawyers seldom neglect; by this
means we hung up our Plaintiff about two Years, in *Chancery*,
'till we were at full Leisure to come to a Hearing before the
Lord-Chancellor *Cooper;* which did not happen 'till after the
Accession of his late Majesty. The issue of it was this. *Dogget*
had about fourteen Days allow'd him to make his Election,
whether he would return to act, as usual: But he declaring,
by his Counsel, That he rather chose to quit the Stage, he
was decreed Six Hundred Pounds for his Share, in our Property, with 15 *per Cent.* Interest, from the Date of the last
License: Upon the Receipt of which, both Parties were to
sign General-Releases, and severally to pay their own Costs.
By this Decree, *Dogget*, when his Lawyer's Bill was paid,
scarce got one Year's Purchase, of what we had offered him
without Law, which (as he survived but seven Years after it)
would have been an Annuity of Five Hundred Pounds, and a
Sine cure for Life.

Tho' there are many Persons living, who know every Article
of these Facts, to be true: Yet it will be found, that the strongest
of them, was not the strongest Occasion of *Dogget*'s quitting the

Stage. If therefore the Reader should not have Curiosity enough to know, how the Publick came, to be depriv'd of so valuable an Actor, let him consider, that he is not oblig'd to go through the rest of this Chapter, which I fairly tell him before-hand, will only be fill'd up with a few idle Anecdotes, leading to that Discovery.

After our Law-suit was ended, *Dogget*, for some few Years, could scarce bear the Sight of *Wilks*, or myself; tho' (as shall be shewn) for different Reasons: Yet it was his Misfortune to meet with us almost every Day. *Button*'s Coffee-house, so celebrated in the *Tatlers*, for the Good-Company, that came there, was at this time, in its highest Request. *Addison, Steele, Pope*, and several other Gentlemen of different Merit, then made it their constant *Rendezvous*. Nor could *Dogget* decline the agreeable Conversation there, tho' he was daily sure to find *Wilks*, or myself, in the same Place, to sour his Share of it: For as *Wilks*, and He were differently proud; the one rejoycing in a captious, overbearing, valiant Pride; and the other, in a stiff, sullen, Purse-Pride, it may be easily conceiv'd, when two such Tempers met, how agreeable the Sight of one was to the other. And as *Dogget* knew, I had been the chief Conductor of our Defence, against his Law-suit, which had hurt him more, for the Loss he had sustain'd, in his Reputation of understanding Business, which he valued himself upon, than his Disappointment had, of getting so little by it; it was no wonder if I was intirely out of his good Graces, which I confess, I was inclin'd, upon any reasonable Terms, to have recover'd; he being of all my Theatrical Brethren, the Man I had most delighted in: For when he was not in a Fit of Wisdom, or not over-concern'd about his Interest, he had a great deal of entertaining Humour: I therefore, notwithstanding his Reserve, always left the Door open to our former Intimacy, if he were inclin'd to come into it. I never fail'd to give him my Hat, and, *Your Servant*, wherever I met him; neither of which he would ever return, for above a Year after; but I still persisted, in my usual Salutation, without observing, whether it was civilly receiv'd, or not. This ridiculous Silence between two Comedians, that had so lately liv'd in a constant

course of Raillery, with one another, was often smil'd at, by our
Acquaintance, who frequented the same Coffee-house: And one
of them carried his Jest upon it so far, that when I was at some
distance from Town, he wrote me a formal Account, that *Dog-*
get was actually dead. After the first Surprize, his Letter gave
me, was over, I began to consider, that this coming from a droll
Friend to both of us, might possibly be written, to extract some
Merriment out of my real Belief of it: In this I was not unwilling
to gratify him, and return'd an Answer, as if I had taken the
Truth of his News for granted; and was not a little pleas'd, that I
had so fair an Opportunity of speaking my Mind freely of *Dog-*
get, which I did, in some Favour of his Character; I excus'd his
Faults, and was just to his Merit. His Law-suit with us, I only
imputed to his having naturally deceiv'd himself in the Justice of
his Cause. What I most complain'd of was, his irreconcileable
Disaffection to me, upon it, whom he could not reasonably
blame, for standing in my own Defence; that not to endure me,
after it, was a Reflexion upon his Sense, when all our Acquaintance had been Witnesses of our former Intimacy; which my Behaviour in his Life-time, had plainly shewn him, I had a mind to
renew. But since he was now gone (however great a Churl he
was to me) I was sorry my Correspondent had lost him.

This Part of my Letter, I was sure, if *Dogget*'s Eyes were still
open, would be shewn to him; if not, I had only writ it to no
purpose. But about a Month after, when I came to Town, I
had some little Reason to imagine it had the Effect I wish'd from
it: For one Day sitting over-against him, at the same Coffee-
house, where we often mixt at the same Table, tho' we never
exchang'd a single Syllable, he graciously extended his Hand, for
a Pinch of my Snuff: As this seem'd, from him, a sort of breaking
the Ice of his Temper, I took courage upon it, to break Silence
on my side, and ask'd him how he lik'd it? To which, with a slow
Hesitation, naturally assisted by the Action of his taking the
Snuff, he reply'd ---*Umh! the best ---Umh! ---I have tasted*
a great while! ---If the Reader, who may possibly think all this
extremely trifling, will consider, that Trifles sometimes shew
Characters in as strong a Light, as Facts of more serious Importance, I am in hopes he may allow, that my Matter less needs an

Excuse, than the Excuse itself does; if not, I must stand condemn'd at the end of my Story. ------- But let me go on.

After a few Days of these coy, Lady-like Compliances, on
his side, we grew into a more conversable Temper: At last,
I took a proper Occasion, and desired he would be so frank with
me, as to let me know, what was his real Dislike, or Motive, that
made him throw up so good an Income, as his Share with us
annually brought him in? For tho' by our Admission of *Booth*,
it might not probably amount to so much by a Hundred, or
two a Year, as formerly; yet the Remainder was too considerable, to be quarrel'd with, and was likely to continue more, than
the best Actors before us, had ever got, by the Stage. And farther, to encourage him to be open, I told him, If I had done any
thing, that had particularly disoblig'd him, I was ready, if he
could put me in the way, to make him any amends in my Power;
if not, I desired he would be so just to himself, as to let me know
the real Truth, without Reserve: But Reserve he could not,
from his natural Temper, easily shake off. All he said came from
him, by half Sentences, and *Inuendos*, as --- No, he had not
taken any thing particularly ill ---- for his Part, he was very
easy, as he was; but where others were to dispose of his Property
as they pleased --- if you had stood it out, as I did, *Booth* might
have paid a better Price for it.--- You were too much afraid of
the Court --- but that's all over.--- There were other things in
the Playhouse.--- No Man of Spirit.--- In short, to be always
pester'd, and provok'd by a trifling Wasp --- a --- vain --- shallow! --- A Man would sooner beg his Bread, than bear it. ----
(Here it was easy to understand him: I therefore ask'd him, what
he had to bear, that I had not my Share of?) No! it was not the
same thing, he said.--- You can play with a Bear, or let him alone,
and do what he would; but I could not let him lay his Paws upon
me, without being hurt; you did not feel him, as I did.--- And
for a Man to be cutting of Throats, upon every Trifle, at my
time of Day! --- If I had been as covetous, as he thought me,
may be I might have born it, as well as you --- but I would not be
a Lord of the Treasury, if such a Temper, as *Wilks*'s, were to
be at the Head of it.---

Here, then, the whole Secret was out. The rest of our Conversation was but explaining upon it. In a Word, the painful Behaviour of *Wilks* had hurt him so sorely, that the Affair of *Booth* was look'd upon, as much a Relief, as a Grievance, in giving him so plausible a Pretence to get rid of us all, with a better Grace.

Booth too, in a little time, had his Share of the same Uneasiness, and often complain'd of it to me: Yet as we neither of us could, then, afford to pay *Dogget*'s Price, for our Remedy; all we could do, was to avoid every Occasion, in our Power, of inflaming the Distemper: So that we both agreed, tho' *Wilks*'s Nature was not to be chang'd, it was a less Evil to live with him, than without him.

Tho' I had often suspected, from what I had felt myself, that the Temper of *Wilks* was *Dogget*'s real Quarrel, to the Stage; yet I could never thoroughly believe it, 'till I had it from his own Mouth. And I, then, thought the Concern he had shewn at it was a good deal inconsistent with that Understanding, which was generally allow'd him. When I give my Reasons for it, perhaps the Reader will not have a better Opinion of my own: Be that, as it may, I cannot help wondering, that he, who was so much more capable of Reflexion, than *Wilks*, could sacrifice so valuable an Income, to his Impatience of another's natural Frailty! And tho' my Stoical way of thinking may be no Rule, for a wiser Man's Opinion; yet if it should happen to be right, the Reader may make his Use of it. Why then should we not always consider, that the Rashness of Abuse is but the false Reason of a weak Man? and that offensive Terms are only us'd, to supply the want of Strength in Argument? Which, as to the common Practice of the sober World, we do not find, every Man, in Business, is oblig'd to resent, with a military Sense of Honour: Or if he should, would not the Conclusion amount to this? Because another wants Sense, and Manners, I am oblig'd to be a Madman? For such every Man is, more, or less, while the Passion of Anger is in Possession of him. And what less can we call that proud Man, who would put another out of the World, only for putting him out of humour? If Accounts of the Tongue were always to be made up with the Sword, all the Wisemen in the World might be brought in Debtors, to Blockheads. And when Honour pretends, to be Witness, Judge, and Executioner, in its own Cause, if Honour were a Man, would it be an Untruth, to say Honour is a very impudent Fellow? But in *Dogget*'s Case, it may be ask'd, How was he to behave himself? Were passionate Insults, to be born, for Years together? To these Questions, I can only answer with two, or three more, Was he to punish himself, because another was in the wrong? How many sensible Husbands endure the teizing Tongue of a froward Wife, only because she is the weaker Vessel? And why should not a weak Man have the same Indulgence? Daily Experience will tell us, that the fretful Temper of a Friend, like the Personal Beauty of a fine Lady, by Use, and Cohabitation, may be brought down, to give us neither Pain, nor Pleasure. Such, at least, and no more, was the Distress I found myself in upon the same Provocations, which I generally return'd with humming an Air to my self; or if the Storm grew very high, it might, perhaps, sometimes ruffle me enough, to sing a little out of Tune. Thus too (if I had any ill Nature to gratify) I often saw the unruly Passion of the Aggressor's Mind punish itself, by a restless Disorder of the Body.

What inclines me, therefore, to think the Conduct of *Dogget* was as rash, as the Provocations he complain'd of is, that in some time after he had left us, he plainly discover'd he had repented it. His Acquaintance observ'd to us, that he sent many a long Look after his Share, in the still prosperous State of the Stage: But, as his Heart was too high to declare (what we saw too) his shy Inclination to return, he made us no direct Overtures. Nor, indeed, did we care (tho' he was a golden Actor) to pay too dear for him: For as most of his Parts had been pretty well supply'd, he could not, now, be of his former Value, to us. However to shew the Town, at least, that he had not forsworn the Stage, he, one Day, condescended, to play for the Benefit of Mrs. *Porter*, in the *Wanton Wife*,[13] at which he knew his late Majesty was to be present. Now (tho' I speak it not of my own Knowledge) yet it was not likely Mrs. *Porter* would have ask'd that Favour of him, without some previous Hint, that it would be granted. His coming among us, for that Day only, had a strong

appearance of his laying it in our way, to make him Proposals, or
that he hoped the Court, or Town, might intimate us, their Desire of seeing him oftner: But as he acted only to do a particular
Favour, the Menagers ow'd him no Compliment for it, beyond
common Civilities. And, as that might not be all he propos'd by
it, his farther Views (if he had any) came to nothing. For after
this Attempt, he never return'd to the Stage.

To speak of him, as an Actor: He was the most an Original,
and the strictest Observer of Nature, of all his Contemporaries.
He borrow'd from none of them: His Manner was his own: He
was a Pattern to others, whose greatest Merit was, that they had
sometimes tolerably imitated him. In dressing a Character to the
greatest Exactness, he was remarkably skilful; the least Article
of whatever Habit he wore, seem'd in some degree to speak
and mark the different Humour he presented; a necessary
Care in a Comedian, in which many have been too remiss, or
ignorant. He could be extreamly ridiculous, without stepping
into the least Impropriety, to make him so. His greatest Success
was in Characters of lower Life, which he improv'd, from the
Delight he took, in his Observations of that Kind, in the real
World. In Songs, and particular Dances too, of Humour, he had
no Competitor. *Congreve* was a great Admirer of him, and found
his Account, in the Characters he expresly wrote for him. In
those of *Fondlewife*, and his *Old Batchelor;* and *Ben*, in *Love for
Love*, no Author, and Actor could be more oblig'd to their mutual masterly Performances. He was very acceptable to several
Persons of high Rank, and Taste: Tho' he seldom car'd to be the
Comedian, but among his more intimate Acquaintance.

And now, let me ask the World a Question. When Men have
any valuable Qualities, why are the generality of our modern
Wits so fond of exposing their failings only, which the wisest
of Mankind will never wholly be free from? Is it of more use to
the Publick, to know their Errors, than their Perfections? Why
is the Account of Life to be so unequally stated? Tho' a Man
may be sometimes Debtor to Sense, or Morality, is it not doing
him Wrong, not to let the World see, at the same time, how far
he may be Creditor to both? Are Defects and Disproportions,

to be the only labour'd Features in a Portrait? But perhaps such Authors may know how to please the World better than I do, and may naturally suppose, that what is delightful to themselves, may not be disagreeable to others. For my own part, I confess myself a little touch'd in Conscience, at what I have, just now, observ'd to the Disadvantage of my other Brother-Menager.

If therefore, in discovering the true Cause of the Publick's losing so valuable an Actor, as *Dogget*, I have been oblig'd to shew the Temper of *Wilks*, in its natural Complexion, ought I not, in amends, and balance of his Imperfections, to say at the same time of him, That if he was not the most correct, or judicious, yet (as *Hamlet* says of the King his Father) *Take him* for *All, in All,*[14] *&c.* he was certainly the most diligent, most laborious, and most useful Actor, that I have seen upon the Stage, in Fifty Years.

Upon the Death of the Queen, Plays (as they always had been on the like Occasions) were silenc'd for six Weeks. But this happening on the first of *August*, in the long Vacation of the Theatre, the Observance of that Ceremony, which at another Juncture would have fallen like wet Weather upon their Harvest, did them now no particular Damage. Their License however being of course to be renewed, that Vacation gave the Menagers Time to cast about, for the better Alteration of it: And since they knew the Pension of seven hundred a Year, which had been levied upon them for *Collier*, must still be paid to somebody, they imagin'd the Merit of a *Whig* might now have as good a Chance for getting into it, as that of a *Tory* had for being continued in it: Having no Obligations, therefore, to *Collier*, who had made the last Penny of them; they applied themselves to Sir *Richard Steele*, who had distinguish'd himself, by his Zeal for the House of *Hanover*, and had been expell'd the House of Commons, for carrying it (as was judg'd at a certain Crisis) into a Reproach of the Government. This we knew was his Pretension to that Favour, in which he now stood, at Court: We knew too, the Obligations the Stage had to his Writings; there being scarce a Comedian of Merit, in our whole Company, whom his *Tatlers* had not made better, by his publick Recommendation of them. And many Days had our House been particularly fill'd, by the Influence, and Credit of his Pen. Obligations of this kind from a Gentleman, with whom they all had the Pleasure of a personal Intimacy, the Menagers thought could not be more justly return'd, than by shewing him some warm Instance of their Desire, to have him, at the Head of them. We therefore beg'd him to use his Interest, for the Renewal of our License, and that he would do us the Honour of getting our Names to stand with His, in the same Commission. This, we told him, would put it still farther into his Power of supporting the Stage, in that Reputation, to which his Lucubrations had already so much contributed; and that therefore we thought no Man had better Pretences to partake of its Success.

Though it may be no Addition to the favourable Part of this Gentleman's Character, to say with what Pleasure he receiv'd this Mark of our Inclination to him, yet my Vanity longs to tell you, that it supriz'd him into an Acknowledgment, that People, who are shy of Obligations, are cautious of confessing. His spirits took such a lively Turn upon it, that had we been all his own Sons, no unexpected Act of filial Duty could have more endear'd us to him.

It must be observ'd, then, that as *Collier* had no Share, in any Part of our Property, no Difficulties, from that Quarter, could obstruct this Proposal. And the usual Time of our beginning to act for the Winter-Season, now drawing near, we press'd him not to lose any Time in his Sollicitation of this new License. Accordingly Sir *Richard* apply'd himself to the Duke of *Malborough*, the Hero of his Heart, who, upon the first mention of it, obtain'd it of his Majesty, for Sir *Richard*, and the former Menagers, who were Actors.[2] *Collier* we heard no more of.

The Court, and Town, being crowded very early, in the Winter-Season, upon the critical Turn of Affairs, so much expected from the *Hanover* Succession, the Theatre had its particular Share of that general Blessing, by a more than ordinary Concourse of Spectators.

About this Time the Patentee, having very near finish'd his House, in *Lincolns-Inn-Fields*, began to think of forming a new Company; and in the mean Time, found it necessary to apply for Leave to employ them. By the weak Defence he had always made against the several Attacks upon his Interest, and former Government of the Theatre, it might be a Question, if his House had been ready, in the Queen's Time, whether he would, then, have had the Spirit to ask, or Interest enough to obtain Leave to use it: But in the following Reign, as it did not appear he had done any thing to forfeit the Right of his Patent, he prevail'd with Mr. *Craggs*[3] the younger, (afterwards Secretary of State) to lay his Case before the King, which he did in so effectual a manner, that (as Mr. *Craggs* himself told me) his Majesty was pleas'd to say upon it, "That he remember'd, when he had been in *England* before, in King *Charles* his Time, there had been Two Theatres in *London;* and as the Patent seem'd to be a lawful Grant, he saw no Reason, why Two Play-houses might not be continued."

The Suspension of the Patent being thus taken off, the younger Multitude seem'd to call aloud for two Play-houses! Many desired another, from the common Notion, that *Two* would always create Emulation, in the Actors (an Opinion, which I have consider'd in a former Chapter.) Others too, were as eager for them, from the natural Ill-will that follows the Fortunate, or Prosperous, in any Undertaking. Of this low Malevolence we had, now and then, had remarkable Instances; we had been forced to dismiss an Audience of a hundred and fifty Pounds, from a Disturbance spirited up, by obscure People, who never gave any better Reason for it, than that it was their Fancy, to support the idle Complaint of one rival Actress, against another, in their several Pretensions to the chief Part in a new Tragedy. But as this Tumult seem'd only to be the Wantonness of *English* Liberty, I shall not presume to lay any farther Censure upon it.[4]

Now, notwithstanding this publick Desire of re-establishing two Houses; and though I have allow'd the former Actors greatly our Superiors; and the Menagers I am speaking of, not to have been without their private Errors. Yet, under all these Disadvantages, it is certain, the Stage, for twenty Years before this time, had never been in so flourishing a Condition: And it was as evident to all sensible Spectators, that this Prosperity could be only owing to that better Order, and closer Industry, now daily observ'd; and which had formerly been neglected by our Predecessors. But that I may not impose upon the Reader a Merit, which was not generally allow'd us, I ought honestly to let him know, that about this time, the publick Papers, particularly *Mist*'s

Journal,[5] took upon them very often to censure our Menagement, with the same Freedom, and Severity, as if we had been
so many Ministers of State: But so it happen'd, that these unfortunate Reformers of the World, these self-appointed *Censors*
hardly ever hit upon what was really wrong, in us; but taking
up Facts upon Trust, or Hear-say, piled up many a pompous
Paragraph, that they had ingeniously conceiv'd was sufficient
to demolish our Administration, or at least, to make us very uneasy in it; which, indeed, had so far its Effect, that my equally-
injur'd Brethren *Wilks*, and *Booth*, often complain'd to me of
these disagreeable Aspersions, and propos'd, that some publick
Answer might be made to them, which I always oppos'd, by
perhaps, too secure a Contempt of what such Writers could do
to hurt us; and my Reason for it was, that I knew but of one
way to silence Authors of that Stamp; which was, to grow insignificant, and good for nothing, and then we should hear no more
of them: But while we continued in the Prosperity of pleasing
others, and were not conscious of having deserv'd what they
said of us, why should we gratify the little Spleen of our Enemies, by wincing at it, or give them fresh Opportunities to dine
upon any Reply they might make to our publickly taking Notice
of them? And though Silence might, in some Cases, be a sign of
Guilt, or Error confess'd, our Accusers were so low, in their
Credit and Sense, that the Content we gave the Publick, almost
every Day, from the Stage, ought to be our only Answer to
them.

However (as I have observ'd) we made many Blots, which
these unskilful Gamesters never hit: But the Fidelity of an
Historian, cannot be excus'd the Omission of any Truth, which
might make for the other Side of the Question. I shall therefore
confess a Fact, which, if a happy Accident had not intervened,
had brought our Affairs, into a very tottering Condition. This
too, is that Fact, which in a former Chapter, I promis'd to set
forth as a Sea-Mark of Danger, to future Menagers, in their
Theatrical Course of Government.

When the new-built Theatre, in *Lincolns-Inn Fields* was ready
to be open'd, seven or eight Actors, in one Day, deserted from

us, to the Service of the Enemy, which oblig'd us to postpone
many of our best Plays, for want of some inferior Part in them,
which these Deserters had been used to fill: But the Indulgence of the Royal Family, who then frequently honour'd us,
by their Presence, was pleas'd to accept of whatever could be
hastily got ready for their Entertainment. And though this
critical good Fortune prevented, in some measure, our Audiences falling so low, as otherwise they might have done, yet it
was not sufficient to keep us in our former Prosperity: For that
Year, our Profits amounted not to above a third Part of our
usual Dividends; though in the following Year we intirely recover'd them. The Chief of these Deserters were *Keene*, *Bullock*,
Pack, *Leigh*,[6] Son of the famous *Tony Leigh*, and others of less
note. 'Tis true, they none of them had more than a negative
Merit, in being only able to do us more Harm by their leaving us,
without Notice, than they could do us Good, by remaining
with us: For though the best of them could not support a Play,
the worst of them, by their Absence, could maim it; as the Loss
of the least Pin, in a Watch, may obstruct its Motion. But to
come to the true Cause of their Desertion: After my having discover'd the (long unknown) Occasion that drove *Dogget* from
the Stage, before his settled Inclination to leave it; it will be
less incredible, that these Actors, upon the first Opportunity to
relieve themselves, should all, in one Day, have left us from the
same Cause of Uneasiness. For, in a little time after, upon not
finding their Expectations answer'd, in *Lincolns-Inn-Fields*, some
of them, who seem'd to answer for the rest, told me, the greatest
Grievance they had, in our Company, was the shocking Temper
of *Wilks*, who, upon every, almost no Occasion, let loose the
unlimited Language of Passion upon them, in such a manner as
their Patience was not longer able to support. This, indeed, was
what we could not justify! This was a Secret, that might have
made a wholesome Paragraph, in a critical News-Paper! But as
it was our good Fortune, that it came not to the Ears of our
Enemies, the Town was not entertain'd, with their publick Remarks upon it.

After this new Theatre had enjoy'd that short Run of Favour,

which is apt to follow Novelty; their Audiences began to
flag: But whatever good Opinion we had of our own Merit, we
had not so good a one of the Multitude, as to depend too much
upon the Delicacy of their Taste: We knew too, that this Company being so much nearer to the City, than we were, would
intercept many an honest Customer, that might not know a
good Market, from a bad one; and that the thinnest of their Audiences, must be always taking something from the Measure of our
Profits. All these Disadvantages, with many others, we were
forced to lay before Sir *Richard Steele,* and farther to remon-
strate to him, that as he now stood in *Collier*'s Place, his Pension
of 700 £. was liable to the same Conditions, that *Collier* had receiv'd it upon; which were, that it should be only payable during
our being the only Company permitted to act, but in case another
should be set up against us, that then this Pension was to be liqui-
dated into an equal Share with us; and which we now hoped
he would be contented with. While we were offering to proceed, Sir *Richard* stopt us short, by assuring us, that as he came
among us, by our own Invitation, he should always think himself
oblig'd, to come into any Measures, for our Ease, and Service:
That to be a Burthen to our Industry, would be more disagreeable to him, than it could be to us; and as he had always taken a
Delight, in his Endeavours for our Prosperity, he should be still
ready on our own Terms, to continue them. Every one who
knew Sir *Richard Steele,* in his Prosperity (before the Effects
of his Good-nature had brought him to Distresses) knew that
this was his manner of dealing with his Friends, in Business:
Another Instance of the same nature will immediately fall in
my way.

   When we propos'd to put this Agreement, into Writing, he
desired us not to hurry ourselves; for that he was advis'd, upon
the late Desertion of our Actors, to get our License (which only
subsisted during Pleasure) enlarg'd into a more ample, and dura-
ble Authority, and which he said he had reason to think would
be more easily obtain'd, if we were willing, that a Patent for the
same purpose might be granted to Him only, for his Life, and
three Years after, which he would then assign over to us. This was

a Prospect beyond our Hopes; and what we had long wish'd for; for tho' I cannot say, we had ever Reason to grieve at the Personal Severities, or Behaviour, of any one Lord-Chamberlain, in my Time, yet the several Officers, under them, who had not the Hearts of Noblemen, often treated us (to use *Shakespear*'s Expression) with all the *Insolence* of *Office*,[7] that narrow Minds are apt to be elated with; but a Patent, we knew, would free us from so abject a State of Dependency. Accordingly, we desired Sir *Richard* to lose no time; he was immediately promis'd it: In the Interim, we sounded the Inclination of the Actors remaining with us; who had all Sense enough to know, that the Credit, and Reputation we stood in, with the Town, could not but be a better Security for their Sallaries, than the Promises of any other Stage, put into Bonds, could make good to them. In a few Days after, Sir *Richard* told us, that his Majesty being apprised that others had a joint Power with him, in the License, it was expected, we should, under our Hands, signify, that his Petition for a Patent was preferr'd, by the Consent of us all. Such an Acknowledgement was immediately sign'd, and the Patent thereupon pass'd the Great Seal; for which I remember the Lord-Chancellor *Cooper*, in Compliment to Sir *Richard*, would receive no Fee.

We receiv'd the Patent *January* 19, 1718, and (Sir *Richard* being oblig'd the next Morning to set out for *Burrowbridge* in *Yorkshire*, where he was soon after elected Member for the new Parliament)[8] we were forc'd that very Night, to draw up in a hurry ('till our Counsel might more advisably perfect it) his Assignment to us of equal Shares, in the Patent, with farther Conditions of Partnership: But here I ought to take Shame to myself, and at the same time to give this second Instance of the Equity, and Honour of Sir *Richard:* For this Assignment (which I had myself the hasty Penning of) was so worded, that it gave Sir *Richard* as equal a Title to our Property, as it had given us to his Authority in the Patent: But Sir *Richard*, notwithstanding, when he return'd to Town, took no Advantage of the Mistake, and consented in our second Agreement, to pay us Twelve Hundred Pounds, to be equally intitled to our Property, which at his Death, we were oblig'd to repay (as we afterwards did) to his Executors; and which, in case any of us had died before him, the Survivors were equally oblig'd to have paid to the Executors of such deceased Person, upon the same Account. But Sir *Richard*'s Moderation with us, was rewarded with the Reverse of *Collier*'s Stiffness: *Collier*, by insisting on his Pension, lost Three Hundred Pounds a Year; and Sir *Richard*, by his accepting a Share in lieu of it, was, one Year with another, as much a Gainer.

The Grant of this Patent having assur'd us of a competent Term, to be relied on, we were now emboldened, to lay out larger Sums, in the Decorations of our Plays: Upon the Revival of *Dryden*'s *All for Love*, the Habits of that Tragedy amounted to an Expence of near Six Hundred Pounds; a Sum unheard of, for many Years before, on the like Occasions. But we thought such extraordinary Marks of our Acknowledgment were due to the Favours, which the Publick were now, again pouring in upon us. About this time we were so much in fashion, and follow'd, that our Enemies (who they were, it would not be fair to guess, for we never knew them) made their Push of a good round Lye upon us, to terrify those Auditors, from our Support, whom they could not mislead by their private Arts, or publick Invectives. A current Report, that the Walls, and Roof of our House, were liable to fall, had got such ground in the Town, that on a sudden, we found our Audiences unusually decreas'd by it: *Wilks* was immediately for denouncing War, and Vengeance on the Author of this Falshood, and for offering a Reward, to whoever could discover him. But it was thought more necessary first to disprove the Falshood, and then to pay what Compliments might be thought adviseable to the Author. Accordingly an Order from the King was obtain'd, to have our Tenement survey'd by Sir *Thomas Hewit*, then the proper Officer; whose Report of its being in a safe, and sound Condition, and sign'd by him, was publish'd in every News-Paper. This had so immediate an Effect, that our Spectators, whose Apprehensions had lately kept them absent, now made up our Losses, by returning to us, with a fresh Inclination, and in greater Numbers.[9]

When it was first publickly known, that the New Theatre would be open'd against us; I cannot help going a little back to remember the Concern that my Brother-Menagers express'd at what might be the Consequences of it. They imagin'd, that now, all those who wish'd Ill to us, and particulalrly a great Party, who had been disoblig'd, by our shutting them out, from behind our Scenes, even to the Refusal of their Mony, would now exert themselves, in any partial, or extravagant Measures, that might either hurt us, or support our Competitors: These too were some of those farther Reasons, which had discourag'd them, from running the hazard of continuing to Sir *Richard Steele* the same Pension, which had been paid to *Collier*. Upon all which I observed to them, that for my own Part, I had not the same Apprehensions; but that I foresaw as many good, as bad Consequences from two Houses: That tho' the Novelty might possibly at first abate a little of our Profits; yet if we slacken'd not our Industry, that Loss would be amply balanc'd, by an equal Increase of our Ease, and Quiet: That those turbulent Spirits which were always molesting us, would now have other Employment: That the question'd Merit of our Acting would now stand in a clearer Light, when others were faintly compared to us: That tho' Faults might be found, with the best Actors, that ever were, yet the egregious Defects, that would appear in others, would now be the effectual means to make our Superiority shine, if we had any Pretence to it: And that what some People hoped might ruin us, would in the end reduce them to give up the Dispute, and reconcile them to those who could best entertain them.

In every Article of this Opinion, they afterwards found that I had not been deceiv'd; and the Truth of it may be so well remember'd by many living Spectators, that it would be too frivolous and needless a Boast, to give it any farther Observation.

But, in what I have said, I would not be understood to be an Advocate, for two Playhouses: For we shall soon find that two Sets of Actors, tolerated in the same Place, have constantly ended in the Corruption of the Theatre; of which the auxiliary Entertainments, that have so barbarously supply'd the Defects of weak Action, have for some Years past, been a flagrant Instance;

it may not therefore, be here improper to shew how our childish Pantomimes first came to take so gross a Possession of the Stage.

I have upon several Occasions already observ'd, that when one Company is too hard for another, the lower, in Reputation, has always been forc'd to exhibit some new-fangled Foppery, to draw the Multitude after them: Of these Expedients, Singing and Dancing had formerly been the most effectual; but, at the Time I am speaking of, our *English* Musick had been so discountenanc'd, since the Taste of *Italian* Operas prevail'd, that it was to no purpose, to pretend to it. Dancing therefore was, now, the only Weight in the opposite Scale, and as the New Theatre sometimes found their Account in it, it could not be safe for us, wholly to neglect it. To give even Dancing therefore some Improvement, and to make it something more than Motion without Meaning, the Fable of *Mars* and *Venus*,[10] was form'd into a connected Presentation of Dances in Character, wherein the Passions were so happily express'd, and the whole Story so intelligibly told, by a mute Narration of Gesture only, that even thinking Spectators allow'd it both a pleasing, and a rational Entertainment; tho', at the same time, from our Distrust of its Reception, we durst not venture to decorate it, with any extraordinary Expence of Scenes, or Habits; but upon the Success of this Attempt, it was rightly concluded, that if a visible Expence in both, were added to something of the same Nature, it could not fail of drawing the Town proportionably after it. From this original Hint then (but every way unequal to it) sprung forth that Succession of monstrous Medlies, that have so long infested the Stage, and which arose upon one another alternately, at both Houses outvying, in Expence, like contending Bribes on both sides at an Election, to secure a Majority of the Multitude. But so it is, Truth may complain, and Merit murmur with what Justice it may, the Few will never be a Match for the Many, unless Authority should think fit to interpose, and put down these Poetical Drams, these Gin-shops of the Stage, that intoxicate its Auditors, and dishonour their Understanding, with a Levity, for which I want a Name.

If I am ask'd (after my condemning these Fooleries, myself)
how I came to assent, or continue my Share of Expence to them?
I have no better Excuse for my Error, than confessing it. I did
it against my Conscience! and had not virtue enough to starve,
by opposing a Multitude, that would have been too hard for
me. Now let me ask an odd Question: Had *Harry the Fourth* of
France a better Excuse, for changing his Religion? I was still
in my Heart, as much as he could be, on the side of Truth and
Sense, but with this difference, that I had their leave to quit
them, when they could not support me: For what Equivalent
could I have found for my falling a Martyr to them? How far
the Heroe, or the Comedian, was in the wrong, let the Clergy,
and the Criticks decide. Necessity will be as good a Plea for the
one, as the other. But let the Question go which way it will,
Harry IV. has been always allow'd a Great Man: And what I
want of his Grandeur, you see by the Inference, Nature has
amply supply'd to me, in Vanity; a Pleasure which neither the
Pertness of Wit, or the Gravity of Wisdom, will ever persuade
me to part with. And why is there not as much Honesty in
owning, as in concealing it? For though to hide it may be Wisdom, to be without it is impossible; and where is the Merit of
keeping a Secret, which every Body is let into? To say we have
no Vanity then, is shewing a great deal of it; as to save we *have*
a great deal, cannot be shewing so much: And tho', there may
be Art, in a Man's accusing himself, even then it will be more
pardonable, than Self-commendation. Do we not find, that even
good Actions have their Share of it? that it is as inseparable, from
our Being, as our Nakedness? And tho' it may be equally decent
to cover it, yet the wisest Man can no more be without it, than
the weakest can believe he was born, in his Cloaths. If then what
we say of ourselves be true, and not prejudicial to others, to be
called vain upon it, is no more a Reproach, than to be called a
brown, or a fair Man. Vanity is of all Complexions; 'tis the
growth of every Clime, and Capacity; Authors of all Ages have
had a Tincture of it; and yet you read *Horace, Montaign,* and
Sir *William Temple,* with Pleasure. Nor am I sure, if it were cur-
able by Precept, that Mankind would be mended by it! Could

Vanity be eradicated, from our Nature, I am afraid, that the
Reward of most human Virtues, would not be found, in this
World! And happy is he, who has no greater Sin to answer for,
in the next!

But what is all this to the Theatrical Follies I was talking of?
Perhaps not a great deal; but it is to my Purpose; for though I
am an Historian, I do not write to the Wise, and Learned only;
I hope to have Readers of no more Judgment, than some of my
quondam Auditors; and I am afraid they will be as hardly contented, with dry Matters of Fact, as with a plain Play, without
Entertainments: This Rhapsody, therefore, has been thrown in,
as a Dance between the Acts, to make up for the Dullness of
what would have been by itself only proper. But I now come
to my Story again.

Notwithstanding, then, this our Compliance with the vulgar Taste; we generally made use of these Pantomimes, but as
Crutches to our weakest Plays: Nor were we so lost to all Sense
of what was valuable, as to dishonour our best Authors, in
such bad Company: We had still a due Respect to several select
Plays, that were able to be their own Support; and in which we
found our constant Account, without painting, and patching
them out, like Prostitutes, with these Follies, in fashion: If therefore we were not so strictly chaste, in the other part of our
Conduct, let the Error of it stand among the silly Consequences
of Two Stages. Could the Interest of both Companies have been
united, in one only Theatre; I had been one of the Few, that
would have us'd my utmost Endeavour of never admitting to the
Stage any Spectacle, that ought not to have been seen there;
the Errors of my own Plays, which I could not see, excepted.
And though probably, the Majority of Spectators would not
have been so well pleas'd with a Theatre so regulated; yet Sense,
and Reason cannot lose their intrinsick Value, because the
Giddy, and the Ignorant, are blind and deaf, or numerous; and
I cannot help saying, it is a Reproach to a sensible People, to let
Folly so publickly govern their Pleasures.

While I am making this grave Declaration of what I *would*
have done, had One only Stage been continued; to obtain an

easier Belief of my Sincerity, I ought to put my Reader in mind of what I *did* do, even after Two Companies were again establish'd.

About this Time *Jacobitism* had lately exerted itself, by the most unprovoked Rebellion, that our Histories have handed down to us, since the *Norman* Conquest:[11] I therefore thought that to set the Authors, and Principles of that desperate Folly in a fair Light, by allowing the mistaken Consciences of some their best Excuse, and by making the artful Pretenders to Conscience, as ridiculous, as they were ungratefully wicked, was a Subject fit for the honest Satire of Comedy, and what might, if it succeeded, do Honour to the Stage, by shewing the valuable Use of it. And considering what Numbers, at that time, might come to it, as prejudic'd Spectators, it may be allow'd that the Undertaking was not less hazardous, than laudable.

To give Life, therefore, to this Design, I borrow'd the *Tartuffe* of *Moliere*, and turn'd him, into a modern *Nonjuror*:[12] Upon the Hypocrisy of the *French* Character, I ingrafted a stronger Wickedness, that of an *English* Popish Priest, lurking under the Doctrine of our own Church, to raise his Fortune, upon the Ruin of a worthy Gentleman, whom his dissembled Sanctity had seduc'd into the treasonable Cause of a *Roman Catholick* Out-law. How this Design, in the Play, was executed, I refer to the Readers of it; it cannot be mended, by any critical Remarks, I can make, in its favour: Let it speak for it self. All the Reason I had to think it no bad Performance, was, that it was acted eighteen Days running, and that the Party, that were hurt by it (as I have been told) have not been the smallest Number of my back Friends ever since. But happy was it for this Play, that the very Subject was its Protection; a few Smiles of silent Contempt were the utmost Disgrace, that on the first Day of its Appearance it was thought safe to throw upon it; as the Satire was chiefly employ'd on the Enemies of the Government, they were not so hardy, as to own themselves such, by any higher Disapprobation, or Resentment. But as it was then probable I might write again, they knew it would not be long before they might with more Security give a Loose to their Spleen, and make up Accounts with me. And to do them Justice, in every Play I afterwards produced, they paid me the Balance, to a Tittle. But to none was I more beholden, than that celebrated Author Mr. *Mist*, whose *Weekly Journal*, for about fifteen Years following, scarce ever fail'd of passing some of his Party Compliments upon me: The State, and the Stage, were his frequent Parallels, and the Minister, and *Minheer Keiber* the Menager, were as constantly droll'd upon: Now, for my own Part, though I could never persuade my Wit to have an open Account with him (for as he had no Effects of his own, I did not think myself oblig'd to answer his Bills) Notwithstanding, I will be so charitable to his real *Manes*, and to the Ashes of his Paper, as to mention one particular Civility, he paid to my Memory, after he thought he had ingeniously kill'd me. Soon after the *Nonjuror* had receiv'd the Favour of the Town, I read, in one of his Journals, the following short Paragraph, *viz. Yesterday died Mr.* Colley Cibber, *late Comedian of the Theatre-Royal, notorious for writing the* Nonjuror. The Compliment, in the latter part, I confess, I did not dislike, because it came from so impartial a Judge; and it really so happen'd, that the former part of it was very near being true; for I had that very Day just crawled out, after having been some Weeks laid up by a Fever: However, I saw no use, in being thought to be thoroughly dead, before my Time, and therefore had a mind to see, whether the Town cared to have me alive again: So the Play of the *Orphan* being to be acted that Day, I quietly stole myself into the Part of the *Chaplain*, which I had not been seen in, for many Years before. The Surprize of the Audience at my unexpected Appearance on the very Day, I had been dead in the News, and the Paleness of my Looks, seem'd to make it a Doubt, whether I was not the Ghost, of my real Self departed: But when I spoke, their Wonder eas'd itself by an Applause; which convinc'd me, they were then satisfied, that my Firend *Mist* had told a *Fib* of me. Now, if simply to have shewn myself in broad Life, and about my Business, after he had *notoriously* reported me dead, can be called a Reply, it was the only one, which his Paper, while alive, ever drew from me. How far I may be vain, then in supposing that this Play brought me into the Disfavour of so many Wits, and valiant Auditors, as afterwards appear'd against me, let those who may think it worth their Notice, judge. In the mean time, till I can find a better Excuse for their, sometimes particular, Treatment of me, I cannot easily give up my Suspicion:[13] And if I add a more remarkable Fact, that afterwards confirm'd me in it, perhaps it may incline others to join in my Opinion.

On the first Day of the *Provok'd Husband*, ten Years after the *Nonjuror* had appear'd; a powerful Party, not having the Fear of publick Offence, or private Injury before their Eyes, appear'd most impetuously concern'd for the Demolition of it;[14] in which they so far succeeded, that for some Time I gave it up for lost; and to follow their Blows, in the publick Papers of the next Day, it was attack'd, and triumph'd over, as a dead, and damn'd Piece; a swinging Criticism was made upon it, in general invective Terms, for they disdain'd to trouble the World with Particulars; their Sentence, it seems, was Proof enough of its deserving the Fate it had met with. But this damn'd Play was, notwithstanding, acted twenty-eight Nights together, and left off, at a Receipt of upwards of a hundred and forty Pounds, which happen'd to be more, than in fifty Years before, could be then said, of any one Play whatsoever.

Now, if such notable Behaviour could break out upon so successful a Play (which too, upon the Share Sir *John Vanbrugh* had in it, I will venture to call a good one) what shall we impute it to? Why may not I plainly say, it was not the Play, but Me, who had a Hand in it, they did not like? And for what Reason? if they were not asham'd of it, why did not they publish it? No! the Reason had publish'd itself, I was the Author of the *Nonjuror!* But, perhaps, of all Authors, I ought not to make this sort of Complaint, because I have Reason to think, that that particular Offence has made me more honourable Friends than Enemies; the latter of which I am not unwilling should know (however unequal the Merit may be to the Reward) that Part of the Bread I now eat, was given me, for having writ the *Nonjuror*.

And yet I cannot but lament with many quiet Spectators, the

helpless Misfortune, that has so many Years attended the Stage! That no Law has had Force enough to give it absolute Protection! for till we can civilize its Auditors, the Authors, that write for it, will seldom have a greater Call to it, than Necessity; and how unlikely is the Imagination of the Needy, to inform, or delight the many, in Affluence? or how often does Necessity make many unhappy Gentlemen turn Authors, in spite of Nature?

What a Blessing, therefore, is it! what an enjoy'd Deliverance! after a Wretch has been driven by Fortune, to stand so many wanton Buffets of unmanly Fierceness, to find himself at last, quietly lifted above the Reach of them!

But let not this Reflection fall upon my Auditors, without Distinction; for though Candour, and Benevolence, are silent Virtues, they are as visible, as the most vociferous Ill-nature; and I confess, the Publick has given me more frequent Reason to be thankful, than to complain.

Having brought the Government of the Stage through such various Changes, and Revolutions, to this settled State, in which it continued to almost the Time of my leaving it;[2] it cannot be suppos'd, that a Period of so much Quiet, and so long a Train of Success, (though happy for those, who enjoy'd it) can afford such Matter of Surprize, or Amusement, as might arise, from Times of more Distress, and Disorder. A quiet Time, in History, like a Calm, in a Voyage, leave us, but in an indolent Station: To talk of our Affairs, when they were no longer ruffled, by Misfortunes, would be a Picture without Shade, a flat Performance, at best. As I might, therefore, throw all that tedious Time of our Tranquillity, into one Chasm, in my History, and cut my Way short, at once, to my last Exit, from the Stage, I shall, at least, fill it up with such Matter only, as I have a Mind should be known, how few soever may have Patience to read it: Yet, as I despair not of some Readers, who may be most awake, when they think others have most occasion to sleep; who may be more pleas'd to find me languid, than lively, or in the wrong, than in the right; why should I scruple (when it is so easy a Matter too) to gratify their particular Taste, by venturing upon any Error, that I like, or the Weakness of my Judgment misleads me to commit? I think too, I have a very good Chance, for my Success, in this passive Ambition, by shewing myself in a Light, I have not been seen in.

By your Leave then, Gentlemen! let the Scene open, and, at once, discover your Comedian, at the Bar! There you will find him a Defendant, and pleading his own Theatrical Cause, in a Court of *Chancery:* But, as I chuse, to have a Chance of

pleasing others, as well as of indulging you, Gentlemen; I
must first beg leave, to open my Case to them; after which,
my whole Speech, upon that Occasion, shall be at your Mercy.

In all the Transactions of Life, there cannot be a more painful Circumstance, than a Dispute at Law, with a Man, with
whom we have long liv'd, in an agreeable Amity: But when
Sir *Richard Steele*, to get himself out of Difficulties, was
oblig'd to throw his Affairs, into the Hands of Lawyers, and
Trustees, that Consideration, then, could be of no weight:
The Friend, or the Gentleman, had no more to do in the
Matter! Thus, while Sir *Richard* no longer acted, from himself, it may be no Wonder, if a Flaw was found in our Conduct, for the Law to make Work with. It must be observ'd
then, that about two, or three Years, before this Suit was
commenc'd, upon Sir *Richard*'s totally absenting himself, from
all Care, and Menagement of the Stage (which by our Articles
of Partnership he was equally, and jointly oblig'd with us,
to attend) we were reduc'd to let him know, that we could not
go on, at that Rate; but that if he expected to make the Business a *sine Cure*, we had as much Reason to expect a Consideration for our extraordinary Care of it; and that during his Absence, we therefore intended to charge our selves at a Sallary
of 1 £. 13s. 4d. every acting Day (unless he could shew us Cause,
to the contrary) for our Menagement: To which, in his
compos'd manner, he only answer'd; That to be sure, we knew
what was fitter to be done, than he did; that he had always
taken a Delight, in making us easy, and had no Reason to doubt
of our doing him Justice. Now whether, under this easy Stile
of Approbation, he conceal'd any Dislike of our Resolution, I
cannot say. But, if I may speak my private Opinion, I really
believe, from his natural Negligence of his Affairs, he was
glad, at any rate, to be excus'd an Attendance, which he was
now grown weary of. But whether I am deceiv'd, or right in
my Opinion, the Fact was truly this, that he never once,
directly, nor indirectly, complain'd, or objected to our being
paid the above-mention'd daily Sum, in near three Years together; and yet still continued to absent himself from us, and

our Affairs. But notwithstanding, he had seen, and done all this with his Eyes open; his Lawyer thought here was still a fair Field, for a Battle, in Chancery, in which, though his Client might be beaten, he was sure his Bill must be paid for it: Accordingly, to work with us he went. But not to be so long, as the Lawyers were in bringing this Cause to an Issue, I shall, at once, let you know, that it came to a Hearing, before the late Sir *Joseph Jekyll*, then Master of the Rolls, in the Year 1726.[3] Now, as the chief Point, in dispute, was, of what Kind, or Importance, the Business of a Menager was, or in what it principally consisted; it could not be suppos'd, that the most learned Council could be so well appris'd of the Nature of it, as one, who had himself gone through the Care, and Fatigue of it. I was therefore encourag'd by our Council, to speak to that particular Head myself; which I confess I was glad he suffer'd me to undertake; but when I tell you, that two of the learned Council against us, came, afterwards, to be successively Lord Chancellors, it sets my Presumption in a Light, that I still tremble to shew it in: But however, not to assume more Merit, from its Success, than was really its Due, I ought fairly to let you know, that I was not so hardy, as to deliver my Pleading without Notes, in my Hand, of the Heads I intended to enlarge upon; for though I thought I could conquer my Fear, I could not be so sure of my Memory: But when it came to the critical Moment, the Dread, and Apprehension of what I had undertaken, so disconcerted my Courage, that though I had been us'd to talk to above Fifty Thousand different People every Winter, for upwards of Thirty Years together; an involuntary, and unaffected Proof of my Confusion, fell from my Eyes; and, as I found myself quite out of my Element, I seem'd rather gasping for Life, than in a Condition to cope with the eminent Orators, against me. But however, I soon found, from the favourable Attention of my Hearers, that my Diffidence had done me no Disservice: And as the Truth, I was to speak to, needed no Ornament of Words, I delivered it, in the plain manner following, *viz.*

In this Cause, Sir, I humbly conceive, there are but two

Points, that admit of any material Dispute. The first is, Whether Sir *Richard Steele*, is as much oblig'd to do the Duty, and Business of a Menager, as either *Wilks, Booth*, or *Cibber:* And the second is, Whether, by Sir *Richard*'s totally withdrawing himself from the Business of a Menager, the Defendants are justifiable, in charging to each of themselves the 1 £. 13*s.* 4*d. per Diem*, for their Particular Pains, and Care, in carrying on the whole Affairs of the Stage, without any Assistance from Sir *Richard Steele*.

As to the First, if I don't mistake the Words of the Assignment, there is a Clause in it, that says, All Matters relating to the Government, or Menagement of the Theatre, shall be concluded by a Majority of Voices. Now I presume, Sir, there is no room left to alledge, that Sir *Richard* was ever refus'd his Voice, though in above three Years, he never desired, to give it: And I believe there will be as little room to say, that he could have a Voice, if he were not a Menager. But, Sir, his being a Menager is so self-evident, that it seems amazing how he could conceive, that he was to take the Profits, and Advantages of a Menager, without doing the Duty of it. And I will be bold to say, Sir, that his Assignment of the Patent, to *Wilks, Booth*, and *Cibber*, in no one Part of it, by the severest Construction in the World, can be wrested to throw the heavy Burthen of the Menagement only upon their Shoulders. Nor does it appear, Sir, that either in his Bill, or in his Answer to our Cross-Bill, he had offer'd, any Hint, or Glimpse of a Reason, for his withdrawing from the Menagement, at all; or so much as pretend, from the Time complained of, that he ever took the least part of his Share of it. Now, Sir, however unaccountable this Conduct of Sir *Richard* may seem, we will still allow, that he had some Cause for it; but whether or no, that Cause, was a reasonable one, your Honour will the better judge, if I may be indulg'd in the Liberty of explaining it.

Sir, the Case, in plain Truth and Reality, stands thus: Sir *Richard*, though no Man alive can write better of Oeconomy than himself, yet, perhaps, he is above the Drudgery of practising it: Sir *Richard*, then, was often in want of Mony; and while

we were in Friendship with him, we often assisted his Occasions:
But those Compliances had so unfortunate an Effect, that they
only heightened his Importunity, to borrow more, and the more
we lent, the less he minded us, or shew'd any Concern for our
Welfare. Upon this, Sir, we stopt our Hands, at once, and per-
emptorily refus'd to advance another Shilling, 'till by the Balance of our Accounts, it became due to him. And this Treatment
(though we hope, not in the least unjustifiable) we have reason
to believe so ruffled his Temper, that he at once, was as short
with us, as we had been with him; for from that Day, he never
more came near us: Nay, Sir, he not only continued to neglect,
what he *should* have done, but actually did what he ought *not* to
have done: He made an Assignment of his Share, without our
Consent, in a manifest Breach of our Agreement: For, Sir, we
did not lay that Restriction upon ourselves, for no Reason: We
knew, before-hand, what Trouble, and Inconvenience it would
be, to unravel, and expose our Accounts to Strangers, who if
they were to do us no hurt, by divulging our Secrets, we were
sure could do us no good, by keeping them. If Sir *Richard*
had had our common Interest at heart, he would have been
as warm in it, as we were, and as tender of hurting it: But
supposing his assigning his Share to others, may have done us
no great Injury, it is at least, a shrewd Proof, that he did not
care whether it did us any, or no. And if the Clause was not
strong enough, to restrain him from it, in Law, there was
enough in it, to have restrain'd him, in Honour, from breaking
it. But take it, in its best Light, it shews him as remiss a
Menager, in our Affairs, as he naturally was in his own. Suppose, Sir, we had all been as careless as himself, which I can't
find he has any more Right to be, than we have, must not
our whole Affair have fallen to Ruin? And may we not, by a
parity of Reason suppose, that by his Neglect a fourth Part
of it *does* fall to Ruin? But, Sir, there is a particular Reason
to believe, that, from our want of Sir *Richard*, more, than a
fourth Part *does* suffer by it: His Rank, and Figure, in the
World, while he gave us the Assistance of them, were of
extraordinary Service to us: He had an easier Access, and a

more regarded Audience at Court, than our low Station of Life could pretend to, when our Interest wanted (as it often did) a particular Solicitation there. But since we have been depriv'd of him, the very End, the very Consideration of his Share in our Profits, is not perform'd on his Part. And will Sir *Richard*, then, make us no Compensation, for so valuable a Loss, in our Interests, and so palpable an *Addition* to our Labour? I am afraid, Sir, if we were all to be as indolent, in the Menaging Part, as Sir *Richard* presumes he has a Right to be; our Patent would soon run us, as many Hundreds, in Debt, as he has had (and still seems willing to have) his Share of, for doing of nothing.

Sir, our next Point, in question, is whether *Wilks*, *Booth*, and *Cibber*, are justifiable, in charging the 1 £. 13s. 4d. *per diem*, for their extraordinary Menagement, in the Absence of Sir *Richard Steele*. I doubt, Sir, it will be hard to come to the Solution of this Point, unless we may be a little indulg'd, in setting forth, what is the daily, and necessary Business, and Duty of a Menager. But, Sir, we will endeavour to be as short, as the Circumstances will admit of.

Sir, by our Books, it is apparent, that the Menagers have under their Care, no less than One Hundred, and Forty Persons, in constant, daily Pay: And among such Numbers, it will be no wonder, if a great many of them are unskilful, idle, and sometimes untractable; all which Tempers are to be led, or driven, watch'd, and restrain'd by the continual Skill, Care, and Patience of the Menagers. Every Menager, is oblig'd, in his turn, to attend two, or three Hours every Morning, at the Rehearsal of Plays, and other Entertainments for the Stage, or else every Rehearsal would be but a rude Meeting of Mirth and Jollity. The same Attendance, is as necessary at every Play, during the time of its publick Action, in which one, or more of us, have constantly been punctual, whether we have had any part, in the Play, then acted, or not. A Menager ought to be at the Reading of every new Play, when it is first offer'd to the Stage, tho' there are seldom one of those Plays in twenty, which upon hearing, proves to be fit for it, and upon such

Occasions the Attendance must be allow'd, to be as painfully tedious, as the getting rid of the Authors of such Plays, must be disagreeable, and difficult. Besides this, Sir, a Menager is to order all new Cloaths, to assist in the Fancy, and Propriety of them, to limit the Expence, and to withstand the unreasonable Importunities of some, that are apt to think themselves injur'd, if they are not finer than their Fellows. A Menager, is to direct and oversee the Painters, Machinists, Musicians, Singers, and Dancers; to have an Eye upon the Door-keepers, Under-Servants, and Officers, that without such care, are too often apt to defraud us, or neglect their Duty.

And all this, Sir, and more, much more, which we hope will be needless to trouble you with, have we done every Day, without the least Assistance from Sir *Richard*, even at times when the Concern, and Labour of our Parts, upon the Stage, have made it very difficult, and irksome to go thro' with it.

In this Place, Sir, it may be worth observing, that Sir *Richard*, in his Answer to our Cross-Bill, seems to value himself, upon *Cibber*'s confessing, in the Dedication of a Play, which he made to Sir *Richard*, that he (Sir *Richard*) had done the Stage very considerable Service, by leading the Town to our Plays, and filling our Houses, by the Force and Influence of his *Tatlers*. But Sir *Richard* forgets, that those *Tatlers* were written in the late Queen's Reign, long before he was admitted to a Share in the Playhouse: And in truth, Sir, it was our real Sense of those Obligations, and Sir *Richard*'s assuring us they should be continued, that first and chiefly inclin'd us to invite him to share the Profits of our Labours, upon such farther Conditions, as in his Assignment of the Patent to us, are specified. And, Sir, as *Cibber*'s publick Acknowledgment of those Favours is at the same time an equal Proof of Sir Richard's Power to continue them; so Sir, we hope, it carries an equal Probability, that without his Promise to *use* that Power, he would never have been thought on, much less have been invited by us, into a Joint-Menagement of the Stage, and into a Share of the Profits: And indeed what Pretence could he have form'd, for asking a Patent from the Crown, had he been pos-

sess'd of no eminent Qualities, but in common with other
Men? But, Sir, all these Advantages, all these Hopes, nay Cer-
tainties of greater Profits, from those great Qualities, have we
been utterly depriv'd of by the wilful, and unexpected Neglect of Sir *Richard*. But we find, Sir, it is a common thing,
in the Practice of Mankind, to justify one Error, by committing
another: For Sir *Richard* has not only refus'd us the extraordinary Assistance, which he is able, and bound to give us; but on
the contrary, to our great Expence, and loss of Time, now
calls us to account, in this Honourable Court, for the Wrong
we have done him, in not doing his Business of a Menager, for
nothing. But, Sir, Sir *Richard* has not met with such Treatment from us: He has not writ Plays for us, for *Nothing*, we
paid him very well, and in an extraordinary manner, for his
late Comedy of the *Conscious Lovers:* And though, in writing
that Play, he had more Assistance from one of the Menagers,[4]
than becomes me to enlarge upon, of which Evidence has been
given upon Oath, by several of our Actors; yet, Sir, he was
allow'd the full, and particular Profits of that Play, as an
Author, which amounted to Three Hundred more, which he
receiv'd as a Joint-Sharer of the general Profits, that arose
from it. Now, Sir, though the Menagers are not all of them
able to write Plays, yet they have all of them been able to do
(I won't say, as good, but at least) as profitable a thing. They
have invented, and adorn'd a Spectacle, that for forty Days
together has brought more Mony, to the House, than the best
Play that ever was writ. The Spectacle I mean, Sir, is that of
the Coronation-Ceremony of *Anna Bullen:*[4a] And though we
allow a good Play to be the more laudable Performance, yet,
Sir, in the profitable Part of it, there is no Comparison. If
therefore, our Spectacle brought in as much, or more Mony,
than Sir *Richard*'s Comedy, what is there, on his side but Usage,
that intitles him, to be paid for one, more, than we are, for
t'other? But then Sir, if he is so profitably distinguish'd for
his Play, if we yield him up the Preference, and pay him, for his
extraordinary Composition, and take nothing for our own, tho'
it turn'd out more to our common Profit; sure, Sir, while we

do such extraordinary Duty, as Menagers, and while he neglects his Share of that Duty, he cannot grudge us the moderate Demand we make for our separate Labour?

To conclude, Sir, if by our constant Attendance, our Care, our Anxiety (not to mention the disagreeable Contests, we sometimes meet with, both within, and without Doors, in the Menagement of our Theatre) we have not only sav'd the whole from Ruin, which, if we had all follow'd Sir *Richard*'s Example, could not have been avoided; I say, Sir, if we have still made it so valuable an Income to him, without his giving us the least Assistance for several Years past; we hope, Sir, that the poor Labourers, that have done all this for Sir *Richard*, will not be thought unworthy of their Hire.

How far our Affairs, being set in this particular Light, might assist our Cause, may be of no great Importance to guess; but the Issue of it was this: That Sir *Richard* not having made any Objection, to what we had charg'd for Menagement, for three Years together; and as our Proceedings had been all transacted, in open Day, without any clandestine Intention of Fraud; we were allow'd the Sums, in dispute, above-mention'd; and Sir *Richard* not being advis'd, to appeal to the Lord-Chancellor, both Parties paid their own Costs, and thought it their mutual Interest, to let this be the last of their Lawsuits.

And now, gentle Reader, I ask Pardon, for so long an Imposition on your Patience: For though I may have no ill Opinion of this Matter myself; yet to you, I can very easily conceive it may have been tedious. You are therefore, at your own Liberty of charging the whole Impertinence of it, either to the Weakness of my Judgment, or the Strength of my Vanity; and I will so far join in your Censure, that I farther confess, I have been so impatient to give it you, that you have had it, out of its turn: For, some Years, before this Suit was commenc'd, there were other Facts, that ought to have had a Precedence in my History: But that, I dare say, is an Oversight you will easily excuse, provided you afterwards find them worth reading. However, as to that Point, I must take my chance, and shall therefore proceed to speak of the Theatre, which was

order'd by his late Majesty to be erected in the Great old
Hall at *Hampton-Court;* where Plays were intended to have
been acted twice a Week, during the Summer-Season. But
before the Theatre could be finish'd, above half the Month of
September being elaps'd, there were but seven Plays acted
before the Court return'd to *London.* This throwing open a
Theatre, in a Royal Palace, seem'd to be reviving the Old *English*
hospitable Grandeur, where the lowest Rank of neighbouring
Subjects might make themselves merry at Court, without being
laugh'd at themselves. In former Reigns, Theatrical Entertainments at the Royal Palaces, had been perform'd at vast Expence,
as appears by the Description of the Decorations, in several of
Ben. Johnson's Masques, in King *James,* and *Charles the First*'s
time; many curious, and original Draughts of which, by Sir *Inigo
Jones,* I have seen, in the Museum of our greatest Master, and
Patron of Arts, and Architecture, whom it would be a needless
Liberty to name.[5] But when our Civil Wars ended in the Decadence of Monarchy, it was then an Honour to the Stage, to
have fallen with it: Yet, after the Restoration of *Charles* II.
some faint Attempts were made to revive these Theatrical Spectacles at Court: but I have met with no Account of above one
Masque acted there, by the Nobility; which was that of *Calisto,*
written by *Crown,* the Author of Sir *Courtly Nice.* For what
Reason *Crown* was chosen to the Honour, rather than *Dryden,*
who was then Poet-Laureat, and out of all comparison his
Superior, in Poetry, may seem surprizing: But if we consider
the Offence which the then Duke of *Buckingham* took at the
Character of *Zimri,* in *Dryden*'s *Absalom,* &c. (which might
probably be a Return, to his Grace's *Drawcansir,* in the *Rehearsal*) we may suppose the Prejudice and Recommendation
of so illustrious a Pretender to Poetry, might prevail, at Court,
to give *Crown* this Preference.[6] In the same Reign, the King
had his Comedians at *Windsor,* but upon a particular Establishment; for tho' they acted in St. *George*'s Hall, within the
Royal Palace yet (as I have been inform'd by an Eye-witness)
they were permitted to take Mony at the Door, of every
Spectator; whether this was an Indulgence, in Conscience, I

cannot say; but it was a common Report among the principal
Actors, when I first came into the Theatre-Royal, in 1690, that
there was then, due to the Company, from that Court, about
One Thousand Five Hundred Pounds, for Plays commanded,
&c. and yet it was the general Complaint, in that Prince's Reign,
that he paid too much Ready-mony, for his Pleasures: But these
Assertions I only give, as I receiv'd them, without being answerable, for their Reality. This Theatrical Anecdote, however,
puts me in mind of one of a more private nature, which I had
from old solemn *Boman*,[7] the late Actor of venerable Memory.
Boman, then a Youth, and fam'd for his Voice, was appointed
to sing some Part, in a Concert of Musick at the private Lodg-
ings of Mrs. *Gwin*;[7a] at which were only present, the King, the
Duke of *York*, and one, or two more, who were usually admitted upon those detached Parties of Pleasure. When the
Performance was ended, the King express'd himself highly
pleas'd, and gave it extraordinary Commendations: Then, Sir,
said the Lady, to shew you don't speak like a Courtier, I hope
you will make the Performers a handsom Present: The King
said, he had no Mony about him, and ask'd the Duke if he had
any? To which the Duke reply'd, I believe, Sir, not above a
Guinea, or two. Upon which the laughing Lady, turning to the
People about her, and making bold with the King's common Expression, cry'd, *Od's Fish! What Company am I got
into!*

Whether the reverend Historian of his *Own Time*,[8] among
the many other Reasons of the same Kind, he might have for
stiling this Fair One the *indiscreetest, and wildest Creature,
that ever was in a Court*, might know This to be one of them,
I can't say: But if we consider her, in all the Disadvantages
of her Rank, and Education, she does not appear to have had
any criminal Errors more remarkable, than her Sex's Frailty
to answer for: And, if the same Author, in his latter end of
that Prince's Life, seems to reproach his Memory, with too
kind a Concern for her Support, we may allow, that it becomes
a Bishop to have had no Eyes, or Taste for the frivolous Charms
or playful *Badinage* of a King's Mistress: Yet, if the common

Fame of her may be believ'd, which in my Memory was not
doubted, she had less to be laid to her Charge, than any other
of those Ladies, who were in the same State of Preferment:
She never meddled in Matters of serious Moment, or was
the Tool of working Politicians: Never broke into those
amorous Infidelities, which others, in that grave Author are
accus'd of; but was as visibly distinguish'd, by her particular
Personal Inclination to the King, as her Rivals were, by their
Titles, and Grandeur. Give me leave to carry (perhaps, the
Partiality of) my Observation a little farther. The same Author,
in the same Page, 263, tell us, That "Another of the King's Mistresses, the Daughter of a Clergyman, Mrs. *Roberts*, in whom
her first Education had so deep a Root, that tho' she fell into
many scandalous Disorders, with very dismal Adventures in
them all, yet a Principle of Religion was so deep laid in her, that
tho' it did not restrain her, yet it kept alive in her, such a constant Horror of Sin, that she was never easy, in an ill course, and
died with a great Sense of her former ill Life."[8a]

To all this let us give an implicit Credit: Here is the Account
of a frail Sinner made up, with a Reverend Witness! Yet I
cannot but lament, that this Mitred Historian, who seems to
know more Personal Secrets, than any that ever writ before
him, should not have been as inquisitive after the last Hours
of our other Fair Offender, whose Repentance I have been
unquestionably inform'd, appear'd in all the contrite Symptoms of a Christian Sincerity. If therefore you find I am so
much concern'd to make this favourable mention of the one,
because she was a Sister of the *Theatre*, why may not --- But
I dare not be so presumptuous, so uncharitably bold, as to suppose the other was spoken better of, merely because she was
the Daughter of a *Clergyman*. Well, and what then? What's
all this idle Prate, you may say, to the matter in hand? Why,
I say your Question is a little too critical; and if you won't give
an Author leave, now and then, to embellish his Work, by a
natural Reflexion, you are an ungentle Reader. But I have
done with my Digression, and return to our Theatre at *Hampton-Court*, where I am not sure the Reader, be he ever so wise,

will meet with any thing more worth his notice: However, if he happens to read, as I write, for want of something better to do, he will go on; and perhaps, wonder when I tell him, that

A Play presented at Court, or acted on a publick Stage, seem to their different Auditors, a different Entertainment. Now hear my Reason for it. In the common Theatre, the Guests are at home, where the politer Forms of Good-breeding are not so nicely regarded: Every one there, falls to, and likes or finds fault, according to his natural Taste, or Appetite. At Court, where the Prince gives the Treat, and honours the Table with his own Presence, the Audience is under the Restraint of a Circle, where Laughter, or Applause, rais'd higher than a Whisper, would be star'd at. At a publick Play they are both let loose, even 'till the Actor is, sometimes, pleas'd with his not being able to be heard, for the Clamour of them. But this Coldness or Decency of Attention, at Court, I observ'd had but a melancholy Effect, upon the impatient Vanity of some of our Actors, who seem'd inconsolable, when their flashy Endeavours to please had pass'd unheeded: Their not considering where they were, quite disconcerted them; nor could they recover their Spirits, 'till from the lowest Rank of the Audience, some gaping *John*, or *Joan*, in the fullness of their Hearts, roar'd out their Approbation: And indeed, such a natural Instance of honest Simplicity, a Prince himself, whose Indulgence knows where to make Allowances, might reasonably smile at, and perhaps not think it the worst part of his Entertainment. Yet it must be own'd, that an Audience may be as well too much reserv'd, as too profuse of their Applause: For though, it is possible a *Betterton* would not have been discourag'd, from throwing out an Excellence, or elated into an Error, by his Auditors being too little, or too much pleas'd, yet as Actors of his Judgment are Rarities; those of less Judgment may sink into a Flatness, in their Performance, for want of that Applause, which from the generality of Judges, they might perhaps, have some Pretence to: And the Auditor, when not seeming to feel what ought to affect him, may rob himself

of something more, that he might have had, by giving the
Actor his Due, who measures out his Power to please, according to the Value he sets upon his Hearer's Taste, or Capacity.
But however, as we were not, here, itinerant Adventurers, and
had properly but one Royal Auditor to please; after that
Honour was attain'd to, the rest of our Ambition had little
to look after: And that the King was often pleas'd, we were
not only assur'd, by those who had the Honour to be near
him; but could see it, from the frequent Satisfaction in his
Looks at particular Scenes, and Passages: One Instance of
which I am tempted to relate, because it was at a Speech, that
might more naturally affect a Sovereign Prince, than any private Spectator. In *Shakespear*'s *Harry the Eighth;* that King
commands the Cardinal to write circular Letters of Indemnity,
into every County, where the Payment of certain heavy Taxes
had been disputed: Upon which the Cardinal whispers the
following Directions to his Secretary *Cromwell:*

------- A Word with you:
Let there be Letters writ to every Shire,
Of the King's Grace, and Pardon: The griev'd Commons
Hardly conceive of me. Let it be nois'd,
That through our *Intercession*, this Revokement,
And Pardon comes. --- I shall anon advise you
Farther, in the Proceeding.[9]

The Solicitude of this Spiritual Minister, in filching from his
Master the Grace, and Merit of a good Action, and dressing
up himself in it, while himself had been Author of the Evil
complain'd of, was so easy a Stroke of his Temporal Conscience,
that it seem'd to raise the King into something more than a
Smile, whenever that Play came before him: And I had a more
distinct Occasion, to observe this Effect; because my proper
Stand on the Stage, when I spoke the Lines, required me to be
near the Box, where the King usually sate. In a Word, this
Play is so true a Dramatick Chronicle of an old *English* Court,
and where the Character of *Harry the Eighth* is so exactly
drawn, even to a humourous Likeness, that it may be no won-

der why his Majesty's Particular Taste for it, should have commanded it three several times in one Winter.

This too calls to my Memory an extravagant Pleasantry of Sir *Richard Steele*, who being ask'd by a grave Nobleman, after the same Play had been presented at *Hampton-Court*, how the King lik'd it; reply'd, *So terribly well, my Lord, that I was afraid I should have lost all my Actors! For I was not sure, the King would not keep them to fill the Posts at Court, that he saw them so fit for in the Play.*

It may be imagin'd, that giving Plays to the People at such a distance from *London*, could not but be attended with an extraordinary Expence; and it was some Difficulty, when they were first talk'd of, to bring them under a moderate Sum; I shall therefore, in as few Words, as possible, give a particular of what Establishment they were then brought up to, that in case the same Entertainments, should at any time hereafter be call'd to the same Place, future Courts may judge, how far the Precedent may stand good, or need an Alteration.

Though the stated Fee, for a Play acted, at *Whitehall* had been formerly, but Twenty Pounds; yet, as that hinder'd not the Company's acting on the same Day, at the Publick Theatre, that Sum was almost all clear Profits to them: But this Circumstance not being practicable, when they were commanded to *Hampton-Court*, a new, and extraordinary Charge was unavoidable: The Menagers, therefore, not to inflame it, desired no Consideration, for their own Labour, farther than the Honour of being employ'd, in his Majesty's Commands; and, if the other Actors might be allow'd, each their Days Pay, and travelling Charges, they should hold themselves ready, to act any Play, there, at a Day's Warning: And that the Trouble might be less, by being divided, the Lord-Chamberlain was pleas'd to let us know, that the Household-Musick, the Wax Lights, and a *Chaise-Marine*,[9a] to carry our moving Wardrobe to every different Play, should be under the Charge of the proper Officers. Notwithstanding these Assistances, the Expence of every Play amounted to Fifty Pounds: Which Account, when all was over, was not only allow'd us, but his Majesty was graciously pleas'd to give the

Menagers Two Hundred Pounds more, for their particular Performance, and Trouble, in only seven times acting. Which last Sum, tho' it might not be too much, for a Sovereign Prince to give, it was certainly more than our utmost Merit ought to have hop'd for: And I confess, when I receiv'd the Order for the Mony, from his Grace the Duke of *Newcastle*, then Lord-Chamberlain, I was so surpris'd, that I imagin'd his Grace's Favour, or Recommendation of our Readiness, or Diligence, must have contributed to so high a Consideration of it, and was offering my Acknowledgments, as I thought them due; but was soon stopt short, by his Grace's Declaration, That we had no Obligations for it, but to the King himself, who had given it, from no other Motive, than his own Bounty. Now whether we may suppose that Cardinal *Wolsey* (as you see *Shakespear* has drawn him) would silently have taken such low Acknowledgments to himself, perhaps may be as little worth consideration, as my mentioning this Circumstance has been necessary: But if it is due to the Honour and Integrity of the (then) Lord-Chamberlain, I cannot think it wholly impertinent.

Since that time, there has been but one Play given at *Hampton-Court*, which was for the Entertainment of the Duke of *Lorrain;* and for which his present Majesty was pleas'd to order us a Hundred Pounds.

The Reader may, now, plainly see, that I am ransacking my Memory, for such remaining Scraps of Theatrical History, as may not, perhaps, be worth his Notice: But if they are such as tempt me to write them, why may I not hope, that in this wide World, there may be many an idle Soul, no wiser than myself, who may be equally tempted to read them?

I have so often had occasion to compare the State of the Stage to the State of a Nation, that I yet feel a Reluctancy to drop the Comparison, or speak of the one, without some Application to the other. How many Reigns, then, do I remember, from that of *Charles* the Second, through all which, there has been, from one half of the People, or the other, a Succession of Clamour, against every different Ministry for the Time being? And yet, let the Cause of this Clamour have been never so well grounded, it is impossible, but that some of those Ministers must have been wiser, and honester Men, than others: If this be true, as true, I believe it is, why may I not then say, as some Fool in a *French* Play does, upon a like Occasion--- *Justement, comme chez nous!* 'Twas exactly the same with our Menagement! let us have done never so well, we could not please every body: All I can say, in our Defence, is, that though many good Judges, might possibly conceive how the State of the Stage might have been mended, yet the best of them never pretended to remember the Time when it was better! or could shew us the way to make their imaginary Amendments practicable.

For though I have often allow'd, that our best Merit, as Actors, was never equal to that of our Predecessors, yet I will venture to say, that in all its Branches, the Stage had never been under so just, so prosperous, and so settled a Regulation, for forty Years before, as it was at the Time I am speaking of. The most plausible Objection to our Administration, seem'd to be, that we took no Care to breed up young Actors, to succeed us; and this was imputed as the greater Fault, because it was taken for granted, that it was a Matter as easy as planting so many Cabbages: Now might not a Court be as well reproach'd, for not breeding up a Succession of complete Ministers? And yet it is evident, that if Providence, or Nature don't supply us with both, the State, and the Stage will be but poorly supported. If a Man of an ample Fortune should take it into his Head, to give a younger Son an extraordinary Allowance, in order to breed him a great Poet, what might we suppose would be the Odds, that his Trouble, and Mony would be all thrown away? Not more, than it would be, against the Master of a Theatre, who should say, this, or that young Man, I will take care shall be an excellent Actor! Let it be our Excuse then, for that mistaken Charge against us; that since there was no Garden, or Market, where accomplish'd Actors grew, or were to be sold, we could only pick them up, as we do Pebbles of Value, by Chance: We may polish a thousand, before we find one, fit to make a Figure, in the Lid of a Snuff-Box. And how few soever we were able to produce, it is no Proof, that we were not always in search of them: Yet, at worst, it was allow'd, that our Deficiency of Men Actors, was not so visible, as our Scarcity of tollerable Women: But when it is consider'd, that the Life of Youth and Beauty is too short for the bringing an Actress to her Perfection; were I to mention too, the many frail fair Ones, I remember, who, before they could arrive to their Theatrical Maturity, were feloniously stoln from the Tree, it would rather be thought our Misfortune, than our Fault, that we were not better provided.

Even the Laws of a Nunnery, we find, are thought no sufficient Security against Temptations, without iron Grates, and high Walls to inforce them; which the Architecture of a Theatre will not so properly admit of: And yet, methinks, Beauty that has not those artificial Fortresses about it, that has no Defence but its natural Virtue (which upon the Stage has more than once been met with) makes a much more meritorious Figure, in Life, than that immur'd Virtue, which could never be try'd. But alas! as the poor Stage, is but the Show-glass to a Toy-shop, we must not wonder, if now and then, some of the Bawbles should find a Purchaser.

However, as to say more, or less than Truth, are equally unfaithful in an Historian; I cannot but own, that in the Government of the Theatre, I have known many Instances, where the Merit of promising Actors has not always been brought forward, with the Regard, or Favour, it had a Claim to: And if I put my Reader in mind, that in the early Part of this Work, I have shewn, through what continued Difficulties, and Discouragements I myself made my way up the Hill of Preferment; he may justly call it, too strong a Glare of my Vanity: I am afraid he is in the right; but I pretend not to be one of those chaste Authors, that know how to write without it: When Truth is to be told it may be as much Chance, as Choice, if it happens to turn out in my favour: But to shew that this was true of others, as well as myself, *Booth* shall be another Instance. In 1707, when *Swiney* was the only Master of the Company in the *Hay-Market; Wilks,* though he was, then, but an hired Actor himself, rather chose to govern, and give Orders, than to receive them; and was so jealous of *Booth*'s rising, that, with a high Hand, he gave the Part of *Pierre*, in *Venice Preserv'd*, to *Mills* the elder, who (not to undervalue him) was out of Sight, in the Pretensions that *Booth*, then young, as he was, had to the same Part: And this very Discouragement so strongly affected him, that not long after, when several of us became Sharers with *Swiney*, *Booth* rather chose to risque his Fortune, with the old Patentee in *Drury-Lane*, than come into our Interest, where he saw he was like to meet with more of those Partialities. And yet again, *Booth* himself, when he came to be a Menager, would sometimes suffer his Judgment to be blinded by his Inclination to Actors, whom the Town seem'd to have but an indifferent Opinion of. This again, inclines me to ask another of my odd Questions, *viz.* Have we never seen the same Passions govern a Court! How many white Staffs, and great Places do we find, in our Histories, have been laid at the Feet of a Monarch, because they chose not to give way to a Rival, in Power, or hold a second Place in his Favour? How many *Whigs*, and *Tories* have chang'd their Parties, when their good or bad Pretensions have met with a Check to their higher Preferment?

Thus, we see, let the Degrees, and Rank of Men, be ever so unequal, Nature throws out their Passions, from the same Motives; 'tis not the Eminence, or Lowliness of either, that makes the one, when provok'd, more or less a reasonable Creature than the other: The Courtier, and the Comedian, when their Ambition is out of Humour, take just the same Measures to right themselves.

If this familiar Stile of talking should, in the Nostrils of Gravity, and Wisdom, smell a little too much of the Presumptuous, or the Pragmatical, I will, at least, descend lower, in my Apology for it, by calling to my Assistance the old, humble Proverb, *viz.* *'Tis an ill Bird that, &c.*[10] Why then should I debase my Profession, by setting it in vulgar Lights, when I may shew it to more favourable Advantages? And when I speak of our Errors, why may I not extenuate them by illustrious Examples? or by not allowing them greater, than the greatest Men have been subject to? Or why, indeed, may I not suppose, that a sensible Reader will rather laugh, than look grave, at the Pomp of my Parallels?

Now, as I am tied down to the Veracity of an Historian, whose Facts cannot be supposed, like those in a Romance, to be in the Choice of the Author, to make them more marvellous, by Invention, if I should happen to sink into a little farther Insignificancy, let the simple Truth of what I have farther to say, be my Excuse for it. I am oblig'd, therefore, to make the Experiment, by shewing you the Conduct of our Theatrical Ministry in such Lights, as on various Occasions it appear'd in.

Though *Wilks* had more Industry, and Application, than any Actor I had ever known, yet we found it possible that those necessary Qualities might sometimes be so misconducted, as not only to make them useless, but hurtful to our Commonwealth; for while he was impatient to be foremost, in every thing, he frequently shock'd the honest Ambition of others, whose Measures might have been more serviceable, could his Jealousy have given way to them. His own Regards for himself, therefore, were, to avoid a disagreeable Dispute with him, too often comply'd with: But this leaving his Diligence, to his own Conduct, made us, in some Instances, pay dearly for it: For Example; he would take as much, or more Pains in forwarding to the Stage, the Water-gruel Work of some insipid Author, that happen'd rightly to make his Court to him, than he would for the best Play, wherein it was not his Fortune to be chosen for the best Character. So great was his Impatience to be employ'd, that I scarce remember, in twenty Years, above one profitable Play, we could get to be reviv'd, wherein he found he was to make no considerable Figure, independent of him: But the *Tempest* having done Wonders formerly, he could not form any Pretensions, to let it lie longer dormant: However, his Coldness to it was so visible, that he took all Occasions to postpone, and discourage its Progress, by frequently taking up the morning Stage with something more to his Mind. Having been myself particularly sollicitous for the reviving this Play, *Dogget* (for this was before *Booth* came into the Menagement) consented that the extraordinary Decorations, and Habits, should be left to my Care, and Direction, as the fittest Person, whose Temper could jossle through the petulant Opposition, that he knew *Wilks* would be always offering to it, because he had but a middling Part in it, that of *Ferdinand:* Notwithstanding which, so it happen'd, that the Success of it shew'd (not to take from the Merit of *Wilks*) that it was possible to have good Audiences, without his extraordinary Assistance. In the first six Days of acting it, we paid all our constant, and incidental Expence, and shar'd each of us a hundred Pounds: The greatest Profit, that in so little a Time had yet been known within my Memory! But, alas! what was paltry Pelf, to Glory? That was the darling Passion of *Wilks*'s Heart! and not to advance in it, was, to so jealous an Ambition, a painful Retreat, a meer Shade to his Laurels! and the common Benefit was but a poor Equivalent, to his want of particular Applause! To conclude, not Prince *Lewis* of *Baden*, though a Confederate General, with the Duke of *Malborough*, was more inconsolable, upon the memorable Victory at *Blenheim*, at which he was not present, than our Theatrical Hero was, to see any Action prosperous, that he was not himself at the Head of. If this then was an Infirmity in *Wilks*, why may not my shewing the same Weakness in so great a Man, mollify the Imputation, and keep his Memory in Countenance?

This laudable Appetite for Fame, in *Wilks*, was not, however to be fed, without that constant Labour, which only himself was able to come up to: He therefore bethought him of the means, to lessen the Fatigue, and at the same time, to heighten his Reputation; which was by giving up now, and then, a Part to some raw Actor, who he was sure would disgrace it, and consequently put the Audience in mind of his superior Performance: Among this sort of Indulgences to young Actors, he happen'd once to make a Mistake, that set his Views in a clear Light. The best Criticks, I believe, will allow, that in *Shakespear*'s *Macbeth*, there are in the Part of *Macduff* two Scenes, the one of Terror, in the second Act; and the other of Compassion, in the fourth, equal to any that dramatick Poetry has produc'd: These Scenes *Wilks* had acted with Success, tho far short of that happier Skill and Grace, which *Monfort* had formerly shewn, in them. Such a Part, however, one might imagine would be one of the last, a good Actor would chuse to part with: But *Wilks* was of a different Opinion; for *Macbeth* was thrice as

long, had more great Scenes of Action, and bore the Name of
the Play: Now, to be a second in any Play, was what he did
not much care for, and had been seldom us'd to: This Part of
Macduff, therefore, he had given to one *Williams*,[11] as yet no extraordinary, though a promising Actor. *Williams*, in the Simplicity of his Heart, immediately told *Booth*, what a Favour *Wilks*
had done him. *Booth*, as he had Reason, thought *Wilks* had
here carried his Indulgence, and his Authority, a little too far;
for as *Booth* had no better a Part, in the same Play, than that of
Banquo, he found himself too much disregarded, in letting so
young an Actor take Place of him: *Booth*, therefore, who knew
the Value of *Macduff*, proposed to do it himself, and to give
Banquo to *Williams;* and to make him farther amends, offer'd
him any other of his Parts, that he thought might be of Service
to him. *Williams* was content with the Exchange, and thankful
for the Promise. This Scheme, indeed, (had it taken Effect)
might have been an Ease to *Wilks*, and possibly no Disadvantage to the Play; but softly--- That was not quite what we had
a Mind to! No sooner then, came this Proposal to *Wilks*, but
off went the Masque, and out came the Secret! For though *Wilks*
wanted to be eas'd of the Part, he did not desire to be *excell'd*
in it; and as he was not sure but that might be the case, if *Booth*
were to act it, he wisely retracted his own Project, took *Macduff*
again to himself, and while he liv'd, never had a Thought of
running the same Hazard, by any farther offer to resign it.

Here, I confess, I am at a Loss for a Fact in History, to which
this can be a Parallel! To be weary of a Post, even to a real Desire of resigning it; and yet to chuse, rather to drudge on in it,
than suffer it to be well supplied (though to share in that Advantage) is a Delicacy of Ambition, that *Machiavil* himself has
made no mention of: Or if in old *Rome*, the Jealousy of any
pretended Patriot, equally inclin'd to abdicate his Office, may
have come up to it; 'tis more than my reading remembers.

As nothing can be more impertinent, than shewing too frequent a Fear, to be thought so, I will, without farther Apology,
rather risque that Imputation, than not tell you another Story
much to the same purpose, and of no more consequence than

my last. To make you understand it however, a little Preface
will be necessary.

If the Merit of an Actor (as it certainly does) consists more
in the Quality, than the Quantity of his Labour; the other Menagers had no visible Reason to think, this needless Ambition of
Wilks, in being so often, and sometimes so unnecessarily employ'd, gave him any Title to a Superiority; especially when our
Articles of Agreement, had allow'd us all to be equal. But what
are narrow Contracts to great Souls with growing Desires?
Wilks therefore, who thought himself lessen'd, in appealing to
any Judgment, but his own, plainly discovered, by his restless
Behaviour (though he did not care to speak out) that he thought
he had a Right to some higher Consideration, for his Performance: This was often *Booth*'s Opinion, as well as my own. It
must be farther observ'd, that he actually had a separate Allowance of Fifty Pounds a Year, for writing our daily Play-Bills,
for the Printer: Which Province, to say the Truth, was the
only one we car'd to trust to his particular Intendance, or could
find out for a Pretence to distinguish him. But, to speak a plainer
Truth, this Pension, which was no part of our original Agreement, was merely paid to keep him quiet, and not that we
thought it due to so insignificant a Charge, as what a Prompter
had formerly executed. This being really the Case, his frequent
Complaints of being a Drudge to the Company, grew something
more, than disagreeable to us: For we could not digest the Imposition of a Man's setting himself to work, and then bringing
in his own Bill for it. *Booth*, therefore, who was less easy, than
I was, to see him so often setting a Merit upon this Quantity of
his Labour, which neither could be our Interest, or his own,
to lay upon him; proposed to me, that we might remove this
pretended Grievance, by reviving some Play, that might be
likely to live, and be easily acted, without *Wilks*'s having any
Part in it. About this time, an unexpected Occasion offer'd itself,
to put our Project, in practice: What follow'd our Attempt,
will be all (if any thing be) worth Observation, in my Story.

In 1725, we were call'd upon, in a manner, that could not be
resisted, to revive the *Provok'd Wife*, a Comedy,[12] which, while

we found our Account, in keeping the Stage clear of those loose Liberties, it had formerly, too justly been charg'd with; we had laid aside, for some Years. The Author, Sir _John Van-brugh_, who was conscious of what it had too much of, was prevail'd upon, to substitute a new-written Scene in the Place of one, in the fourth Act, where the Wantonness of his Wit, and Humour, had (originally) made a Rake talk like a Rake, in the borrow'd Habit of a Clergyman: To avoid which Offence, he clapt the same Debauchee, into the Undress of a Woman of Quality: Now the Character, and Profession of a Fine Lady, not being so indelibly sacred as that of a Churchman; whatever Follies he expos'd, in the Petticoat, kept him, at least clear of his former Prophaneness, and were now innocently ridiculous, to the Spectator.

This Play being thus refitted for the Stage, was, as I have ob-serv'd, call'd for, from Court, and by many of the Nobility. Now, then, we thought was a proper time to come to an Ex-planation with _Wilks:_ Accordingly, when the Actors were summon'd to hear the Play read, and receive their Parts; I ad-dress'd myself to _Wilks_, before them all, and told him, That as the Part of _Constant_, which he seem'd to chuse, was a Character of less Action, than he generally appear'd in, we thought this might be a good Occasion to ease himself, by giving it to an-other. --- Here he look'd grave. --- That the Love-Scenes of it were rather serious, than gay, or humourous, and therefore might sit very well upon _Booth_. --- Down dropt his Brow, and furl'd were his Features. --- That if we were never to revive a tolerable Play, without him, what would become of us, in case of his Indisposition? --- Here he pretended to stir the Fire. --- That as he could have no farther Advantage, or Advancement, in his Station to hope for, his acting in this Play was but giving himself an unprofitable trouble, which neither _Booth_, or I, de-sired to impose upon him. --- Softly. --- Now the Pill began to gripe him. --- In a Word, this provoking Civility, plung'd him into a Passion, which he was no longer able to contain; out it came, with all the Equipage of unlimited Language, that on such Occasions his Displeasure usually set out with; but

when his Reply was stript of those Ornaments, it was plainly
this: That he look'd upon all I had said, as concerted Design,
not only to signalize our selves, by laying him aside; but a Con-
trivance to draw him into the Disfavour of the Nobility, by
making it suppos'd his own Choice, that he did not act in a Play
so particularly ask'd for; but we should find, he could stand upon
his own Bottom, and it was not all our little caballing should
get our Ends of him: To which I answer'd with some Warmth,
That he was mistaken in our Ends; for Those, Sir, said I, you
have answer'd already, by shewing the Company, you cannot
bear to be left out of any Play. Are not you every Day complain-
ing of your being over-labour'd? And now, upon our first offering to ease you, you fly into a Passion, and pretend to make
that a greater Grievance, than t'other: But, Sir, if your being In,
or Out of the Play, is a Hardship, you shall impose it upon yourself: The Part is in your Hand, and to us, it is a Matter of Indifference now, whether you take it, or leave it. Upon this he
threw down the Part upon the Table, cross'd his Arms, and sate
knocking his Heel, upon the Floor, as seeming to threaten most,
when he said least; but when no body persuaded him to take it
up again, *Booth*, not chusing to push the matter too far, but
rather to split the difference of our Dispute, said, That for his
Part, he saw no such great matter in acting every Day; for he
believed it the wholesomest Exercise in the World; it kept the
Spirits in motion, and always gave him a good Stomach. Tho'
this was, in a manner, giving up the Part to *Wilks*, yet it did not
allow, he did us any Favour in receiving it. Here, I observ'd Mrs.
Oldfield began to titter, behind her Fan: But *Wilks* being more
intent, upon what *Booth* had said, reply'd, Every one could
best feel for himself, but he did not pretend to the Strength of
a Pack-horse; therefore if Mrs. *Oldfield* would chuse any body
else to play with her, he should be very glad to be excus'd: This
throwing the Negative upon Mrs. *Oldfield*, was, indeed, a sure
way to save himself; which I could not help taking notice of,
by saying, It was making but an ill Compliment, to the Company,
to suppose, there was but one Man in it, fit to play an ordinary
Part with her. Here Mrs. *Oldfield* got up, and turning me half

round to come forward, said with her usual Frankness, Pooh!
you are all a Parcel of Fools, to make such a rout about nothing!
Rightly judging, that the Person, most out of humour, would
not be more displeas'd at her calling us all, by the same Name.
As she knew, too, the best way of ending the Debate, would
be to help the Weak; she said, she hop'd Mr. *Wilks* would
not so far mind what had past, as to refuse his acting the Part,
with her; for though it might not be so good, as he had been
us'd to; yet, she believed, those who had bespoke the Play,
would expect to have done to the best Advantage, and it would
make but an odd Story abroad, if it were known, there had been
any Difficulty in that point among ourselves. To conclude,
Wilks had the Part, and we had all we wanted; which was an
Occasion to let him see, that the Accident, or Choice of one
Menager's being more employ'd than another, would never be
allow'd a Pretence, for altering our Indentures, or his having
an extraordinary Consideration for it.

However disagreeable it might be, to have this unsociable
Temper daily to deal with; yet I cannot but say, that from the
same impatient Spirit, that had so often hurt us, we still drew
valuable Advantages: For as *Wilks* seem'd to have no Joy, in
Life, beyond his being distinguish'd on the Stage; we were not
only sure of his always doing his best, there, himself; but of
making others more careful, than without the Rod of so irascible
a Temper over them, they would have been. And I much question, if a more temperate, or better Usage of the hired Actors,
could have so effectually kept them to Order. Not even *Betterton* (as we have seen) with all his good Sense, his great Fame,
and Experience, could, by being only a quiet Example of Industry himself, save his Company from falling, while neither Gentleness could govern, or the Consideration of their common
Interest reform them. Diligence, with much the inferior Skill,
or Capacity, will beat the best negligent Company, that ever
came upon a Stage. But when a certain dreaming Idleness, or
jolly Negligence of Rehearsals gets into a Body of the Ignorant,
and Incapable (which before *Wilks* came into *Drury-Lane*,
when *Powell* was at the Head of them, was the Case of that

Company) then, I say, a sensible Spectator might have look'd upon the fallen Stage, as *Portius* in the Play of *Cato*, does upon his ruin'd Country, and have lamented it, in (something near) the same exclamation, *viz.*

----- O ye Immortal Bards!
What Havock do these Blockheads make among your Works!
How are the boasted Labours of an Age,
Defac'd, and tortur'd, by Ungracious Action?

Of this wicked Doings, *Dryden* too complains in one of his Prologues, at that time, where speaking of such lewd Actors, he closes a Couplet with the following Line, *viz.*

And murder Plays, which they miscall Reviving.[13]

The great Share, therefore, that *Wilks*, by his exemplary Diligence, and Impatience of Neglect, in others, had in the Reformation of this Evil, ought in Justice to be remember'd; and let my own Vanity here take Shame, to itself, when I confess, That had I had half his Application, I still think I might have shewn myself twice the Actor, that in my highest State of Favour, I appear'd to be. But, if I have any Excuse for that Neglect (a Fault, which if I loved not Truth, I need not have mentioned) it is that so much of my Attention was taken up in an incessant Labour to guard against our private Animosities, and preserve a Harmony, in our Menagements, that I hope, and believe, it made ample Amends, for whatever Omission, to my Auditors might sometimes know it cost me some pains to conceal. But Nature takes care to bestow her Blessings, with a more equal Hand than Fortune does, and is seldom known to heap too many upon one Man: One tolerable Talent, in an Individual, is enough to preserve him, from being good for nothing; and, if that was not laid to my Charge, as an Actor, I have in this Light too, less to complain of, than to be thankful for.

Before I conclude my History, it may be expected, I should give some further View of these my last Contemporaries of the Theatre, *Wilks*, and *Booth*, in their different acting Capacities. If I were to paint them in the Colours they laid upon one another,

their Talents would not be shewn with half the Commendation,
I am inclin'd to bestow upon them, when they are left to my own
Opinion. But People of the same Profession, are apt to see themselves, in their own clear Glass of Partiality, and look upon their
Equals through a Mist of Prejudice. It might be imagin'd too,
from the difference of their natural Tempers, that *Wilks* should
have been more blind, to the Excellencies of *Booth*, than *Booth*
was to those of *Wilks;* but it was not so: *Wilks* would sometimes commend *Booth* to me; but when *Wilks* excell'd, the
other was silent: *Booth* seem'd to think nothing valuable, that
was not tragically Great, or Marvellous: Let that be as true, as
it may; yet I have often thought, that from his having no Taste
of Humour himself, he might be too much inclin'd to depreciate
the Acting of it in others. The very slight Opinion, which in
private Conversation with me, he had of *Wilks's* acting Sir
Harry Wildair, was certainly more, than could be justified; not
only from the general Applause that was against that Opinion
(though Applause is not always infallible) but from the visible Capacity which must be allow'd to an Actor, that could
carry such slight Materials to such a height of Approbation:
For though the Character of *Wildair*, scarce in any one Scene,
will stand against a just Criticism; yet in the Whole, there are so
many gay, and false Colours of the fine Gentleman, that nothing
but a Vivacity in the Performance, proportionably extravagant,
could have made them so happily glare, upon a common Audience.

Wilks, from his first setting out, certainly form'd his manner
of Acting, upon the Model of *Monfort;* as *Booth* did his, on that
of *Betterton*. But --- *Haud passibus aequis:* [14] I cannot say, either
of them came up to their Original. *Wilks* had not that easy regulated Behaviour, or the harmonious Elocution of the One, nor
Booth that conscious Aspect of Intelligence, nor requisite Varia-
tion of Voice, that made every Line the Other spoke seem his
own, natural, self-deliver'd Sentiment: Yet there is still room for
great Commendation of Both the first mentioned; which will not
be so much diminsh'd, in my having said, they were only excell'd
by such Predecessors, as it will be rais'd, in venturing to affirm,

it will be a longer time, before any Successors will come' near them. Thus one of the greatest Praises given to *Virgil* is, That no Successor in Poetry came so near *Him*, as *He* himself did to *Homer*.

Tho' the Majority of Publick Auditors are but bad Judges of Theatrical Action, and are often deceiv'd into their Approbation of what was no solid Pretence to it; yet, as there are no other appointed Judges to appeal to, and as every single Spectator has a Right to be one of them, their Sentence will be definitive, and the Merit of an Actor must, in some degree, be weigh'd by it: By this Law then, *Wilks* was pronounc'd an Excellent Actor; which if the few true Judges did not allow him to be, they were at least too candid to slight, or discourage him. *Booth* and he were Actors so directly opposite in their Manner, that, if either of them could have borrow'd a little of the other's Fault, they would Both have been improv'd by it: If *Wilks* had sometimes too violent a Vivacity; *Booth* as often contented himself with too grave a Dignity: The Latter seem'd too much to heave up his Words, as the Other to dart them to the Ear, with too quick, and sharp a Vehemence: Thus *Wilks* would too frequently break into the Time, and Measure of the Harmony, by too many spirited Accents, in one Line; and *Booth*, by too solemn a Regard to Harmony, would as often lose the necessary Spirit of it: So that (as I have observ'd) could we have sometimes rais'd the one, and sunk the other, they had both been nearer to the Mark. Yet this could not be always objected to them: They had their Intervals of unexceptionable Excellence, that more, than balanc'd their Errors. The Master-piece of *Booth* was *Othello:* There, he was most in Character, and seem'd not more to animate, or please himself, in it, than his Spectators. 'Tis true he ow'd his last, and highest Advancement, to his acting *Cato:* But it was the Novelty, and critical Appearance of that Character, that chiefly swell'd the Torrent of his Applause: For let the Sentiments of a declaiming Patriot have all the Sublimity, that Poetry can raise them to; let them be deliver'd too, with the utmost Grace, and Dignity of Elocution, that can recommend them to the Auditor: Yet this is but one Light, wherein the Excellence of an Actor can shine: But in *Othello* we may see him, in the Variety of Nature: There the Actor is carried through the different Accidents of domestick, Happiness, and Misery, occasionally torn, and tortur'd by the most distracting Passion, that can raise Terror, or Compassion, in the Spectator. Such are the Characters, that a Master Actor would delight in; and therefore in *Othello*, I may safely aver, that *Booth* shew'd himself thrice the Actor, that he could in *Cato*. And yet his Merit in acting *Cato* need not be diminsh'd by this Comparison.

Wilks often regretted, that in Tragedy, he had not the full, and strong Voice of *Booth* to command, and grace his Periods with: But *Booth* us'd to say, That if his Ear had been equal to it, *Wilks* had Voice enough to have shewn himself a much better Tragedian. Now though there might be some Truth in this; yet these two Actors were of so mixt a Merit, that even, in Tragedy, the Superiority was not always on the same side: In Sorrow, Tenderness, or Resignation, *Wilks* plainly had the Advantage, and seem'd more pathetically to feel, look, and express his Calamity: But, in the more turbulent Transports of the Heart, *Booth* again bore the Palm, and left all Competitors behind him. A Fact perhaps will set this Difference, in a clearer Light. I have formerly seen *Wilks* act *Othello*, and *Booth* the *Earl of Essex*,[15] in which they both miscarried: Neither the exclamatory Rage, or Jealousy of the one, or the plaintive Distresses of the other, were happily executed, or became either of them; tho' in the contrary Characters, they were both excellent.

When an Actor Becomes, and naturally Looks the Character he stands in, I have often observ'd it to have had as fortunate an Effect, and as much recommended him to the Approbation of the common Auditors, as the most correct, or judicious Utterance of the Sentiments: This was strongly visible, in the favourable Reception *Wilks* met with in *Hamlet*, where I own the Half of what he spoke, was as painful to my Ear, as every Line, that came from *Betterton* was charming; And yet it is not impossible, could they have come to a Poll, but *Wilks* might have had a Majority of Admirers: However, such a Division had been no Proof, that the Præeminence had not still remain'd in *Better-*

ton; and if I should add, that *Booth* too, was behind *Betterton* in *Othello*, it would be saying no more, than *Booth* himself had Judgment, and Candour enough to know, and confess. And if both he, and *Wilks*, are allow'd, in the two above-mention'd Characters, a second Place, to so great a Master, as *Betterton*, it will be a Rank of Praise, that the best Actors, since my Time, might have been proud of.

I am now come towards the End of that Time, through which our Affairs had long gone forward in a settled course of Prosperity. From the visible Errors of former Menagements, we had, at last, found the necessary Means to bring our private Laws, and Orders, into the general Observance, and Approbation of our Society: Diligence, and Neglect, were under under an equal Eye; the one never fail'd of its Reward, and the other, by being very rarely excus'd, was less frequently committed. You are now to consider us in our height of Favour, and so much in fashion, with the politer Part of the Town, that our House, every *Saturday*, seem'd to be the appointed Assembly of the First Ladies of Quality: Of this too, the common Spectators were so well apprized, that for twenty Years successively, on that Day, we scarce ever fail'd of a crowded Audience; for which Occasion we particularly reserv'd our best Plays, acted in the best manner we could give them.

Among our many necessary Reformations; what not a little preserv'd to us the Regard of our Auditors, was the Decency of our clear Stage; from whence we had now, for many Years, shut out those idle Gentlemen, who seem'd more delighted to be pretty Objects themselves, than capable of any Pleasure, from the Play: Who took their daily Stands, where they might best elbow the Actor, and come in for their Share of the Auditor's Attention. In many a labour'd Scene of the warmest Humour, and of the most affecting Passion, have I seen the best Actors disconcerted, while these buzzing Muscatos have been fluttering round their Eyes, and Ears. How was it possible an Actor, so embarrass'd, should keep his Impatience, from entering into that different Temper which his personated Character might require him, to be Master of?

Future Actors may perhaps wish I would set this Grievance, in a stronger Light; and, to say the truth, where Auditors are ill-bred, it cannot be well expected, that Actors should be polite. Let me therefore shew, how far an Artist in any Science is apt to be hurt by any sort of Inattention to his Performance.

While the famous *Corelli*, at *Rome*, was playing some Musical Composition of his own, to a select Company in the private Apartment of his Patron-Cardinal, he observed, in the height of his Harmony, his Eminence was engaging, in a detach'd Conversation; upon which he suddenly stopt short, and gently laid down his Instrument: The Cardinal, surpriz'd at the unexpected Cessation, ask'd him, if a String was broke? To which, *Corelli*, in an honest Conscience of what was due to his Musick, reply'd, No, Sir, I was only afraid I interrupted Business. His Eminence, who knew that a Genius could never shew itself to Advantage, where it had not its proper Regards, took this Reproof in good part, and broke off his Conversation, to hear the whole *Concerto* play'd over again.

Another Story will let us see, what Effect a mistaken Offence of this Kind had upon the *French* Theatre; which was told me by a Gentleman of the long Robe, then at *Paris*, and who was himself the innocent Author of it. At the Tragedy of *Zaire;* while the celebrated Mademoiselle *Gossin*[16] was delivering a Soliloquy, this Gentleman was seized with a sudden Fit of Coughing, which gave the Actress some Surprize, and Interruption; and his Fit increasing, she was forced to stand silent so long, that it drew the Eyes of the uneasy Audience upon him; when a *French* Gentleman leaning forward to him, ask'd him, If this Actress had given him any particular Offence, that he took so publick an Occasion to resent it? The *English* Gentlemen, in the utmost Surprize, assur'd him, So far from it, that he was a particular Admirer of her Performance; that his Malady was his real Misfortune, and if he apprehended any Return of it, he would rather quit his Seat, than disoblige either the Actress, or the Audience.

This publick Decency in their Theatre, I have myself seen carrid so far, that a Gentleman in their *second Loge*, or Middle-

Gallery, being observ'd to sit forward himself, while a Lady sate behind him, a loud Number of Voices call'd out to him, from the Pit, *Place à Dame! Place à Dame!* When the Person so offending, either not apprehending the Meaning of the Clamour, or possibly being some *John Trott*, who fear'd no Man alive, the Noise was continued for several Minutes; nor were the Actors, though ready on the Stage, suffer'd to begin the Play, till this unbred Person was laugh'd out of his Seat, and had placed the Lady before him.

Whether this Politeness, observ'd at Plays, may be owing to their Clime, their Complexion, or their Government, is of no great Consequence; but, if it is to be acquired, methinks it is pity our accomplish'd Countrymen, who every Year, import so much of this Nation's gawdy Garniture, should not, in this long course of our Commerce with them, have brought over a little of their Theatrical Good-breeding too.

I have been the more copious upon this Head, that it might be judged, how much it stood us upon, to have got rid of those improper Spectators, I have been speaking of: For whatever Regard we might draw by keeping them, at a Distance, from our Stage, I had observ'd, while they were admitted behind our Scenes, we but too often shew'd them the wrong Side of our Tapestry; and that many a tollerable Actor was the less valued, when it was known, what ordinary Stuff he was made of.

Among the many more disagreeable Distresses, that are almost unavoidable, in the Government of a Theatre, those we so often met with from the Persecution of bad Authors, were what we could never intirely get rid of. But let us state both our Cases, and then see, where the Justice of the Complaint lies. 'Tis true, when an ingenious Indigent, had taken, perhaps, a whole Summer's Pains, *invitâ Minervâ*,[17] to heap up a Pile of Poetry, into the Likeness of a Play, and found, at last, the gay Promise of his Winter's Support, was rejected, and abortive, a Man almost ought to be a Poet himself, to be justly sensible of his Distress! Then, indeed, great Allowances ought to be made for the severe Reflections, he might naturally throw upon those pragmatical Actors, who had no Sense, or Taste of good Writing. And yet,

if his Relief was only to be had, by his imposing a bad Play upon
a good Set of Actors, methinks the Charity that first looks at
home, has as good an Excuse for its Coldness, as the unhappy Object of it, had a Plea for his being reliev'd, at their
Expence. But immediate Want was not always confess'd their
Motive for Writing; Fame, Honour, and *Parnassian* Glory
had sometimes taken a romantick Turn in their Heads; and then
they gave themselves the Air of talking to us, in a higher Strain
------ Gentlemen were not to be so treated! the Stage was like
to be finely govern'd, when Actors pretended to be Judges of
Authors, *&c*. But dear Gentlemen! if they were good Actors,
why not? How should they have been able to act, or rise to any
Excellence, if you suppos'd them not to feel, or understand what
you offer'd them? Would you have reduc'd them, to the meer
Mimickry of Parrots, and Monkies, that can only prate, and
play a great many Tricks, without Reflection? Or how are you
sure, your Friend, the infallible Judge, to whom you read your
fine Piece, might be sincere in the Praises he gave it? Or, indeed,
might not you have thought the best Judge a bad one, if he had
dislik'd it? Consider too, how possible it might be, that a Man of
Sense would not care to tell you a Truth, he was sure you would
not believe! And, if neither *Dryden, Congreve, Steele, Addison,*
nor *Farquhar,* (if you please) ever made any Complaint of their
Incapacity to judge, why is the World to believe the Slights
you have met with from them, are either undeserv'd, or particular? Indeed! indeed, I am not conscious that we ever did you, or
any of your Fraternity the least Injustice! Yet this was not all
we had to struggle with; to supersede our Right of rejecting,
the Recommendation, or rather Imposition of some great Persons (whom it was not Prudence to disoblige) sometimes came
in, with a high Hand, to support their Pretensions; and then,
cout que cout[18] acted it must be! So when the short Life of this
wonderful Nothing was over, the Actors, were, perhaps, abus'd
in a Preface, for obstructing the Success of it, and the Town
publickly damn'd us, for our private Civility.

I cannot part, with these fine Gentlemen Authors, without
mentioning a ridiculous *Disgraccia,* that befell one of them,

many Years ago: This solemn Bard, who, like *Bayes*, only writ for Fame, and Reputation; on the second Day's publick Triumph of his Muse, marching in a stately full-bottom'd Perriwig into the Lobby of the House, with a Lady of Condition in his Hand, when raising his Voice to the Sir *Fopling* Sound, that *became the Mouth of a Man of Quality*, and calling out --- Hey! Box-keeper, where is my Lady such-a-one's Servant, was unfortunately answer'd, by honest *John Trott*, (which then happen'd to be the Box-keeper's real Name) Sir, we have dismiss'd, there was not Company enough to pay Candles. In which mortal Astonishment, it may be sufficient to leave him. And yet had the Actors refus'd this Play, what Resentment might have been thought too severe for them?

Thus was our Administration often censured for Accidents, which were not in our Power to prevent: A possible Case, in the wisest Governments. If therefore some Plays have been preferr'd to the Stage, that were never fit to have been seen there, let this be our best Excuse for it. And yet, if the Merit of our rejecting the many bad Plays, that press'd hard upon us, were weigh'd against the few, that were thus imposed upon us, our Conduct, in general, might have more Amendments of the Stage to boast of, than Errors to answer for. But it is now Time to drop the Curtain.

During our four last Years, there happen'd so very little unlike what has been said before, that I shall conclude with barely mentioning those unavoidable Accidents, that drew on our Dissolution. The first, that for some Years had led the way to greater, was the continued ill State of Health, that render'd *Booth* incapable of appearing on the Stage. The next was the Death of Mrs. *Oldfield*, which happen'd on the 23d of *October*, 1730. About the same Time too Mrs. *Porter*, then in her highest Reputation for Tragedy, was lost to us, by the Misfortune of a dislocated Limb, from the overturning of a *Chaise*. And our last Stroke was the Death of *Wilks*, in *September*, the Year following, 1731.[19]

Notwithstanding such irreparable Losses; whether, when these favourite Actors, were no more to be had, their Successors

might not be better born with, than they could possibly have
hop'd, while the former were in being; or that the generality
of Spectators, from their want of Taste, were easier to be pleas'd,
than the few that knew better: Or that, at worst, our Actors
were still preferable to any other Company, of the several, then
subsisting: Or to whatever Cause it might be imputed, our
Audiences was far less abated, than our Apprehensions had suggested. So that, though it began to grow late in Life with me;
having still Health, and Strength enough, to have been as useful
on the Stage, as ever, I was under no visible Necessity of quitting
it: But so it happen'd that our surviving Fraternity having got
some chimaerical, and as I thought, unjust Notions into their
Heads, which though I knew they were without much Difficulty to be surmounted; I chose not, at my time of Day, to
enter into new Contentions; and, as I found an Inclination in
some of them, to purchase the whole Power of the Patent into
their own Hands; I did my best, while I staid with them, to make
it worth their while to come up to my Price; and then patiently
sold out my Share, to the first Bidder, wishing the Crew, I had
left in the Vessel, a good Voyage.

What Commotions the Stage fell into the Year following, or
from what Provocations, the greatest Part of the Actors revolted, and set up for themselves, in the little House, in the *Hay-
Market*, lies not within the Promise of my Title-Page to relate:
Or as it might set some Persons living, in a Light, they possibly
might not chuse to be seen in, I will rather be thankful, for the
involuntary Favour they have done me, than trouble the Publick, with private Complaints of fancied, or real Injuries.

FINIS.

NOTES

The intention of my annotation has been to provide clarity for Cibber's often vague references, establish correct chronology for his haphazard dating, and identify his allusions. Latin quotations are translated and correctly attributed, dramatic allusions traced and corrected when in error. For these things I have been greatly aided by Lowe, who traced many of Cibber's sources. Dates and correct titles of plays are provided, as well as identification of characters in them. Lowe has again been useful here, but I have checked his notes against the information in *The London Stage: 1660-1800*, as indeed, I have accepted none of his information without verification wherever possible.

In the notes, the following are referred to by author only.

Avery, E. L., *et al. The London Stage 1600-1800*. Carbondale: Southern Illinois University Press, 1960–.

Barker, Richard H. *Mr. Cibber of Drury Lane*. New York, 1939.

Bellchambers, Edmund. (ed.). *An Apology for the Life of Colley Cibber, Comedian*. London, 1822.

Boswell, James. *Life of Johnson*, ed. G. N. Hill, revised by L. F. Powell. 6 vols. Oxford, 1934-50.

Burney, Charles. *History of Music*. 4 vols. London, 1776-89.

Davies, Thomas. *Dramatic Miscellanies*. 3 vols. London, 1783-1874.

Doran, John. *Their Majesties Servants*. London, 1897.

324   AN APOLOGY FOR THE

Downes, John. *Roscius Anglicanus*. London, 1708.

Genest, John. *Some Account of the English Stage from the Restoration in 1660 to 1830.* 10 vols. Bath, 1832.

Lowe, Robert W. (ed.). *An Apology for the Life of Colley Cibber.* London, 1889.

Victor, Benjamin. *History of the Theatres of London and Dublin from the Year 1730 to the Present Time.* 2 vols. London, 1761.

INTRODUCTION

1. The controversy between Pope and Cibber and Fielding and Cibber has been so well documented that it seems pointless to repeat the lengthy tale here. The best discussion of the Pope-Cibber feud is found in Norman Ault, *New Light on Pope* (London, 1949). R. H. Barker, *Mr. Cibber of Drury Lane*, pp. 221-32, and L. R. N. Ashley, *Colley Cibber* (New York, 1966), pp. 140-51 have both given good accounts of the Fielding-Cibber quarrel. See Barker also (pp. 111-32) for good material on the Cibber-Dennis rivalry.

2. Boswell, I, 149. The poem was probably written in 1741. See D. N. Smith, E. L. McAdam, Jr. *Johnson's Poems* (Oxford, 1941), p. 114.

3. Norman Ault and John Butt note that "the probabilities point to Pope's authorship." *Poems of Alexander Pope* (London, 1954), VI, 302.

4. See *Apology*, Chap. VI, n. 3.

5. *Love's Last Shift* has generally been considered the first of the sentimental comedies. Ernest Bernbaum discusses the play in this light in *The Drama of Sensibility* (Boston, 1915), as does Joseph Wood Krutch in *Comedy and Conscience After the Restoration* (New York, 1924). An excellent article on the play is Paul Parnell's "Equivocation in *Love's Last Shift*," *SP*, LVII (July 1960), 519-34. A discussion of the play as sentimental for reasons other than the conversion scene is Byrne R. S. Fone, *Colley Cibber's "Love's Last Shift": An Edition with Notes and Commentary* (Ann Arbor: University Microfilms, 1968). A dissenting view on the sentimental primacy of the play is in Arthur Sherbo's *English*

Sentimental Drama (East Lansing: Michigan State University Press, 1957).

6. *Love's Last Shift* is "a comedy with a just design, distinguished characters, and a proper dialogue. . . ." But Cibber's vanity, "when he was a boy" prevailed "upon him to own what an unknown, tho' very ingenious gentleman writ." John Dennis, letter to Henry Cromwell, June 14, 1720 in *Letters Familiar, Moral, and Critical* (London, 1721), p. 140.

7. There has always been some question as to the honesty of this transaction. Cibber had at first resigned his share to his scapegrace son Theophilus. After the patent was sold to Highmore, Theophilus led most of the actors to the rival playhouse, thus leaving Highmore with, for the time, a worthless investment. See Barker, pp. 165-76.

8. Boswell, I, 402.

9. *Ibid.*, III, 184.

10. Horace Walpole, *Correspondence*, ed. W. S. Lewis (New Haven: Yale University Press, 1941), I, 115.

11. Barker, 194, n. 1.

12. For £52/10. See Watson Nicholson, "Colley Cibber's 'Apology,'" *Notes and Queries*, Eleventh Series, No. III (Jan.-June 1911), 266.

13. See the anonymous pamphlet, *The Laureat* (London, 1740), p. 96.

14. Anthony Aston was perhaps an actor, and certainly intimate with Drury Lane. His *Brief Supplement to Colley Cibber, Esq. His Lives of the Late Famous Actors and Actresses* (London, n.d.) is a useful addition to Cibber. James Wright's *Historia Histrionica* (London, 1699) gives an account of the theater before the Civil War.

15. Benjamin Victor, *The History of the Theatres of London and Dublin from the Year 1730 to the Present Time* (London, 1761), I, 1-2—an excellent supplement to Cibber.

16. Walpole, X, 298.

17. Boswell, III, 72.

18. *The Laureat*, p. 58.

19. Alexander Pope, *Correspondence*, ed. George Sherburn (Oxford, 1956), IV, 437-38.

20. *The Laureat*, p. 2.

21. *Ibid.*, p. 15.

22. *Ibid.*, p. 14.

23. "T. Johnson," *The Tryal of Colley Cibber* (London, 1740), pp. 6-7.

24. *Ibid.*, p. 9.

25. *Ibid.*, p. 11.

26. Fielding may have contributed as well to another pamphlet, *An Apology for the Life of T.* [heophilus] *C.* [ibber], *Comedian. Being a Proper Sequel to the Apology for the Life of Mr. Colley Cibber, Comedian. With an Historical View of the Stage to the Present Year. Supposed to Be Written by Himself. In the Style and Manner of the Poet Laureate* (London, 1740). Theophilus did not write the pamphlet, though he had earlier promised to write an autobiography. This work parodies the *Apology* and then turns into a resumé, and adds considerable information about the theater in the 1730's.

27. Bellchambers, p. v.

28. Bellchambers, p. xi.

29. Lowe, I, v.

30. William [Carew] Hazlitt, "An Appreciation" in the Everyman *An Apology for His Life* (London, 1914), p. vii.

31. Edgar Johnson, *One Mighty Torrent* (New York, 1937), p. 106.

32. Barker urges this point as well (p. 197).

33. *Tryal*, p. 14.

34. Barker, p. 197.

DEDICATION

1. Henry Pelham (1695?-1754), brother of Cibber's friend, the Duke of Newcastle, and in 1743, prime minister.

2. Esher Place, in Surrey, purchased by Pelham in 1729.

3. "Simple in respect to wordly style." Horace *Carmina* 1.5.5.

CHAPTER I

1. Events of Chapter I: 1671: Cibber's birth. 1682: enters school.

2. "There is strength in numbers." Juvenal *Satires* II. 46.

3. Cibber earned 1500 guineas from the *Apology* before he sold the copyright to Dodsley in 1750.

4. Anne Oldfield (1683-1730), Robert Wilks (c.1665-1732), and Barton Booth (1681-1733). Mrs. Oldfield was one of the great actresses of her day. She first became known, Bellchambers says (p. 508), in Cibber's *The Careless Husband*. Cibber had seen her in Crowne's *Sir Courtly Nice* and had encouraged her. She was eminent both in comedy and tragedy, the latter being her forte. The *Authentick Memoirs* (1731) and Egerton's *Faithful Memoirs* (1731) are the lives to which Cibber refers. Wilks came to Drury Lane from Dublin in 1698. Edmund Curll wrote an account of Wilks after the actor's death and branded all others false. Cibber gives a full picture of Booth in Chapter XVI. He too acted in Dublin and joined Lincoln's Inn Fields in 1700. Benjamin Victor's memoir of Booth appeared in 1733.

5. Cibber's official exit was in 1733.

6. "Bayes" is Dryden in Villiers's *The Rehearsal.* "Poo! That is not because he has a mind to be his son, but for fear he should be thought nobody's son at all" (III, iv).

7. Cibber's christening is recorded in the baptismal register of the Church of St. Giles-in-the-Fields: "November 1671 Christenings 20. Colley sonne of Gabriell Sibber and Jane...."

8. Caius Gabriel Cibber (1630-1700) was sent by the king of Denmark to study in Italy. He was named sculptor-in-ordinary to King William III in 1693 and executed figures and decorations for Hampton Court, Windsor, the Royal Exchange, and St. Paul's. He

built the Danish Church in Wellclose Square, and there, under a
memorial of his own design, Gaius, Jane, and Colley were buried.
See Harald Faber, *Caius Gabriel Cibber: 1630-1700* (Oxford,
1926).

9. Jane Colley was Caius' second wife, whom he married November
24, 1670.

10. *glout:* to pout, look sullen.

11. Bellchambers identifies them as Lord Chesterfield and Bubb
Doddington, Lord Melcombe. Lowe (I, 14, n. 1) insists that the
second was Erskine and quotes *The Laureat* (p. 18) as saying that
the portraits were "L--d C--d and Mr. E--e."

12. By the feet of Hercules. You can judge of Hercules' stature by
his foot.—Proverb.

13. Spoken of Yorick whose "flashes of merriment . . . were wont to
set the table on a roar." *Hamlet*, V, 209-10.

14. "To be mad by method." Terence *Eunuch* I. 63.

15. "Let it remain to the last as it was at the first." Horace *Ars
Poetica* 126.

16. A Spartan king (c. 400-360 B.C.).

17. The Emperor Hadrian (76-138 A.D.).

18. In William Byrd's collection "Psalmes, Sonets, & Songs of Sadnes
and pietie" (1588) is a song "My Minde to Me a Kingdome is,"
probably by Edward Dyer. See C. L. Day and E. B. Murrie, *English Song Books: 1651-1702* (London, 1940), p. 292.

19. Cibber means Pope. The reference is to Desdemona's speech to
Othello (III, iii, 70-74): "What? Michael Cassio,/ That came
a-wooing with you, and so many a time,/ When I have spoken of
you dispraisingly,/ Hath ta'en your part. . . ."

20. "I should prefer to be thought a foolish and clumsy scribbler, if
only my failings please, or at least escape me, rather than be wise
and unhappy." Horace *Epistles* II. 2. 126.

21. "It is sweet at the fitting time to cast serious thoughts aside."
Horace *Odes* IV. 12. 28.

22. "Os homini sublime dedit." "He gave to man an uplifted face, that is, lofty expression. Ovid *Metamorphosis* I. 85.

CHAPTER II

1. Events of Chapter II: 1685: Death of King Charles II. 1730: Cibber chosen poet laureate.

2. Cibber, who was sixty-eight when he wrote the *Apology*, was admitted to the best company in London. Dr. Johnson said about his company that "It is wonderful that a man, who for forty years had lived with the great and the witty, should have acquired so ill the talents of conversation: and he had but half to furnish; for one half of what he said was oaths." *Life*, II, 340.

3. Arlington died July 28, 1685, five months after the king.

4. His post as laureate.

5. "Forsan et haec olim meminisse juvabit." "Perhaps it will help to remember these things one day." Virgil *Aeneid* I. 203.

6. "Sing, Sing the day, and Sing the Song": not identified.

7. Bellchambers believed this to be an illusion to a pamphlet entitled, as he printed it, "Lick at the Laureat." However, as Lowe observes (I, 35, n. 2), there is no work of that title published before 1740. Cibber may have had in mind the anonymous "*A Lash for the Laureate: or An Address . . . to . . . Mr. Rowe . . .*" (London, 1718). After the *Apology* appeared there was published "*A Blast Upon Bays: or, A New Lick at the Laureat* (London, 1742).

8. To enrapture the public.

9. Pope's portrait of Addison in *The Epistle to Dr. Arbuthnot* (1735), ll. 209-14.

10. The 242d *Tatler*, October 26, 1710. The line in *The Tatler* correctly reads: "Where the sentence . . . ."

11. "Indignation will prompt my verse." Juvenal *Satires* I. 79.

12. He plays with emotions.

13. Cinna wants to seem poor, and so he is.

14. Cibber succeeded Laurence Eusden as poet laureate. Ambrose Philips, Theobald, Dennis, and Stephen Duck were contestants for the post, with Duck as favorite. Cibber was chosen, however, and his appointment announced the third week in November 1730. His official appointment came on December 3, 1730.

15. Poetical Knight Errant—unidentified. No copy of this issue seems to be available.

16. The lines from the Epilogue to *The Non-Juror* (1717) read: "These Blows I told him/ On his Play would fall,/ But he un-mov'd, cry'd/ Blood! We'll stand it all."

17. "Deciens repetita placebit." This will please ten times over. Horace *Ars Poetica* 365.

18. The last lines of Young's *Second Epistle to Mr. Pope* (1730).

CHAPTER III

1. Events: 1687: Cibber unsuccessful in entering college. 1688: The Revolution. Cibber joins. 1689: Cibber goes to London.

2. Lewis Cibber's piety was not as strong as his dissolute nature. He died broken in health and spirit in 1711.

3. William Cavendish, Earl of Devonshire, was one of the Whig lords who invited William to the throne.

4. November 5, 1688.

5. "So potent was religion in persuading to evil deeds." Lucretius I. 101.

6. Prince George of Denmark married Princess Anne in 1682. Anne, influenced by the Churchills, wrote to William, and fled Whitehall on November 25, 1688. Macaulay says that she was met at Nottingham by a "bodyguard of gentlemen." Cibber does not make it clear whether he was one of these gentlemen or not.

7. Sarah Churchill, afterward Duchess of Marlborough. Lady Fitz-harding may be Henrietta Anne, wife of John Berkeley, or Hen-rietta, daughter of George Fitzharding, Earl of Berkeley.

8. Macaulay describes her as "that most odious and miserable of human beings, an ancient crone at war with her whole kind . . .

great indeed and rich, but valuing greatness and riches chiefly because they enabled her to brave public opinion and to indulge
without restraint her hatred of the living and the dead." *History
of England*, II, 196.

9. Devonshire was made lord steward and lord-lieutenant of Derbyshire in March 1689. He did not become duke until May 1694.
Cibber corrected his error in the second edition.

10. No other.

11. *The Laureat* (p. 28) identifies the trio in this farce as Miss Santlow, who was to become Mrs. Booth, Captain Montague, and her
defender, Secretary Craggs, i.e., James Craggs the Younger (1686-
1721), in 1718 one of the principal secretaries of state.

12. William Smith joined the Duke's Company in 1662/63 and acted
in both comedy and tragedy. Bellchambers insists (p. 56) that
Cibber was in error and that Smith appeared as late as the year of
his death. He did return to the stage after leaving it in April 1684,
for he is listed in Tate's adaptation of Fletcher's *The Island Princess* in 1687. He died in December 1695.

13. "As where's that palace whereinto foul things/ Sometimes in-
trude not?" *Othello*, III, iii, 137-38.

14. A charge that might be leveled at Cibber for *Love's Last Shift*.
At least if not ready money, he got quick fame.

15. Thomas Betterton (1635-1710). Cibber has much to say of Betterton, perhaps the greatest actor of his time. His Shakespearean roles
were praised by Dryden and later by Pope. See Robert W. Lowe,
Thomas Betterton (New York, 1891). Of William Mountfort (c.
1660-92) Downes (pp. 40-41) observes that his Sir Courtly Nice,
in Crowne's play, "was so nicely performed" that of his successors
only Cibber equaled him. Bellchambers gives an account (p. 135)
of his violent death in defense of Mrs. Bracegirdle. See Albert S.
Borgman, *The Life and Death of William Mountfort* (Cambridge:
Harvard University Press, 1935). There were two Griffins, Edward, and Captain Philip, one of which appeared with the King's
Company in 1672/73. The name last appears in June 1698 as Manly
in *The Plain Dealer*. Anne Bracegirdle (c. 1674-1748) appeared on
the stage as a child, perhaps in March 1680, when she was seen as
Cordelio in Otway's *The Orphan*. Her forte was comedy, and

though one of the best actresses of the day, she retired early in
1709.

16. James Carlile is mentioned by Downes, with Mountfort, as having "grown to the maturity of good actors" (p. 39) by 1682. He is
last heard of in Tate's *A Duke and No Duke* in 1684 and was killed
in 1691. John Wiltshire was, Lowe says, "a useful actor of the
second rank" (I, 84, n. 1). He joined the United Company in 1691/
92 and Lincoln's Inn Fields in 1695/96. He is last mentioned in
1697; therefore, Cibber is in error about his death, since King
William's wars in Flanders and Ireland were in 1689-90.

Fredson Bowers charts Jonson's career, which was short, and if
we believe Dekker (*Satiro-Mastix*, 1601), not especially brilliant.
See Fredson Bowers, "Ben Jonson the Actor," *SP*, xxxiv (1937),
392-406.

CHAPTER IV

1. Events: 1660-90: Stage History. 1689-90: Cibber enters Drury
Lane as an apprentice.

2. That is, in 1682, the union of Betterton's and Killigrew's company at Drury Lane.

3. Cibber is confusing and in error. William Davenant (1606-88)
received a patent in August 1660, and a second on January 15, 1663,
to manage his players, the Duke's Company, at Lincoln's Inn
Fields, not Dorset Garden, which was not opened until 1671.
Thomas, not Henry, Killigrew, received his patent April 25, 1662
and his company, the King's Players, acted at the Theatre-Royal,
Drury Lane. Killigrew died in 1683.

4. Genest (I, 404) says Jonson's plays were not shared.

5. Charles Hart had acted in pre-Commonwealth times and was
with the King's Company from the first. He was, legend says,
Nell Gwynn's first lover, and one of the principal tragedians of
the Theatre-Royal. He died August 18, 1683.

6. The Licensing Act of 1737 closed Goodman's Fields and the
Haymarket.

7. Cibber meant operas, and, Lowe says, pantomimes (I, 93, n. 1.),
for which he had no love.

8. *The Tempest* was first adapted by Davenant and Dryden in 1667 and then by Shadwell in 1674. Shadwell followed his success with *Psyche* (1674) and *Circe* (1677).

9. "Probitas laudatur at alget." "Honesty is praised and neglected." Juvenal *Satires* I. 74.

10. In the Prologue to *Hecyra.*—Lowe, I, 95, n. 3.

11. Michael Mohun (c. 1625-84), "from his inferior height and muscular form, generally acted grave, solemn, austere parts."—Bellchambers, p. 82. A pre-Commonwealth actor, Mohun joined the King's Company in 1660. He appeared in Flecknoe's *Ermina* in that year. In 1676-77 he was, with Hart and Kynaston, appointed temporary manager of Drury Lane. He died in October 1684.

12. Cardell Goodman is listed in the King's Company in 1673. His greatest role was in Lee's *Alexander the Great*. He died in exile after being involved in a plot to assassinate King William. Clark appeared in *The Plain Dealer* in 1674.

13. Cibber meant 1682.

14. The adventurers subscribed to the building of the theater in Dorset Garden and had shares in Drury Lane.

15. Only Benjamin Johnson was alive in 1740.—Lowe, I, 99, n. 1.

16. "The actor pointed at is, no doubt, Wilks."—Lowe, I, 100, n. 1. The allusion is to *Hamlet,* III, ii, 8-11: "Oh, it offends me to the soul to hear a robustious periwig-pated fellow tear a passion to tatters, to very rags . . . ."

17. III, ii, 18 ff.

18. "If you want me to weep, you must first feel grief yourself." Horace *Ars Poetica* 102-3.

19. "This is doubtless directed at Booth, who was naturally of an indolent disposition, and seems to have been, on occasions, apt to drag through a part."—Lowe, I, 103, n. 2.

20. *Julius Caesar*, IV, ii, 39-40 and 64. "There is no terror, Cassius, in your threats . . . ."

21. "And if thou wouldst paint my likeness, paint sound." Ausonius *Epigrams* xxxii.

22. *The Rival Queens, or, The Death of Alexander the Great* (1677), II, i, 156-62.

23. Charles Le Brun (1619-90).

24. Drury Lane, October 1690.

25. Richard Estcourt (1668-1712). Bellchambers (p. 181) defends him as an able actor, but Lowe (I, 115, n. 2) observes that his "ability seems to have been at least questionable."

26. In Otway's *The Orphan* (1680).

27. "The wealthy curled darlings of our nation." *Othello*, I, ii, 68.

28. Sir Godfrey Kneller (1646-1723).

29. *Hamlet*, III, i, 160-61.

30. The benefit of Beaumont and Fletcher's play was on April 13, 1710. Betterton was buried May 2.

CHAPTER V

1. John Fletcher, *Rule a Wife and Have a Wife* (1624, 1640).

2. 1676 and 1691, respectively.

3. "Spirat tragicum satis et felicitur audet." "He has tragic inspiration and is happy in his ventures." Horace *Epistles* II. i, 166.

4. Act IV.

5. "You hold back your jeering?"

6. *1 Henry IV*, I, iii, 124.

7. *The Spanish Friar* (1681), II, ii, 76-77.

8. Willmore is the rover in Aphra Behn's *The Rover, or The Banished Cavaliers* (in two parts, 1677-81).

9. In Crowne's *Sir Courtly Nice, or It Cannot Be* (1685).

10. Mountfort died at the hands of a Captain Hill in 1692/93.

11. Samuel Sandford appeared in 1661 as Worm in Cowley's *The Cutter of Coleman Street*. Though Cibber stresses his tragic roles, Bellchambers (p. 140) says that he was a comedian as well. Cibber

mentions that Sandford acted in 1700, but he is heard of no more after 1706. Cibber probably refers to the Spanish painter José Ribera (1588-1656), known as Lo Spagnoletto.

12. Creon in Dryden and Lee's *Oedipus* (1679); Maligni in Porter's *Villain* (1662); Machiavil in Lee's *Caesar Borgia* (1680).

13. "Probably the Earl of Shaftesbury."–Lowe, I, 134, n. 1.

14. "The play in question is *The Triumph of Virtue* produced at Drury Lane in 1697, and the actress is Mrs. Rogers, who afterward lived with Wilks."–Lowe, I, 136, n. 1.

15. All characters in Addison's *Cato* (1713). Cibber himself played Syphax the "General of the Numidians."

16. *Richard III* was produced at Drury Lane in Dec.-Jan. 1699/1700. Cibber's adaptation, which held the stage for 150 years, is a stage-worthy piece.

17. Lowe (I, 141, n. 1.) points out that it is James, not Robert Nokes to whom Cibber refers. Robert Nokes died in 1673. James was with the Duke's Company in 1660 and died in September 1696.

18. Anthony Leigh joined the Duke's Company about 1672. He played in *The Man of Mode*, and the part of Dominic in *The Spanish Friar*. He died in December 1692. Cave Underhill was one of the great low comedy players whose career embraced some fifty years. He retired in 1710.

19. The plays are: Dryden's *Sir Martin Mar-All* (1668) and *The Spanish Friar* (1681); Etherege's *The Comical Revenge*, or *Love in a Tub* (1664); Betterton's *The Wanton Wife* (1668); Otway's *The Soldier's Fortune* (1680/81); Dryden's *Amphytrion* (1690).

20. "His life was gentle, and the elements
     So mixed in him that Nature might stand up
     And say to all the world, 'This was a Man.' "
                    Julius Caesar, V, v, 73-75.

21. Coligni in Porter's *The Villain* (1662); Ralph in John Caryll's *Sir Solomon Single* (1670). The other plays are by Otway and Shadwell and appeared in 1681 and 1688, respectively.

22. *Rest:* returning a tennis ball from player to player.

23. William Penkethman was an eccentric but able actor who often padded his parts with his own additions. He acted in Dublin with the United Company in 1692 and with Drury Lane in 1694.

24. Thomas D'Urfey's *Fond Husband,* or *The Plotting Sisters* (1677), and John Crowne's *City Politiques* (1683).

25. Fletcher's *The Prophetess* (c. 1620), made into an opera by Betterton with music by Purcell, was produced in 1690.

26. By Aphra Behn. Produced in March 1687 at Dorset Garden.

27. *Art and Nature* by James Miller was acted at Drury Lane in 1738. Into the comedy was introduced the principal character of *Harlequin Sauvage.* The play closed after one night. See Lowe, I, 152, n. 1.

28. Cibber refers to an incident, recounted later in Davies' *Dramatic Miscellanies* and reprinted in Lowe (I, 153, n. 1.), in which, after a stage gaffe, Penkethman made the remark attributed to him and so turned the wrath of the audience.

29. Shadwell. Acted in 1673.

30. June 3, 1709.

31. George Powell (1658-1714) was highly regarded by his contemporaries and was probably a better actor than Cibber makes him out to be. See *Spectator,* No. 40. John Verbruggen (d. c.1708) and Cibber entered the theater at about the same time. Bellchambers (p. 169) considers that Cibber depreciated the merit of Williams, who is not heard of after 1698.

32. After several attempts Elizabeth Barry went on stage. She first appeared in 1675 and eventually became an actress of great brilliance. She died on November 7, 1713.

33. 1692.

34. In Otway's *The Orphan* and Shadwell's *Venice Preserved* (1682).

35. In Dryden's *All for Love* (1678) and Lee's *The Rival Queens* (1677).

36. There is evidence that Mrs. Barry had a benefit each year. See *London Stage,* I, xxx.

37. The Queen created twelve new peers in 1711. Mrs. Barry however, died in 1713. See Doran, p. 56.

38. Mary Sanderson married Thomas Betterton about 1663. She had appeared before her marriage in Shakespearean roles and continued to do so until her death, some eighteen months after that of her husband, in 1712.

39. By Nathaniel Lee (1678).

40. See Lowe (I, 163, n. 1) for the confusion surrounding this very minor matter. An Elinor Dixon Leigh did play Lady Wishfort in *The Way of the World* in 1700. She was, quite likely, the wife of Anthony Leigh.

41. John Fletcher, about 1615. Adapted by Buckingham in 1666/67.

41a. Charlotte Butler, or Boteler, is listed in the Duke's Company in 1673. She acted, danced, and sang and is last heard of in 1692 when she sang in Settle's *The Fairy Queen*.

42. Betterton's *The Prophetess; or, The History of Dioclesian* (1690). *King Arthur* by Dryden and Purcell was acted in 1691.

43. Joseph Ashbury (1638-1720) managed the theater in Dublin and was reputed to be the best acting teacher then alive.

44. Susanna Percival married Mountfort on July 2, 1686/87. He was murdered in 1692 and she became Mrs. Verbruggen about 1694. She acted in *The Old Bachelor* and *The Double Dealer* and died in 1703.

45. In *The Scornful Lady* (1616).

46. Dryden's comedy was produced in 1672.

47. "Rowe and Congreve."—Lowe, I, 172, n. 1.

48. In *The Way of the World*.

49. Betterton's benefit took place on April 7, 1709. Her name last appears in February 1707.

50. Probably Michel Baron (1653-1729), actor, and son of the famous Andre Baron (1602-55), tragedian and comedian.

51. I, not unaware of evil, have learned to help those in distress. Virgil *Aeneid* I. 630.

52. Lowe (I, 179, n. 1) theorizes that Cibber retired, basing his comments on Davies, because of ill-treatment and the increasing impatience of the public with his ill-played attempts at tragic roles.

CHAPTER VI

1. Events: 1690-95: Cibber's first years at Drury Lane. 1694: Begins *Love's Last Shift*. 1695: Division of the theaters. 1696: *Love's Last Shift* produced.

2. Charles Killigrew, heir of Thomas Killigrew, and Alexander Davenant, who had his interest from Charles Davenant, heir of Sir William. Christopher Rich, a lawyer, acquired Davenant's interest in 1691 and became the effective manager of the united companies. Rich will appear as one of the villains of Cibber's tale, and he was indeed grasping and miserly, caring nothing for the theater, everything for profit.

3. Cibber received his first salary when he bungled a small part when acting with Betterton. The old actor furiously asked who the young man was. Told it was Cibber, Betterton commanded "forfeit him." "But he has no salary." "No," Betterton is supposed to have replied, "why put him down for ten shillings and forfeit him five." See Davies, *Dramatic Miscellanies*, III, 444.

4. "He was in stature of the middle Size, his Complexion fair, inclinable to the Sandy, his Legs somewhat of the thickest, his Shape a little Clumsy, not irregular, and his Voice rather shrill than loud or articulate, and crack'd extremely, when he endeavour'd to raise it. He was in his younger Days so lean as to be known by the Name of *Hatchet Face*." This description should be accepted with some care since it comes from *The Laureat* (p. 103).

5. Cibber married Katherine Shore on May 6, 1693. Daughter of Mathias Shore, sergeant trumpeter to the King, Katherine studied music with Purcell and later played the original Hillaria in *Love's Last Shift*.

6. Those critics who speak of Cibber's reforming zeal in connection with *Love's Last Shift* should listen closely here.

7. The date of the performance was January 13, 1694 at Drury Lane.

8. Leigh died on December 22, 1692, and Mountfort was murdered in 1692; however, Nokes died in 1696.

9. "This is no doubt a hit at Wilks whose temper was extremely impetuous."–Lowe, I, 191, n. 1.

10. December 28, 1694.

11. William Bullock (d. 1733). At the Theatre-Royal in 1695, left in 1714. He was considered one of the best comedians of the time. Benjamin Johnson (d. 1742) entered the Theatre-Royal in 1695. He played the first Sir William Wisewoud in *Love's Last Shift*.

12. March 25, 1695.

13. 1676. The play, an adaptation of Marlowe's *Lust's Dominions* was performed Monday, April 1, 1695.

14. Rich, certainly.

15. The end of April 1695.

16. "Mrs. Mountfort was now Mrs. Verbruggen."–Lowe, I, 200, n. 2.

17. The first line correctly reads: "Forbear your wonder . . . ."

18. Genest (II, 65) warns us that Cibber's dislike for Powell may be the cause for some exaggeration even though "there can be no doubt but that the acting . . . was miserably inferior to what it had been . . . ."

19. These events occurred in the latter part of May 1695.

20. "Without objection."

21. Cibber probably refers to Jakob Appel, born in Amsterdam in 1680. He died in 1751.

22. "Quicquid agunt homines, votum, timor, ira, voluptas,/ Gaudia, discursus, nostri est farragi libelli." "Whatever is human, a promise, a fear, an anger, a delight, a satisfaction, gadding about, that is the subject of my page." Juvenal *Satires* I. 85.

23. Richard Brome, *A Jovial Crewe, or; The Merry Beggars* (1641).

24. 1696.

25. January 1695/96.

26. Sir Novelty Fashion the fop.

27. Thomas Southerne (1660-1746), the dramatist, was a valuable ally to have at Drury Lane.

28. Though the Lord Chamberlain was probably overgenerous, his comment is an index to the critical reception of the play. Langbaine and Gildon, in *The Lives and Characters of the English Dramatic Poets* (1698), called the comedy "surprising and admirable" and forgave the improbability of Loveless' not recognizing Amanda. They observed that "the beauty of incident and the excellent moral that flows from it, abundantly outweigh the faults" (p. 20). This judgment was repeated a few years later by the anonymous author of *A Comparison Between the Two Stages* (1702), whose character, Sullen, refers to the play as a "philosopher's stone" that "did wonders." These wonders Sullen calls deserved, "there being few comedies that come up to't for purity of plot, manners and moral."—Staring B. Wells, ed., *Princeton Studies in English*, 26 (1942), 16.

29. The dedication, to Richard Norton, assures us that "the Fable is intirely my own; nor is there a Line or Thought, throughout the whole for which I am Wittingly oblig'd either to the Dead or Living; For I cou'd no more be pleas'd with a stol'n Reputation, than with a Mistress who yielded only upon the Intercession of my Friend: it satisfies me, Sir, that you believe it mine ...."

30. At Drury Lane, November 21, 1696.

31. Lincoln's Inn Fields, April 1697.

32. Given in December 1696 at Drury Lane. Cibber played Aesop.

33. Between 1696 and 1773, the last recorded performance, *Love's Last Shift* was given over two hundred performances.

34. It was generally conceded that, as Davies (III, 496) points out, "Cibber was endured in ... tragic parts, on account of his general merit in comedy."

CHAPTER VII

1. Events: 1698: Wilks comes to Drury Lane. 1700-1704: Cibber becomes close to Rich, 1728: Cibber rejects *Beggars Opera*. 1729: *Love in a Riddle* played.

2. Cibber means 1695.

3. In Nathaniel Lee's tragedy (1680).

4. The dates were 1698-1700; 1706-7; 1707-8. Doggett, who later shared management of the theater with Cibber, had been on the stage since the beginnings.

5. Cibber neglects to mention that he, too, looked for a safer ship. He left Rich and joined the more popular theater of Betterton in 1696. He soon returned, however, since it was illegal for actors to desert, and since he probably realized that his real success would lie with Rich. In the preface to *Woman's Wit* (1697), he says: "During the time of my writing the first two acts I was entertained at the New Theatre . . . . In the middle of the third act, not liking my station there, I returned again to the Theatre Royal."

6. In 1697. The privilege was abolished in 1737.

7. Wilks returned in 1698.

8. In Addison's *Cato*, Cato addresses his foes: "Am I distinguished from you but by toils,/ Superior toils, and heaven weight of cares:/ Painful pre-eminence." III, v, 21-23.

9. In Lee's *The Rival Queens* (1677) and Etherege's *The Man of Mode* (1676).

10. The events discussed here occurred in 1728. Cibber's rejection of the *Beggar's Opera* in that year, and his subsequent composition of a similar piece, led to the attacks against him by Mist. When *Polly* (1729), sequel to the *Beggar's Opera* was suppressed and Cibber suspected of influence in its suppression, the fate of *Love in a Riddle* was sealed. At its first performance, January 7, 1729, it was roundly hissed.

11. Lincoln's Inn Fields, January 29, 1728.

12. Drury Lane, January 7, 1729. A pastoral.

13. "We know these things are of no consequence." Martial *Epigrams* xiii. 2, 8.

14. "Cibber should have written *Catiline*."—Lowe, I, 245, n. 2.

15. *Polly* was suppressed on December 12, 1729. It was published the next year, but not seen until June 19, 1777.

16. Departed spirits.

16a. *Fleers:* mocking comments.

17. Lowe (I, 251, n. 1) speculates that the actress was Mrs. Barry.

18. *Bite:* to deceive, to take in.

19. Cibber's close association with Rich began about 1700. Contemporary pamphlets indicate his importance. Cf. *Visits from the Shades* (1704) in which Cibber is made to call himself a "viceroy in the theatres," Mrs. Manley's *The New Atlantis* (1709), and Dennis' *The Characters and Conduct of Sir John Edgar* (1720).

20. This event shows Cibber's close alliance with Rich. The events referred to: the arrival of Wilks in 1698, the replacement of Powell by Wilks as rehearsal director in 1702, and Wilks' contract of £4 a week in 1704 attest to this. Cibber himself received a similar contract at £3/10 with an additional 30 shillings for further services. He thus became, as Barker (p. 61) notes, the "most influential and highest paid actor in the company."

21. Characters in Jonson's *Epicoene, or, The Silent Woman* (1609).

22. John Mills, tragedian, with Drury Lane in 1694. He died in 1736.

23. 1700.

CHAPTER VIII

1. Events: 1698: Collier's attack on the theater. 1715: Steele granted the patent.

2. Steele's comedy was acted in December 1701. Cibber played Lord Hardy.

3. It was *Woman's Wit, or, The Lady in Fashion*, Drury Lane, 1697. Cibber intended to capitalize on the success of *Love's Last Shift, or, The Fool in Fashion*, though the similarity is small.

4. "Aut podesse volunt aut delectare poetae." "Artists wish to be either beneficial or delightful." Horace *Ars Poetica* 333. "Omne tulet punctum qui miscuit utile dulce." *Ars Poetica* 343.

5. The ill consequences were that masking became synonymous with being a prostitute.

6. A farce by Edward Ravenscroft, produced in 1682 and revived annually on Lord Mayor's Day.

7. The earliest performance may have been on April 29, 1700, since, by tradition, Dryden is supposed to have died on the third day (May 1, 1700). Genest (II, 179) thinks the play was revived March 25, 1700, and Lowe (I, 268, n. 1), that Cibber is in error. Since Dryden's masque was attached to the play in 1700, Vanbrugh, who revived the piece, Lowe suggests, probably gave Dryden the third night; however, the earliest known performance of the masque was not until July 6, 1700.

8. Jeremy Collier.

9. 1698.

10. Joe Haines was a popular low-comedy player. He was with the King's Company from 1667-80, and with Rich's actors in 1695. He died in 1701.

11. Congreve furiously answered Collier in *Amendments of Mr. Colliers False and Imperfect Citations* .... (1699), and Vanbrugh, in the same year, in *A Short Vindication of the Relapse ... from Immorality and Prophaneness* ....

12. A writ of noncontinuance.

13. They were Sir John Friend and Sir William Perkins who had plotted against the king.

14. Sir Charles Killigrew was master of the revels in 1698.

15. Acted possibly in February 1699/1700.

16. I wish it so.

17. January 19, 1715.

18. Cibber writes in 1738. Goodman's Fields was, however, opened in 1729.

19. "This was John Harper .... His trial was on November 20, 1733. Harper was a low comedian of some ability but of no great note." —Lowe, I, 283, n. 2.

20. A character in Vanbrugh's *The Provoked Husband, or, A Journey to London*. It was finished by Cibber and acted in 1728.

21. Fielding opened his Haymarket Theater in 1736, but with the Licensing Act the next year, was forced to close. This is the cause of Fielding's final ire.

22. "If you want to make anything of yourself, you must dare some crime that merits prison." Juvenal *Satires* I. 73.

23. Drawcansir in Buckingham's *The Rehearsal* (1671), IV, 1, habitually speaks with other men's lines.

24. The temple of Diana at Ephesus was burned in 356 B.C., supposedly by Herostratus who confessed that he did it only to insure his fame. Cibber used the allusion in Act I of *Love's Last Shift*.

25. "Lord Chesterfield."—Lowe, I, 289, n. 1. *The Laureat* (p. 51) notes this too.

26. "Less vividly is the mind stirred by what finds entrance through the ears than by what is brought before the trusty eyes." Horace *Ars Poetica* 180-81.

27. Guiscard attacked Robert Harley, Earl of Oxford, in 1711.

28. He received 3000 guineas from Highmore for his share.

CHAPTER IX

1. Events: 1698: Wilks to Drury Lane from Dublin. 1699: Mrs. Oldfield to Drury Lane. 1705: Opening of the Haymarket. 1706: Swiney takes over Haymarket under Rich's control. November 1706: Cibber deserts Drury Lane for Haymarket and feud between Swiney's and Rich's companies begins.

2. Again, Cibber should have said 1682.

3. The first performance was on January 13, 1708.

4. Southerne's tragedy was first acted at Drury Lane in 1696. Vanbrugh's *The Relapse* followed in 1697.

5. Cibber tells us almost all we know of Horden. Burgesse was a captain.

6. Horden was killed on May 18, 1696, and Wilks did not appear until 1698, and Estcourt not until 1704. "Cibber, who is very reckless in his dates, is here particularly confused."—Lowe, I, 304, n. 1.

7. Drury Lane, December 7. Cibber played Lord Foppington.

8. Vanbrugh's *A Journey to London* was completed by Cibber as *The Provoked Husband*. It was performed at Drury Lane on Janu-

ary 10, 1728. Cibber played Sir Francis Wronghead to Mrs. Old-field's Lady Townly.

9. "Verum ubi plura nitent in carmine, non ego paucis offendar maculis." "When the beauties in a poem are more in number, I shall not take offense at a few blots." Horace Ars Poetica 351-52.

10. Cibber says that "her voice was sweet, strong . . . and melodious . . . . The qualities she had acquired, were the genteel and elegant; the one in her air, and the other in her dress, never had her equal on the stage . . . ."

11. Nicholas Rowe's tragedy, The Ambitious Stepmother acted at Lincoln's Inn Fields in December 1700. The lines, from the epilogue, are, "Show but a Mimick Ape or French Buffoon,/ You to the other House in Shoals are gone,/ And leave us here to Tune our Crowds alone . . . ."

12. In Farquhar's The Constant Couple (1699) and its sequel Sir Harry Wildair (1701).

13. Cibber is wrong. The Haymarket opened on April 9, 1705, and the "little whig" was Lady Sunderland. However, Percy Fitzgerald in his New History of the English Stage (London, 1882), p. 238, says that when the cornerstone was uncovered in 1825 the inscription showed that it had been laid by the Duke of Somerset.

14. October 30, 1705.

15. The dates are: Squire Trelooby (1704) in collaboration with Congreve and Walsh and The Mistake (1705). The Cuckold in Conceit was never printed (Lowe, I, 326, n. 4), though it was acted in 1707. Cibber probably meant The Confederacy (1705). Since The Triumph of Love, an opera consisting of music by Albinoni, Scarlatti, and others was first performed on November 12, 1712, Cibber is in error here. What he probably means is the Loves of Ergasto performed on April 9, 1705.

16. Cibber tries to enlarge upon Swiney's success; however, the company failed, and Swiney was far less independent of Rich than Cibber would have us believe.

17. Lowe rightly points out (I, 332, n. 2) that Estcourt should not have been included on this list for his name appears on a Drury Lane bill for 1706/7. Theophilus Keen acted in Dublin in 1695 and

joined Drury Lane in that or the following year. He was a tragedian and died in 1719.

18. Colonel Brett, who received from Sir Thomas Skipwith a share
in Drury Lane.

19. "The chief actors left at Drury Lane were Estcourt, Penkethman, Powell, Capt. Griffin, Mrs. Tofts, Mrs. Mountfort (that is
the great Mrs. Mountfort's daughter), and Mrs. Cross: a miserably
weak company."—Lowe, I, 334, n. 1.

20. Cibber first appeared at the Haymarket on November 7, 1706, as
Lord Foppington in his own *The Careless Husband* (1705).

CHAPTER X

1. Events: 1706: Haymarket opposes Drury Lane's operas with
plays.

2. Farquhar's *The Beaux' Stratagem;* Cibber's *The Lady's Last
Stake; or, The Wife's Resentment,* and his, *The Double Gallant;
or, the Sick Lady's Cure,* all in 1707.

3. Cibber used Susanna Centlivre's comedy *Love at a Venture*
(1706) and William Burnaby's *The Lady's Visiting Day* (1701)
and *The Reformed Wife* (1707). Actually, *The Double Gallant*
was published in 4to November 8, 1708, as "Written by Mr.
Cibber."

4. These scenes became Cibber's *Marriage a la Mode; or, the Comical Lovers.* The play appeared in January and February 1707, at
Queen's.

5. *The Maid's Tragedy* (1619), *Lucius Junius Brutus* (1681). Lowe
(II, 13, n. 3) says the lines alluded to in Dryden's prologue to
Fletcher's *The Prophetess* are "Never content with what you had
before,/ But true to change, and Englishman all o'er." He further
notes (II, 14, n. 1) that *Mary Queen of Scotland* was in fact *The
Island Queens; or, the Death of Mary Queen of Scots,* by John
Banks, printed in 1684, finally acted in 1704 as *The Albion Queens.*

6. That is, John Banks, *The Unhappy Favorite; or, the Earl of
Essex* (1681); *Virtue Betray'd, or, Anna Bullen* (1682), and *The
Island Queens* (1684).

7. On May 3, 1698. All performances were suspended at Drury Lane "because Powell had been allowed to play." He had "drawn his sword on Colonel Stanhope and young Davenant."—Lowe, II, 20, n. 1.

CHAPTER XI

1. Events: 1707: Sir Thomas Skipwith offers his right in the patent to Colonel Brett. Brett accepts. 1708: Haymarket and Drury Lane again united by order of the Lord Chamberlain.

2. "Si quid novisti rectius istis, Candidus imperti; si nil, his utere mecum." "If you know something better than these precepts, pass it on my good fellow. If not, join me in following these." Horace *Epistles* 1. 6, 68.

3. Shakespeare says: "for the play, I remember, pleas'd not the million, 'twas caviary to the general . . . ." *Hamlet,* II, ii, 424-25.

4. The deed is dated October 6, 1707.

5. That is 1696 N.S.

6. The Countess of Macclesfield, who married Brett about 1698.

7. By the actor Mountfort. 1688; Drury Lane 1691.

8. In 1707.

9. The Cavalier Nicolo Grimaldi called Nicolini; he was first a soprano and then a contralto. See Burney, IV, 207.

CHAPTER XII

1. Events: 1708: Brett assigns his share to Wilks, Estcourt, and Cibber. 1709: Rich seeks to reduce power of the three and takes for his own use one third of the profits of the actor's benefits. June 1709: The Queen closes Drury Lane; Rich's power is broken. November 1709: William Collier obtains license to reopen Drury Lane.

2. Nicolo Haym's *Pyrrhus and Demetrius,* December 1708.

3. Valentini Urbani, a castrato. See Burney, IV, 205. For Cibber's account of Mrs. Tofts, see following pages. She died about 1760.

4. Carlo Broschi—Farenelli—(1705-82), appeared in London about 1734.

5. 115th *Tatler* for January 2, 1709/10.

6. Senesino was Francesco Bernardi (1680-1739), a male soprano; he appeared in London in November 1720.

7. However, Brett had, on March 31, 1708, made Wilks, Cibber, and Estcourt his deputies in the management, and as Cibber tells us, the actors then began the plots which led to June 6, 1709, when the Queen closed Drury Lane.

8. Clitus, or Cleitus, was a friend of Alexander the Great whom Alexander killed in a quarrel.

9. *Indulto:* a duty or tax.

10. April 30, 1709.

11. Mrs. Bracegirdle retired in February 1707. Mrs. Barry, however, can be found with the Haymarket in 1709/10.

12. Barker (p.77) suggests that "Cibber himself was almost certainly the actor in question."

13. Lowe quotes in full the order which finally ended Rich's domination. Signed by the Duke of Kent, the Lord Chamberlain, it notes Rich's refusal to pay his actors at the Lord Chamberlain's direction. It continues: "I do therefore . . . hereby silence you from further acting & require you not to perform any plays . . ." See Lowe, II, 73, n. 1.

14. *Tatler*, No. 193, July 4, 1710. The letter, supposed to be by John Downes, draws Rich as a schemer set out to destroy the stage with his "Harlequins, *French Dancers*, and *Roman* Singers . . ." and who fomented disorder among the younger actors. See George Aitken, ed., *The Tatler* (London, 1899), III, 406-8, on the doubtful authorship of the letter.

15. Booth remained with Rich. "Among the others were Powell, Bickerstaffe, Pack, Keene, Francis Leigh, Norris, Mrs. Bignell, Mrs. Moor, Mrs. Bradshaw, and Mrs. Knight."—Lowe, II, 77, n. 1.

16. Lincoln's Inn Fields opened on December 18, 1714.

16a. The first structure at Bridges Street, Drury Lane, opened May 7, 1663, and was destroyed by fire on January 25, 1671/72. The Theatre Royal, Drury Lane, was opened March 26, 1674. Wren probably designed the second theater since in a collection of his theater designs, a sectional design exists which corresponds to the dimensions and appearance of the Theatre Royal.

16b. The Elizabethan platform stage and the Restoration apron stage were very little different. In the old structure of which Cibber speaks, the apron extended some seventeen feet into the pit. Rich shortened the apron, enlarged the pit, and narrowed the stage by adding the side boxes. This innovation, of course, was in the direction of the modern picture, or proscenium, stage. Cibber correctly points out the advantages of the older form, which we are now beginning to recognize again.

17. Drury Lane did not open under Aaron Hill's management until November 23, 1709. The Haymarket had opened on September 15, 1709. Cibber does not mention William Penkethman's successful theater at Greenwich which was open between June 15, 1710 to the end of September of that year.

18. Lowe (II, 88, n. 1) quotes Bellchambers, who identifies the monarch as Victor Amadeus, of Sardinia.

19. Francesca Cuzzono, soprano, and Faustina Bordoni Hasse, mezzo, were rivals in 1726-27.

20. "Suis et ipsa Roma viribuis ruit." "Rome through her own strength is tottering." Horace *Epodes* xvi. 2.

21. Sacheverall's trial opened February 27, 1710.

22. November 1709.

23. November 26, 1709. The piece describes the attack on Drury Lane, amusingly, as a mock battle.

24. Shadwell's play was acted at Drury Lane on February 25, 1710.

25. Hester Santlow, a dancer and actress at Drury Lane, left the stage about 1733. Genest (III, 375) describes her as "a pleasing actress with no great powers."

CHAPTER XIII

1. Events: 1709: Actors again divided, those loyal to Rich now under Collier at Drury Lane. Those under Swiney and the actor-managers, Wilks, Doggett, and Cibber at the Haymarket. Rich begins to rebuild the theater at Lincoln's Inn Fields. 1709-11: Swiney quarrels with the actors, loses theater. 1711: Cibber, with Doggett, granted a license to manage Drury Lane. 1712: Swiney, hounded by creditors, goes to the continent.

2. November 6, 1710. The parties were Cibber, Wilks, Doggett, and Swiney.

3. As often.

4. The Earl of Pembroke.—Lowe, II, 105, n. 1.

5. Aaron Hill (1685-1750) was a poet and minor dramatist whose plays, among them *Elfrid* (1710), and *The Fatal Vision* (1716), and whose essays on the theater, put him in a position of some authority. He was an advocate of experiment in the theater, and his plans for the Haymarket included presentation of plays which would be successful not only commercially but excellent artistically, a consideration not always paramount at the time.

6. Cibber, Wilks, and Doggett, had signed an agreement on March 10, 1709, with Swiney. The three became suspicious of Swiney's management of the finances. Swiney had come to control the opera, as well. The events which Cibber describes eventually led to Swiney's departure for the continent in the season of 1712-13.

7. "This is to live two lives: to be able to enjoy one's earlier life." Martial *Epigrams* X. 23. 7-8.

CHAPTER XIV

1. Events: Season of 1712-13. November 11, 1713. Barton Booth admitted into partnership by order of the Lord Chamberlain. Doggett opposes, begins legal action, and finally leaves Drury Lane forever.

2. Anthony Aston wrote a *Brief Supplement* to the *Apology*, in which he adds to Cibber's anecdotes of actors of the period. It is not likely that he is the person of whom Cibber speaks, however.

Benjamin Victor's *The History of the Theatres* appeared in 1761, but it did not seem to be intended as a supplement to the *Apology*, though it is effectively that.

3. Drury Lane, April 14, 1713, actually. Cibber played Syphax.

4. Lowe says the actors were Elrington and Evans (II, 121, n. 1), *The Laureat* (p. 78), Elrington and Griffith. All three first appeared at Drury Lane in 1714-15.

5. "Impatient, passionate, ruthless, fierce." Horace *Ars Poetica* 121.

5a. Though *Cato* was to be an expression of Whig sentiment, or so the party leaders hoped, it soon became the object of Tory attention as well. Rumors of Tory plotting with the Pretender were many, and political feeling was strong. When *Cato* was acted both Whigs and Tories applauded the play with fervor, for the story of a banished leader's virtue appealed to both factions, though for different reasons. The playhouse became the scene of contests and dissensions between Whig and Tory over which party could more loudly approve Addison's praises to liberty. Pope observed that Addison's own lines: "Envy itself is dumb, in wonder lost, / And factions strive who shall applaud him most," were especially applicable to the situation.

6. "The Duke of Marlborough is the person pointed at."—Lowe, II, 130, n. 1.

7. Sir Robert Howard's *The Committee* played at the new theater in Lincoln's Inn Fields in 1661/62 or 1662/63.

8. That is, 1713. Cibber insists on the error.

9. Attic salt.

10. November 11, 1713.

11. Thomas Coke.

12. "So I demand."

13. Mary Porter died in 1762. Bellchambers (p. 422) places her in "the very first class of theatrical performers." Thomas Betterton's *The Amorous Widow; or, The Wanton Wife* (1670).

14. " 'A was a man, take him for all in all." *Hamlet*, I, ii, 87.

CHAPTER XV

1. Events: 1714: Death of Queen Anne. Sir Richard Steele becomes partner with the actor-managers. 1715: Steele and managers given patent. 1717: *The Non-Juror* acted. 1718: *All for Love* revived. 1719: Cibber suspended. He neglects to mention this incident, but apparently he had refused to give a part to an actor, Elrington, who appealed to the Lord Chamberlain, who questioned Cibber's conduct. Cibber insisted that he, not the Lord Chamberlain, was a judge of actor's merits. 1720: Steele excluded from the patent. Cibber, Wilks, and Booth given new patent. 1721: Steele returned to partnership. Quarrels ensue for several years. 1728: *The Provoked Husband* acted. Disputes between Steele and the managers finally settled.

2. License dated October 18, 1714.

3. James Craggs (1686-1721), secretary of state in 1718.

4. The supporters of Mrs. Rogers rioted when Mrs. Oldfield was cast as Andromache in Phillips' *The Distressed Mother* in March 1714 (Lowe, II, 166-67, n. 2). *The Distressed Mother* was performed on October 24, 1713, April 1, 1714, and February 19, 1715. In the last performance Mrs. Oldfield played Andromache.

5. Nathaniel Mist published the Jacobite *Weekly Journal*, later, *Mist's*, and *Fog's Journal*.

6. George Pack appeared first at Lincoln's Inn Fields in 1700 and continued on the stage until 1724. Francis Leigh is probably the actor referred to.

7. The "insolence of office." *Hamlet*, III, i, 273.

8. Steele was elected in 1715 and received the patent January 19, 1715. He granted equal shares to Cibber, Wilks, and Booth.

9. Cibber's chronology in the last two paragraphs is confusing. The patent was granted on January 19, 1715. Steele was elected in that year, not in 1718. The revival of *All for Love* was in December 1718, and Hewitt's report is dated January 1721.

10. "This is no doubt John Weaver's dramatic entertainment called *The Love of Mars and Venus*, which was published as acted at Drury Lane, in 1717."—Lowe, II, 180, n. 2.

11. The Scottish rebellion of 1715.

12. *The Non-Juror* opened at Drury Lane on December 6, 1717. Cibber played the villainous nonjuror, Dr. Wolf.

13. Pope was certainly offended by *The Non-Juror* and the attacks of Dennis and Mist were strengthened by it. However, Cibber was unpopular since, aside from his tactlessness and snobbery, as first reader of the company, he was often in the position to discourage new playwrights, which he did with some relish.

14. January 10, 1728. The powerful party is no doubt Mist. In *Mist's Journal* for January 13, 1728: "On Wednesday last a most . . . barbarous . . . Murder was committed . . . upon a posthumous Child of the late Sir John Vanbroog [sic], by one who . . . has gone by the name of Keyber."–*London Stage*, II, Pt. 2, 954.

CHAPTER XVI

1. Events: 1728: The three actor managers, Cibber, Wilks, and Booth, in full control. 1728: Cibber speaks before Court of Chancery over dispute with Steele. 1730: Cibber elected poet laureate. 1733: Cibber retires.

2. Cibber moves from 1717 to 1728. Cibber explains that the theater was in a peaceful state, but this was not entirely so. Profits were low, and there was competition from French actors and from a revived Lincoln's Inn Fields. The decade was not generally successful, and Cibber himself saw several plays fail.

3. Cibber errs. The date was 1728.

4. Cibber himself.

4a. *The London Stage*, Allardyce Nicoll, and other sources reveal nothing about an unusual spectacle in Bank's *Virtue Betrayed, or Anna Bullen*. It is likely, however, that if considerable expense had been given to the play, it was for the season of 1713 and 1714, when the play was often acted.

5. The Earl of Burlington.–Lowe, II, 209, n. 3.

6. *Calisto* was written in 1675, *Absolom and Achitophel* in 1681. Cibber's comments are, then, pointless.

7. John Bowman (1651-1739) was on stage for sixty-five years.

7a. Mrs. Gwin. Nell Gywnn, actress and mistress of the king. She excelled in sprightly roles. Her last stage appearance was in 1682.

8. Bishop Gilbert Burnet, *History of My Own Time* (London, Vol. I, 1723; Vol. II, 1734).

8a. Mrs. Roberts, or Jane Roberts, was a minor actress of whose fame on the stage nothing remains.

9. *Henry VIII*, I, ii, 103-8.

9a. *Chaise-marine:* a seat hung on straps, on a ship, and so rigged that it does not pitch or role. Here, Cibber probably means a chaise or carriage, the body of which is suspended on straps so that it can be used to carry scenery or costumes without damage to them.

10. 'Tis an ill bird that bewrays its own nest.

11. Charles Williams (d. 1731).

12. Vanbrugh's play was revived January 11, 1726, as revised by the author.

13. "Ye gods, what havoc does ambition make/ Among your works!" *Cato*, I, i, 11-12. The Dryden work is in "Address to Granville on his tragedy Heroic Love." The lines are: "And, in despair their empty pit to fill,/ Set up some Foreign monster in the bill./ Thus they jog on still tricking, never thriving/ And murdering plays, which they miscall reviving."

14. With paces not at all equal.

15. In Bank's *Unhappy Favorite* (1682).

16. Jeanne Catherine Gaussin of the *Comédie Française*. She first appeared in 1731, and died in 1767.

17. Without inspiration.

18. Cost what it may.

19. Mrs. Porter died in 1731; Wilks on September 27, 1732.

THE COLLATION

The editions collated are the first and second of 1740, the third of 1750, and the fourth of 1756. They are identified in the notes as 1, 2, 3, 4, respectively. Collational notes include: 1—page and line reference; 2—the element in question taken from the copy text; 3—the variant form. The edition number of the variant follows each element; 4—if an emendation has been made, it is indicated by (*emend.*) followed by the number of the edition from which the emendation is drawn. If no such number follows, the emendation is editorial. Emendations have been made only where the sense of the text is clearly imperfect.

Of the four editions, the second edition was clearly revised by Cibber. The third, published by Dodsley, seems to have been set directly from the second edition with no authorial change. A random collation of the fourth edition shows no changes, and it is unlikely that in 1756, a year before his death, Cibber would have spent any time revising a book from which he could receive little pleasure.

page: line
  10:5.   farther] further 2, 3, 4
  12:20. became one of his] became his 2, 3, 4
  13:17. one that has] one who has 2, 3, 4
  14:21. time to] time enough to 2, 3, 4
  17:14. other hard Conditions] other Conditions 2, 3, 4
  21:1.   have sate] have set 2, 3, 4
  21:10. here, where] here, when 2, 3, 4
  21:29-30. conversing; a Quality] conversing; which is a
               Quality 2, 3, 4

23:1.   among 'em] among them 2, 3, 4
23:3.   any of 'em 1, 2] any of them 3, 4
23:34.   most mind] most a mind 2, 3, 4
28:24.   I say] I can say 2, 3, 4
29:27.   as from what] as what 2, 3, 4
33:24.   of perhaps] perhaps of 2, 3, 4
42:10.   Concern; lest (*emend.*)] Concern; let 1, 2, 3, 4
45:9-10. Honours of Duke of Devonshire, Lord] Honours of
         Lord 2, 3, 4
47:27.   no great Pretence] no Pretence 2, 3, 4
55:1.   after so long] after the so long 2, 3, 4
55:36.   Agreement] Argument 2, 3, 4
61:24.   be so often tempted] be also tempted 2, 3, 4
63:7.   Powers united] Powers at once united 2, 3, 4
76:11.   had he not (*emend.*) 3, 4] he had not 1, 2
99:6.   any one Theatre] any Theatre 2, 3, 4
135:10. to have been as] to be as 2, 3, 4
152:26. his late Majesty . . . George I.] his Majesty . . . George
         the First 2, 3, 4
158:35. not to suffer (*emend.*) 2, 3, 4] not suffer 1
159:4-5. or Mis-rule] and Mis-rule 2, 3, 4
164:15. 1708] 1707 2, 3, 4
166:12. at this time] at that time 2, 3, 4
167:4.   she grew more] she got more 2, 3, 4
169:23-24. and Wilks] and Mr. Wilks 2, 3, 4
173:10. under greater Disadvantages] under great
         Disadvantages 2, 3, 4
176:1.   upon any other] upon every other 2, 3, 4
183:3.   of 'em all] of them all 2, 3, 4
184:24. large Elephant] fine Elephant 3, 4
185:3.   and acquainted the] and acquaint the 2, 3, 4
198:33. of our Publick] of the Publick 2, 3, 4
205:10. upon the raising] upon raising 2, 3, 4
207:1.   he was suffer'd] he were suffer'd 2, 3, 4
211:28. then but an] then not an 2, 3, 4
211:32. and the exquisitely] and exquisitely 2, 3, 4
213:33. probably might make] probably make 2, 3, 4
224:12. 1714, and which] 1714, which 2, 3, 4
245:14. as from a] as a 2, 3, 4
245:17. from the *Dublin*] from *Dublin* 2, 3, 4

246:14. Behaviour of Wilks] Behaviour in Wilks 2, 3, 4
263:21. the chief Conductor] the Conductor 2, 3, 4
263:28. I had most] I most 2, 3, 4
276:25. Member for the new Parliament] Member of
    Parliament 2, 3, 4
280:26. Do we not] Do not we 2, 3, 4
289:18. it seems amazing] it is amazing 2, 3, 4
291:10. he has had] he had 2, 3, 4
302:21. Court be as well reproach'd] Court as well be
    reproach'd 2, 3, 4
302:35. we find] we can find 2, 3, 4

INDEX

(References in the text are followed immediately by the page and note number of the text footnote reference.)

Abbee, M.l', 170
Abdelazar (Behn), 109, 339 n.13
Achilles (Gay), ix
Actors
    benefits for, 218 ff.
    desert Rich for Collier, 229-30
    female roles still played by men, 71
    formation of new company by Swiney, 219 ff.
    -managers, established at Drury-Lane, 243 ff.
    -managers, Wilks, Doggett, Cibber, with Collier, receive license, 236
    patent no longer authority over, 221-22
    principal actors of the United Company, listed, 59
Addison, Joseph, Cibber on Pope's "Atticus" portrait of, 26
    on acting of *Hamlet*, 60, 249-50, 255, 263, 319
"Address to Granville" (Dryden), quoted, 312, 354 n.13
Adventurers, 58, 199, 231, 238
Aesop (Vanbrugh), 121
Agesilaus, 16, 328 n.16
Alexander the Great, 217
Alexander the Great, see *The Rival Queens*
All for Love (Dryden), 277
Ambitious Stepmother, The (Rowe), ix
    quoted, 171, 345 n.11
Amorous Widow, The; or, The Wanton Wife (Betterton), 267
Amphytrion (Dryden), 67, 334 n.24, 83
Anne, Princess, later Queen, 42-44, 59, 93, 166, 189

359

Vergil, 314
  The Aeneid, quoted, 23, 329 n.5; 101
Victor, Benjamin, xviii, 325 n.15
Villain, The (Porter), 86, 335 n.21
Villiers, George, Duke of Buckingham, 94, 295
Virtue Betray'd (Banks), 190, 347 n.6; 293

Walker, Robert, xvi
Walker, Obadiah, 253
Walpole, Horace, xiv, xviii, 325 n.16
Wanton Wife, The (Betterton), 83
Watte, John, xvi
Way of the World, The (Congreve), 111
Western Lass, The (D'Urfey), 95
Whitehall Evening Post, 31-33, 330 n.15-16
Wilks, Robert, xxii, xxv, 7, 327 n.4; 60, 333 n.16; 90, 107, 339 n.9; 130-34,
    139-44, 150, 165, 169, 179, 191, 220, 236, 238-39, 245, 251-52,
    257-58, 260 ff., 266 ff., 273-74, 287-94, 305-16, 320
William, Prince of Orange, later King, 39, 42, 44, 52, 59, 151, 188, 205, 216
Williams, Charles, 90, 336 n.31; 111, 307
Will's Coffee House, 192
Wiltshire, John, 52, 332 n.16
Woffington, Margaret (Peg), xv
Wright, James, *History of Rutlandshire,* 8
Wycherley, William, 76

Young, Edward, *Second Epistle to Mr. Pope,* 35, 330 n.18